William Alexander

Johnny Gibb of Gushetneuk in the Parish of Pyketillim

With glimpses of the parish politics about A.D. 1843. Seventh Edition

William Alexander

Johnny Gibb of Gushetneuk in the Parish of Pyketillim
With glimpses of the parish politics about A.D. 1843. Seventh Edition

ISBN/EAN: 9783337075750

Printed in Europe, USA, Canada, Australia, Japan

Cover: Foto ©Lupo / pixelio.de

More available books at **www.hansebooks.com**

JOHNNY GIBB OF GUSHETNEUK

BY WILLIAM ALEXANDER

Printed by R. & R. Clark

FOR

DAVID DOUGLAS, EDINBURGH.

LONDON . . .	HAMILTON, ADAMS, AND CO.
CAMBRIDGE . .	MACMILLAN AND BOWES.
GLASGOW . .	JAMES MACLEHOSE AND SONS.
ABERDEEN . .	LEWIS SMITH AND SON.

The Author

JOHNNY GIBB

OF GUSHETNEUK IN THE

PARISH OF PYKETILLIM

WITH

Glimpses of the Parish Politics about A.D. 1843

BY

WILLIAM ALEXANDER

AUTHOR OF 'SKETCHES OF LIFE AMONG MY AIN FOLK,'
'NOTES AND SKETCHES ILLUSTRATIVE OF NORTHERN RURAL LIFE IN
THE EIGHTEENTH CENTURY,' ETC.

SEVENTH EDITION

EDINBURGH: DAVID DOUGLAS
1881

PREFACE TO THE SEVENTH EDITION.

FOLLOWING on the successive publication of several editions of *Johnny Gibb*, in a cheap and popular form, a fine edition in royal octavo was published at the commencement of 1880. The feature of the work, as thus issued, was the series of illustrations executed by Mr. George Reid, R.S.A. By all competent judges these have been admitted to be, not only admirable as samples of art, but strikingly characteristic and truthful as visible embodiments, by the pencil, of the life and its surroundings sought to be portrayed by the pen. The portrait sketches, while eminently felicitous interpretations of the characters in the text, are, at same time, "genuine typical Aberdeenshire faces," such as, at the date of the story, were to be found, without difficulty, among the dwellers in many a quiet rural scene. And the charming vignette illustrations from actual localities, of which the larger part are mentioned in their literal connection in the text, need no word of commendation.

In the previous edition, which ran speedily out of print, the illustrations were most successfully engraved by M. Durand, Paris, and their present careful reproduction in lithographic form will, it is believed, be appreciated by those who have not been able to possess themselves of the more expensive volume.

ABERDEEN, *October* 1881.

CONTENTS.

CHAP.		PAGE
I.	Johnny Gibb sets out for the Wells	1
II.	The Journey to the Wells	7
III.	Rustic Courtship	13
IV.	Johnny Gibb's Political Education	20
V.	Life at the Wells	26
VI.	Mrs. Birse of Clinkstyle	32
VII.	Back from the Wells	38
VIII.	Tam Meerison Flits	45
IX.	Pedagogical	54
X.	Benjie's Classical Studies	61
XI.	The Kirk Road	68
XII.	The Smiddyward Prayer Meeting	75
XIII.	The Distribution Meeting — Ecclesiastical Opinions	83
XIV.	Tam Meerison's Private Affairs	90
XV.	Sandy Peterkin's School	96
XVI.	A Start in Life	102
XVII.	Sandy Peterkin is warned	109
XVIII.	The Public Meeting	115
XIX.	Meg Raffan, the Henwife	128
XX.	Mrs. Birse and her Own	135
XXI.	Patie's Plush Waistcoat	141
XXII.	Mainly Polemical	146
XXIII.	Jonathan Tawse and Dawvid Hadden	152

CONTENTS.

CHAP.		PAGE
XXIV.	Preparing for the Conflict	158
XXV.	The Gushetneuk Meeting	163
XXVI.	Sandy Peterkin's Fortune	173
XXVII.	Mains of Yawal at the Synod	179
XXVIII.	The Free Kirk of Pyketillim	185
XXIX.	A Change of Time	192
XXX.	Meg Raffan entertains Dawvid Hadden	197
XXXI.	The Election of Elders	202
XXXII.	Dawvid Hadden visits at Clinkstyle	208
XXXIII.	The Merchant's Shop	214
XXXIV.	Dawvid Hadden reports to Sir Simon	221
XXXV.	The Settlement of Mr. MacCassock	227
XXXVI.	The Settin' of Gushetneuk	234
XXXVII.	Clinkstyle again	240
XXXVIII.	Meg Raffan goes to the Shop	246
XXXIX.	Patie's Wedding	253
XL.	The News of the Marriage	259
XLI.	The Manse Scheme	265
XLII.	Sir Simon instructs Dawvid Hadden	274
XLIII.	Dawvid Hadden consults the Henwife	280
XLIV.	Johnny Gibb discusses the Situation	284
XLV.	Dawvid Hadden makes two Business Calls	290
XLVI.	Hairry Muggart goes to the Toon	297
XLVII.	Johnny Gibb makes his Will	302
XLVIII.	The Climax of Gentility	306
XLIX.	The Conclusion	312
	Glossary	319

LIST OF PLATES.

AUTHOR	*Frontispiece.*
JOHNNY GIBB	*To face page* 4
BLACK BULL INN	,, 10
MACDUFF	,, 12
PETER BIRSE	,, 34
TARLAIR	,, 42
JONATHAN TAWSE	,, 56
MRS. BIRSE	,, 62
PYKETILLIM KIRK	,, 70
SMIDDYWARD	,, 76
BENACHIE	,, 118
GEORDIE WOBSTER	,, 124
MEG RAFFAN	,, 132
DAWVID HADDEN	,, 154
RODERICK M'AUL	,, 168
WEST KIRK, ABERDEEN	,, 182
ANDREW LANGCHAFTS	,, 194
HAIRRY MUGGART	,, 206
SAMIE PIKSHULE	,, 260
GUSHETNEUK	,, 318

CHAPTER I.

JOHNNY GIBB SETS OUT FOR THE WELLS.

"Heely, heely, Tam, ye glaiket stirk—ye hinna on the hin shelvin o' the cairt. Fat hae ye been haiverin at, min? That cauff saick 'll be tint owre the back door afore we win a mile fae hame. See 't yer belly-ban' be ticht aneuch noo. Woo, lassie! Man, ye been makin' a hantle mair adee aboot blaikin that graith o' yours, an kaimin the mear's tail, nor balancin' yer cairt, an' gettin' the things packit in till 't."

"Sang, that 's nae vera easy deen, I can tell ye, wi' sic a mengyie o' them. Faur 'll aw pit the puckle girss to the mear?"

"Ou, fat 's the eese o' that lang stoups ahin, aw wud like tae ken? Lay that bit bauk across, an' syne tak' the aul' pleuch ryn there, an' wup it ticht atween the stays; we canna hae the beast's maet trachel't amo' their feet. Foo muckle corn pat ye in?"

"Four lippies—gweed mizzour—will that dee?"

"We 'se lat it be deein. Is their trock a' in noo, aw won'er?"

"Nyod, seerly it is."

It was in the latter part of June 1839, and Johnny Gibb was preparing to set out on his annual journey to the "Walls" at Macduff. He was, at the moment of the reader's introduction to him, employed, with the assistance of his servant man, Tam Meerison, in yokin the cairt, preparatory to starting *en route*. The time was 4.30 A.M.

Johnny Gibb was the tacksman of Gushetneuk, a two-horse haudin on the property of Sir Simon Frissal of Glensnicker; and he and his wife had spent the greater part of a very industrious lifetime on the place.

Mrs. Gibb, in personal appearance, looked to be a woman somewhere approaching sixty, in an exceedingly good state of preservation. Dumpy in figure, inclining slightly to obesity in condition, and with cheeks of the exact hue of a high-coloured apple, she was, nevertheless, understood to be far fae stoot; she was, indeed, nervish, and apt to take drows. Hence this yearly resort to the Wells at Macduff, renowned for their restorative and invigorating virtues, had come to be a necessity for her. When Johnny Gibb had got the neeps doon, he took his carts to the mill-dam, had them backed into the water, where they were first well soaked and then scrubbed clean, after the defilement of driving out the neep muck. And then one of the first things, ordinarily, was to prepare for the usual journey to the Wells.

In the district where Johnny Gibb lived, they believed in the Walls, old and young of them. Elderly people, male and female, went to Macduff to benefit by the bracing effects of sea-bathing, combined with a course more or less rigorous of sea water taken internally, followed up by the mineral water of Tarlair; sturdy bairns were taken thither in troops for the cure of scabbit faces and sic like; youths and maidens, whose complaints seemed often not of a deadly nature, went to the Walls as they could contrive to get; Jamie Hogg went there for the benefit of his sair een; Peter Tough to mitigate the rheumatics; Mains of Yawal, when he had occasion to gae doun throu on business, actually drove his square wooden-looking gig five miles out of his direct route in order that he might have the opportunity of merely once dookin at Macduff. He lows't the gig and put his horse in to rest and feed, and I recollect distinctly seeing his tall gaunt figure in bottle-green surtout, as, despising ceremony, he strode away straight down from the fisher town, or rather the ropery, through hillocks of slippery ware and knablick stanes till he found water enough to dook in; and a tedious walk he had, for the tide was out. The *modus operandi* of Mains's dookin was, that he first laid aside his hat and the bottle-green surtout, and, by the aid of a good handful of sea-ware scrubbed the upper part of his person. He then resumed the hat and surtout, and divesting himself of the remaining part of his garments, completed the operation in the like fashion. The farm servants even were fain to follow the prevailing custom; and this, their belief, had not been discouraged by the physician in ordinary, the elder Dr. Drogemweal. The doctor had a semi-military reputation, inasmuch as, when the first Bonaparte was disturbing people by threats of invading our Island and so on, the doctor had been attached to the local militia; and he was wont to accompany the fencibles to Fraserburgh at the time of their annual drill. It was related of him how he would make the delinquent soldier drink a quart-bottle of sea water by way of punishment, believing that, while the thing had a penal effect, it also conserved the man's constitution. To his latest day, when a chap went to him for advice, he would prescribe twa unce o' salts, and, if the case were grave, would take out his lance and bleed him; winding up by a general exhortation to go to the Wells the first opportunity. And thus, in the very year before that of which I am about to write, when Johnny Gibb went over to Pitmachie to fee a man, he encountered a stoot young folla, from the Upper Garioch, who would suit his purpose admirably well, but was determined to have sax poun ten of fee. Johnny offered sax poun and a shilling of arles, after much threepin, as his ultimatum. They tuggit and ruggit to no purpose, till at last a compromise was reached, and the bargain concluded, on the chap throwing in this stipulation, "Weel, weel, than, aw'll tak' the siller; but ye maun gie's an ouk at the Walls aifter the neep seed."

Such was the repute of the Wells at Macduff in my day, but that is long ago; and to me the modern Macduff is a place all but totally unknown.

"Come awa', noo; come awa', an' nae loss the mornin'."

continued Johnny Gibb, in an impatient tone—patience was not Johnny's prime virtue,—when he had satisfied himself that the cart was properly packed and adjusted. His words were addressed, in the first place, to Mrs. Gibb, who had been hoverin' between the door and the kitchen for some time, one part of her thoughts resting on Johnny and the cart, and another on Jinse Deans, the servant girl, to whom she continued still to address another and another exhortation, to be sure "an' plot 'er milk dishes weel, in this byous weather; an' get the kye pitten oot ear'," so that they might "get a caller mou'fu', an' win in afore they ran a-heat;" to see that "the caufies warna negleckit," and give due heed to sundry other matters that concerned the proper ongoing of the place during the absence of its mistress.

Mrs. Gibb was dressed in a home-made gray wincey gown, a very precisely made up and very well starched close mutch (they were old-fashioned people the Gibbs), and a tartan plaid that had been in the family for at least a generation. She was assisted into the cart with due ceremony, and with the help of a chair—Jinse, the trusty, bare-headed, bare-armed maid, handing up after her a reticule basket, crammed with provisions for consumption by the way, and a big blue umbrella.

"Faur's the lassie noo?" quoth Johnny.

"Ou, I gart 'er rin roun' the neuk o' the wood a filie syne, to Smiddyward, to see 'at Eppie was up, and nae keep 's wytin."

"That 'll dee. Go on, Jess," and Johnny pulled the whip from the britchen as he spoke. "Ye may be leukin for me hame afore sindoon the morn's nicht."

"Weel, weel, tak' care o' yersel's," replied Tam Meerison, as he turned leisurely away to complete his stable operations, and tie his points, before he and the servant loon, who was not yet out of bed, should call on Jinse for their pottage.

I have not yet described Johnny Gibb's personal appearance, and, if the reader in the least cares to know, let me say that he was a short, thick-set man, or mannie rather,

with broad, sun-tanned countenance, whereof the shaggy eyebrows, and somewhat large, but well-set mouth, were not the least prominent features. He was slightly bow-legged, which rather added to the stability of his appearance; his dress was blue home-spun, crowned with a blue bonnet, for though Johnny was not a man who would altogether ignore the deference due to the conventionalities of society, he averred "that hats is a perfect mertyreesin to the heid, oonless them 't's wearin' them daily day." And so it came to pass that, except on the occasion of a funeral, or the Communion Sunday, Johnny's hat was seldom to be seen. And my private opinion is that, even on these occasions, it had been better left in its usual limbo. It was such an uncouthly shaped, brown, and hairy structure, that Johnny was hardly recognisable under it; he certainly looked much better and more gatefarrin in his blue bonnet.

As Johnny strode stoutly on alongside of his bonny bay mare, Jess, ilka blade o' grass tipped with its ain drap o' dew, and the orient sun just beginning to struggle through masses of gray cloud, and to gild the tree tops with occasional glimpses of his face, while the lark poured forth his song overhead in streams of rich melody, and a stray hare now and then hirpled up the dykeside—the scene was, undoubtedly, one fresh enough, and lovely enough to stir the blood of any but the most mouldy and ungrateful of human beings.

Round the corner of the wood from Gushetneuk, and a little beyond where a trotting burnie came down the hollow, there stood a small hamlet, consisting of about half-a-dozen unpretending edifices, scattered here and there, and including the smith's and shoemaker's places of abode and workshops, with an old-fashioned toon loan fringed by a few large ash and plane trees. At the top of the loan there was a very rustic-looking schoolhouse, and one or two small rape-thackit cottages. This was Smiddyward. By the roadside here, there stood waiting the arrival of the cart, Eppie Will, a widow 'oman, and friend of Mrs. Gibb, and her only son, Jock, a fite-heidet youth of fourteen or thereby, tender eyed, with a bandage round his head longitudinally, and tightly encased from head to foot in a suit of gray moleskin, garnished with abundance of brass buttons. With them stood a girl of about Jock's age, dressed almost as quaintly as Jock, though with feminine tact, she had set off her primitive gingham frock for the occasion with a fresh nosegay pinned in the front. In point of physical features, too, she had the advantage of him. In contrast to Jock's rather flabby face and sheepish look, "the lassie," as Johnny and Mrs. Gibb invariably called her, had a face which, though somewhat high in point of colour, possessed that regularity of feature and pleasantness of contour, which, in a different rank of life, would have been held to give promise of ultimately maturing into unmistakable womanly beauty. The lassie, whose name was Mary Howie, was the niece of Mrs. Gibb; and being the daughter of parents whose poverty, if not their wills, could very well consent to spare her, she had become, in a sort, the adopted child of the Gibbs, who had no family of their own.

Johnny Gibb stopped Jess, got the whole hypothec into the cart; and then, mounting the forebreist himself, started again, fairly under way for the Wells.

CHAPTER II.

THE JOURNEY TO THE WELLS.

IF need were, I could describe the entire course of the journey from Gushetneuk to the Wells at Macduff. But perhaps to do so would be an undue trifling with a busy public, whose manner of travelling, for health and pleasure, as well as for business, is so different now. The railway system had not penetrated to Aberdeen even, then. Long strings of carriers' carts, jogging on night and day, each with its creel atop, and here and there a jolly carrier lying in the same half or wholly asleep, and perhaps, a more watchful mastiff under the axletree—these did the heavy and slow part of the business; and then there was the mail coach, and the rattling Defiance; and now and again such a vehicle as the Tallyho, for speedy conveyance of passengers, at the average rate of eight miles an hour, stoppages not always included; also the "Flyboat," or "Swift Gig Boat," plying on the Aberdeenshire Canal, whose sideway draught, to the unfortunate horses that ran on the bank, with a laddie rider, dexterously joukin inward and downward at every villanously low bridge under which they went, was the extreme of cruelty to animals.

These things are not only obsolete, but almost completely forgotten, and the idlest, laziest man in the shire grumbles loudly at the unconscionably slow rate of those trains that do not run faster than twenty miles an hour.

Such is the progress of the human race; not to speak of

the electric telegraph, which threatens to land us in a material millennium before we have had time to abrogate the Ten Commandments, and do whatever else advanced minds may think needful to getting our moral equilibrium steadied at a point commensurate with the advance of natural science.

However, I must return to Johnny Gibb, who, in taking a near cut at the outset, had guided his cart and its freight through one or two yetts, the bars of which he took painfully out, and put as painfully in again, and after gaining the high road, had received the salutations of sundry servant lads, early out either on their way to the peat moss, or from which they were already returning with loaded carts. By and by, the voyagers had passed out of kent bounds—bounds kent to the junior passengers, that is to say, for to Johnny Gibb the whole way was as familiar as his oxter pouch; and great was the delight of the lassie and Jock Will, as the scene changed and changed, and first one gentleman's seat and then another, came in view. And Johnny would tell the name of each, and, in sententious phrase, give a brief sketch of the owner.

"Ay, ay, the fader o' 'im was a lang-heidit schaimin carle, an' weel fells the sin for that," was the remark in one case; and in the next, "A braw hoose that, isnint? But, an' ilka ane hed their nain, I wudna say nor the laird wud hae to forhoo's bit bonny nest."

"Eh, sirs: sic a weary wardle," said Eppie Will. "Fa cud 'a thocht it?"

"The tae half o' oor lairds is owre the lugs in a bag o' debt. I wud hae them roupit oot at the door, and set to some eesefu trade."

"Na, sirs," ejaculated Eppie; and Mrs. Gibb put in a deprecatory "Hoot man!"

"Stechin up a kwintra side wi' them, wi' their peer stinkin' pride," pursued Johnny, "an' them nedder able to manage their awcres themsel's, nor can get ither fowk that can dee 't for them. Ye 're leukin, Jock; gin ever ye be a factor, loon, see an' leern the eese o' the grun, an' keep baith laird an' tenan' straucht i' the theets."

"Eh, John Gibb; for shame to the laddie," quoth Eppie Will. Jock himself gave a soft laugh, looked askance, and rubbed the chaff sack with the palm of his hand.

And thus they moved on mile after mile.

"Gi'e the bairns a bit piece noo, 'oman," continued Johnny, changing the theme, when they had journeyed for a matter of three hours; "the like o' them's aye yap, an' it'll be twall o'clock ere we win doon to Turra to lowse."

"Hear ye that noo, Eppie?" said Mrs. Gibb, affecting the jocular. "That's to lat 'imsel' get a gnap no!"

"Aweel, sae be't. It's an ill servan' t's nae worth's maet. Here's a bit coblie o' fine clear caller water; we'll gie the beast a drink, an' lat 'er get a mou'fu' o' girss till we see fat's i' that bit basketie."

And so Jess was set to the grassy bank, with a wisp of half-dried hay strewn before her, and the bearing reins thrown loose. Mrs. Gibb produced an abundant store of cakes and butter ready spread, and the cakes placed face to face, with several kneevlics of tempting blue cheese. The party regaled themselves sumptuously on their wholesome fare, and drank of the caller water to which Jess had been treated.

And, verily, he hath but an imperfect acquaintance with the true philosophy of locomotion, who shall affect to sneer at the mode in which Johnny Gibb and his charge journeyed. Grant but fitting company, favourable weather, and a fair allowance of fresh straw, and the art of man hath not yet devised a more rational and truly enjoyable method of "voyaging" by land than by the use of a common cart, drawn by a willing and intelligent cart horse. Of this truth all practised visitors to the Wells had an intuitive perception; if reliance on it was not, indeed, essential to the integrity of their belief in the entire institution. And how well they could furnish out the cart for the comfortable accommodation and sustenance of those who journeyed therein! Time would fail me to speak of the compendious outfit they could stow away within and about the vehicle. I recollect well seeing one arrival of a large family, the head of which had boxed up the sides of his cart with rough boards till he had achieved a kind of two storeys, the ground floor containing sundry kitchen utensils, and the upper one the live passengers; and he had actually built in a fixed stair in the hind part of the cart! But this was an extreme experiment, and the usual mode was simply to pack well on the basis of the cart itself.

Resuming their journey, the party plodded on through the romantic den of Gask, and down on the handsome little town of Turriff, with its bleachfield along the quiet burn side, and its common herd, who touted his horn as he wended along, and gradually gathered out the town's kine to feed on the pleasant haughs adjoining.

At Turriff Johnny lows't the mare, and put up for refreshment at the Black Bull Inn, where he and the hostler discussed a gill of the national liquor, very amicably, between them. As the gentlest drink for the ladies, he called a bottle of mulled porter; and, leaving them to sip and sip of the same in the little back parlour of the Inn, with its sanded floor and crockery-shop statuary, he sallied forth to exhibit the lions of the place to the youngsters, not omitting to point out to them the Toon's Hoose, and the Cross, the geographical position of which he took care to explain, as equally distant from Aberdeen and Elgin. As saith the popular distich—

> "Choose ye, choise ye, at the Cross o' Turra,
> Either gang to Aberdeen, or Elgin o' Moray."

That was a delightsome road down by Knockiemill, and along the pleasant banks of the Deveron, in full view of Forglen House, Denlugas, and so forth. This Johnny Gibb knew, and he preferred it to the turnpike road accordingly. I do not know that he escaped a toll by adopting this route, for there was a passport system in force in those days, whereby the man who went through the Turriff bar was armed with a ticket that gave him the privilege of passing the next bar without pecuniary mulct. However that may be, the water-side road was chosen as the more picturesque

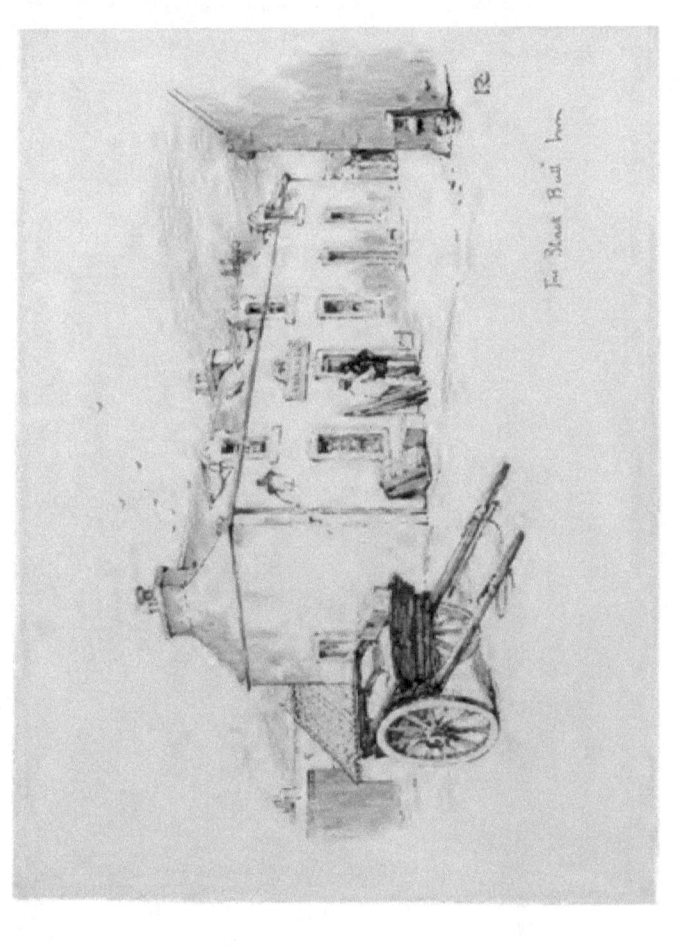

—a most legitimate consideration surely with those who travelled for health and pleasure. Up they came again near by Eden, along the turnpike road for some miles, and again diverging to the right, on Johnny and his cart went under the westering sun, till the hill-top was reached; when, lo! there lay before them the calm blue sea, with slight ripples of white here and there, and here and there on its bosom a brave schooner scudding along the Firth, with fully spread canvas, or a boat, with brown sail newly hoisted, speeding away from the harbour mouth; wherein lay sundry craft, the top-masts of which were fully visible as the eye wandered inward over the irregular field of red-tiled roofs, and settled on the vista afforded by the long steep street leading down to the shore.

"Eh, that's the sea!" exclaimed the lassie, in a rapture of admiration.

"Is 't the sea, mither?" said Jock, not quite assured. "It's surely nae that colour?"

"'Deed an' it's jist the saut sea, whaur mony ane's gotten a watery shrood."

"Divnin ye see the ships sailin on 't?" said the lassie.

"Weel, they're nae vera muckle anes," replied Jock.

"But they're maybe hyne awa.'"

"Ho! but a muckle ship sud hae three masts," said Jock, desirous of vindicating his nautical knowledge, "an nane o' that has mair nor twa."

"Will we get a sail on 't?" was the lassie's next question.

"'Serve's, lassie, ye little ken fat ye're speakin o'. Lat alane the fear o' the boat coupin an' you gyaun to the boddom o' the sea, ye wud seen be as deid 's a door nail wi' sea-sickness." And Mrs. Gibb, as a warning to the young people to beware of trusting themselves on the bosom of the heaving deep, related how, long ago, when Johnny and she were young, and Johnny headstrong and reckless, he would have himself and his wife conveyed from Macduff to Banff by water; and what of peril and fright the voyage involved, the boat rising up and down on its very ends, and leaning over till the spray actually skirpit her face, while, to crown all, the monster of a skipper sat coolly at his helm laughing at her terror.

As this crack went on in the cart, Johnny stumped along by Jess's head, scanning the countenances of those he met, in search of any stray kent face. By and by his eye caught a formal inscription, in the usual street-corner style, "Duff Street." "Fat whigmaleerie's this noo?" quoth Johnny. "The fowk o' this place wud ca' their vera tykes aifter the Yerl o' Fife. This is fat we hed ees't to ca' the 'Main Street'—Duff Street; fat sorra ither."

The explanation was that, since Johnny's last journey to the Wells, the good people of Macduff had adopted the modern practice of systematically naming and numbering their streets. It was then in the region of Market Street, I do not say that it was in that particular thoroughfare itself, that Johnny found a lodging-house for his charge. Their landlord was Donald M'Craw, a blind old pensioner, who had followed the gallant Abercromby into Egypt, and whose industrious helpmeet occupied her leisure time in keeping a dame's school in the kitchen of their habitation. And while she energetically pursued her pedagogical duties among her noisy charge, the blind Donald was wont to sit in his arm chair in the corner, a not uninterested listener to what was going on, and always ready at an emergency to come in full shout with his military word of command to enforce obedience or silence, as the case might be.

CHAPTER III.

RUSTIC COURTSHIP.

TAM MEERISON had been servant to Johnny Gibb only from the term of Whitsunday, that is to say for about three weeks previous to the date of which I have been writing. He was a stout fellow of six or seven and twenty, with a broad, good-natured face, and straggling, but very promising whiskers of light complexion fringing his cheeks. On his head he wore a sort of nondescript blue bonnet, and going downward on his person you found a remarkably substantial sleeved vest of moleskin and a pair of cord trousers, narrow at the knees, and spreading somewhat about the ankles, with about half-a-dozen buttons at bottom overhanging the heavy beetikin on either foot. The servant lass, Jinse Deans, a sedate-looking, red-haired damsel of fully Tam's age, had been a resident at Gushetneuk for a couple of twelvemonths bygone; and when Johnny had set out for the Wells the two were master and mistress of the place for the time being. Tam pursued his work industriously afield during the day, along with the orra man, Willy M'Aul, a youth of sixteen or seventeen, and son of the souter of Smiddyward. When six o'clock p.m. had come, Tam incontinently lows't. Then came supper of kail and kail brose, of which the three partook in company, amid no little badinage, consisting mainly of equivocal compliments to Jinse on her housekeeping capabilities, from Willy M'Aul, or as he was more commonly designated, the loon, who was of that particular character fitly described as a roy't nickum. Tam next lighted his pipe and blew clouds of smoke to the kitchen roof, as he watched Jinse " washing up " her dishes, an operation which Jinse invariably performed with an amount of clattering and noise that made the beholder marvel how it happened that she did not break at least one half of the crockery as it passed through her hands. Whether Tam was admiring Jinse's dexterity and vigour in going through her work or not I cannot say; I rather think, at any rate, that Jinse was not altogether unconscious that she was making a considerable display of these qualities before the new ploughman. At last she had finished, when, addressing the loon, she said—

"Gae 'wa', ye haveril, an' fesh hame the kye, till I get them milket."

"An' fat 'll aw get for that, Jinse?"

"Gin ye get fat ye deserve, ye winna braig aboot it."

"Wud ye gi'e 's a kiss gin aw war to dee 't?"

"Ye 're a bonny ablich to seek a kiss. I 'se rug yer lugs t' ye gin ye dinna gae this minit."

"Hoot man, ye 've nae pluck ava," exclaimed Tam, as the loon retreated towards the door to escape from Jinse, who had shown a distinct intention of suiting the action to the word. "Canna ye tak' a grip o' 'er?"

"I wudna advise you to dee that, Tam, or ye 'll maybe fin' 't she 's a sauter," replied Willy, as he marched off for the cows.

Later in the evening, when the cows had been milked, the calves properly attended to, and the work of the day fully concluded, Johnny Gibb's three servants were to be seen loitering about the kitchen door, and talking over the countra clatter. Tam, who was seated on the big beetlin stone by the door cheek, had spoken once and again of going to bed, and had given the loon emphatic warning of the expediency of his immediately seeking repose, as he might depend on it that he, Tam, would pull him out of the blankets by the heels if he were not astir by five o'clock next morning. Notwithstanding his urgency with the loon,

Tam did not himself give any distinct indication of hurrying to bed. But as the loon failed to "obtemper" his repeated hints, he at last started to his feet, and went clanking across the causeway and up the trap stair to the chaumer over the stable. And while the loon proceeded to undress, Tam yawned once and again portentously. He then, very deliberately, wound up his watch, and, seating himself on his kist began, by and by, to sowff over "My love she's but a lassie yet." When he had got Willy fairly into bed, Tam next rose, and under pretence of going to the stable, slipped down the trap and out by the door, which he quietly locked, to make sure that Willy M'Aul would not follow him. In somewhat less than two minutes thereafter, Tam Meerison and Jinse Deans were seated side by side on the deece in Johnny Gibb's kitchen.

I don't know all what Tam Meerison said to Jinse Deans that summer gloamin. How should I? The whispers of lovers are hard to catch. Nor am I able to say how far Johnny Gibb would have approved of the sort of sederunt that took place on this occasion, in his absence, between his servant maid and his servant man. But certain it is that this was not the first time that Jinse had been wooed in a similar manner, and in that same place. Not by the same wooer, certainly, for until three weeks ago she had been utterly unaware that such a man as Tam Meerison existed.

At any rate, if Jinse saw no harm in receiving a little attention from an additional sweetheart, Tam evidently found her company the reverse of disagreeable. The time fled swiftly past, as it is wont to do in such circumstances. It had "worn on" to twelve o'clock; to one o'clock; and the lonely corncraik, which had so long kept up its rasping, yet cheery, note, to break the stillness of the summer twilight, had at last ceased its cry, and gone to sleep. It was still and quiet as quiet could be, when footsteps were surely heard approaching the house of Gushetneuk.

"Wheesht!" exclaimed Jinse, in a low whisper. "Fat's that?—I hear a fit."

"Nonsense," said Tam; "it's some o' the horse i' the park at the back o' the hoose."

"It's naething o' the kin'. Here, I say—there's somebody comin' up the close! In aneth the deece wi' ye this minit!" whispered Jinse, in great excitement.

Tam felt there was nothing for it but to do as he was bid; not that he liked the idea of doing it, or that his judgment was fully convinced of the propriety of the course prescribed, but he failed in getting up any valid negative to oppose to Jinse's urgency; and so, giving way to the force of her exhortation, Tam proceeded to squeeze his inconveniently-bulky person under the deece, among a horde of old shoes, dilapidated brooms, and sic like, with all the celerity he could achieve. And he was not a moment too soon, for the head and shoulders of some person were already dimly discernible at the front window. The deece stood opposite to this window, at the back wall. A tap or two on the pane were immediately heard, followed by a loudly-whispered "Jinse!"

Now, Jinse's position at the moment *was* a little awkward. With womanly tact she had remained by the deece to cover Tam's retreat, which had been accomplished with tolerable success; but here there were one, if not two pairs of eyes staring through the uncurtained window, and there was yet light enough to enable the owners of those eyes to follow the movements of any one inside, and even to discover their whereabouts, if they happened to be fully in view of the window, which the occupant of the deece unluckily was. She hesitated, yet remained still; but the call was persistently kept up, "Jinse! I'm sayin, Jinse!" Jinse's wits could scarcely have been calmed to the point of keeping continued silence under the increasingly-violent demand of the assailants of the window to have audience of her; to pretend that she was in bed was hopeless; and so, starting up in a fashion to knock over one or two chairs and stools—not a bad feint either—Jinse advanced to the window, and indignantly demanded what the midnight brawlers wanted.

"Ou, Jinsie, 'oman, dinna tak' the huff—nae fear o' the aul' cock the nicht. We ken brawly that Gushets an' 's wife tee 's awa' fae hame."

"Father they be awa' fae hame or no, ye hae nae bizness comin here at this time o' nicht disturbin fowk."

"Wus ye sleepin terrible soun', Jinse?"

"Sleepin!" exclaimed a second voice; "the fowk o' Gushetneuk sleeps noo oot o' their beds, an' wi' a' their claes on!" And at this sally of wit the two men laughed loudly.

"Gae wa' this minit, I tell ye," exclaimed Jinse, with increased vehemence.

"I wauger she has a man wi' 'er, the jaud," was the only reply that proceeded from the first speaker.

Jinse, who either did not hear, or pretended not to hear, this remark, then, in a rather less indignant tone, asked, "Fat are ye wuntin here, I'm sayin?"

"Fat are we wuntin! Wuntin in tae see ye, Jinse; fat ither," said the voice that had spoken most.

"Gae awa' hame, I tell ye."

But, at this juncture, Jinse to her great horror, heard the latch of the door softly lifted, and the door itself, which of course had never been locked, evidently opening—a doubtful illustration, I daresay, of the saying that "love laughs at locksmiths." Before she could hinder it the two men were inside, and advancing towards the kitchen. They were quite well known to Jinse to be two of the servants at the farm of Mains of Yawal—one of them, indeed, averred that he had been "here afore"—but, for all this, it was decidedly inconvenient to have them in the house with the avowed intention of searching out the man who, as they asserted, was there before them, and all to see "fat like" he was.

"Faur hae ye pitten 'im noo, Jinsie?" exclaimed the more demonstrative of the two; "jist tell 's, 'oman—we winna hurt 'im."

"I say!" cried Jinse, excitedly, endeavouring to push him back.

c

"Jock, min," continued the man, addressing his friend, who had not yet emerged from the trance; "Jock, canna ye come ben an' gi'e Jinse the fawvour o' yer company. Oh-ho! he'll be i' the bed, I wauger," and the fellow darted across, and opened the doors of the bun bed in which Johnny Gibb's servant maid slept. Partly through vexation and excitement, partly perhaps as a stroke of policy, Jinse had resort now to a woman's last defence—her tears. Her tormentor, failing to find the man he groped for in the bed, and with his compunctions slightly stirred, perhaps, seized her round the neck.

"Weel-a-wuns, than, Jinsie," exclaimed the equivocal comforter, "we 'se lat 'im rest 's banes in peace an quaetness;" saying which he swung Jinse round, and they both together came down on the deece with ponderous force. Now, Johnny Gibb's deece, though a substantial piece of furniture on the whole, did yield slightly, perhaps, under severe pressure; and, moreover, in the process of pushing himself under it, Tam had unsettled the deece from the two fragments of thin slate on which its front legs stood. The result of this was that, inasmuch as Tam Meerison was bulky enough to require in any case all the accommodation he could find between the deece seat and the floor, the doosht of the two persons falling on it had the effect of bringing his person into such violent contact with a three-cornered ironing heater, which happened to be under him, that Tam uttered an involuntary "Go-ch!" with considerable emphasis. The general noise going on fortunately prevented this exclamation being heard; but, as Tam lay there a very close prisoner indeed, without the power of stirring a hair's-breadth, the sweat gathered on his brow plentifully, and he began seriously to reflect what was to be the end of it, for the second man had now also taken his seat on the deece, and horrible pictures of being squeezed as flat as a skate rose in his mind; still he hoped the deece would hold out, and so long as it did so, he might hold out too, seeing he certainly had not more than half the superimposed burden to sustain.

No doubt it was a weary lie for Tam, for a full hour and a half had elapsed before Jinse managed to get rid of the two intruders. In the course of the conversation overhead of him, Tam had the pleasure of hearing his sweetheart questioned in a very direct and unceremonious fashion about himself, under the title of "Gushets' new man," the interrogator adding, as his own private opinion, "He's a queer-leukin hurb, at ony rate." It need hardly be said that Jinse answered discreetly in the circumstances.

When the unsought visitors had left, I daresay she and her companion exchanged some words of mutual congratulation and comfort; but daylight was already showing itself, and the feelings of both Tam and Jinse had been too rudely disturbed to admit of their settling down again at that time to a quiet and loving conference. Tam hung about for a little after he had risen from below the deece, and spoke widely of giving the two disturbers of his enjoyment their "kail throu' the reek some day," and then he slipped out to the stable, and crept cannily up the chaumer stair. Tam had hoped to get quietly to bed, at any rate; but, just as he had deposited the last article of his removable garments on his kist lid, and stood in nocturnal attire, ready to creep in amongst the plaids, his bed-fellow, Willy M'Aul, turned himself with a drowsy grane, and muttered, "Ay, ay ! ye 're a gey boy, comin to yer bed at three o'clock i' the mornin."

"Haud yer jaw, min!" was Tam's abrupt response.

CHAPTER IV.

JOHNNY GIBB'S POLITICAL EDUCATION.

THE reader who has followed me thus far has, I hope, obtained a sort of general notion of Johnny Gibb's character; but, while the worthy farmer of Gushetneuk is jogging leisurely home from Macduff in the cart all alone, leaving his charge to enjoy their eight-days' bathing till he should return again for them, I may be allowed to indicate a little further the stamp of man that Johnny was.

In point of worldly circumstances the goodman of Gushetneuk, by dint of honest industry and the possession of a reasonably-conditioned old tack, had come long ago to be very comfortable. He had the repute, indeed, of being rich; but to what figure his wealth really reached nobody could exactly say, or even very definitely guess, because he and his goodwife belonged to that worthy and unsophisticated order of people, now becoming rare, I fear, with whom increase of wealth brings no change either in tastes or habits of life. Johnny's table was not, in any noticeable degree, more sumptuously furnished than it had been thirty years before, when he began life on little beyond the mere lawbour o' his han's. He still duly every morning sat down by the little back table on the kitchen deece, whereof I have already spoken, and having put aside his bonnet and said grace, took up his horn spoon and suppit his porridge from a dainty wooden caup, the milk that seasoned it being contained in a smaller timmer luggie. The only difference between him and the lads at the front dresser was, that Johnny had tea, and oat cakes and butter daily, whereas the lads got butter an' breid only on Sabbath mornings. At Klyack, Yule, and other festivals, master and servant feasted royally together at the same table, along with sundry invited guests, usually from among the residenters at Smiddyward. Johnny's clothing, moreover, was of exactly the same type as it had ever been; indeed, some pieces of it still extant and in use had been worn since he was a young man. What is yet more wonderful, when we think of the general habit of the prosperous part of society in this particular, Johnny had never once dreamed of "cutting" an old acquaintance because of the stigma attaching to him on account of his poverty. There was he, a man perfectly "independent" in pecuniary matters (and not less independent in his opinions and feelings), who certainly had a very good balance at his banker's, and, as was pretty broadly hinted, had, under a strong appeal, at one time actually lent money to his laird, and who yet, at kirk or market, would accost any dyker or ditcher in the parish on terms of perfect equality. The odd thing, too, was that all this did not seem in the least to lower Johnny in the respect of these poor folks, who accepted his opinions with greater deference than they were sometimes disposed to accord to those of people making much higher pretensions.

In politics, Johnny Gibb was what would be called an advanced Liberal,—only the term, I rather think, had not been invented then. When the first Reform Bill was under discussion he became conspicuous by his vehement declarations in its favour. The smith and the souter of Smiddyward had been wont to meet and discuss the subject, and to read, for mutual edification, all the Radical opinions they could find in print in the serial literature of the time. Johnny became a casual hearer, and, by and by, a not inapt pupil. And thus, when the Bill had passed and a contested election had come, Johnny went down to the polling place at the "Broch," and threw up his blue bonnet among the excited burghal crowd, who had rigged out the toon's drummer to head their scattered procession and beat for victory. He stoutly shouted "Bruce for ever! Gordon never!" and, in place of accepting, like the other newly-enfranchised tenants in the lan', the directions of his laird, Sir Simon Frissal of Glensnicker, to vote for Captain Gordon, he resented the hint given, and at the polling place reminded Sir Simon, in very plain terms, that they two stood now, politically, on an equality.

"Step forward, John," said the rather pompous laird, when they met at the front of the polling-table. Sir Simon was inclined to hang on and see whether his presence would not overawe his refractory tenant even at the eleventh hour.

"Savin yer presence, sir," said Johnny, "I wud raither gi'e you the prefairence."

"Step forward," said the laird, severely.

"Weel, weel, sir," was the reply,—"to please you. We're a' voters alike noo, ye ken, Sir Seemon—ay, ay, we're a' alike noo. Fa is't, said ye?—Sir Mykaeal Breece!" shouted Johnny, in the ears of his astonished neighbours, and under the nose of his frowning laird. Then Johnny clapt on his bonnet, and strode away out unconcernedly.

Johnny Gibb's political opinions undoubtedly damaged his ecclesiastical prospects. The eldership in the parish, apart from Jonathan Tawse, the schoolmaster, had got worn down to two members, whereof one was much incapacitated by old age and deafness, and the other was but an unstable pillar at best, seeing that he not unfrequently got publicly tipsy on the market-day, and had been known to ride his pony belly-deep in a neighbour's dunghill on his way home, and then, when the animal could get no farther on, sit up in the saddle and shout to some supposed waitress, "Anither half-mutchkin, lassie!" The necessity of recruiting the eldership was patent, and the eyes of not a few were directed to Johnny Gibb as one fit and suitable person for the office. Others hinted at Roderick M'Aul, the souter; but, in those days, in the parish of Pyketillim, we liked to select men of substance for the eldership. Besides, the souter was reckoned very wild in his religious opinions, inasmuch as he had agitated the question of a Sunday-School, and was believed to maintain family worship in his household.

The parish minister, the Rev. Andrew Sleekaboot, was a very peaceable man in the main, albeit a man that liked extremely well to have his own way, which, indeed, he generally got among his parishioners. The idea had been suggested to him before by Jonathan Tawse that, in order to keep Johnny Gibb docile and submissively attached to the Kirk, he should have him made an elder; and Mr. Sleekaboot was not indisposed to think that this might have prevented certain aberrations on the part of Johnny, who had been guilty of the irregularity of hearing and even entertaining as his guest a "missionar" minister, that came to the quarter occasionally on the invitation of the souter—a thing which no elder, so far as known in that region, had ever presumed to do. But now the daring course taken by Gushetneuk in setting his laird's political opinions and wishes at defiance fairly staggered Mr. Sleekaboot, and he determined to try the effect of indirect discipline in the matter. So he preached a sermon ostensibly on the qualities of those fitted to hold office in the Church, but in which his main strength was expended in picturing the dreadful offence of which they were guilty who refused in any manner of way to be subject to the powers that be. The allusions, though rather laboriously roundabout in their putting, were clear enough to the meanest capacity. The laird, Sir Simon Frissal, who, being in the quarter, had come to countenance the occasion, and who, from his boxed-in, or pumphel seat, as it was called by the irreverent youth of the parish, had nodded approval frequently during the delivery of the sermon, pronounced it "an excellent discourse," and spoke vaguely of getting it published. The general remark among the parishioners was of this sort, "Nyod, didnin he tak a gey fling at the 'lectioneerin' the day?" "Aw doot Gushetneuk cam in for a bit scaad yon'er."

Johnny Gibb met Mr. Sleekaboot in a day or two after the delivery of this famous discourse, when Johnny bluntly accosted him thus:—

"Weel, I daursay ye thocht ye hed me o' the steel o' repentance on Sunday, sir?"

"John! John! what do you mean by that?"

"Ou, brawly ken ye that, sir; ye're nae so blate—yer discoorse was mair like a hash o' Tory poleetics, nor an expoondin' o' the Gospel."

"John! let me warn you,—these Radical and irreverent notions of yours can end in no good."

"That's preceesely fat ye taul me fae the poopit on Sunday, sir."

"I simply deduced from the passages of Scripture founded upon those general principles that ought to guide men in certain relations of life."

"Maybe; but I think, wi' a' respeck, it cudna be coontit muckle short o' a wrestin' o' the Word o' Gweed to apply some o' the remarks as ye did."

"Mr. Gibb," said the Rev. Mr. Sleekaboot, with some severity, "that's a style of remark I have not been accustomed to from any parishioner."

"Sae muckle the waur for ye, maybe," was the undaunted reply.

"Will you be kind enough to condescend upon any remarks of mine that were not warranted by the Scripture?" added the minister.

"Weel, sir," replied Johnny, "ye made a hantle o' the poo'ers that be, an' the duty o' absolute subjection to them. Noo, sir, lat me tell ye that the Apos'le never inten'et to set up either the laird or the minaister as ane o' the poo'ers ordeen't to bear rowle owre's i' the fashion that ye seem't to approve so muckle o'. The laird jist sets me a bit grun, an' as lang as I keep my bargain an' pay my rent, he has nae bizness wi' maitters o' conscience, temporal or spiritooal. As for the minaister, I gi'e him a' due deference as my spiritooal instructor, gin he pruv 'imsel worthy o't; but fat mak' ye o' the text that he s'all be 'servant of all'?"

Mr. Sleekaboot did not stay to make much of it one way or another, at that time at any rate. He mumbled out something about people being "opinionative" and "impracticable," and with a face expressive of a good deal more than he said, bade Johnny Gibb Good day.

A few Sundays thereafter it was announced from the pulpit that a batch of three new elders had been chosen; by whom was not stated, but the electing body was believed to consist of Mr. Sleekaboot and the office-bearers already referred to. Anyhow the batch did not include the name of John Gibb. The new pillars of the church were our old friend Mains of Yawal, Braeside (who was the brother-in-law of Peter Birse of Clinkstyle, hereafter to be introduced), and Teuchitsmyre. They were all men of reputable substance, and gifted with the minimum of liability to do or say anything original or remarkable.

As was fully to be anticipated, several expectant elders (and their wives) were highly exasperated at being passed over, and canvassed the gifts of the newly-ordained with some asperity. Johnny Gibb said nothing, though his unexpected exclusion caused more talk in the parish than even Mr. Sleekaboot altogether liked. And thus it came about, by and by, that, in quarters in amicable affinity with the manse, the confidentially-whispered averment was freely circulated that the unhappy tenant of Gushetneuk, greatly to the distress of his excellent pastor, had been found to be a good way from soun' on various fundamental points of doctrine; indeed, a man of violent and somewhat dangerous opinions generally.

CHAPTER V

LIFE AT THE WELLS.

My last note of Johnny Gibb's excursion to the Wells left Johnny and his good mare Jess plodding on their way homeward. They reached Gushetneuk in due time, safe and sound; and there we shall leave them meantime, while I describe shortly the habits of the bather and water-drinker.

The daily round was uniform and systematic. You were expected to drink the salt water as an aperient once in two days at least, and to bathe every day. The water was drunk in the morning—the patients helping themselves out of the Moray Firth at such spots as they found most convenient, and then walking along the bare, bluff beach to the valley of Tarlair, where they supplemented the salt water by drinking of the mineral stream that discharged itself at the little well-house, covered with several large Caithness flags, that stood there. There was a little house, too, at the foot of the north bank, where a drop of whisky could be got somehow in cases of emergency, as when the patient got hoven with the liberal libations of salt water previously swallowed, or where the taste lay strongly in that direction; but this was no part of the recognised regimen.

Then about midday was the season for bathing. The women—perhaps I should say ladies—bathed at the part nearest the town, and the men farther eastward; and, on the whole, very excellent and safe bathing ground it is;

with, I rather think, the addition of baths built for public accommodation since the date of which I write. But I speak of the old fashion of things. Bathing served to whet the appetite for dinner, as water-drinking may be supposed to have whetted the appetite for breakfast! and the former important meal over, the bathers spent the latter part of the day in pleasure; daundering about the quays, observing the operations going on there amongst the gallant tars and hardy fishermen, at the risk of having an uncomplimentary designation referring to their present mode of life occasionally applied to them; sauntering out to the hill of Doune to watch the ceaseless breakers on the bar of Banff, and wonder how the waters of the Deveron ever managed to make their way into the sea through the sandy deposits that all but shut up its mouth; or perhaps an excursion would be undertaken to Banff or beyond it: and, in those days everybody made a specialty of visiting Duff House, wandering about the fine grounds at pleasure, and, if ill luck forbade it not, contriving to get some good-natured domestic to guide them over the interior of that noble mansion.

The circumstances being as I have said, Widow Will set herself to find out a prudent and experienced person of the male sex to whose care she might entrust Jock, her son, for, at any rate, the bathing part of the course.

"An' deed tat 'll no be ill to get," quoth Mrs. M'Craw, "for there 's a vera discreet, weel-livin' man fae the parish o' Marnoch bidin at my gweedbreeder's sister's, near the Buchan toll yett."

"Eh, but aw cudna think o' tribblin a body that kens nae mair aboot me an' mine nor the man o' France," said the widow.

"Och, an' he 'll be muckle waur o' tat! Maister Saun'ers 'll no be so easy fash't, I 'se warran. For a won'er he 'll be in for a crack wi' Donal', an' we 'se see."

"He 's an acquantens o' your goodman's, than?"

"Fat ither," said Mrs. M'Craw. "An' a weel-leern't man he is. There 'll be few as I 've seen cud haud the can'le to Donal' at argifyin aboot Kirk maitters; but I b'lieve ye he'll no loup the stank so easy wi' Maister Saun'ers."

"Na, sirs!" sagely observed Widow Will.

"An' aw b'lieve he's here o' ta vera word," added the good woman, as a ruddy-cheeked, well-conditioned man of middle age, dressed in a comfortable suit of gray, and a cloth cap of large dimensions on his head, passed the window and entered. The stranger, who proved to be in reality Maister Saun'ers from Marnoch, at once agreed to take charge of Jock, both for water-drinking and dookin; and, finding that his friend Donald had crept out to the garden to enjoy the soft air of a fine summer evening, and feel the declining beams of that sun which he had long ceased to see, he went in search of him; no doubt to hold high debate on some of their favourite topics, in preference to wasting his time with mere women's chatter.

And thus Jock was entrusted to the responsible care of the gentleman from Marnoch.

Maister Saun'ers, as the Celtic landlady had called him, had enjoined on the lad the necessity of being out of bed betimes to accompany him. By six o'clock next morning, accordingly, the two were stalking leisurely along the beach on the east side of the town. At a convenient point they picked their steps down, as other people of both sexes were doing, to where the tide was washing fresh and clear into sundry irregular rocky pools. At the margin of one of these Jock's guide, philosopher, and friend, stooped down, filled a tin jug of the salt water, and then, standing bolt upright, solemnly drank off the whole quantity. The jug contained a pint, ample measure; and when Maister Saun'ers had emptied it, he observed to Jock—"Noo, laddie, I'm easy physicket. I'll need no more; but an ordinar' dose for a stoot healthy man's aboot half as muckle again as I've ta'en. Here noo, I'll full the juggie to you." And, suiting the action to the word, he filled the tin jug and presented it to Jock, who lifted the vessel to his head with a dubious and tardy sort of movement.

"Drink hardy, noo!" cried Maister Saun'ers, as Jock

made a gruesome face, and threatened to withdraw the jug from his lips.

He made a fresh attempt, but could get no farther with the process of drinking.

"Hoot, toot, laddie, that 'll never do. That wud hardly be aneuch for a sookin bairn."

The jug was hardly half emptied.

"But it's terrible coorse," pleaded Jock, with a piteous and imploring look.

"Coorse! awa' wi' ye, min! Gweed, clean saut water. Ye sud gae at it hardier, an' ye wud never think aboot the taste o' 't. Come noo!"

Jock made another and not much more successful attempt.

"Hoot, min! Dinna spull the gweed, clean, halesome water—skowff 't oot!"

"Weel, but aw canna—it 'll gar me spue," said Jock in a tone approaching the greetin.

"An' altho', fat maitter?" argued his more experienced friend; "that 'll help to redd your stamack, at ony rate. Lat me see ye tak' jist ae ither gweed waucht o' 't, and syne we 'se be deein for a day till we see. But min' ye it 's nae jeesty to tak' owre little—speeshally to begin wi'."

Jock made a portentous and demonstrative gulp, which, I fear, had more show than effect, so far as swallowing the remaining contents of the tin jug was concerned. However, he was reluctantly allowed to spill the remainder.

"Come awa' noo, an' pluck a gweed han'fu o' caller dilse, an' tak' a bite o' them—they 're a prime thing for the constitution," continued Jock Will's new guardian.

This order was more grateful than the former had been, and Jock floundered over the slippery tide-washed boulders with alacrity, to gather dulse. "Tak' the shally anes aye fan ye can get them noo," said Maister Saun'ers, as Jock came up towards him with a bundle of rather rank-looking material. "They 're a vera halesome thing ta'en wi' the water. Leuk at that noo!" And he exhibited a bunch of short, crisp dulse, powdered about the root ends with clusters of tiny shells of the mussel species. "That's the richt thing;" and Maister Saun'ers, after dipping the dulse afresh in a little briny pool, swung them into his mouth. As the shells cracked and crunched away between his excellent grinders, he added, "That shalls has a poo'erfu effeck o' the stamack. We'll awa' roon to Tarlair noo."

When they had walked on to Tarlair, Jock was exhorted to drink as much of the mineral water as he could be persuaded to have thirst for, and to "gyang aboot plenty," but to "tak' care an' keep awa' fae the edges o' that ooncanny banks."

The scene at Tarlair was pretty much what I daresay it often was. About the Well-house were gathered a cluster of visitors, male and female, of various ages, mostly country people, but including a couple of well-dressed sailors, who had evidently been out the night previous on the spree, and had come there to shake off the effects of their debauch, if one might judge from the disjointed exclamations of one of them, who lay stretched at full length on his face on a long stone seat, occasionally complaining of the physical discomfort he was suffering, cursing the day of his return to Macduff, and cursing himself as an unmitigated fool. At a little distance along the valley was a group of sturdy water-drinkers of the male sex, with their coats off, exercising themselves at putting the stone; others, male and female, were to be encountered walking hither and thither, or returning to the Well for another drink; and some lay sluggishly on the brow of the steep grassy banks that shut in Tarlair on the landward side, enjoying the pleasant morning sun, watching any craft that might happen to be in view, or trying to make out as much as they could of the blue hills of Caithness across the Firth. And thus it went on till the several water-drinkers found themselves ready to go home to breakfast.

Of Jock Will's bathing experiences, I daresay, I need say nothing. His guardian was admitted by his compeers to be himself a "hardy dooker," a quality in which, notwithstanding his utmost exhortations, Jock continued to be rather deficient, I fear. The first gluff of the cold water, when it crept up on his person, was a trial which his nerves could hardly withstand; and the oft-repeated injunction to "plype doon fan the jaw's coming" embodied a lesson which Jock invariably shrank from, unless the iron grasp of his preceptor happened to be on his shoulder. Truth to say, Jock had always the feeling that the reflux of the wave would carry him away into some deep unfathomed cave of the Moray Firth. Nevertheless, there are hundreds of nice convenient baylets about the Macduff bathing ground, where even the most inexperienced may safely take a dip; and at any rate no harm came to Jock Will during the period of his stay at the Wells.

CHAPTER VI.

MRS. BIRSE OF CLINKSTYLE.

In the quiet region about Gushetneuk, comparatively unimportant events attracted no inconsiderable amount of public attention; and furnished topics of news that would circulate for a wonderful length of time. And thus the annual visit of Johnny Gibb's family to the Wells was naturally known to the neighbourhood, and formed the topic of conversation for the time being. It was also a means of getting a certain amount of useful news direct from "the Shore."

And so it came about that, on the evening after his return from Macduff alone, Johnny had a visit from his neighbour, Peter Birse, the farmer of Clinkstyle. Peter's errand was partly one of friendship, and partly one of business. But here it will be proper shortly to define, somewhat more exactly, who Mr. Peter Birse was.

Clinkstyle, next to Mains of Yawal, which lay on the west as it did on the east side of the road, and a little nearer to the Kirktown of Pyketillim, was the largest farm in the vicinity. The tenant of Clinkstyle kept two pairs of horses and a stout shalt, or orra beast, which "ran in the gig," the latter being a recently-added voucher for the respectability of Peter Birse, or rather, I should say, the respectability of his wife. She was a managing woman, Mrs. Birse, a very managing woman; extremely desirous of being accounted "genteel;" moreover, for thrift none in the parish could beat her. Perhaps it would be wrong to say that she boasted of her thrift; but at any rate the unapproachable sums she realised off her cows every summer in the shape of butter and cheese, in addition to fostering the calves, were no secret. Yet it was understood that Mr. Andrew Langchafts, the new merchan' at the Kirktown, who, with the intention of distancing all his rivals in the district, and securing the lion's share of the custom going, had prominently avowed his intention of giving the highest prices for butter and eggs, did not altogether admire her mode of transacting business. When the sturdy sunburnt servant damsel from Clinkstyle, in chack apron and calico wrapper, came to his shop deeply freighted with a basket of butter weighing thirty-six pounds, for which he paid at the rate of eightpence a pound—(a halfpenny in excess of the other shops)—and when Mrs. Birse, by her messenger, bought in return "an unce o' spice, a pennyworth o' whitet broons, half a peck o' saut, an' a stane o' whitenin," one can easily imagine that the merchan' did not deem it encouraging. And it would be difficult to believe that he could feel greatly flattered when the girl, having got her erran's and her goodly nugget of shillings in her hand, added, "The mistress bad 's seek some preens fae ye. Ye gyauna's neen last—she says she never saw a merchan' 't cudna affoord to gie 's customers preens."

"Well," quoth Andrew Langchafts, gravely, "I have really no margin—I 'm afraid I 'll have loss, for the butter 's declining."

"That 's fat she said at ony rate," answered the damsel; "an' she said she expeckit there wud be some ootgang o' the butter, forbye 't ye sud say 't it 's scrimp wecht."

"I tell you, young woman, if I press the buttermilk out of each of these lumps, I would lack well nigh a pound avoirdupois."

"Weel, weel, ye better come awa' wi' oor preens at ony rate, an' lat 's be gyaun, or I 'll get up my fit for bidin sae lang."

The merchant, a stiff gousty-lookin' stock, who had but recently begun business in the shop at Pyketillim, whose

D

experience heretofore had, it was understood, been mainly in a tolerably populous back street in Aberdeen, and who was thus not quite conversant with the peculiarities of thrifty country life, had no help for it but comply with the request.

Mrs. Birse had a family of three sons and one daughter, whose ages ran from ten to seventeen, and she had already begun to lay plans for their future establishment in life. The eldest son, Peter junior, was destined to succeed his father as farmer of Clinkstyle; the second, Rob, must be provided with a farm as soon as he was ready for it; the youngest, Benjamin, was to get leernin: and the daughter would, of course, be married off in due season to the best advantage.

Well, as I have said, Peter Birse called at Gushetneuk on the gloamin after Johnny Gibb's return. Along with him came his collie dog, and his eldest son; and Peter's conversation took somewhat of this turn—

"Weel, Gushets, ye've wun redd o' the goodwife noo, hae ye?"

"I' the meantime, Clinkies—mithna ye try something o' the kin' to get on the breeks yersel' for a fyou days, jist for a cheenge?"

Clinkies did not altogether relish the retort seemingly, so he gave up the jocular vein and continued—

"Weel, foo's the crap leukin doon the wye o' Turra?"

"Ou brawly; bits o' the corn wud be neen waur o' a gweed shooer, but the feck o' 't's settin' for a gey fair crappie."

"D'ye think that, though, Gushets?—it's blate, blate, a hantle o' 't, hereabout."

"Ou ay, ye've a gey puckle i' the laft, an' twa 'r three aul' rucks to thrash oot, Peter; but I wudna advise you to keep up, expeckin an ondeemas price for 't—the corn's comin' doon," said Johnny.

"Eh, man, is 't?" exclaimed Peter Birse. "An' fat are they gi'ein at the Shore?"

"Four-an'-twenty for gweed, weel-colour't stuff; an'

gettin' slack at that," said Johnny Gibb. "There's sic cairns o' 't pourin' in sin' the neep seed was finish't."

Peter Birse senior could scarcely conceal his chagrin at this announcement, the truth being that he had been sent over by Mrs. Birse to find out from Johnny what was being paid for the quarter of oats at Macduff; and also what was being charged for the boll of lime and coals, the object of these inquiries being to obtain the necessary data for deciding whether it would be prudent and advantageous to send off a couple of cart-loads of grain from Clinkstyle, for sale at that port, and to bring the carts home laden with either of the articles just named.

"An' divnin ye think four-an'-twenty a terrible little simmer price, Gushets?" pleaded Peter.

"'Deed, Peter, it's aboot daar aneuch for them that has 't to buy. Dinna ye be keepin' up, lippenin till a muckle price afore hairst,—ye may get a less, an nae blessin' wi' 't."

"Aweel, a' the toosht about our toon 'll mak' little odds. We wusna jist seer gin we wud thrash oot the bit huickie or twa 't we hae, or no. Is there mony fowk at the Walls this sizzon?"

"Muckle aboot the ordinar'."

"There 'll be mair neist month, I daursay,—the water winna be at its strength till near aboot Lammas, ye ken. Fan div ye gae doon again to fesh hame the goodwife?"

"This day ouk."

"An' ye 'll tak' a day or twa o' the water yersel', like?"

"Fae Wednesday till Saturday lickly,—we 'll come hame on Saturday."

"Jist that. They 'll be begun to the herrin' gin than?"

"I kenna."

"Sawna ye nae appearance o' the fishers gettin the muckle boats hurl't doon to the water aff o' the chingle, or the nets rankit oot?"

"Weel, I really tyeuk little notice, Peter; but I 'se keep my een apen fan I gae back."

"Jist that," added Peter. "It's a sturrin place Macduff: speeshally aboot the time o' the herrin'."

Peter had an object in all the questions he had put. He had got a commission of inquiry from his spouse, and his business when he had fulfilled it was to go home and report to her. When he had done so faithfully, Mrs. Birse pronounced, almost with indignation, against the idea of selling corn at twenty-four shillings a quarter; and more than hinted that if Johnny Gibb's granary and stackyard had not been pretty well emptied, he would not have been so communicative of the sort of advice he had tendered to the goodman of Clinkstyle. "Man, ye're a saft breet; cudna ye 'a speer't fat he wad tak' for a dizzen o' quarters oot o' the bing on *his* barn laft?" added Mrs. Birse, in the way of personal compliment to Peter; and having delivered herself of her sentiments on the grain question, she next heard Mr. Birse's statement about the general run of things at Macduff, and the fishing in particular.

The truth was, Mrs. Birse contemplated troubling Johnny Gibb with a small order when he returned to the seaport just named to fetch home his own. And on the evening before Johnny set forth on that journey, the lad Rob Birse was entrusted with the delivery of this order to the person who was to be honoured with its execution. Rob came across to Gushetneuk accordingly, and, having found Johnny, discharged his trust in these words—

"My mither bad 's tell ye—gin ye wad be good aneuch —fan ye gang to Macduff, to fesh hame till her fan yer comin back twa dizzen o' fresh herrin'. An' gin there binna herrin', gin ye cud get a gweed chape skate till her, an' twa-three bawbee partans."

"An' is that a', laddie—has she nae ither bits o' erran's?" asked Johnny, with a slight tinge of sarcasm, which the youthful Birse hardly appreciated.

"No, aw dinna think it," answered the lad. "She was gyaun to bid ye fesh half-a-gallon o' dog-oil till her, but she hedna a pig teem that wud haud it."

During these eight days of temporary celibacy, while

his wife was absent at the Wells, Johnny Gibb persisted in taking most of his meals with his three servants. He partook along with Tam Meerison and the loon of whatever Jinse Deans saw fit to make ready; and when Jinse ventured to ask his advice about some part of her household work, Johnny got something very like crusty, and said he "kent nedder aucht nor ocht about it;" and that if she "didna ken better aboot hoosewifeskip" than he did, she "wad mak' a peer bargain" to the man that got her; at which Jinse giggled, tossed her head slightly, and professed that there "was fyou seekin' 'er."

But Jinse was a competent servant as well as a gate-farrin damsel; and, though she had consulted Johnny once out of deference to him, she was quite capable of discharging her household duties satisfactorily without special guidance; and, in point of fact, she did so discharge them at this time, in so far as both Johnny and the other members of the household were concerned.

CHAPTER VII.

BACK FROM THE WELLS.

JOHNNY GIBB's return visit to the Wells, in 1839, was to him a somewhat memorable one; not for any remarkable events by which it was distinguished, but in this wise. Johnny had the fortune then to make the incidental acquaintance of two men, each in his way not a little after his own heart. These were Donald M'Craw, and the gentleman from Marnoch, of whom the reader has already heard somewhat. Donald, like many another Celt, was a keen hand in the discussion of all questions of a theologico-polemical cast, and a staunch upholder of the Church's exclusive jurisdiction in matters spiritual. And while the Marnoch man held similar sentiments with Donald theoretically, the progress of events was just then bringing to his own door the opportunity of illustrating his theory by a practical testimony.

And thus it was that when Johnny Gibb, Donald M'Craw, and "Maister Saun'ers," as Mrs. M'Craw called him, had got fairly yokit on the subject of the Kirk, a lengthened and engrossing confabulation was the result. When general principles had beeen sufficiently expounded—Donald and the Marnoch man being so thoroughly well up in the subject that Johnny was reduced to the position very much of a listener and learner—Maister Saun'ers entered on the history of the Marnoch case with all the exactitude of personal knowledge. Johnny had heard of it in a general way before, and sympathised with the protesting parishioners, but as his information grew through the communications of Maister Saun'ers, his sympathy also waxed in intensity, till it merited the name of righteous indignation against those who had sought to deprive them of their rights and privileges.

"Ay," said Maister Saun'ers, "faur's the richts o' conscience there, I wud like to ken? A man wi' nae gifts fittin' 'im for the wark forc't upon an unwillin' people i' the vera teeth o' the Veto Act."

"An' was there naebody in fawvour o' this Edwards?" asked Johnny.

"Judge ye, Maister Gibb—oot o' three hunner heids o' faimilies, members o' the congregation, nae less nor twa hunner an' sixty-one protestit against his bein' sattl't."

"An' the lave sign't for 'im?"

"'Deed no—I dinna like to speak oot o' boun's: but I'm seer there's nae half-a-dizzen, that hae ony richt to meddle i' the maitter, in fawvour o' him—leavin' oot Peter Taylor, the innkeeper at Foggieloan, I ken hardly ane."

"Dear me, man: but lat yer Presbytery be fat they like, the Assembly 'll never thole sic ongaens."

"Ay, Maister Gibb, but that's jist faur the creesis lies. The Assembly o' last year—thirty-aucht, ye ken—ordeen't the Presbytery to throw the presentee oot: aweel, that's been deen sinsyne. But nae doot ye've heard o' the Auchterarder case, faur the Coort o' Session was call't into play, an' the vera Presbytery o' Dunkeld brocht till its bar in person—it's aneuch to gar ane's bleed boil to think o' 't, aifter the noble struggles an' sufferin's o' oor covenantin' forebears to mainteen spiritooal independence."

"It leuks like a joodgment o' ta lan' for oor oonfaithfu'ness," said Donald.

"Aweel," continued Maister Saun'ers, "the Apos'le says, 'evil communications corrupt good menners,' an' so although the Presbytery hae been prohibitet fae takin' ony forder steps fatsomever to induck this 'stranger' that the flock will never follow, fa sud hin'er him to gae to the Coort o' Session neist an' seek a decree authoreesin the Presbytery to gae on wi' the sattlement?"

"I' the vera teeth o' the Assembly?" exclaimed Johnny.

"Ay, Maister Gibb, that's the pass we're brocht till at Marnoch noo."

"An' has the airm o' ta secular poo'er raelly been streetch't oot to touch ta ark o' ta Kirk's spiritooal independence?" asked Donald, with an air of solemnity.

"Judge ye, Donal'—This vera ouk this Edwards has gotten a legal dockiment fae the shoopreme ceevil Coort, requarin the Presbytery forthwith to tak' 'im on his trials."

"Alas! alas!" said the blind pensioner, shaking his head, "sic unhallow't wark bodes ill for oor coontra. We may some o' us leeve to see ta day when the faithfu' people o' God maun worship on the hill-sides again."

"But," interposed Johnny, "your Presbytery—they'll see you richtit. They winna daur to disobey the Assembly."

"Oor Presbytery! Jist wait ye," said Maister Saun'ers. "We've hed owre gweed preef o' their quality in the times bygane. They've deen ocht but befrien'et the people; an' I'll gi'e the lugs fae my heid gin they dinna gae on noo, neck-or-naething, to cairry out this sattlement—that's to say, the majority; for aiven in Stra'bogie we've a faithfu' minority protestin' against sic iniquity."

"An' will ye stan' to hae this man Edwards forc't upo' ye, neck an' heels?" said Johnny Gibb, warmly.

"Never!—I tell ye the fowk o' Marnoch 'll never submit to that, come fat will. They'll leave the kirk wa's to the owls an' the bats seener, an' gae forth oonder the firmament o' heaven to worship."

"Praise to Him that rules ta hearts o' men that we hae faithfu' witnesses i' the lan'!" quoth Donald M'Craw, with something of the fervour of an old Covenanter.

"Ay," replied Johnny; "it wud be a gran' sicht to see a congregation mairch oot, an' leave the bare wa's o' the desecratit kirk, raither nor bide still, un'er the minaistry o' ane that hed nae better call till 's office nor fat the poo'ers o' this earth can gi'e 'im by dent o' the strong airm o' the law—owreridin' the saacred richts o' men's consciences."

"Mark my words weel," said Maister Saun'ers; "if ye dinna see sic a sicht as fat ye speak o' in Marnoch, afore ony o' 's is muckle aul'er, I'm far mista'en."

"Wae, wae, to ta men that forder sic unsanctifiet wark," said Donald; "an' may ta Christian people nae be foun' faint-hertit i' the day o' trial."

"Never fear," exclaimed Maister Saun'ers stoutly; "we hae stood to oor prenciples as yet, an' we'll dee't still, i' maugre o' an Erastian Presbytery, wha ken nae heicher homage nor renderin' to Cæsar the things that are God's."

"Ay, ay, man," said Johnny, reflectively, and I rather think the image of Mr. Sleekaboot crossed his mind. "There's owre mony o' them tarr't wi' the same stick—war'dly, time-servin' characters; mair concern't aboot pleasin' the lairds nor sairin their Maister."

"Weel, weel," added Maister Saun'ers, "depen' ye upon 't, though it may begin at hiz, it canna en' there. There maun be a clearin' oot, an' an estaiblishment o' the true prenciples that oor forefaders focht an' suffer't for, afore the Kirk o' Scotlan' can be set on her richt foondations."

"Ah, but ye 're speakin' ta Gospel truth noo," exclaimed Donald M'Craw, who delighted in sombre prediction. "'I will overturn, overturn, overturn,' saith ta prophet. An' ta Kirk has been too lang sattl't on her lees—her day o' joodgment must come."

As may be imagined, the spirit of Johnny Gibb was not a little stirred within him by the discourse he had held with Maister Saun'ers and Donald M'Craw. For the day or two that he remained at Macduff, Maister Saun'ers was his constant companion. They took their walks together, and Jock Will trotted behind; they sat on the braes in the sun, and talked together, and Jock traversed the pebbly part of the beach in search of bonny buckies, half of which Jock had destined for the adornment of his mother's mantelpiece at home; the other half—well, Jock was gallant enough to meditate a surprise for the lassie, by presenting to her, should a favourable opportunity occur, as they journeyed home, a choice collection of the finest shells that the Macduff beach afforded. When the two new-made friends parted there was a vigorous handshaking, and Johnny Gibb avowed, as indeed turned out to be the case, that from that day forward his zeal in the Non-intrusion cause would be quickened in a degree that should bear no relation to his previous state of hazy, half-informed rebellion against Moderate domination, as it had been attempted to be exercised by Mr. Sleekaboot.

The journey home from the Wells was necessarily very much of the character of the journey thither; only that the patients were a little more tanned, if possible, by the sun, and the stores they now carried were chiefly of a maritime nature—a few dried cod; herrings; partans; dulse, and a bottle of sea water taken along by Widow Will to perfect her son's cure. In due course they arrived at Gushetneuk.

"Hae, lassie," quoth Johnny Gibb, handing out a decrepit-looking wicker basket, "that's the wife o' Clinkstyle's herrin'. Ye'll better tak' them owre at ance, or we'll be hearin' aboot it."

"Wudna ye sen' a puckle o' the dilse to the goodwife, man—an' a partan?"

"Please yersel', 'oman; but I sud partan neen wi' 'er. They war owre dear bocht till agree wi' her constiteetion."

"Hoot, ye sudna be sae nabal wi' fowk," answered the goodwife.

Johnny gave an expressive pech, and proceeded with the dismantling of the cart.

The compromise made was to send along with Mrs. Birse's parcel of herrings a goodly bundle of dulse; and the lassie went off to Clinkstyle freighted accordingly.

"An' that's my herrin' is't, Mary?" said Mrs. Birse, on seeing the basket. "An' dilse, nae less? Na, sirs, but ye'll be a far-traivell't 'oman noo. Did the wifie Wull come hame wi' yer aunt an' you, no?"

"Ay."

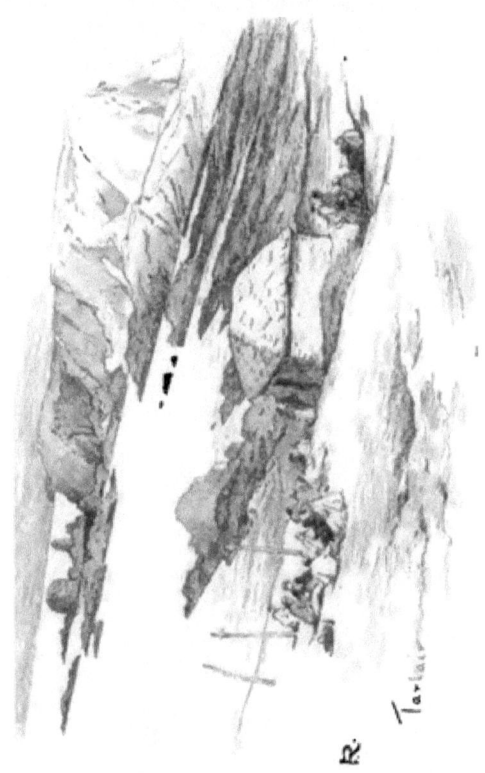

"An' Jock, nae doot—Is his sair chafts better noo?"

"I think they are," said the lassie.

"An' ye've bidden a' thegither at Macduff, I 'se warran'?"

"Na; auntie an' me bidet oor lanes in ae hoose, an' Widow Wull at anither."

"Ou yea, I thocht ye wud 'a maetit a' throu' ither—'t wud 'a made it chaeper for Jock an' 's mither, maybe. They cam' in files to see you, an' bade throu' the aifterneen?"

"Ay, files."

"An' fa did yer aunt an' you bide wi', syne?"

"They ca'd them Mr. and Mrs. M'Craw."

"A muckle house, I wauger, an' braw fowk?—brawer nor the fowk that Jock Wull an' 's mither bade wi'?"

"Ay, it was middlin' muckle."

"It wusna neen o' the fisher tribe 't ye bade wi,' than?"

"Na, the man was an aul' sojer."

"An aul' sojer! He 's keepit ye in order, no?"

"But he was blin'."

"An' 's wife made a livin' by keepin' lodgers—she wud hae mair nor you?"

"Na; she keepit a skweel for little littleanes."

"An' lodg't you i' the room en'?—jist that. She wud mak' a gweed penny i' the coorse o' the sizzon that wye, I 'se warran'."

As the goodwife of Clinkstyle leisurely undid the basket, she plied the girl with these and sundry other queries, marked by the like laudable intention of finding out the inner history of the journey to the Wells; and in particular whether Widow Will had not only been conveyed to and fro by the Gushetneuk folks, but had also shared in their bounty while at Macduff. At last the basket was emptied and its contents scrutinised.

"Ay, lassie, an' that 's my twa dizzen? They 're some saft, an' nae gryte sizes, weel-a-wat—Hoot, lassie, there 's only sax an' twenty there! Keep me, there sud 'a been foorteen to the dizzen—I never tyeuk less nor foorteen fae aul' Skairey the cadger, lat aleen Macduff itsel'. Aweel, tak' ye hame yer creelie noo. I sanna be speerin' the price o' them eenoo, but fan I see yer uncle I *sall* lant him the richt gate. He's a het buyer o' fish—nae to ken the cadger's dizzen!"

It is not quite certain that Mrs. Birse had any matured intention of ever asking the price of the herrings, if no one else stirred the question. Anyhow she deemed it politic to let it rest meanwhile; and politic also, in a wider sense, to dismiss the lassie graciously.

"Na, Mary, but ye *are* growin' a lang lassie. Oor 'Liza an' you ees't to be heid-y-peers, but ye're tynin her a' thegither. I dinna believe but ye're near as heich's Peter there. Come 'ere, min," continued Mrs. Birse, addressing the young gentleman in question, who had applied himself industriously to the mastication of the dulse. "Awat, but ye mak' a winsome pair. Gae 'wa' noo, Patie, an' convoy Mary a bit; tak' 'er basket i' yer han', and see 't ye help her owre the stank afore ye turn."

Peter, a thriving but on the whole slightly softish-looking lad, hirsled off his seat with rather evident reluctance, and after groping about for his bonnet, proceeded to do as his mother had ordered him. And with this lesson in gallantry to her eldest born, the goodwife of Clinkstyle turned her to the continued prosecution of her domestic duties.

CHAPTER VIII.

TAM MEERISON FLITS.

THE style of life that prevails at such places as Gushetneuk would not, I can well believe, suit the taste of the sensational story-teller. He might wait a very long time for "thrilling incidents" of any sort, and wait in vain; and the sober realities of every-day life, as there exemplified, would be certain so to conflict with his spasmodic conceptions of human existence as to drive him to distraction. Nevertheless, I am prepared, after full trial, to deny that such a style of life is in reality, or necessarily, either dull or uninteresting. But, what is more to the point, it is just the very thing that suits my present purpose, inasmuch as I can take my narrative in the most leisurely way, and jump over twelve months or so, which I now do, with the bare remark that I have performed that exploit, fully trusting to pick up my characters *in statu quo* just as I left them.

When the Martinmas term of 1840 was drawing near, Johnny Gibb wanted to know of Tam Meerison whether he was disposed to remain as his servant through the winter. Tam's answer to this question, addressed to him while he was busy currying the bay mare, was not decisive either way.

"Aw cudna say," quoth Tam, drily; "aw wudna care a great heap, gin we can 'gree aboot the waages, an' a' ither thing confeerin."

"Confeerin or no confeerin," said Johnny, testily, "I wunt a mair direck answer—fat siller are ye seekin'?"

"It depen's a gweed hantle on a body's neebours tee," continued Tam.

"Ou ay, I ken the loon an' you's been aye haein bits o' sharries noo and than; but he's a weel-workin', weel-conduckit loon, an' ye winna pit an aul' heid upo' young shou'ders."

"Will he be bidin?" asked Tam.

"Lickly, though he hasna been speer't at yet; an' Jinse's bidin—hae ye ony faut to fin' wi' her?"

"I've naething adee wi' women's wark, an' never meddles wi' 't," said Tam, pursuing his grooming very industriously. "Roun', Jess—wo—still, you thing." The latter part of the sentence was of course addressed to the animal, then undergoing its daily trimming.

"Weel, weel, but tell me, ay or no, an' fat fee yer seekin'," insisted Johnny Gibb.

"I cudna say foo the fees 'll be rinnin this term; an' aw wudna like to name siller till the mornin' o' the market."

"A puddin' lug, min," exclaimed Johnny. "That's aye the gate wi' you chiels; tum'le aboot a haill kwintra side, sax month or so here, sax month or so there, for half o' your life-time, an never save a saxpence to bless yoursel's wi'."

"I cudna dee 't, though," said Tam, who still carried in his mind Johnny's demand to know what fee he wanted.

Johnny at once turned him about and left the stable.

Now the truth of the matter was that Tam Meerison did not wish to leave Gushetneuk. The loon, of whom the reader has formerly heard, and who was still Tam's fellow-servant, was just a little of a thorn in his side occasionally, by his lack of reticence in speech on certain subjects; but then there was much seemingly to balance this very partial grievance. If Johnny Gibb was occasionally a little hasty, he was on the whole a kind and indulgent master. The horses Tam drove were handsome, well appointed, and well fed—an important consideration, and properly so, with every man in Tam's position. Tam admitted that the servants were "weel ees't" in the way of food; and then the presence of Jinse Deans had come to be something that seemed to be essential to Tam's perfect serenity of mind. But for all that Tam was so far the slave of habit that he could not clearly see his way to departing one jot from what, among his compeers, had come to be considered the correct mode of bargain-making in covenanting for their services; he had a kind of general idea that it was on the whole an effeminate sort of thing to "bide owre lang i' the same place," and he had now been eighteen months at Gushetneuk.

On the morning of the feeing market day, Johnny Gibb no doubt asked, once more, what wages Tam required, but evidently Johnny was in a decidedly more indifferent mood than when he had previously mooted the subject. And, accordingly, when Tam, who by that time had begun seriously to doubt his previous policy, "socht," he somewhat curtly "bade" ten shillings less than the sum Tam mentioned. With few more words they separated, and each went away to the market in his own interest, but with a vague notion on Tam's part that they "wud lickly meet afore they were lang there." Early in the day, however, Johnny had a stoot gudge, anxious to "work a pair o' horse," pressed on his notice, and easily arranged with him. Tam hung in the market for good part of the day, receiving only indifferent offers, and the upshot was, that he at last, reluctantly enough, engaged himself to be foreman at Clinkstyle. Peter Birse, as was not an unusual case with him, was about to make what is understood by "a clean toon" of his servants, and, according to his invariable practice, had been endeavouring to fill up the vacancies in his establishment at the cheapest rate; so he managed to pick up Tam Meerison at an advanced period of the market, at a crown less fee than Johnny Gibb had offered Tam on the morning of the same day.

The change from Gushetneuk to Clinkstyle was one that Tam Meerison did not find exactly conducive to his comfort. In explaining his reasons for making the change, Tam, to put the best face upon it, told his friends that he was desirous of getting to a "muckler toon" than Gushetneuk, where he would have more "company" and so on. But, poor lad, the company he got were a cause of no little trouble to him. It so happened that Mrs. Birse's notions about the proper mode of feeding servants were not such as to command the approval generally, of those servants who had had practical experience of them, or to procure for Mrs. Birse herself a favourable reputation among that class where she was known. The new servants—second horseman, orra man, and cow bailie—were disposed not merely to grumble but to break out into open insurrection, on the ground of the unsatisfactory character of the victuals supplied to them. And they expected Tam to vindicate their rights in the matter; a duty which he found by no means easy or pleasant. So far as mere inarticulate growling, or the utterance of an incidental anathema against the victuals in the hearing of the servant maid went, Tam found no difficulty in going fully along with his companions. But a crisis came by and by. The goodwife, in her thrifty way, had for a good many nights in succession supplied boiled turnips and turnip brose to the lads as the staple of their supper. And in testimony of their appreciation of the fare thus furnished, they latterly had no sooner smelt the odour thereof as they entered the kitchen night after night, than they duly commenced to low like as many oxen. Then it was that Mrs. Birse seized the occasion to catch them *flagrante delicto*, by bursting into the kitchen as they were bellowing away; and a very stiff onset she gave them about this unbecoming behaviour.

"An' fat hae ye to say against gweed sweet neeps to yer sipper, I sud like to ken?" demanded the irate matron.

"Oh weel, it's owre af'en to hae them ilka night 'cep Sunday for a haill ouk," said Tam.

"Owre af'en! Birst the stamacks o' ye; fat wud ye hae!"

"A cheenge files."

"For fat, no? There's fowk maybe 't kens their place better nor set their servan's doon at the same table wi' themsel's; and gin ye hinna leern't that muckle gweed breedin' yet, the seener ye 're taucht it the better; fat sorra div ye wunt?"

"We wunt naething but a fair diet," answered Tam.

"A fair diet! An' weel 't sets ye—aw wud thank ye to tell me fan *your* fader, the roch dyker,"—and here Mrs. Birse looked directly in Tam Meerison's face—"was able to gi'e 's faimily aneuch o' onything to ate. But that 's aye the gate; them that 's brocht up like beggars 's aye warst to please."

This outburst took the wind so considerably out of Tam that he utterly failed to make any reply; and Mrs. Birse, after a brief pause, went on, "'Deed, they 're but ower gweed for ye—wi' weel hir't brose, an' plenty o' as gweed milk to yer kyaaks as ever cam' oot o' a byre."

"Sang, it needs 't a'—near aucht days aul', an' as blue as blaeworts;—but it 's nae the milk 't we 're compleenin o' eenoo," said the second horseman, after another pause.

"Na, an' ye wud be baul' to compleen, ye ill-menner't pack; but ye 'll jist tak' yer neeps there, an' nae anither cheep oot o' the heids o' ye; or gin ye dinna, we 'll ken fat wye to tak' an order o' ye."

"Tak' an order o' the aul' Smith, an' ye like; neeps sax nichts oot o' the seyven winna stan' law at ony rate," said the former speaker.

"An' it 's muckle *ye* ken aboot law," replied the goodwife, scornfully. "Jist gae ye on till I need to gar yer maister tak' ye afore the Shirra, an' ye 'll maybe hae some diffeekwalty in stannin yer grun for refeesin a gweed halesome diet."

With this deliverance, and unheeding the rejoinder, "Aweel, aw daursay ye 've hed the chance o' hearin' the Shirra afore noo," Mrs. Birse turned, and bounced away ben to the parlour, where she proceeded to make tea for her husband and hopeful progeny, now gathered round the table, at the same time letting the unspent balance of her wrath blow off in a general way, to ease her mind; the head of the household getting a slight incidental scorching, when he happened to come in the way.

"I'm sure, man, I'm jist keepit in a fry wi' ae coorse pack aifter anither; ye seerly wile the vera warst that ye can get fan ye gae to the market."

"Hoot, 'oman, ye sudna vex yersel' aboot them."

"Easy to ye; but an' ye had the maetin o' them's I hae, ye wud tell anither story. A vulgar, ill-fashion't set."

"Fat's been adee eenoo?"

"Adee! refeesin their neeps, an' makin' a din like as mony nowte fan they cam' in."

"Hoot awa'."

"Yes," interjected Miss Eliza Birse, "an' I heard the second horseman cursin' about the kitchie cakes."

"An' fat did he say, my dear?" asked Mrs. Birse.

"He bann't at Betty, an' said they werena fit for swine to eat."

"An' fat did Betty say, 'Liza?"

"She said 't hoo 't she cudna help it; that it was your orders to mak' them weet i' the hert to keep the men fae eatin' owre muckle."

"The dooble limmer!" exclaimed Mrs. Birse. "An' her leukin a' the time 't a bodie speaks till 'er as gin butter wudna melt in her cheek."

"Weel, I heard 'er at ony rate; for I was jist gaen up the stair, an' stoppit and hearken't at the back o' the inner kitchie door."

"The oongratefu ill-menner't jaud 't she is," continued Mrs. Birse. "But I'll sort 'er for that. She'll be expeckin to get some leavin's i' the teapot, to be a cup till 'er fan the men gae oot to sipper the beasts, as eeswal; but she 'll leuk wi' clear een ere she see that again, I doot. That's the reward 't fowk gets for their kin'ness to the like o' 'er."

While this conversation was going on, the tea was proceeding apace. The three young Masters Birse and Miss Birse, with their respected parents, were seated round a somewhat clumsily set out table, containing in the way of solids, an ample store of bread, oatcakes, cheese, and butter. The olive plants were all at school, except Peter junior, who, being designed for agriculture, was understood to have the literary part of his education about finished, and was taking to farming operations, including some minor attempts at cattle-dealing, at which he had been allowed to try his hand, very kindly. Suddenly Peter senior called across the table to his youngest born, Benjamin—

"Benjie! fat are ye deein pirlin aboot at yer breid that gate?"

"Weel," answered Benjie, sulkily, "'Liza's gi'en 's a nae gweed bit, an' winna hae 't 'ersel'."

"The breid's a' perfeckly gweed—ate it this moment, sir!" said Peter Birse senior, severely.

Benjie put on a look more dour and dolorous than before, but failed to fulfil the parental mandate.

"Fat is 't, my pet?" asked Mrs. Birse, in her most sympathising tones, addressing Master Benjamin.

"Weel, it's nae gweed," answered Benjie, proffering his mamma the unacceptable bit of cakes—a thick, rather sodden-looking piece. The worthy lady examined it for a second, and said, "'Liza! that's a bit o' the kitchie kyaaks —fat wye has that come here?"

"I dinna know," answered Miss Birse; "it was upo' the truncher."

"Is there mair o' 't? Eh ay—here's twa korters! Betty cudna but 'a kent that she was pittin 't upo' oor maun'. I sudna won'er nor she's stown as muckle o' the parlour breid till hersel'. Sic creatures wi' oonhonesty. Lay that twa korters by, 'Liza, till we see better in till 't. I 'se be at the boddom o' that, though it sud cost her 'er place." The careful mother added, "There's a better bittie to ye, my dautie," and as she said this, she handed to Benjie a full half of one of the quarters of parlour cakes, which bore about the same relation to the kitchie kyaaks that a well-browned biscuit does to a lump of dough.

"Hoot, 'om—an," Peter Birse had commenced to utter, in the way of deprecation of this proceeding, when Mrs. Birse cut him short by tossing the lump of kitchie kyaaks towards him, and exclaiming—

"Weel, weel, try 't yersel', gin ye hae onything to say. But ye canna expeck the bairn's stamackie to be able to disjeest the like o' that."

"Humph, I cud ate it brawly," said Peter Birse senior; and in proof of the truth of his assertion he did eat it. Only his next helping was taken, not from the remaining bit of kitchie kyaaks, but from the parlour cakes.

The result of the turnip controversy was that Tam Meerison and his companions did get an occasional supper of kail, very purely prepared with salt and water; only as the three lads coincided in holding decidedly that Tam ought to have "stuck'n up better to the aul' soo," his influence and authority as foreman were correspondingly diminished. And the less Tam was disposed to renew the quarrel with his mistress, the more did the others swear "at lairge" when they happened to be about the kitchen. Not seldom was this done, with the evident intention of provoking warfare, as well as of manifesting the slight degree of respect they entertained for Tam, and for everbody else connected with Clinkstyle; the general result being that Tam would sit, mainly dumb, a good part of the evening, hearing no end of jibes indirectly launched at himself; while Betty, the hard-worked bedraggled kitchen damsel, would at one time giggle and laugh with the rough fellows, and be at next turn coarsely tormented till she was in a state of the highest wrath; or be made the butt of their oaths and obscene allusions. As for Mrs. Birse, bauld woman as she was, even she found it to her comfort to make as few errands to the kitchen as might be, while "the boys," as her husband termed them, were about.

And here, good reader, I bethought me of giving utterance to a few moral reflections on the degraded character of our farm-servant class; and how blameworthy they are for being such immoral and unmannerly boors. But somehow my line of vision came always to be obstructed by a full-figure image of Mrs. Birse of Clinkstyle, who, you will perceive, is a very particular and intimate acquaintance of mine. Mrs. Birse *would* come into the forefront, and her husband,

Peter, was vaguely discernible in the background. So I gave up the attempt. You may make it on your own account; but I doubt whether you will be able to search thoroughly into the causes of this social evil without being also troubled with the image of Mrs. Birse of Clinkstyle.

CHAPTER IX.

PEDAGOGICAL.

THE parish which forms the theatre of the principal scenes in this history, if not amply furnished with the means of education, had, at any rate, the advantage of a couple of schools. There was, first of all, the parochial school; a sample of that noble institution which is understood to have done so much for the enlightenment of our native country. And I should be the last to depreciate the value of the parochial school, though I have a strong impression that the statutory dominies of a quarter of a century ago, up and down, were, as a rule, highly inefficient for educational purposes. The improvement in the general style of teaching since that time is, I also believe, much greater than is imagined by many people.

The Rev. Jonathan Tawse, of the parochial school of Pyketillim, whose name has been previously mentioned, was considered, on the whole, a superior educationist, as compared with his brethren throughout the Presbytery. What the parishioners said about him in the early part of his career was, that his ambition lay too much toward the pulpit to admit of an efficient discharge of his duties as a teacher. And certain it is that the Rev. Jonathan Tawse was not destitute of a desire to wag his pow in some particular poopit which he could call his own, as his prompt readiness to officiate for any absent or sick brother of the Presbytery testified. And he usually sought opportunity to air his gifts still farther afield about the time of the annual vacation. It had even been bruited that he made bold, on one occasion, to offer himself in this way to the suffrages of a vacant town's congregation. But whether it was that the people were inappreciative, or patrons unaccommodating to the influence that he could command, the Rev. Jonathan Tawse settled down as a dominie, and a confirmed old bachelor, and took rather kindly and freely to toddy and snuff. I don't think that the Church lost much in respect of the Rev. Jonathan Tawse's failure to reach the dignity of formal ordination. For even in my time he preached at rare intervals in Mr. Sleekaboot's absence; and we juniors liked him; only it was for reasons which I greatly fear did not tend to edification. Firstly, his sneeshinie habits were a sort of pulpit novelty that tended to liveliness as contrasted with the stiff and demure solemnity of the usual minister. And then Mr. Tawse's services were short as compared with those of Mr. Sleekaboot. Not that he said less, either in prayer or in the sermon, but he had remarkable rapidity of utterance. There are religionists, I believe, in the East at any rate, who pray by machinery. Now, the Rev. Jonathan Tawse, in prayer, behaved exactly like an instrument which had been wound up, and must run down. With an exactitude that was remarkable, the well-worn phrases fell in in rapid succession to each other, each in its own due order, as cog answers to cog in the mill wheel and pinion. Thus were daily mercies, and the weekly returning day of rest with gratitude acknowledged; thus was our beloved Queen (a recent change from his Majesty the King) prayed for, with the high court of Parliament, the Assemblies of our national Zion, and all judges and magistrates of the land, that we (the parishioners of Pyketillim) under them might lead quiet and peaceable lives, that they might be a terror to evil doers, and a praise and protection to such as do well. Then, when Mr. Tawse came to the sermon, he tackled it with corresponding impetus. They were not new sermons that he used, but productions of a long bygone time, when he had considered himself a probationer, and they were framed after the manner of Blair, though marked by an occasional juvenile efflorescence of style that was rather out of keeping with the now mature age of the preacher. Such as they were, Mr. Tawse read them off with a monotonous rapidity that did great violence to all those principles of elocution and punctuation which he was wont to exemplify with impressive emphasis in the audience of his pupils. The only breaks in the discourse were when he made a halt to take snuff, or when the exigencies of the case compelled him to lift his head for the purpose of blowing his nose with his speckled silk handkerchief.

But, as I have said, Mr. Tawse was reckoned an able teacher; and he laboured away in his vocation with tolerable assiduity, the monotony of the ordinary routine being broken by occasional outbursts of a rather irritable temper, and the less frequent coruscations of a sort of dry humour that lay within him. He had usually a class of two or three "Laitiners," on whom he bestowed much pains, and a good deal of chastisement. These were intended to be the parsons and lawyers of the future; only the results did not always fulfil the expectations cherished, for I could point to sundry of the Latiners of my time who, at this day, are even less reverend and learned than myself, which is saying a good deal. As to his classes generally, Mr. Tawse had not much that deserved the name of method in their management; and still less was there of thoroughness in the little that he had. English grammar was one of the modern improvements which he prided himself on having introduced, and against which not a few of the more practical sort of parents loudly protested, as implying an unwarranted curtailment of the time that should have been devoted to the more useful branches, particularly coontin. And I know of one pupil at any rate, who, being much more earnestly bent on play than work at that period of his life, managed to maintain a decent grammatical reputation and a respectable position in the class, without his having ever possessed a copy of any Grammar whatever of his own, or ever looked in the most cursory way at the day's lesson out of the im-

perative school hours. The mode adopted was to keep one's acquirements modestly in subordination, and of set purpose avoid being inconveniently near the top of the class. Then when lesson time drew near, one could ordinarily manage to obtain a furtive glance of some other body's beuk, and hastily scan the lesson. With the thing very fresh on the mind, and a deft calculation, based on the number between you and the top, of the particular bit you would have to repeat, you stood a fair chance of getting over the first round creditably; and that accomplished, it was your own fault if you could not get sufficiently up in the subject by the time the whole class had been gone over to enable you to meet with impunity any further demands on your erudition at the hands of the dominie. This was a practicable course with both the Grammar and "Catechis;" and in the arithmetic department it was quite possible, by judicious guess-work, and "copyin" from others as opportunity offered, to have gone well through the inevitable "Gray," rule by rule, and yet be unable to face a very plain question in Proportion or Practice without heartfelt dread, if it happened to lie outside of Mr. Gray's "examples." The annual Presbytery examination has been said to be very much of a farce. In my day it was felt to be anything but that; for we had one vehement member of Presbytery who broke freely out in scolding fits, which were much dreaded; while another had an appalling facility in scribbling down arithmetical problems that made the hair stand on end to think of, much more to face in the way of attempting their solution; and thus the yearly appearances of the "minaisters" came to be the most formidable ordeal to which we were subjected. In the ordinary course we dozed away very comfortably, and the pupil who was alive to the current dodges of the time might have as much trifling and remain about as ignorant as he chose, for there was no real system of testing his acquirements, and he only needed to dread being "brought to the scratch" when some extreme aberration on his part had put Mr. Tawse in a thorough rage. Then he might expect a severe overhaul, with a certain amount of punishment by having his lugs ruggit, the sides of his head cuffed, or a few strokes with the tawrds implanted on his palms; and thereafter things settled down again to the ordinary routine.

Now, as I have indicated, it had been felt by many judicious parishioners that the parochial school of Pyketillim, under Mr. Tawse, was too much of a mere high-class academy. The complaint was not that Mr. Tawse's system, as administered, was lacking in general efficiency and thoroughness, but that he "took up his heid owre muckle wi' that Laitin and Gremmar, an' ither beuk leernin—a mixter-maxter o' figures wi' the letters o' the A B C, aneuch to turn the creaturs' heids." And indeed it was cautiously averred by some, that the dominie had really driven one pupil doited by the distance he had endeavoured to lead him into the abstruse region of Mathematics. Mr. Tawse himself said the lad was a natural born dunce; that he had hoped to make a decent scholar of him by dint of hard drilling, but that his harns, after deducting the outer case, might have been contained in an eggshell, and that his own muddled stupidity was the only disaster of an intellectual kind that was ever likely to befall him. The boy was the elder son of Mains of Yawal. Of course, Mains did not relish the insinuation, and complained to Mr. Sleekaboot of Jonathan's rude style of speech.

"Oh, well, you know his temper is a little hasty; but he is a man of sterling principle, and a very competent teacher," said Mr. Sleekaboot.

"Still an' on," replied Mains, "it's nae ceevil eesage to speak that wye aifter he gat 's nain gate wi' the laddie."

"In what branches has the boy failed?"

"Weel, aw cudna say; he hisna been makin naething o' 't; he 's jist a kin' o' daumer't i' the heid like."

"He has perhaps increased his tasks too much for the boy's capacity?"

"I cudna say aboot 's capacity—ye canna pit an aul' heid upo' young shou'ders, ye ken. I suppose he 's jist like ither laddies."

"H—m, yes; well, I'll speak to Mr. Tawse, and get him to modify his tasks."

"My rael opingan is," said Mains of Yawal, resolved to have a hit at Mr. Tawse, "that the dominie's nae gryte deykn at the common coontin 'imsel'; an' that mak's 'im sae fond to get them on to some o' that rowles, that works by a kin' o' slicht o' han'."

"Sleight of hand!" said Mr. Sleekaboot, with a smile, "what works by sleight of hand?"

"Weel, I'll tell ye, sir," answered Mains, pulling up; "fan I wuntit him to gi'e Sawney a raith at lan' mizzourin, to qualify 'im for a lan' steward or siclike, gin it ever happen't sae—there's naebody wud ken, ye ken—he begood aboot deein 't by Algaibra an' Jiggonometry, an' threepit owre me 't it was sic an advantage to dee 't that gate. Noo, I'm seer fan Dawvid Hadden, the grun offisher—an' there's nae a capitaller mizzourer o' grun in a plain wye i' the seyven pairis'es—cam' owre to lay aff a bit o' oor ootfeedles last year, he not naething but jist the chyne an' 's poles, an' a bit sclaittie an' skaillie. An' him an' me keest it up in a han' clap."

Mr. Sleekaboot perceived that Mains was rather gratified by his own success in the delivery of this speech. So, instead of attempting further elaborate argument with him, he crept up his soft side by ostensibly deferring to Mains's opinions on the practical question of land measuring; and then promising that he would talk the whole matter over with Jonathan Tawse, and bring him to a right frame of mind toward the younger Mains of Yawal. And Mr. Sleekaboot, without much difficulty, succeeded in healing this breach. But he failed in eradicating the opinion that obtained, especially in the west side of the parish, that it was desirable to have a school better adapted to meeting the wants of those who were bent on a purely practical education—the modern side in their view, in short.

And thus it came about that the side school of Smiddyward was established. Sandy Peterkin was one of those original geniuses who seem born with an extremely good capacity for acquiring knowledge, and no capacity whatever for turning the knowledge so acquired to any noticeable account, so far as bettering their own position, or benefiting other people connected with them, is concerned. In his boyhood he had sucked in knowledge with a sort of good-natured ease and avidity; and then, when he came within sight of a practical application of the same, Sandy disappointed the hopes of his friends by changing his mind, and turning out a kind of "sticket doctor." I really don't think that Sandy could ever have had sufficient nerve for the medical profession. Then, in an equally erratic fashion, he had gone abroad to seek his fortune, and after twenty years, returned without finding it. In a general way, then, Sandy had again made his appearance in the locality, willing to settle down, but without any particular vocation, or well-defined idea as to what he would desire to apply himself to. Luckily for Sandy, the agitation on the subject of Mr. Tawse's shortcomings was at that particular time pretty keen, and the notion of another school rather popular. I would not insinuate that it was because Mr. Sleekaboot opposed the project that Johnny Gibb lent his aid so zealously in patching up the old maltbarn at Smiddyward—which they pierced with two windows of four panes each, at the same time converting the ingle into a hearth—in order to adapt the place as a school. But Johnny certainly did take an active part in planning the structural works, and defraying the cost of material and workmanship, as well as in recommending the new teacher as a "byous clever chiel, a feerious gweed coonter, an' a prencipal han' at mizzourin grun."

At the date of my story, Sandy Peterkin had conducted his school for only a few years, the usual winter attendance numbering about thirty pupils. In summer it naturally decreased, and in order to eke out his stipend for that part of the year, Mr. Peterkin was wont, when the "hairst play" came, to hire himself out as a raker, or general errand man, to some of the neighbouring farmers.

Such were the two schools and schoolmasters of Pyketillim.

CHAPTER X.

BENJIE'S CLASSICAL STUDIES.

It was to Jonathan Tawse, such as I have described him, that the goodwife of Clinkstyle took her youngest son, Benjie, with the view of his addicting himself to the profession of the law. She had unfolded to the dominie her plans regarding the future of the young man, and wished his advice as to the requisite curriculum of study.

"Ou, weel," said Jonathan, "we'll jist hae to set him on for the regular coorse in classics."

"I wudna won'er," answered the goodwife. "An' foo mony classes will he hae to gae throu' syne?—ye ken he's i' the foort class, an' complete maister o' the muckle spell-beuk, 'cep some unco kittle words 't 's nain fader can mak' naething o'."

"Hoot-toot-toot, ye 're wrang i' the up-tak'—it 's classics —nae classes. Mair plainly, an' he war a wee thing better grun'it in English—through Mason's Collection may be— we maun pit him to Latin an' so on."

"Dis lawvyers need muckle o' 't, noo?"

"The mair the better, whan they want to bamboozle simple fowk," said the dominie. "Like Davie Lindsay's carman, that gat 's gray mare droon't whan he ran to the coort:—

> They gave me first **ane thing** they call *citandum,*
> Within aucht days I gat but *libellandum;*
> Within ane month I gat *ad oppenendum;*

> In half ane year I gat *inter loquendum*,
> An' syne I gat—how call you it?—*ad replicandum*;
> But I cud never ane word yet understand him."

"Keep me, Maister Tawse! ye 've sic a heid o' leernin' yersel'. I dinna believe but ye cud mak' up a prent beuk an' ye war to try. But mithnin he dee wi' the less coontin?"

"No; certainly not; he maun hae Mathematics confeerin."

"An' that be the gate o' 't, the seener he 's begun the better, I wud think, to nae loss time. Cudna ye begin 'im at ance wi' a bit lesson? 'Leern ear', leern fair,' they say, an' Benjie's a gran' scholar o' 's size. He wud bleck 's breeder that 's twa year aul'er nor him, ony day"

"Aweel, lat me see," said Mr. Tawse, who, having at the time no Latin class, had begun to cast about as to the possibility of setting one agoing for the winter, "I 'll see if I can get anither ane or twa, an' try them wi' the Rudiments—ye may jist get a Ruddiman i' the meanwhile, till we see."

"That 's the beuk that they get the Latin oot o', is 't?"

"No, no; jist the grammar—the rules o' the language."

"It cudna be deen wuntin, cud it? I dinna care aboot owre muckle o' that gremmar, 's ye ca' 't."

"Care or no care, it 's quite indispensable; an' it 's utter nonsense to speak o' wantin 't," said Mr. Tawse, in an irritated tone.

"They 're sic a herrial, that beuks," pursued Mrs. Birse. "Aye, aye needin' new beuks; but maybe ye mith hae an aul' Kroodymans lyin' aboot? I'm seer Benjie wudna blaud it—he 's richt carefu' o' 's beuks, peer thing."

"No, no, Mrs. Birse. I 'm nae a dealer in aul' beuks "—

"Eh, forbid 't I sud mint at that, Maister Tawse; but an' ye hed hed ane 't ye cud 'a len'it the laddie, I 'm seer we wud 'a been richt muckle obleeg't."

"If ye dinna value yer son's edication sufficiently to think it worth yer while to pay for the necessary beuks, jist train 'im for the pleuch stilts at ance."

"'Deed, Maister Tawse, I 'll dee naething o' the kin'.

There's neeu o' 's fader's faimily requarin to work wi' their han's for a liveliheid, an' it cam' to that, no. Peter 'll get the tack at hame, 's breeder Robbie 'll be pittin in till a place, an' his sister sanna wunt 'er providin'; an' gin that war 't a' we cud manage to plenish the best fairm i' the laird's aucht for Benjie; but fan craiturs has pairts for leernin, it 's a temp'in o' Providence to keep them back."

"Oh, *rara avis in terris!*"

"Fat said ye?"

"Oh, that 's only the Latin way o' expressin' my admiration o' the boy's pairts," said Mr. Tawse, "an' it shows ye vera weel what a comprehensive an' elegant tongue it is. It wud be a perfect delight to ye to hear Benjie rattlin' aff sentences fae Latin authors—I 'm sure it wud."

"Is that Kroodymans a dear beuk, Maister Tawse?"

"A mere trifle—a maitter o' twa shillin's or half-a-croon."

"Weel, I think ye mith jist get it the first time 't ye 're sen'in to the toon—they 'll maybe gi'e some discoont to the like o' you—an' we can coont aboot the price o' 't at the en' o' the raith."

Ruddiman was procured in due course, and Benjie set to the study of it, along with a lad whom Mr. Tawse had got as a boarder, and who was understood to be the natural son of—nobody knew exactly who. He was an idle boy, but quick enough when he chose to apply himself. And thus he and Benjie made, as Mr. Tawse confessed, an extremely bad team. For if the truth must be told, notwithstanding Mrs. Birse's eulogistic estimate of Benjie's literary capacity, as compared with that of his paternal parent and elder brothers, none of the Messrs. Birse junior had manifested exactly brilliant intellectual parts; and any capacity or predilection they had shown had been very distinctly in the direction of intermeddling with cattle and horses, and concerning themselves with the affairs of the farm. I don't think that Mr. Birse senior was in the least disappointed at this, though of course he had long ago reconciled himself to the idea that Benjie was somehow to be the great and learned man of the family. Howbeit Ruddiman agreed but ill with Benjie's tastes, and the consequence was that when the first raith was almost ended, he had scarcely got past *Ego Amo, Tu Amas*, and certainly had not the remotest conception of what it was all about. But this was not all. The effect of Benjie's studies had been to drive him home from school, over and over again, and with growing frequency, in a shattered state of health. Now it was his head that was in a dreadful state, and next his wyme, and Benjie shed many salt tears over his deplorable condition.

This state of things could not go on. Clinkstyle growled, and averred that his youngest son would be killed by too much learning; and the goodwife coaxed and coddled with no beneficial result. Then she went to Mr. Tawse to ascertain whether he was not tasking the excellent youth too severely, as it was alleged he had done in the case of Mains of Yawal's eldest son and heir; and she came back in a great rage, for Mr. Tawse had been curt and uncomplimentary, and had hinted very plainly something about Benjie "shamming," after which he abruptly left Mrs. Birse standing outside the door, and proceeded to the interior of the school to finish his day's labours.

"Weel, weel, 'oman," said Peter Birse senior, "they wud need a heid o' iron 't could gae throu' that stuff; ye'll need to pit a stop till 't some gate."

"Gae 'wa' wi' yer buff; it's muckle 't ye ken aboot it," answered Peter's dutiful spouse, determined not to be convinced by him at any rate.

"Jist wyte than till ye see the upshot. I sudna won'er nor he mak' the laddie an' objeck for life—min' fat naar happen't wi' Mains's laddie."

"Mains's laddie! Humph! An' my son hinna some mair smeddum aboot 'm nor the like o' that gawkie trypal, it's time 't he war set to herd the laird's geese instead o' followin' aifter edication. Ye micht hae some regaird for ither fowk's feelin's, man, gin ye hae neen for yer nain!"

"But I'm nae sayin' 't Benjie hisna a better uptak' nor the like o' him," pleaded Peter, apologetically.

"Better uptak'!" exclaimed Mrs. Birse. "Sma' thanks t' ye for that! Foo af'en hiv I seen 'im, peer innocent, bleck you an''s breeders tee, readin' namie chapters oot o' the Word o' Gweed. An' that's fat he gets for's pains! I'm seer he sets an example to aul'er fowk."

"Hoot, 'oman! I wusna meanin' to misca' oor nain laddie."

"An' foo did ye dee't than, Peter Birse? Tell me that?"

Peter had not an answer ready—in time at any rate—and Mrs. Birse went on, "I'm seer ye ken brawly fat wye my uncle, 't deet Can'lesmas was a year, wan in to be a lawvyer aboot Aiberdeen, an' made jist an ondeemas thing o' siller—as the feck o' them does. Awat he len'it a hantle to the toonship, an' leeft a vast o' property forbye. Peer man, he did little gweed wi''t i' the hin'er en'; or some o''s mith 'a been in a vera different seetivation fae slavin' on till ony ane, takin' chairge o' bestial, and milkness, an' a pack o' vulgar trag o' fairm servan's. But's wife's freens raive a heap o''t aff o''im fan he was livin', an' manag't to get the muckle feck o' fat was leeft fan he weer awa'."

"But aw doot he hed a hantle o' enfluence, or he wudna come on sae weel," said Peter.

"Aw won'er to hear ye speak, man. Fat enfluence cud he hed; fan he gaed to the toon, as I've heard 'im tellin' a dizzen o' times, a laddie wi' a tartan plaid aboot 's shou'ders, an' a''s spare claise i' the neuk o''t? Forbye, isna there Maister Pettiphog't fell into my uncle's biziness, an' was oor awgent fan ye pat awa' yer second horseman fernyear for stravaigin fae the toon o' the Sabbath nicht, an' gyaun in owre 's bed wi' 's sharnie beets on—a vera respectable man—didna he begin, as he taul's himsel', upo' the 'sweepin's o' the Shirra Court'?"

"True, true," said Peter, in a half-bewildered tone.

"Aweel, aw think it would be ill 's pairt, an' he wudna tak' Benjie for a 'prentice at ance, an' pit 'im o' the road to mak' a wye o' deein for 'imsel'. He made a braw penny aff o' you at ony rate."

F

It was impossible for Peter to answer such powerful and voluble reasoning; and he had virtually succumbed before Mrs. Birse reached the concluding and more practical portion of her discourse, which revealed a part of the plan of Benjie's future of which he had not hitherto got the faintest glimpse, although as now presented it rather commended itself to him. The effect upon Mrs. Birse herself of so fully expressing her sentiments, was, on the whole, soothing. But on one thing she was fully resolved, come what would—to give Jonathan Tawse a snubbing. So, in addressing our promising young gentleman next morning, she said, "Ye'll tak' my compliments to Maister Tawse, noo, Benjie, an' tell 'im to sen' his accoont wi' ye—the raith's oot at the en' o' this ouk at ony rate—an' gin he canna manage to behave wi' common ceevility to them 't he's makin' 's breid aff o', and teach their bairns withoot brakin' their health, maybe anither will. Will ye min' that, noo?"

What this threat signified exactly, in the mind of the person who uttered it, it would perhaps be difficult to guess. At any rate, when Benjie brought the account, Mrs. Birse's thoughts took quite a practical shape. Jonathan Tawse's fee for the ordinary curriculum of the school was 3s. 6d. a quarter; when Latin was included he made it two shillings more; and when Mrs. Birse saw the enormous charge of 5s. 6d., followed by 2s. 6d. for a half-bound Ruddiman, it was some little time before she could give adequate expression to her feelings. She declared first that she would never pay such an "extortion;" and next that ere she did pay she would certainly make Peter Birse senior face the unconscionable dominie before the Shirra, where the account would be rigorously taxed, and the iniquity of its author exposed in the face of the world. The actual result as regards the account itself was that after a while Peter Birse senior was sent to pay it, with orders to deliver certain sarcastic remarks bearing on the combined greed and professional incapacity of Mr. Tawse; and which orders Peter, as is usual in such circumstances, did not carry out to the letter; but, indeed, mumbled some sort of awkward apology for the withdrawal of Benjie from the school; for, of course, he had been instantly removed—a result which Benjie seemed in no wise to regret during the interregnum that occurred until it should be determined what should be done with him next.

CHAPTER XI.

THE KIRK ROAD.

How shall I describe the Kirk Road of Pyketillim? Of course it is the Kirk Road when the parishioners are assembling for public worship that I mean.

It is a beautiful spring Sunday morning of the year 1842. Samuel Pikshule has duly tolled his eight o'clock bell, which sends its billows of pleasant melody rolling over bank and hollow to the farthest end of the parish, amid the still, dewy sunlight; then he has gone and deliberately discussed his breakfast, and shaved off his beard, and washed his face, before he would ring ten o'clock and turn the key in the kirk door.

It was at a quarter to twelve that Samie began to ring the people in. But for good part of an hour before that they were to be seen wending slowly onward in twos and threes by this and that side path into the 'commodation road, which winds along by Smiddyward, Gushetneuk, and Clinkstyle, and so on over the Knowe and down upon the Kirktown. As they met on the main road they resolved themselves into groups, larger or smaller, according to taste and other circumstances. Here is a knot of three or four women, including one sturdy old dame, with close mutch, ancient shawl of faded hue, and big umbrella planted firmly under her arm, fine as the day is; there another couple, one of indefinitely goodwifely aspect, the other evidently a thrifty spinster, and a lassie clanking on in heavy tacketie shoes at their skirts, anxious to get what comprehension she may of the semi-prophetic gossip, and to discover the individualities referred to in the confidentially-breathed " she says, says she," that occupy the tongues of her seniors. There Dawvid Hadden, ground-officer to Sir Simon Frissal, pulls up, takes off his hat, wipes his brow, lets his wife forgather with whom she may, and the bairns scatter on in front, while he hooks his one thumb in his waistcoat armhole, and puts the other hand below his coat tail to wait for Hairry Muggart, the wright, and get the news as they jog socially on, picking up a fit companion or two by the way. At other points we have knots of sturdy chaps, free from the plough for one day, and done up according to taste in rough gray tweeds, and with the ends of their brilliant neckerchiefs flying loose, tramping along by themselves; and skweel loons, on the alert for idle pranks, and fully conscious that Jonathan Tawse's rule is intermitted for the time, now loitering and next scampering on with utmost speed.

When the journey is about accomplished, we have no end of friendly inquiries to make as we cluster about the kirkyard yett; then slowly filter inward to re-group ourselves on the open space in front of the kirk-door; to sit down with a few cronies on the green slope under the venerable trees, or it may be on a lair stane in God's acre itself, to take snuff, and see how far our notes about the weather and the crops agree. Samie begins to ring at the quarter, but we let him ring on; and it is only when Mr. Sleekaboot is seen coming up the long walk in full canonicals (we had no vestry in those days) that we betake ourselves to the interior of the kirk, crushing in in a somewhat ram-shackle and irreverent fashion it must be allowed, and planting ourselves in attitude to sleep, or observe, as the case may be.

But I will not describe the church services farther than has been already done. Our profiting usually was pretty much, I presume, what might have been expected. At the close Mr. Sleekaboot sat down composedly, and the elders seized the ladles—substantially built ladles they were, and had served their purpose for generations past—and perambulated the kirk. We gave our bawbees like loyal Presbyterians; that is to say, the head of the family always gave one, and sometimes his wife another, or one of the elder bairns—a habit and practice which have been most faithfully adhered to in most congregations, town and country, till this day; insomuch that hundreds of worthy people of fair wealth and position, who would be ashamed to offer less than sixpence to any other good object, proclaim their veneration for the usages of these ancient Christians by carefully abstaining from ever dropping into the brod aught else than a copper counterfeit presentment of Her Majesty. Well, we did this in the parish church of Pyketillim; and I do not recollect more than once seeing a man—it was up i' the laft—put a penny into the brod as it was pushed round, and then adjust his offering to the statutory amount by taking out a bawbee.

When the kirk skail't, the scene was different from the gathering. To be sure, if Samie Pikshule had a roup to scry, or a strayed stirk to "adverteese," there was a general and eager clustering about him at the kirk gable, as Samie yabbled out the particulars. But otherwise we put on double steam to what was in use when we were daundering up to the "courts of the sanctuary," as Mr. Sleekaboot phrased it. Before we were clear of the Kirktown some half-dozen of the male parishioners (usually elderly ones, familiar with the dwellers in the Kirktown, and who cared not to carry fleerish and flint in their Sunday claes) had availed themselves of a het sod to light their pipes; and the result was seen in a cloudlet of blue smoke rising here and there over the streams of people as they moved on in steady flow east and west; everybody now marching onward with something of the air of those who have serious business on hand.

Now, it so happened that on the particular Sunday morning to which I have made reference, Peter Birse had living with him over the day, as a visitor, a particular friend from up-throu,' an ardent agriculturist like himself. The two had been out betimes in the morning and had enjoyed a saunter over Clinkstyle's fields, discussing matters relative

thereto as they went. After the ten o'clock bell had rung in, and long after breakfast, it occurred to Peter as they stood at the top of the garden walk, not knowing well how to occupy themselves further, that a profitable use might be made of the spare time yet between them and the hour of public worship.

"Nyod, fat wud ye say to takin a stap roon b' the back o' the wuds gyaun to the kirk. The laird has a puckle fine stirks i' the Upper Holm park 't the grieve 's aye blawin' aboot?"

"Oot already?"

"Ou ay. They war some scant o' strae, ye see; they keep sae mony horse beasts aboot the place. But they 're fine lythe parks, an' ear' tee; beasts mith live i' them throu' the winter naar."

"I wud like freely weel to see them, man," said the stranger.

"Weel, jist heely till I gi'e a cry in 't we 're awa'."

And they went by the back of the woods—it was a long way round—where the stirks were duly seen, criticised, and admired. Then they stumbled on a field of the laird's which the grieve was preparing to be laid down in turnips, and took a skance of what was going on there.

"It's easy deen for them 't yauchts the grun to try protticks wi' 't," observed Peter.

"He 's been trenchin seerly," said his friend.

"Ou na; but they hed a gryte stren'th o' beasts rivin' 't up wi' fat they ca' a subsoil pleuch."

"The stibble lan', likein?"

"Ay, ay, stibbles."

"Weel, I cudna say; aw wud be some dootfu' aboot it. A bit faugh across the rig i' the en' o' the year, an' syne a gweed deep fur 's better nor turnin' up the caul' boddom."

"Oh, loshie, ay, man," said Peter Birse. "But than ye see it 's a' ae thing to him fat he pit into the grun gin he can raise a crap; an' he 'll haud on the manure to the mast-heid, fatever it may cost. They war sayin' he hed gotten a curn o' that ga-ano stuff 't they speak aboot."

"Yea, man!" replied the stranger in a wondering tone.

They approached the corner of a field off the road, and stood up on the top of the backit dyke, when Mr. Birse exclaimed, "Aw div not believe but here's a hillockie o' that ga-ano i' the neuk o' the park."

Peter was right. Guano was then a newly-introduced manure, which he and his friend, who understood the virtues of bone dust perfectly, had not yet seen. The grieve had got a consignment of the Ichaboe variety, whereof he had deposited a small parcel in the corner of the field to await turnip sowing. In a twinkling our two worthies had leapt off the dyke and were busy examining the guano.

"Eh, man, but it's fushionless-like stuff!" said Peter Birse's friend, after inquiringly crushing a sample or two between his finger and thumb.

"Isnin't a mervel fat wye that cud gar onything grow?" was Peter's reply.

"But does't raelly dee 't, man?"

"Weel, I've nae rizzon to misdoot the grieve's word; an' he taul' me that it sent up some cabbage kail 't he try 't it on fernyear like the very shot o' a gun."

"Man, aw wud like richt weel to try a pucklie o' 't. Mithna a body gae the length o' takin' the fu' o' a sneeshin pen?"

"Awat ye may tak' a nievefu' on-been miss't," said Peter.

"Gin they wudna think it greedy-like, an 't were kent."

"Feint a fears o' that," answered Peter Birse. "But fat wye'll we cairry 't?"

"Ou, that'll be easy deen," said Peter's visitor, shaking out his crumpled cotton pocket handkerchief; "the dud'll haud it fine."

"Weel, its keerious I didna think o' that, no."

"But wunnin ye tak a starn yersel'?" asked the stranger.

"Weel—aw dinna differ. I 'se tell the grieve 't we wus tryin' the quality o' 's ga-ano."

And so Peter next spread out his handkerchief, into which he too put a handful of guano. The samples were duly bestowed in the coat pockets of the two friends, who then resumed their journey to the kirk, at which they arrived in due time, highly pleased with their experiences by the way.

I do not know how far the suggestion may be necessary that the olfactory nerves of Peter Birse and his friend would not seem to have been particularly sensitive. But had the fact been otherwise, it would appear to me highly probable that the two gentlemen would have had some indications before they entered the kirk of the likelihood of a perfume rather more powerful than pleasant proceeding from their pockets. It would appear, however, that nothing of the sort had disturbed their reflections; at any rate, the two had entered and gravely seated themselves before the guano had cost them a second thought. Things did not remain long in this quiescent state, however. Mrs. Birse, who seldom came early, entered next, with Miss Birse. Peter and the stranger did not rise to put the ladies into the pew, but, according to use and wont, simply hirsled yont, and made room for them at the end of it. Miss Eliza Birse seated herself and sniffed; then her mother sniffed, and looked first at the floor and then at her husband. And all at once the situation flashed upon poor Peter's mind! Yes! He did feel the odour of the guano; and the man in front of him, who had turned half round and looked into Peter's pew, evidently felt it too. Samie Pikshule, who was going along the pass to shut the door, felt it, and stopped short with an inquiring glance around him; and it was said by those near him that Samuel uttered something about "some chiel comin' there wi' a foumart in 's pouch, stechin up the kirk." But what could Clinkstyle do? There he was, shut into the top of the pew, and the service going on. To rise and force his way out would be to proclaim his predicament more widely; for he would without fail perform the function of censer to the congregation all the way to the door. And then it would be of no use unless he took his friend with him.

I have no real delight in cruelty to animals, and will not enlarge upon the agony endured by Peter Birse during the sermon. He had no doubt whatever that Mrs. Birse knew him to be guilty—his own imploring look had betrayed him there. He fancied that the eyes of the whole congregation were fixed upon him, and he verily believed that Mr. Sleekaboot was directing part of his observations towards him personally. The stranger, who seemed to be a placid man, sat perfectly unmoved. On the whole, the incident, which, of course, got abroad pretty generally among the people of Pyketillim, did not tend to secure increased respect for Peter; and it may be added that he *was* once or twice thereafter judiciously reminded of it by his spouse, as an illustration of the necessity for a more discreet head than his own to decide in, at any rate, all matters of breeding and etiquette. Thus far on the social aspect of the question. Peter's sole defence when put to it was, that he never for a moment supposed he could be wrong in following the example of his visitor, who, moreover, was a distant relative of Mrs. Birse; and that neither of them dreamt that " the ga-ano cud hae hed sic a rank kneggum."

To his surprise Mrs. Birse replied, with not a little solemnity, " Weel-a-wat, ye needna be surpris't nor it be a jeedgment o' ye for brakin' the Sabbath."

CHAPTER XII.

THE SMIDDYWARD PRAYER MEETING.

EVER since the time of his visit to the Wells in 1839, Johnny Gibb had been applying his mind more actively than before to current ecclesiastical questions. The conversation of his Marnoch friend had given him an impetus in that direction, which occasional epistolary communications from the same quarter, with accounts of the exciting intrusionist scenes enacted there, as recorded in the newspapers, had served to prolong and intensify. And whereas Johnny's burden against a jolly and ease-loving clergy had previously partaken very much of the nature of a general denunciation of them as "dumb dogs who cannot bark," he had now learnt clearly to distinguish between Moderates and Evangelicals, and these words were frequently on his lips. In the person of Mr. Sleekaboot, moreover, Johnny deemed that he found the very incarnation of Moderatism. This fact set the worthy man terribly on edge, and as the sounds of controversy in the Church courts fell ever and anon on his wakeful ears, he felt it only the more incumbent on him to stand boldly up for the good cause. His right-hand man in this crisis was Roderick M'Aul, the souter at Smiddyward, and it so happened that about the date now reached in my narrative, the Rev. Alister Macrory, whom the souter had known in his youth, and of whose gifts and piety he had a good opinion, but who, by some mischance, had hitherto failed in getting tied to any parish in particular, was passing through the region, and felt that he could not do less than call upon his old acquaintance, by whom he was hospitably entertained. Johnny Gibb, of course, was asked over to enjoy the visitor's conversation; and it then occurred to the two friends that, as the Rev. Alister Macrory was not particularly pressed for time, they might retain his services for a few weeks, and give the parishioners of Pyketillim the opportunity for once of hearing the Gospel preached. It was an easy matter to secure the use of Sandy Peterkin's school for the purpose, and it was secured accordingly.

The school at Smiddyward was not an imposing structure, either as regards external appearance or interior decoration. It was straw-thatched, with the door halved transversely, and not longitudinally; and inside there were desks and seats of a very plain sort for about forty pupils. The roof was an "open" one, with the "wood-work" quite "visible" (so far as the accumulation of soot thereon admitted), and not less so the divots that overlaid it. There Sandy Peterkin bore rule. His school, let me say, was thriving in a way that fully equalled Sandy's most sanguine expectations. I don't think, however, that these were very extravagant. The first of Mr. Macrory's services had been held in the school on a week-day evening, with an audience that half filled the place; and the event had caused no little talk in the parish. Johnny Gibb presented, a service which the older parishioners could recollect his having occasionally performed, on emergencies, in the parish kirk, many long years ago; and the energetic oratory of Mr. Macrory, without any "paper" to aid him therein, was fitted to startle, apart altogether from the matter, by the very contrast it presented to the perfectly unimpassioned performance of Mr. Sleekaboot, as he read over once more the well-thumbed MS., which the more attentive parishioners knew so well by head-mark that they could give you day and date of its last preaching, and also predict, with tolerable accuracy, the next time it would be put to the same use. But the Rev. Alister Macrory, albeit a little uncouth and violent in his manner, and given to shaking

his fist and staring directly forward at a particular point in his audience, as if he wanted to single you out individually to be preached at, was, to all appearance, a man really in earnest, and the general impression made by his discourses was something new in the quarter.

Now, it so happened that at the very time Mrs. Birse withdrew her hopeful younger son, Benjie, from the pedagogic rule of Jonathan Tawse, one or two little incidents had occurred fitted to stagger that eminently prudent matron, and even to some extent to shake her belief in the human race generally. Miss Birse had spent the winter in Aberdeen, in attendance at a fashionable ladies' seminary; and, let me say it, had been wonderfully successful in picking up that uneasy polish and those stilted conventional phrases that lend such a charm to the manner of our proper and properly-trained young ladies. She was coming home "finished" in a style that should make her an acquisition in the best society in the parish. So thought her mamma; and the idea had occurred to her, that, as Eliza had boarded with a distant relative whose hospitality was deemed amply repaid by the presentation of a half-stane kebbuckie, once for all, with a dozen of eggs and a pound or two of butter every month, when fresh linen was despatched to the interesting young lady, Benjie might be sent to some school of classic repute, and fill his sister's vacated place as a lodger on the same terms. Mrs. Birse was scandalised when the ungrateful people made it known that they "cudna tak' a countra loon on nae accoont—they hed owre many mou's to fill o' their nain;" and she was more than scandalised at the "dryness" exhibited by them towards Eliza at parting, when the goodman of the house, as it seemed, had had to carry her things past Kittybrewster to the Flyboat house, and to supplement for Miss Birse the sixpence she was short of her fare homeward by that admirable medium of communication.

"I 'm seer fowk wudna ken fat to dee to keep doon the ill crap o' some creaturs. Fan they war onfeelin aneuch to try a pawrent's hert b' refeesin the laddie, peer innocent, they notna 'a latten oot their breath upo' her'; mony a bare aneuch day has she kent wi' them; an' weel may seem—her vera frocks needin' takin' in to keep them onfa'en aff o' her body. An' she hedna hed bawbees to get pieces till 'ersel files, oot o' sicht o' their bairns, aw div not believe but she wud 'a gotten a mischief o' hunger."

So said Mrs. Birse in her indignation.

However, as Benjie could not be transferred to Aberdeen, a dilemma had occurred; and during its continuance Master Benjamin, as has been said, seemed in nowise indisposed to enjoy rural life; in such forms as, for example, those of walking with Tam Meerison at the plough for hours, and riding the pony to water and back, and grooming it, despite the warnings of his mother as to the degrading tendency of such occupations on a young man destined to learned pursuits. His next elder brother being intended for the farm, it mattered less how his education was picked up. So things had gone on for some weeks, when all of a sudden Mrs. Birse announced that Benjie was to be sent to Sandy Peterkin to continue his studies. Peter Birse senior shook his head dubiously and protested. But Mrs. Birse was firm. Finding sundry other arguments unavailing, Peter urged—

"But, ye ken, Sandy disna preten' to be claer o' the Laitin 'imsel', 'oman; an' ye cudna expeck him to leern 't weel till ithers."

"An' fat for no? There's fowk preten's to be claer upon 't that mak's but a peer shot at leernin ithers."

"Ou, but ye ken Maister Tawse hedna Benjie lang."

"An' hedna he Jock Ogg, the gauger's loon, haill twa year at it; an' aifter a' his peer fader was forced to pack 'im awa' to the sea. The fient a flee hed he leern't but a lot o' ill tricks an' lees; for 's nain gweed-mither taul' me oot o' 'er ain mou. An' that aul', greedy, sneeshinie howffin gaen on chairgin' an ondeemas soom for skweel fees a' the time. A bonnie story to say that the peer innocent was feingyin fan he tyeuk a drow! Jist his nain strunge mainner an' ill natur' 't flegs the creaturs."

"Weel, I'm maist seer the minaister 'll be ill pleas't," continued Peter."

"An' fat raiks? It 'll be lang ere ye be made fat aff o' him! I'm seer they gat twa as gweed hens as ever swally't black dist fae this toon at Aul' Yeel; but I b'lieve, though they hed a' the upsettin' trash i' the pairis' at the Manse i' the coorse o' the winter, *we* never bruik breid wi' them."

"But it wudna dee to offen' the minaister, ye ken—gin fowk war in tribble or onything"——

"Peter Birse, fat are ye raelly thinkin' aboot? Fat has that to dee wi' the edication o' fowk's bairns? Maister Sleekaboot may be a gweed aneuch man in 's ain place, an' he war latt'n aleen b' 's nain 't ocht to ken better. Leddies! —they wud need it! But the peer man's siclike led, 't aw raelly believe it's the trowth that Gushetneuk says that he does *not* preach the Gospel."

"Keep me, 'oman, I won'er at ye speakin' that gate. His preachin' 's a hantle better nor we practeese."

"Ou, I daursay some fowk's but speakin' the trowth fan they say that; but he 's a rael wor'dly-min'et person."

"Hoot, I'm seer ye ken he 's a weel-meanin' man, an' a weel-leern't."

"Aweel, gin he get's nain cronies a' richt, he winna care fat the affcasts dee!—hm! So ye 'll jist gae doon wi' me the nicht to the skweel at Smiddyward. We can see Sandy Peterkin aboot Benjie; and there 's to be a preachin' i' the skweel i' the evenin', by ane Macrory fae the wast kwintra. They say he 's weel worth the hearin, an' we 'se jist bide an' get a word fae 'im."

It was in vain for Peter to remonstrate. Mrs. Birse had found cause of offence in both Mr. Sleekaboot and Jonathan Tawse, and she was resolved to open a campaign against both. Jonathan would be punished by the conclusive withdrawal of her sons from his school, and sending them to that of his rival; and she knew that by their going to hear an itinerant preacher Mr. Sleekaboot would be at once incensed in a high degree, which would be likely to give opportunity for at least reminding him, as she knew how, of his shortcomings in tending his flock.

It was on the evening appointed for the second sermon or address that the goodwife of Clinkstyle led her reluctant spouse down to Smiddyward. Their business with Sandy Peterkin was easily despatched, Sandy, who honestly confessed that his classics were a little rusted, undertaking to do the best he could with Benjie; and they were then free to attend the meeting.

"Ou, ay, it's a prayer meetin' the nicht," said Sandy Peterkin, when Mrs. Birse had announced her intention. "I'm gaen awa' to pit up the lichts—they'll be gedderin eenoo. Ye'll jist sit still at the fireside here. I winna be a minute in bein' back."

Sandy groped in his aumry till he got hold of two penny candles, one of which he put in a tin candlestick, while he stuck the lower end of the other into a turnip suitably excavated. He lighted one of them, and when he had sidled away out, endeavouring to keep the wind from it until he should reach the school, Peter Birse made a last despairing appeal to his wife.

"Keep's, 'oman, did ye hear that?"

"Hear fat?"

"Sandy says it's a prayer meetin', an' nae a preachin'."

"Weel; an' fat for no?"

"Ye seerly winna gang till 't, than?"

"There'll naebody tak' a bite o' 's though we dee."

"Hoot, 'oman, it's owre sairious for jokin'. It's as ill's the vera missionars. There wus never the like heard o' in this pairis'."

"This pairis'! humph! This pairis' is some mark or than no."

"Fat will the minaister say, an' my ain gweed-breeder ane o' his el'ers?"

Peter's remonstrances were cut short by the return of Sandy Peterkin, who announced that they were now "feckly gedder't." So at his goodwife's beck and bidding, and in the circumstances, as to public facts and general feeling, which

THE SMIDDYWARD PRAYER MEETING. 81

he had accurately described, Clinkstyle had to do his conscience the direct violence involved in attending a prayer meeting.

When they entered, the audience was found to consist mainly of women and young people, though, as far as might be seen by the dim candle-light, there were six or eight grown-up men present.

Mr. Macrory conducted the opening services, and then read and expounded a chapter, making sundry very pointed applications; and leaving it to be clearly understood that the cold morality which was droned into the ears of the people from Sabbath to Sabbath was of no avail to save either the teacher or the taught from everlasting perdition. The sort of direct onslaught, both in word and look, in which the speaker indulged, made Peter Birse feel a good way short of perfectly comfortable; and, judging by appearances, others of his neighbours could have dispensed with some small part of Mr. Macrory's energy, without complaining. As for Mrs. Birse, she at once adopted an air of edifying demureness; and took care to sidle up far enough to be full in sight of Johnny and Mrs. Gibb, who were seated near by the preacher, their servants, Jinse Deans and Willy M'Aul, with the lassie, occupying the seat next behind them. Mr. Macrory had finished his exposition; he gave out a psalm to be sung, and then, when the singing was concluded, in a very audible and deliberate tone announced that "Our brother, Mr. M'Aul, will engage in prayer." There was a sort of electric start among a considerable part of the audience at this intimation, as much as to say, "The souter engage in prayer!" And, no doubt, if they had known the ancient adage primarily applying to men of his calling, they would have mentally repeated it. All the same, they felt the sentiment therein expressed. It had beforetime been bruited abroad that Roderick M'Aul kept up family worship daily, and two or three customers who had at sundry times accidentally stumbled in when he was about to commence, had gone through sensations which they were shy of attempting to describe, on being asked by Roderick to join in the

G

devotions. But that Roderick M'Aul should stand up before a public audience, and offer up prayer—Roderick M'Aul, who was just a souter, and with not a shred of clerical character about him—the thing was so utterly beyond the scope of the most fervid imagination among the general body of the parishioners of Pyketillim, that not only did several of the audience at the meeting, besides Peter Birse, feel in some doubt whether they stood with their heads or their heels uppermost, but the news of what had occurred spread rapidly through the parish next day. The deed was declared by several to be "daurin'," and by quite as great a number to be "blaspheemous."

Nevertheless, the example set by the souter did not, I think, fail in having its effects. If the simple and fervent, albeit slightly ungrammatical utterance of the devotional feelings within him had the effect of dumfoundering and scandalising some, there were others of his audience that were impressed in a more wholesome way; and among these was Johnny Gibb, who went home with the honest conviction in his breast that Roderick M'Aul was a better man than himself. "For," said Johnny, "he's ready to confess Christ afore men aifter a fashion that I hae never mintit to dee yet."

CHAPTER XIII.

THE DISTRIBUTION MEETING——ECCLESIASTICAL OPINIONS.

OF course, Mr. Sleekaboot was speedily made acquainted with the operations of the Rev. Alister Macrory at Smiddyward; but he took it all very coolly. There had been ranting fanatics in the world long before now, and there would no doubt be so till the end of time, said the Rev. Mr. Sleekaboot.

At the quarterly Distribution, when all the bawbees gathered by the brod for the bygone three months were to be fully reckoned and apportioned, the elders met at the Manse; and each got his share to pay over to the various recipients—quiet, and not particularly uncomfortable old bodies of both sexes; real old residenters; not your modern paupers of the clamorous, thriftless, and unsatisfied sort. And this part of their duty the Session discharged with creditable assiduity, and even more than creditable humanity. Have I not seen Mains of Yawal, who lived farthest from the kirk, time after time, carrying home his portion of the offering, all too bulky to go into any pouch he had, carefully enclosed in his blue-spotted "pocket-napkin," and dangling in his hand with solid weight? And he would thereafter go his round, be it fair night or foul, to see Saun'ers Tapp, and Lizzy Glegg, and their ancient contemporaries, and all to give to each his or her due share of the offering bawbees.

But, meanwhile, I am not concerned with the details of the distribution. Sometimes when the elders met to arrange for it at the Manse—though, I daresay, this formed no part of the *res gestæ* to be minuted by Jonathan Tawse—the sederunt would be wound up by a quiet glass of toddy. Such was the case at the distribution meeting that occurred just two nights after Mr. Macrory's meeting at Smiddyward. And the elders were all present, with the exception of Clinkstyle's sister's husband, Braeside. Of course the subject of the prayer meeting came up.

"An' fa div ye think sud' 'a been there hearin' this ranter but Clinkstyle an' 's wife?" said Mains of Yawal.

"Poor man, poor man," answered Mr. Sleekaboot, with a smile. "I fancy he had hardly been left to the freedom of his own will in the matter."

"Deed, I can believe ye're richt there, sir," said Mr. Tawse, taking a heavy pinch of snuff. "That wife o' his is a perfect Xantippe."

"Oh—I presume she heckled you when she withdrew her precious son from the school."

"For that maitter I can usually gi'e as gweed as I get," said Mr. Tawse. "But she's a rude vulgar hizzie, natheless; an' for the loon, I never ruggit the lugs o' a more complete dunce."

"Did you venture to tell that in the audience of the maternal ears, Jonathan?" asked the minister, the jocularity of the query being shared in by only the dominie and himself, as the rest of the company failed to catch its flavour, couched in such refined English.

"Deed, I believe I fell little short o' 't. But what was that ye was sayin', Mains, aboot this fanatic, Macrory, settin the souter to gi'e a prayer at the meetin' in Sawney Peterkin's hovel?"

"Oh, it was fat they ca' a prayer meetin'; an' aifter he hed roar't on for a file 'imsel', he cries oot 'Some broder 'll engaige noo;' fan up startit the souter an' gya them a screed o' 't by ordinar'. Several o' them hed been sair pitt'n oot aboot it, aw 'm thinkin'."

"An' little won'er," quoth Teuchitsmyre, the other new elder, who was a fat, red-nosed man with a very thick neck. "Ta'en a fup to them wud 'a sair't them richt."

"And heard you who all were present?" asked Mr. Sleekaboot.

"Weel, aw 'm thinkin' Gushetneuk an' 's wife, forbye, 's I was sayin', the fowk o' Clinkstyle. The lave wud be feckly the aul' wives aboot the Ward, an' maybe a fyou young fowk."

"Did John Gibb take any part?"

"Eh—aw didna hear that said; but he 's been ane o' the heid deesters aboot feshin this Macrory to the pairt."

"A fractious, heidstrong creatur," said Jonathan Tawse. "But there's some brains in 'im tee; that was aye my opinion."

"He 's too anxious to make himself and his opinions prominent," answered Mr. Sleekaboot.

"It was a great mistak' in you, Mr. Sleekaboot—savin' the presence o' Mains an' Teuchitsmyre—to keep Gushets an' the souter oot o' the el'ership."

"How, how—men who act thus?"

"Ou ay, but an' they had been made pillars i' the kirk, like the lave o' 's, ye wud hae heard less o' any sic divisive coorses, depen' ye upon 't," said the dominie.

"I don't know; we——"

"My dear sir, fan did ye ever hear o' an el'er in the parish o' Pyketillim gaen aboot a kwintra side cantin' an' prayin', as this souter does, it seems? An', tak' ye my word for 't, ye 'll hae Gushetneuk followin' 's example neist."

"Well, but, Mr. Tawse," said the minister, evidently disposed to get very serious on the point, "as I was saying, and as you know, we must take good care for the order of the Church. There can be nothing more perilous to the peace of our Zion than the presence of unbridled spirits in office within her bosom. And I, in the position of spiritual head of this parish, I being responsible alike to the Presbytery and the patron Sir Simon Frissal, I would never for a moment brook the revolutionary opinions held by those men."

"Ye 're vera richt, Maister Sleekaboot—vera richt," said Mains, with great emphasis. He was getting hot and red in the face; and I think had by this time based his opinion on a tolerably wide induction, when, suddenly changing the theme, and emptying his glass, he added, "Nyod, that's capital fusky."

Teuchitsmyre nodded approvingly, and said, "It's the rael Glendronach, seerly."

"Weel, weel, as ye please, sir," replied Mr. Tawse. "I was half jokin', ye ken. But ye canna won'er though a sair-dung dominie sud try to save 's nain credit by sayin' that it mitha been worth while, as a stroke o' policy, till hae latt'n Clinkstyle on to the el'ership."

"He would have been in nowise a more efficient member of session than his excellent relative, Braeside."

"Neen, neen—jist sax i' the ane an' half-a-dizzen i' the ither. Baith hairmless breets. But ye see Braeside hisna an ambitious wife—D' ye see my drift? Hooever, to pass fae that point, I think ye really ocht, in some way, to tak' an order o' these fanatics."

"Of Gibb and M'Aul?"

"Na, na; ye had better lat ill aleen there. But it mithna be difficult to frichten Peterkin fae gi'ein' that bit hole to lat them meet in."

"Well; it'll die out. There has been in all ages of the Christian Church, as I have said, an ever-recurring tendency, especially among the unlearned, to lapse into fanaticism; though the admirable organisation and discipline of our own Church have effectually repressed serious outbreaks at all times."

"An' may it be for ever sae," said Jonathan Tawse. "But fat are ye to mak' o' a' this uncanny steer o' the Non-intrusion pairty i' the Kirk? Ye'll hae some difficulty, *cæteris paribus*, in disciplinin' the major pairt o' the Kirk itsel'."

"Ay, Mr. Tawse," said the minister, with a half chuckle, "but it's not a case of *cæteris paribus*, my good friend. There is such a thing as the law of the land, and the civil power. With that at our back we need never fear the hot-headed party in the Church. Keep yourself easy."

"Ou, it winna brak' my rest, sir. But I dinna muckle like the leuk o' these bits o' collisions atween the spiritual poo'er as they ca't, an' the civil: siclike as in the bygone case o' Lethendy; an' syne, nearer han' hame, at Marnoch; whaur, in the first case, the Coort o' Session steps in to interdict a sattlement by a Presbytery; an' in the neist its aid is requir't to force an unacceptable presentee on a congregation. An', of coorse, I needna speak o' the starshie sinsyne still nearer oor ain door, at Culsalmond, wi' the goodman o' Teetaboutie."

"Well, I have you there, Jonathan. General arguments are never so convincing as special facts. I'm glad that the brethren in Strathbogie had the firmness to endeavour to vindicate the just rights of presentees. Here you have an instance in my own case. When I had the honour of receiving a presentation from Sir Simon to the Parish of Pyketillim, I met a very cold reception, let me tell you, from the people. I don't believe that, but for the personal presence of Sir Simon—with whom, though I say it myself, I stood high from the first—half-a-dozen people in the parish would have signed the call then. Now, I'm sure, there's not half-a-dozen in the whole parish who would not sign it."

"I'm seer o' that, sir," said Mains of Yawal; and Teuchitsmyre's whole body gave a confirmatory hitch.

"So much for the popular voice—nothing could be more delusive," added Mr. Sleekaboot, with an air of something like triumph.

I do not know that the Rev. Jonathan Tawse would have disputed this last sentiment at any rate; but inasmuch as he in his own case had not been so fortunate as Mr. Sleekaboot in finding a backer to enable him to get over the initial unpopularity incidental to him as a preacher, there was not exactly identity of feeling between him and his respected minister on this particular point. Therefore Jonathan took snuff afresh, refilled his tumbler, and incontinently turned the conversation to topics more congenial to Mains and Teuchitsmyre, who, being unable to follow the high argument that the two divines had got into, had contented themselves by listening with as much of an elderlike and interested air as they could manage to assume.

The weather, and the markets for grain and live stock, subjects of common interest, and on which the whole party could speak with practical intelligence, were discussed *ad longam*, during the latter part of the evening.

The case put by Mr. Sleekaboot, and which had brought the ecclesiastical part of the conversation to a close, had been, all through the early part at least of the Ten Years' Conflict, his standing illustration of the utter fallaciousness of the Non-intrusion principle. He had quoted it repeatedly to his brethren, as well as to outsiders, and had even ventured to direct the attention of Sir Simon Frissal to it. Sir Simon had signified his approval. "Yes, yes, your style was very poor indeed," added the baronet; and Mr. Sleekaboot felt as much gratified as the circumstances allowed.

Now, it so happened in course of this very spring of 1842, and not many weeks after the distribution, that Johnny Gibb was jogging home on a market night on his trusty gray pony, and whom should he overtake but the Rev. Andrew Sleekaboot, jogging home too, from the Presbytery. Johnny's principle of action, as it concerned differences between himself and others, was always to dunt it oot as he went along. Consequently, when he and Mr. Sleekaboot met, Johnny hailed the minister as freely and frankly as if they had never cas'en oot in their lives. And Mr. Sleekaboot, who had a lingering suspicion that it might be otherwise, felt once more somewhat warmed towards his parishioner, of whom he, under the mild impulse of the moment, almost thought there might be hope even yet. Johnny was keen on ecclesiastical matters, at any rate, and perhaps his disposition toward debate had not been lessened by his share in a friendly gill with a neighbour at the stabler's before he took out his shalt. His questions about what the Presbytery had been doing did not elicit much information, but Mr. Sleekaboot could not help being dragged into a discussion on the general Church question, when it became more and more evident to him that Johnny Gibb was a very distinct and confirmed specimen of the Non-intrusionist. So he determined for once to floor Johnny. They had just got to the point where their roads separated, and they and their shalts paused in the gloamin light.

"I tell you it's the greatest delusion in the world. A veto law against a presentee involves the greatest fallacy as well as the greatest injustice;" and then Mr. Sleekaboot began the irrefutable illustration, "When I was settled at Pyketillim I don't believe that I would have got almost any of the parishioners to have signed the call——"

But here Johnny broke in abruptly—

"An' ye kent it weel, sir; feint a vera mony wud ye get yet!"

Mr. Sleekaboot was grievously taken aback. In place of finishing the statement of his favourite illustration, he said something about the "insolence of ignorant uneducated persons," whereat Johnny, who had at least equalled his pastor in the rapidity with which he managed to get up his temper, retorted in words perhaps more vehement than respectful.

And so they parted; Mr. Sleekaboot riding off toward the Manse, while Johnny turned the head of the gray shalt in the direction of Gushetneuk.

CHAPTER XIV.

TAM MEERISON'S PRIVATE AFFAIRS.

SIX months after the date of his removal from Gushetneuk, Tam Meerison had once more to decide on the question of renewing his engagement with his master, or seeking a new one. His experiences at Clinkstyle had not been altogether of the most pleasant sort, whether as regards his master or mistress or his fellow-servants, and the natural conclusion would have been that Tam certainly would not stay longer there. But conclusions in such cases are sometimes affected by circumstances which it is not so easy to guess at. A day or two before the feeing market day it had leaked out that Tam was bidin, and the fact considerably intensified the feeling of contempt which his fellow-servants had been in the habit of occasionally exhibiting towards him. They had hoped to leave Clinkstyle with a clean toon again, and they were angry at being disappointed. While Peter Birse manifested his satisfaction by talking more than usual to Tam, or stalking along for a bit with him at the plough, the lads lost no opportunity of throwing out a taunt at his craven resolution; or reminding him of those bygone interludes when Mrs. Birse had chosen to express her private opinion of him and his. Doubtless these taunts were not pleasant; but I don't know that they weighed most on Tam's mind at that particular juncture. In point of fact, the state of Tam's affections, combined with the adverse influences that seemed to be arraying themselves against him, kept him in a condition of no little anxiety. Tam now bitterly regretted that pig-headed sense of self-importance on his part, which had made him, without the shadow of a valid reason, decline Johnny Gibb's first overture to re-engage him at the previous term; and thus had earned for him a bad situation in place of a good one—precisely the course that I have seen many more of Tam's class follow, to reach exactly the same end. But this was not all. Tam was seriously in love with Jinse Deans. Whether Jinse had hitherto reciprocated his passion in any true sense, I would be loth to venture an opinion. It was certain she received Tam as a suitor; but it was equally certain that Tam was not the only person so favoured. Tam knew this. Nay more, while he had over and over again met with what he reckoned "slichts" at the hands of his enchantress, he had an agonising suspicion that Johnny Gibb's new man, his own successor, and whom Johnny had described as a "stoot gudge an' a gatefarrin," was also stickin' up to Jinse. Ah! poor Tam, thou wert truly out of the frying-pan into the fire! Tam had writhed under and sought to resent the slight scorchings he had to endure from the youth Willy M'Aul on the subject of his courtship; next he had assumed the high horse with Johnny Gibb, and then left Gushetneuk a half-repentant man, allowing his successor to come in and court his sweetheart at leisure. Whereas, had he remained there still, he would have had opportunities for baulking competitors which none other could have had. It was like abandoning a strongly defensive position in face of the enemy.

So thought Tam Meerison, and his meditations were not sweet. When the next term approached, Tam accordingly contrived to get early information about Johnny Gibb's arrangements. Unhappily for him, his successor at Gushetneuk was bidin. "Jist like 'im; inhaudin scoonrel," thought Tam. However that might be, Tam had got a little bocht wit on the subject; and he felt that, if he stood at a certain disadvantage with Johnny Gibb's stoot gudge, inasmuch as the gudge, being at Gushetneuk, had so much readier access to Jinse than he had, being at Clinkstyle; then if he left Clinkstyle, and ran the risk of having to transport himself several miles farther off, his position and prospects would be yet further damaged in proportion to the increased distance.

Therefore it was that Tam Meerison made up his mind to bear the ills he had, and to remain at Clinkstyle.

Another six months had passed and left his courtship much in the same state; but by that time Tam had put his foot in it, by talking disrespectfully of Master Benjamin Birse. It was in the kitchen, and, though Tam was not aware of it, Miss Birse was behind the inner door, where we have heard of her being before. What Tam had said was to the effect that "Benjie was an orpiet, peeakin, little sinner;" and that "he was fitter to be a dog-dirder, or a flunkey, nor to gae to the college;" sentiments which— although they seemed to meet with a rather hearty response from the audience immediately before him—when retailed to Benjie's mother, were productive of a storm, that thereafter burst with no little fury about Tam's ears. Tam's mood, I fear, had been desperate at any rate, and he now retorted on Mrs. Birse by somewhat bluntly telling her she "mith be prood to see 'er loon wi' a pair o' yallow breeks an' a strippet waistcoat on; it wud be ten-faul better nor bein a muckle goodman, wi' a wife that wudna lat 'im ca' 's niz his ain." Mrs. Birse took this as personal. And when the term came, Tam left Clinkstyle, half reckless, as it seemed, of his fate; for surely Jinse's heart was too hard to win, and what else need he care for!

Tam Meerison had gone off to a distance of over a dozen miles, and for the next twelve months the region of Pyketillim saw nothing, and I really believe heard very little of, and still less from, him. For Tam was not a man of the pen. He had, indeed, learnt to write a sort of decent small text at school, but the accomplishment was of wondrous little use to him. He never wrote letters, except on very pressing emergencies, and not more than three or four of these had occurred since he became a man. It was not the mere writing that dismayed him; it was the composition—foo to begin—and the backin'. These were the grand obstacles; and Tam's chief exercise in penmanship had been the occasional copying of some approved receipt for the composition of blacking for horse harness, in the way of friendly interchange with a cronie.

At the Martinmas of 1841, Johnny Gibb changed his principal man-servant. The gudge, whose ambition it was to rise, was leaving on a friendly understanding, with a view to go to school for a quarter with Sandy Peterkin, to rub the rust off his literary and arithmetical acquirements, and then learn the business of a mole-catcher when spring came, and Johnny promoted Willy M'Aul, now grown a stout lad of over nineteen, to his place. The gudge had been at the feeing market, from which he came home at a pretty late hour, and in high spirits, with sweeties in his pockets, not merely for Jinse, but for Mrs. Gibb as well, when fit opportunity should occur for presenting them.

"An' fat's the news o' the market, min?" asked Jinse of the gudge, who had seated himself at the top of the deece to eat his supper.

"Little o' 't; slack feein'; an' plenty o' drunk fowk."

"The waages doon?"

"Doon! Ay are they. Gweed men feein' at seyven-pun-ten; an' women for oot-wark hardly winnin abeen a poun' note. An' dizzens never got an offer."

"It's braw wardles wi' them 't disna need to fee," said Jinse, with a sly reference to the gudge's hopeful prospects.

"Weel, Jinse, fat encouragement is there to the like o' me to bide on an' loss my time at fairm wark? Ye may be the best han' 't ever gaed atween the pleuch stilts, but ye can never get an ondependent or sattlet wye o' deein."

"Div ye mean a place o' yer nain?"

"Weel, gin a body cud hae the chance o' gettin' a bit craftie. But I'll appel to yersel', Jinse—Fat comes o' maist ilka fairm servan' 't gets a wife?"—(and the gudge looked sweetly on Jinse)—"they're forc't to tak' to the dargin, an gae awa' an' bide aboot the Broch, or some gate siclike."

"But hinna ye nae mair news?" said Jinse, desirous of turning the conversation.

"In fack, there's nae chance but slave on to the en' o' the chapter; oonless ye win in to some ither wye o' deein in time," continued the gudge, whose own scheme naturally occupied a favourable place in his thoughts at the time.

"Hoot, min, gi'e 's the news o' the market," said Jinse.

"Weel, fat news wud ye like?"

"Fa's bidin or flittin'?"

"Weel, I didna hear particular. Ye see I was oot o' the throng a gey file arreengin some things o' my nain."

"Gweeshtens, ye've seerly been sair ta'en up. Didna ye traffike neen wi' common fowk the day?"

"Ou weel, ye see, fan a body has some buzness o' their nain to atten' till they're nae sae sair ta'en up wi' fat's gaen on in general."

"Sawna ye nae bargains made ava?"

"Weel, the only bargain 't aw cud say 't aw saw was Mains o' Yawal feein' a third horseman. I was in 'o Kirkie's tent gettin' a share o' a gill wi' a cheelie 't I was ance aboot the toon wi', fan Mains cam' in, skirpit wi' dubs to the vera neck o' 's kwite. I didna ken the chap, naething aboot 'im, but fan they war jist aboot bargain't Mains leuks owre an' refars to me. 'That's an aul' servan' o' mine,' says he to the chap, 'an' ye can speir at him aboot the place.' They hed threepit on a lang time; but an coorse wus comin' nearer 't afore Mains socht the drink, an' at length he bargain't wi' 'im for a croon oot o' seyven poun' to ca' 's third pair; an' that was the only bargain 't I saw."

"Did ye see ony o' oor fowk—or hear onything about them?"

"I didna see neen o' yer breeders."

"I wud like richt to ken gin they be flittin' or no. Neen o' Clinkstyle's fowk bidin', aw reckon?" asked Jinse.

"That's weel min'et," exclaimed the gudge, with some vivacity. "Bidin'! na, nae lickly; but fa div ye think 's comin' there again?"

"Comin' there again? Fa cud tell that—somebody hard up for a place, seerly?"

"Jist guess."

"Ha! fa cud guess that? Like aneuch somebody 't I min' naething aboot—fowk 't's cheengin the feck 't they hae at ilka term."

"Weel," said the gudge, deliberately, "it's jist Tam Meerison!"

The light of Johnny Gibb's old iron lamp, with its one rush wick, was not brilliant at best; and it had been getting worse in consequence of the protracted sederunt in which the gudge had indulged. Therefore, though I rather think Jinse did start slightly, and colour a little at the intimation just made by the gudge, I don't think the gudge observed it; and, truth to say, the gudge himself was a very little agitated.

"Gae 'wa' to yer bed, than, this minit," said Jinse; "see, ye've keepit me sittin' wytein ye till the vera nethmost shall o' the lamp's dry."

And the gudge went to bed accordingly.

CHAPTER XV.

SANDY PETERKIN'S SCHOOL.

The occasion of a muckle scholar coming to the Smiddy-ward school was an event of some importance. And, therefore, when the embryo mole-catcher presented himself on a Monday morning to meet the scrutiny of the thirty odd urchins under Sandy Peterkin's charge, there was a good deal of commotion and whispering. He wore a pair of moleskin leggings, which extended up to the very thigh tops, and were there suspended by a little tag of the same cloth to the side button of his trousers. When he took off his bonnet his head was seen to be huddry; that is, noticeably huddry for such a civilised place as the inside of a school. He had been to Andrew Langchafts' shop at the Kirktown, and had there furnished himself with a sclate and skallie, a pennyworth of lang sheet paper, unruled, and two quills for pens. These, with an old copy of "the Gray," were the furnishings for the ensuing scholastic campaign that was to fit him for entering on the practical study of mole-catching.

"Weel," said the new scholar, laying down his equipments on the side of the maister's desk, "aw'm jist gyaun to be the raith; an' aw wud like to win as far throu' 's aw cud."

"Coontin', ye mean?"

"Oh ay; in fack a body canna weel hae owre muckle o' it at ony rate."

"Fat progress hae ye made in arithmetic?" asked Sandy Peterkin.

The gudge scratched his head for a little; and then, wetting his thumb, proceeded to turn over the dog-eared leaves of his Gray. "Faek, I dinna jist min' richt. It's half-a-dizzen o' year sin' I was at the skweel. That was wi' Maister Tawse; an' I daursay your wye winna be the same 's his wi' the coontin, mair nor ither things; so it winna maitter muckle."

"Ye 've been through the simple rules at ony rate," suggested Sandy.

"Hoot ay; aw 'm seer aw was that. Nyod, I think it was hereaboot," and the aspirant mole-catcher pointed to the place on the book.

"Compound Division?" said the maister, looking at the page.

"Ay," said the scholar, with a sort of chuckle; "but aw 'm nae sayin' 't aw cud work it noo—aw wud better begin nearer the beginnin'."

"Weel—maybe Reduction."

"That wud dee fine. It's an ill-to-work rowle, an' I never oon'ersteed it richt wi' Maister Tawse. Aw won'er gin aw cud win as far through 's wud mak' oot to mizzour aff an awere or twa o' grun, or cast up the wecht o' a hay soo?"

"That 'll depen' on your ain diligence," said Sandy Peterkin, with a smile.

"Weel, I ance was neepours wi' a chap 't cud 'a deen that as exact 's ye like; an' he not nae leems till 't, nedderin, but jist a mason's tape line 't he hed i' the locker o' 's kist."

"It's quite possible to dee that wi' a marked line," answered the dominie.

"It 's richt eesefu' the like o' that," said the gudge; "an' fan a body 's gyaun aboot like, they wud aye be gettin' 't adee noo an' than, and cudna hardly foryet the wye. Noo, Maister Tawse wud never lat 's try naething o' that kin', 'cep we hed first gane throu' a great heap o' muckle rowles; an' that disna dee wi' the like o' hiz 't hisna lang time at a skweel."

"An fat ither lessons wud you like to tak'?" asked the maister.

"Ye ken best; only it was for the coontin 't I cam'; an' leernin' to mak oot accoonts maybe."

"We hae a grammar class noo—wud you try it?"

"Na, na; aw winna fash wi' 't," said the gudge, with a decisive shake of the head. "It's nae for common fowk ava that gremmar."

"Maybe geography than. I've a gweed chart on the wa' here 't ye cud get a skance o' the principal countries upon vera shortly."

"Weel, but is 't ony eese to the like o' me, that geography? I wunna lickly be gyaun to forrin pairts."

If there was one branch more than another on which Sandy Peterkin set a high value, and on which, as a travelled man, he loved to descant, it was geography. So he pressed its importance, and a dubious consent was given to trying an hour at it once a week, it being understood that the future mole-catcher would not be subject to the catechis lesson on Saturdays. Then, as he had a suspicion that his new pupil was not too well up in his general literature, Sandy suggested the propriety of his taking a reading lesson.

"Na; aw hardly think 't I'll fash wi' that edder," was the reply. "I was never that deen ill at the readin', an' I was i' the muckle Bible class afore aw leeft the skweel."

"But ye maybe hinna read muckle sinsyne; an' ye wud get a lot o' usefu' information i' the Collection lesson."

"But the like o' me's nae needin' to read like the minaister," said the muckle scholar, with a laugh, "an' it wud gar 's loss a hantle o' time fae the coontin. An 'oor at that, an' syne the vreetin—the day wud be deen in a han'-clap, afore a body cud get oot mair nor a question or twa."

However, Sandy succeeded in persuading him to take the Collection lesson. When the lesson came, he did not like to bid him stand up among a dozen urchins so much smaller than himself. The muckle scholar sat with his sturdy legs crowded in below the incommodious desk. He floundered through his turn at reading in a style at which his junior class-fellows did not always conceal their mirth. But he was too self-centred to be particularly thin-skinned, and Sandy Peterkin was indulgent, even to the extent of taking care that the graceless young rapscallions should spell every hard word in the muckle scholar's hearing, while Sandy spared him such trials: albeit he improved the time when the gudge's turn came by a short homily on the importance of attention to correct spelling. Then would our mature class-fellow seize his sclate, and gravely set on to the piecemeal solution of "the Gray," from which occupation it was found that none of the ordinary devices would distract him. And at writing time, when the dominie sat in his desk, knife in hand, with a *chevaux de frise* of quill feathers, held in idle or mischief-loving hands, surrounding his nose as he diligently mended, or new-made, pens for a score of writers, the muckle scholar spread himself to his task, and grimly performed his writing exercise. He would also at times stay after the school was dismissed, and get the benefit of Sandy Peterkin's private instructions for an hour or so.

In short, there could be no doubt that the gudge would pass into the world again accomplished beyond many of his contemporaries; and thereafter he could hardly fail of attaining something of distinction in his destined walk, and with that distinction the attendant emoluments.

As Johnny Gibb's late servant moved about Smiddyward (he had got boarded and lodged, for the time, with Widow Will), he could not help reflecting on these things; and it occurred to him that in his own person he presented a very eligible matrimonial bargain for any well-disposed young woman. And why should he not look over occasionally to Gushetneuk to keep up his friendly relations with Johnny and Mrs. Gibb, and let Jinse Deans know how expansive a place the world was to men of enterprise? I rather think that Jinse still needed a little contrivance now and then to prevent undesirable rencontres between certain of her sweethearts. And this was the real explanation which the gudge, who was a simple soul, and still loved to indulge in late sittings, ought to have got to account for the peremptoriness with which he had been once or twice ordered to his home. But Jinse condescended to no explanations on what seemed her capricious treatment of the lad. And, of course, Jinse could not help what might emerge beyond the range of her influence.

So it happened that, on a certain evening, when the gudge had got himself comfortably fixed up on the smiddy hearth, and was talking away full swing in a half-oracular sort of style to several other lads, his old rival, Tam Meerison, came in with a long stack of plough irons on his shoulder to be sharpened. Tam first threw off his burden with a heavy clank; then, after saluting the smith, lifted it into the glowing light of the fire at the edge of the hearth, and, with a hammer he had laid hold of, proceeded to knock the piled coulters and socks out of connection with each other. He next glanced across the hearth, and without addressing anybody very directly, exclaimed—"'Wa' oot o' that; ye 've been birslin yer shins lang aneuch there." The gudge's lessons probably required his attention about that particular period of the evening. At any rate, he soon found that his time would not permit further loitering in the smiddy just then. Tam took the vacated place on the hearth, and lighted his pipe with every appearance of satisfaction. He had just done so when the smith, who was not unaware apparently of the relations between the two, wickedly endeavoured to blow the flame of jealousy, by waggishly informing Tam of the hopeful prospects of his rival.

"Tak' moles!" quoth Tam, whose manner had evidently progressed of late in the direction of brusqueness. "I wud as seen ca' stinkin' fish wi' a horse worth auchteenpence."

"Hoot, min, but he 's gyaun to get Jinse Deans for 's wife fanever his apprenticeship's throu'," said the smith.

"Hah, hah, ha-a-a," roared Tam, with a loud laugh. "It 's been to help 'im wi' that that he heeld in wi' Johnny Gibb sae lang."

"I wudna won'er," said the smith. "But she 's a

muckle thocht o' 'oman, Jinse. They speak o' lads comin' back to the place aifter they 've gane hyne awa', jist for her sake—that's a greater ferlie, seerly. Fat wud ye say to that?"

"Fat! That they 're great geese. Na, na, smith, 'The back o' ane's the face o' twa;' that's the style for me. Hah, hah, ha!"

"An' ye hinna been at Gushetneuk than, sin' ye cam back to the quarter?"

"Nane o' yer jaw, min. Min' yer wark there, an' gi'e that sock a grippie o' yird. Clinkies likes his stibbles weel riven up; an' the set 't he hed hed wi' 'im afore the term's been makin' bonny wark till 'im i' the backfaulds."

"Ou, I thocht young Peter an' him atween them wud 'a manag't to keep them richt—nae to speak o' yer aul freen the mistress."

"I wuss ye hed jist seen the place, than. Nae the vera pattle shafts but was broken, an' the harness gray an' green for wunt o' cleanin'. I b'lieve the wife was at them aboot that, an' got jist a richt nizzin for ance i' the wye o' ill jaw."

"Ye wudna dee the like o' that, Tam?"

"Sang, she 'll better nae try 't, though. But a body's mad to see the wye 't they hed been guidin' the beasts. Yon's a snippit horsie 't was i' the secont pair—yon young beastie—jist clean spoil't. He was some skittish at ony rate, an' the chap hed laid upon 'im an' twistet 'im wi' the ryne till he's a' spoil't i' the mou' completely; an' I 'm seer he hed latt'n 'im oot amon' 's han's i' the theets, for ye cudna lippen till 'im as lang's ye wud turn yer fit. Clinkies gar't me tak' 'im an' pit 'im on to the muckle broon horse, to try and steady 'im. But I can tell ye it's nae gryte job haein' to dee wi' ither fowk's botch't wark."

"'Deed no, Tam; but I 've nae doot ye 'll dee yer best wi' 't. I' the meanwhile ye mith gi'e me a chap to tak' doon the point o' the coulter a bit."

Tam put his pipe in his waistcoat pocket, and started to the forehammer with the greatest promptitude.

CHAPTER XVI.

A START IN LIFE.

On a certain afternoon, about a week before the Whitsunday term of 1842, Johnny Gibb, who had been busy afield, came toddling home when the afternoon was wearing on, and went into the mid house, to look out sundry blue-checked cotton bags with turnip seed, for he meditated sowing of that valued root. He was hot and tired, and his spouse invited him to rest for a little on the deece. Would he take a drink of ale?

"Ay will aw, 'oman," said Johnny, "an' ye hae 't at han'. Lat 's see the caup there."

Mrs. Gibb obeyed the command, and Johnny drank of the reaming liquor with evident satisfaction.

"Rest ye a minit, than, an' drink oot the drap; for ye 've never devall't the haill day," said Mrs. Gibb; and saying so, she lean't her doon, with some intention apparently of entering on a confab with her husband.

"Are ye thinkin' o' gyaun doon to the market on Wednesday?" asked she, with that kind of air which seems directly to provoke an interrogatory answer; and Johnny at once exclaimed—

"No; foo are ye speerin that? Ye ken 't baith the boys is bidin: I've nae erran'."

"Ye never think o' speerin aboot Jinse," replied Mrs. Gibb, still in the key that suggested the necessity for an explanatory note.

"Jinse Deans!" exclaimed Johnny. "Fat's the ecse o' speerin at her? An' she binna pleas't wi' 'er waages she wud seerly 'a tell't ye lang ere noo."

"I doot it's nae the waages a'thegither, peer 'oman. But Jinse's needin' awa'."

Mrs. Gibb had evidently made up her mind now to give some further explanation about this new movement, when, as Fate would have it, the colloquy was broken in upon by Jinse (who had been unaware of her master's presence there) herself at the moment stumbling into the kitchen, from which she had been temporarily absent.

"Fat haiver's this 't ye've ta'en i' yer heid noo?" demanded Johnny, addressing Jinse. "Are ye gyaun clean gyte to speak o' leavin yer place; and it only an ouk fae the term tee? Faur wud ye gae till?"

"Hame to my mither's," answered Jinse, exhibiting somewhat of discomposure at Johnny's vehemence.

Jinse's mother lived not far off Benachie, in a very unpretentious residence.

"An' fat on the face o' the creation wud ye dee gyaun hame?—Yer mither's but a peer 'oman; she has little need o' you wi' 'er," said Johnny.

Jinse, who was making, on the whole, an uneasy defence, averred that her mother "wasna vera stoot."

"But is she wuntin you hame?" was Johnny's demand. "Tell me that."

Here Jinse gave symptoms of breaking into tears, and Mrs. Gibb interposed with a "Hoot, man! ye're aye sac ramsh wi' fowk."

"Weel, weel," quoth Johnny, as he seized his bonnet and marched toward the door; "ye're a' alike. Fa wud ken fat ye wud be at!"

I don't know that Johnny Gibb meant to include his wife. The reference was rather to the class to which Jinse belonged, though, no doubt, he went away with the conviction that women-kind in general are absurdly impracticable in their ways. But be that as it it may, Johnny found that he had to provide a new servant lass.

In private audience Jinse Deans had revealed to Mrs. Gibb, with many sighs and tears, that Tam Meerison had "promis't to mairry her." What more I don't know; but the worthy goodwife, after scolding Jinse as severely as it was in her nature to do, told her to "wash her face, an' nae mair o' that snifterin. An' gae awa' and get ready the sowens. I'se say naething mair aboot it till the term day's by. Nae doot ye'll be i' yer tribbles seen aneuch wuntin that."

Poor Jinse; the prospect of marriage did not seem a cheerful one for her, notwithstanding the number of candidates there had been for her hand. Of her reputed sweethearts, Tam Meerison was the one for whom she had at any rate affected to care the least; and since the time Tam had begun seriously to court her, his jealousy had been again and again roused by the undisguised preference given to others, his rivals. And yet Tam Meerison was to have her to wife. It would be wrong to say that Tam had not a certain feeling of satisfaction in the thought of this; for, notwithstanding his adoption latterly of a more seeming-reckless style, Tam had been from an early date severely smitten by Jinse's charms. Indeed his satisfaction was presumably considerable, else he had probably not formed the laudable resolution to marry. But then there were counterbalancing considerations. The idea of marriage as an actual event had been forced upon him with a kind of staggering suddenness, which caused the approach of the reality itself to awaken a rather uncomfortable feeling of responsibility. Tam began to see that it would be troublesome to go about, and he had but a dim notion of the indispensable technicalities. Then there was the question of a house and home for his wife; and here Tam's case no doubt merited commiseration. There was no house whatever available within a circuit of several miles; for the lairds in the locality, in the plenitude of their wisdom, and foreseeing the incidence of a poor law, had, as a rule, determined that there should be no possibility of paupers seeing the light on their properties. They would rather pull down every cottage on their estates. What could poor Tam do?

Jinse said she would go to her mother's. Where Jinse's mother lived was three miles off; and with her mother Jinse could only get what share she might of a hovel that very barely afforded room for two beds in its dark and diminutive but and ben. And there, also, an unmarried sister and two brothers, all in farm service, claimed to have the only home they possessed. It was not greatly to be wondered at if Tam felt perplexed, and began to consider marrying really a stiff business. It was under this feeling of perplexity that he succumbed once again to Clinkstyle's offer of a renewed engagement, and in order to get one foot at least planted down without more trouble, agreed to bide with Peter Birse for another six months.

Tam had ventured across to Gushetneuk at a suitable hour on the night of which we have been speaking, to talk over with his affianced what most nearly concerned him and her.

The two sat on the deece again; and this time nobody disturbed them. Jinse was sobbing. Tam put his arm about her; and there was genuine feeling in the poor chap's words, I have not the least doubt, as he said in his tenderest tones, "Dinna noo, Jinse—Ye 'se never wunt a peck o' meal nor a pun' o' butter as lang 's I 'm able to work for 't."

By and by Jinse's emotion moderated, and they got into a more business strain; and then Tam asked—

"Does Gushets ken yet?"

"Eh, aw dinna ken richt; aw never got sic a gast 's aw got the nicht i' the aifterneen, fan aw haumer't into the kitchie upo' the mistress an' him speakin' something or anither aboot me gyaun awa'."

"But an' coorse she kent aboot it afore?"

"She jist kent the streen 't I wudna be here aifter the term; I gyauna 'er muckle audiscence fan she speer't foo I was leavin'. But an' ye hed heard the maister fan he brak oot—I cudna 'a haud'n up my heid, Tam, nor been ongrutt'n, deen fat I hed liket!"

"An' did ye tell him onything mair, than?"

"Geyan lickly! Fa wud 'a deen that, noo? But I

tell't her aifter he was awa'—it was rael sair, Tam," and Jinse threatened greetin again.

"Did she say ony ill upo' me?" asked Tam.

"No; but though the maister was in a terrible ill teen, jist aboot 's gyaun awa' an' that, I was waur, gin waur cud win, fan she scault's an' gya's sae muckle gweed advice, tee."

"Ou weel, Jinse, we're nae waur nor ither fowk, nor yet sae ill's plenty."

With this comforting reflection the conversation turned, and Jinse asked—

"But fat are ye gyaun tae dee a' simmer?"

"I'm bidin' again."

"Bidin' at Clinkstyle?"

"Ay."

"But it's a coorse place to bide in, isnin't?"

"Weel," answered Tam, slowly, and not quite willing, in the circumstances, to make that admission, "the wife's some roch an' near b'gyaun, but there's little tribble wi' the maister 'imsel."

"Didna ye hear o' nae ither place at the market?"

"But I wasna there. I bargain't the day afore, and didna seek to gyang. Ye see I taul' the maister 't I wud tak' a day for 't fan the neeps is laid doon."

Tam evidently considered this a stroke of management, and Jinse, brightening up a little, asked—

"An' fan wud it need to be?"

"Jist as seen 's things can be sattl't. We maun be cried on twa Sundays, at ony rate."

"Twa Sundays?"

"Ay, there's nane but puckles o' the gentry gets 't deen in ae Sunday, aw b'lieve."

"Weel, ye maun come up to my mither's on Saiturday's nicht."

"Ou ay, an' we can speak aboot it better than. Your mither'll ken a' aboot the wye o' 't, I'se warran'. But I doot she'll be pitt'n aboot wi' 's bidin' there. I wuss we cud 'a gotten a hoose ony wye."

"Weel, we maun jist pit up wi' things like ither fowk, I suppose."

"But it'll mak' sic a steer in her hoose, ye ken."

"Oh, we'll manage fine for that maitter. There's her but bed, it's nae vera sair in order eenoo; but I've twa fedder pillows o' my nain, an' a patch't coverin', forbye a pair o' blankets 't the mistress helpit 's to spin, an' gya 's the feck o' the 'oo'. There 'll be plenty o' room for my kist i' the but, an' ye maun hae yer ain kist aside ye, ye ken."

"But yer mither winna hae gweed sparin' 'er room constant; it's nae 's gin 't war only a fyou ouks. She winna get nae eese o' 't hersel'."

"Ou, but ye ken there's nane o' oor fowk comes hame eenoo, 'cep Rob, an' Nelly at an antrin time; Jamie's owre far awa'. An' ony nicht 't Rob's there, gin ye chanc't to be the same nicht, you twa cud sleep thegither, seerly; an' I cud sleep wi' my mither, an' Nelly tee, for that maitter."

"Foo af'en does Rob come?"

"Aboot ance i' the fortnicht or three ouks."

"I think I'll win near as af'en 's that mysel'," said Tam, upon whose mind the general effect of this conversation had been rather exhilarating than otherwise. His sweetheart had not merely contrivance; she had also foresight and thrift, evidently, as the general inventory given of her providin' testified. Still he hankered after a house that he could call his own. It was not that Tam's ambition on this point was extravagant. If he could get one end of a but an' a ben cottage, about such a place as Smiddyward, with a cannas-breid of a garden, and the chance of going to see his wife once a week, he would have been well content.

But this Tam found to be impracticable. He made full inquiry; and even invoked the aid of his acquaintance the smith, whose banter was turned into hearty sympathy with the statement of the case now laid before him. The smith tackled Dawvid Hadden, the ground-officer, and urged the reparation of part of the old erections of which Sandy Peterkin's school formed the main wing, as a dwelling for Tam. As the manner of sycophants dressed in a little delegated authority is, Dawvid's answer was a kind of echo of what he imagined Sir Simon would have said, "Na, na, smith, it's a very fallawshus prenciple in fat they ca' poleetical ecomony to encourage the doonsittin' o' the like o' them in a place.—Ou, it's nae the expense. Na, na; the biggin o' a score o' hooses wud be a mere triffle, gin Sir Simon thocht it richt in prenciple—a mere triffle. But there they sit doon, an' fesh up faimilies till they wud thraten to full a destrick wi' peer fowk—the Brod cud never keep the tae half o' them. No; I'm weel seer they'll get nae hoose i' the pairis' o' Pyketillim."

It was not a kindly speech that of Dawvid Hadden; albeit it expressed, firstly, the newest view of political economy in the locality, which was just then beginning to be practically carried out; and, secondly, an accurate statement of Tam Meerison's chances of getting a house within the parish. In this particular, Tam had his strong wish and reasonable desire completely defeated. It may be difficult for the man who lives in a comfortable home with his family about him to estimate with precision either the keenness of feeling, or the deteriorating effects involved in such disappointment. I don't think it should be difficult for any man to make up his mind as to giving a hearty condemnation to the too common land policy which has entailed the like cruel hardship upon hundreds of honest hard-working men in the class to which Tam belonged.

But my business is not to moralise, I daresay; and I have only to add to this chapter that, as better could not be, Tam Meerison and Jinse Deans had no help for it but get married, and commence their career of wedded bliss under the slenderly-equipped conditions already indicated.

CHAPTER XVII.

SANDY PETERKIN IS WARNED.

WHETHER the unceremonious home-thrust administered to the Rev. Andrew Sleekaboot by Johnny Gibb had anything to do with the matter or not, I am not prepared to say, but so it was, that very speedily after that occurrence, the patron of the parish and lord of the manor "had his attention directed" to the current state of opinion, and recent ongoings at Smiddyward School. Sir Simon was one of those lofty individuals whose attention requires to be directed to this or that; or they might for long overlook many commonplace events transacting themselves before their view; and in the present case, it was surmised, rightly or wrongly, that the Rev. Mr. Sleekaboot, in his own quiet way, had, on second thoughts, taken means to stir up the dignified baronet. Anyhow, Sir Simon was stirred up; and he made it known, through his ground-officer, Dawvid Hadden, that the "conventicle" held in Sandy Peterkin's school must forthwith cease and determine.

It would not have been in accordance with Sandy Peterkin's antecedents had he exhibited as much worldly prudence and policy as to jouk an' lat the jaw of Sir Simon's wrath gae owre. So, although the Rev. Alister Macrory was just about finishing a second spell of preaching in the school, and there was no immediate prospect of the place being further occupied in the same way, Sandy chose to return an abrupt and rebellious answer to Sir Simon's order to have the conventicle stopped. Sandy, without consulting any one, replied that he was a citizen of a free country, and would give the use of the school to anybody he pleased.

"Yea, Saun'ers, man," answered Dawvid Hadden. "Ye'll better ca' canny; aw wuss that bit mou'fu' dinna craw i' yer crap or a' be deen."

"We'll tak' oor risk o' that, Mr. Hadden; for even Sir Simon hasna the poo'er o' pot an' gallows noo."

"Maybe no; but it'll be cheeng't wardles an he binna able to haud's nain wi' them 't 's obleeg't till 's leenity for ha'ein a reef o' ony kin' abeen their heids. I 'se jist warn ye ance mair to be cowshus; or ye'll hear mair aboot it."

Along with an abundance of toadyism towards those he reckoned above him, Dawvid Hadden exhibited not a little of the spirit of the petty tyrant on the side seen by the people who, he imagined, came fairly within the compass of his particular authority, and it is not to be supposed that the version given to Sir Simon of Sandy Peterkin's behaviour toward Dawvid as Sir Simon's representative, suffered that behaviour to lose anything of its offensiveness. At any rate, Dawvid very speedily began to let mysterious hints drop about the general connection between attendance at the Smiddyward services and brevity of tenure on the lands of Sir Simon Frissal, and he did not scruple to let it be understood that Sandy Peterkin had put himself entirely at his, Dawvid's, mercy.

I don't know that either the souter or the smith, if they had been consulted, would have advised Sandy Peterkin to do the rash thing he did in contemning Dawvid Hadden; nevertheless, they were both roused at the idea that "the creatur" should insult a man who was so much his superior, as they agreed in considering the dominie of the Ward to be. Probably, however, their indignation would have subsided without any particular result, had it not been that just about the time when it was hottest, Johnny Gibb, who had been advised of Dawvid's general ongoings, but not of this particular act, came across to the smiddy on some lawful errand. The smith was going on at the hearth, for Hairry

Muggart, the wright, had come across from the Toon-en, carrying on his shoulder a plough beam, which he wanted the smith to strap. Hairry was a ponderously built man, with feet much bigger than they were shapely, and a bluish tint in the red with which his face was amply splashed. He was deliberate in his movements, and delivered himself of what he had to say with a certain copious and opinionative egotism which was rather enjoyable to listen to when Hairry was going on full swing. The strappin of Hairry's beam had been completed, when a breathing space occurred, during which the conversation turned upon Dawvid Hadden and his proceedings.

"Fat div ye say?" quoth Johnny Gibb. "Did the creatur raelly gae the length o' thraetenin' the maister?"

"Or, to dee 'im nae oonjustice, we sall suppose that he only deliver't the laird's orders," said the smith.

"Laird or nae laird, he ocht to keep a ceevil tongue in 's heid."

"Weel, I winna say but Sandy spak back in a wye 't was lickly to gar the body cantle up. Ye ken we 've a' oor weyknesses, Gushets!"

"I maun see Sandy aboot this at ance. I'll tell ye fat it is, smith, things are comin' till a heid in this countra, 't fowk can-not pit up wi'. I 'se be at the boddom o' this, though I sud gae to the Place an' see Sir Seemon 'imsel' the morn."

"Aw 'm dootin' ye winna fin' 'im—there, John," said Hairry Muggart, in an oracular way.

"An' fat for no?"

"He 's awa' to the Sooth yesterday. Dawvid cam' up to me afore sax o'clock i' the mornin'. *She* was jist up an' the bar aff o' the door, an' was o' the road oot wi' the aise-backet, an' her nicht mutch nae aff, fan he comes roon by the stack mou' like a man gyaun to redd fire. 'Is the vricht up?' says Dawvid. ''Serve me, fat are ye on sic a chase for at this oor i' the mornin'?' says my wife. I heard the clatter o' them, an' throws on my waistcoat an' staps my feet in'o my sheen, an' gin that time he was at the door. 'Ou, ye 've wun oot owre yer bed,' says he.

'Fan did ever ye get me i' my bed at this time i' the mornin'?" says I, an' wud 'a ta'en a bit fun wi' 'im, ye see. But Dawvid rebats, an' says he, 'That's nedder here nor there, Hairry, man; ye'll need to get your sma' borin' brace an' a fyou ither teels this moment an' ca' a bit framie thegidder, 't's wuntit to keep the loggage steady o' the cairt.'"

"An' heard ye onything aboot Sandy Peterkin an' the skweel?" asked Johnny Gibb, who had listened not too patiently to Hairry.

"I'm comin' to that eenoo, Gushets. Ye see, they sud 'a been at me the nicht afore. Hooever, the butler forgat a' aboot it, an' the cairt hed to be awa' at aucht o'clock i' the mornin.' But I b'lieve gin Dawvid didna soun' them aboot it for ance. Weel, as aw was sayin', the cairt was a' in order in fine time. An' Dawvid was i' the gran'est humour 't cud be. Oh, he wud hae nae na-say, but I wud gae up by the Wast Lodge, faur Meg Raffan the henwife bides, an' tak' my brakfist wi' 'im. Aweel, this fares on, an' we hed oor dram thegidder, like ony twa lairds; an' syne Dawvid got rael crackie aboot this an' that. An' it was than 't he taul me that the laird was gyaun awa' to the Sooth aboot some faimily affairs, an' 't he wudna lickly be hame for a puckle months at ony rate."

"An' Dawvid was to reign in's stead, nae doot!" suggested the smith.

"Weel, he was gey lairge upo' that. 'Ye see it's nae a licht responsibility at nae time,' says he, 'till conduck the buzness o' an estate like this. An' it's aiven mair seriouser at a time like this; for Sir Simon has naebody but mysel'. But I hae full poo'er to ack accordin' to my nain joodgment.'"

"But he saidna naething aboot the skweel than?"

"He jist did that, John. Says he, 'They've been haein' a gey on-cairry doon at the Ward, wi' that non-intrusion meetin's. An' that creatur Peterkin gya me the grytest o' ensolence the tither nicht. But jist bide still, till I get 'im richt i' my poo'er, gin I dinna gi'e 'im a grip that he hisna gotten the like o' 't for some time.'"

SANDY PETERKIN IS WARNED.   113

"An' ye didna tell Dawvid 't ye hed been a regular hearer at the meetin's yersel'?" said the smith, who was now going on at the light and easy job of sharpening the prongs of a graip for Johnny Gibb.

"Ou na," replied Hairry, with a fozy laugh. "Fan he didna appear to ken, I keepit my thoom upo' that. But I 'm maist seer that he has nae orders fae Sir Simon to meddle wi' Sandy Peterkin, fatever he may thraeten."

"That wud only mak' maitters waur an' waur," said Johnny Gibb. "But at ony rate it 's high time to tak' some decidet step to lat oor opingans be kent, an' tak' mizzours for gettin' the commoonity instruckit aboot the richts an' preevileges o' the Kirk o' Scotland, as weel 's fat belongs to the ceevil poo'er. That 's gaen on in a hantle o' places throu' the kwintra."

"At public meetin's? Weel, foo sudna we hae a public meetin'?" asked Hairry.

The smith and Johnny seemed a little taken aback at the novelty of the idea. At last the smith said—

"We 're nae vera public kin' o' characters, Hairry, an' mith mak' but a peer job o' 't—Wud ye tak' the cheer yersel'?"

"Eh—weel, failin' a better, aw dinna differ."

"Cudnin we get Sandy an' the souter in aboot, an' try an' sattle upo' something, as lang 's we 're thegither?" asked Johnny Gibb.

"Naething easier nor that, at ony rate," answered the smith, who speedily had a juvenile messenger despatched for the worthies named.

And so they resolved to have a public meeting. It was the opinion of Roderick M'Aul, the souter, that they should follow up the Rev. Alister Macrory's evangelical services by inviting some prominent members of the non-intrusion section of the clergy to address them on the principles involved in the great controversy now going on within the Church of Scotland. But while there was a general agreement that this ought to be kept in view as an ultimate object, Johnny Gibb expressed a strong opinion in favour of

I

some more immediate demonstration on their own account, as a sort of embodiment of their protest against tyranny and oppression, in whatever shape, or from whatever quarter. Hairry, as in consistency bound, supported his own idea of a public meeting. Of course, the only place where it had entered anybody's head that it could be held, was in Sandy Peterkin's school. The souter and the smith, in view of what had occurred, indirectly suggested a little caution on that point. This the other two deemed quite out of place in the circumstances—(Johnny, in his heat, even defined Dawvid Hadden as a "pushion't ted,")—the only point was, would Sandy Peterkin be willing to give them the use of the school?

"Weel-a-wat ye winna hae't twice to seek," said Sandy, cheerfully. "I'm only sorry that my dask's nae a bit wider an' heicher. It does fine wi' me; but for a public speaker it's unco crampit; an' Mr. Macrory compleen't wil' ill upon 't. Only there's great principles at stake, an' nae doot the man that feels their importance 'll mak' nae words to speak in a gey hameo'er place. I'll be richt prood to think that I can accommodat' a meetin' for sic a gweed purpose."

So there only remained the duty of "adverteesin" the meeting, as Hairry phrased it, which was to be done by every man personally inviting those within his own circle, to attend at the proper time, when the day and hour had been finally agreed upon.

CHAPTER XVIII.

THE PUBLIC MEETING.

It would not be correct to say that the promoters of the Smiddyward meeting omitted preliminary consultation as to the order of business that should be observed when they had got the public assembled in the school; they deliberated and debated much thereanent, only their ideas on the subject were not very definite.

"We maun get the prenciples for which the Kirk o' Scotlan''s conten'in' expoon'it in a wye 't they can oon'erstan," said Johnny Gibb. "It 's a sair pity that Maister Macrory 's awa'; but ye 've heard a hantle o' 's discoorse, an ye 've a gweed memory, souter, mithna ye try an' rin owre the heids o' 't?"

"I wud be richt willin', Gushets, to dee onything within my poo'er; but ye ken I 'm nae gremmarian, an' cudna conneck it nae gate nor ither 't the fowk cud follow me," said the souter.

"Get Sandy Peterkin 'imsel' to pit a bit narrative thegither," interposed the smith. "He 's weel acquaint wi' the subjec' an' aiven though he war to jot doon bits an' read."

"I 'm nae in wi' that ava," answered Hairry Muggart. "Fat expairience cud he hae? never oot owre 's skweel door to ken fat 's been gyaun on. 'Seein' 's believin',' as they say. Lat some ane 't 's been a wutness to the ootrages o' the ceevil poo'er, as Gushets says, tak' up the leems.

Gushets, I've seen you at vawrious Presbytery meetin's; forbye 't ye was up at Culsalmon', tee, at the fawmous intrusion case.—Ay, yon knowe-heid saw a sicht that day 't I wunna foryet in a hurry. Fat for sudna ye gie 's a word?"

"'Wa' wi' ye, Hairry; fa' i' the wardle wud ever think o' me makin' a speech? I mith haud in a back chap till anither; but to attemp' a discoorse—I wud be owre the theets ere we got weel streiket."

"Bless me; fat are we argle-barglin aboot, Rory?" said the smith, who saw the drift of things at a glance.

As the smith spoke, Hairry Muggart hirsled half round—

"There's Hairry, 't 's to be oor cheerman. It fa's to him o' richt to apen the subject; an' fa fitter to gae owre the haill heids an' partic'lars?"

"Weel—no, I mith try a fyou remarks aboot fat I 've seen; but I wunna promise to gae owre the haill subject."

"Never min', Gushets 'll tak' up fat ye leave oot," said the smith.

The truth was, Hairry desired the opportunity of figuring as a public speaker, and had kept that enviable distinction clearly in view from the outset.

So the meeting was called. Johnny Gibb and all his household were there, with the souter, the smith, Sandy Peterkin, and other residenters at Smiddyward, including Widow Will, her son Jock, now developing into a long, lanky loon, and her lodger, the mole-catcher, who had gone through his first campaign, and become a fully-qualified practitioner; also, Andrew Langchafts, the merchan', and a few people from the Kirktown. Mrs. Birse was there, and Miss Birse, with Peter junior. Peter Birse senior was absent, and the fact was sufficiently remarkable to warrant a sentence in explanation thereof; so Mrs. Birse, with affable frankness, informed Johnny Gibb that he "hedna been vera stoot, an' was compleenin war nor eeswal the nicht."

As was fit and proper, the meeting was opened with devotional exercises, the souter taking the chief part, and

Johnny Gibb precenting with edifying birr. Then a slightly embarrassing silence ensued, which came to an end when the smith whispered something to Sandy Peterkin, and Sandy, with his wonted readiness to oblige, stood up, and said he had much pleasure in moving that their respected friend Mr. Muggart take the chair.

Hairry, who was encumbered with his bonnet and a big stick, laid these articles aside, and, with some trouble, forced his way into the maister's dask. He did not seem to be very certain whether it was the right thing to sit or to stand, and ended by a sort of compromise in leaning over the desk. Without the usual prefatory acknowledgment of the honour conferred upon him "in asking him to preside," Hairry went into the heart of his subject at once—"As ye a' ken we've met this evenin' to be instrucket aboot the veto law an' the non-intrusion pairty, as far as oor nain expairience, an' the proceedin's o' the kirk coorts 'll cairry 's; all which it behoves this countra to lay to hert." Hairry then proceeded to give what summary he could of the principles involved in the "Ten Years' Conflict," referring, more or less lucidly, to the cases of Auchterarder, Lethendy, and Marnoch. "An' noo," he continued, "the conflick's comin' nearer oor ain door; the Garioch's seen the veto law trampl't oonder fut. My fader was an upper Garioch man, an' I've heard him tell o' a minaister o' Culsalmon' i' the aul' time 't gaed oot o' the Sunday aifterneens wi' a fup in 's han', an' fuppit the fowk up to the kirk; fan they wud 'a be sittin' in bourachs aboot the lan'stells o' the brig. Hooever, things maybe hedna gane far i' the wye o' men's. An' fat kin' o' a state o' haethen ignorance cud they but be in wi' sic a man as Ferdie Ellis i' the poopit? Ou weel, as I was sayin', the creesis cam', as ye a' ken, i' the en' o' the year; fan the Presbytery made a fashion o' sattlin' this Maister Middleton, that hed been helpener afore to Ferdie. But I'm occupyin' owre muckle o' your time, an' wud request John Gibb to fawvour the meetin' wi' his expairience o' that oonhallow't proceedin'."

"Ye'll dee 't better yersel', Hairry," said Johnny Gibb.

"Ye was there as weel's me, an' kent a hantle mair o' the heid deesters. Say awa', an' I 'se gi'e ony sma' help 't I can i' the wye o' ekein' 't oot."

"Weel," answered Hairry, deliberately wiping his spectacles and putting them on, and thereafter pulling a somewhat crumpled piece of paper from the tail pocket of his coat. Up to this time the chairman had endeavoured to keep up a sort of didactic style; but he now, despite his notes, merged himself in what was more natural to him, and, I humbly think, more entertaining to his audience—whether more instructive or not—the direct narrative style. "Weel, ye see," continued Hairry, "there's naething, as the Presbytery-clark said, 'like dockimentary preef' fan ye come to particulars—I leern't that muckle fae the Presbytery meetin' on the twenty-aucht o' October last past. It was than that they met first i' the kirk o' Culsalmon', an' resolv't to gae on wi' the sattlement o' this bodie, Middleton; an' they carriet it, seyven to five. Hooever, I markit doon a fyou particulars aifterhin, to be siccar wi' 't—aw'm nae gyaun to read them, but jist keep the heids afore me. Aweel, this fares on, an' fan the day cam'—Gushetneuk an' mysel' hed hed the maitter throu' han'—says John to me, 'Mithna we tak' a stap owre to the kirk o' Culsalmon', man, an' see wi' oor ain een fat wye the bools'll row?' It was a slack sizzon, an' I hed promis't to gae up to Colpy to see some aul' acquantances at ony rate. Oot we sets. Awat it was a snell mornin'; Benachie as fite's a washen fleece, an' oorlich shoo'ers o' drift an' hail scoorin' across the kwintra. We wusna weel past the neuk o' the wuds o' Newton till we sees the fowk gedderin fae here an' there, some gyaun up the Huntly road afore's, some comin' fae the Glens, an' some hyne doon as far's we cud see, comin' fae the Ba'dyfash wan. They war feckly o' their feet, though there wus twa-three ridin' an' siclike; I kenna gin they war minaisters—(by their wye o' sittin' their beasts some o' them leukit fell like it no)—or gin they war lawvyers, or shirras, or fat.—But I doot I'm wan'erin' fae the pint immedantly oon'er consideration. Amnin aw, John?"

"Gae on, gae on, Hairry; they'll cry oot fan they tire o' ye," answered Johnny Gibb.

"Allow me to speak for the general owdience," answered Andrew Langchafts, in a solemn key. "We're vera deeply interestit in the whole subjeck, Maister Cheerman. Ye canna be owre minute in the details, lat me assure you. We're arriv't at a creesis, as ye've weel observ't, in the Church's history; an' the facts o' the case canna be too strongly imprentit on the min's o' the risin' generation especially."

Previous to the night of meeting, it had hardly been known on which side the sympathies of Mr. Langchafts, who was not a talkative man, lay; and this explicit declaration raised him not a little in the estimation of Johnny Gibb, who exclaimed, "I'm glaid to hear ye, merchan'. Gae on noo, Hairry."

"Aweel, 's aw was sayin', we wus steppin' on as eident 's we cud. It was ill road, an' we hed a gweed stoot stick the piece; but John was gey soople for me, an' the strap o' ane o' my queetikins brak, an' was like to trachel me waur. 'Heely, Gushets, draw bridle a minit,' says I; an' wi' that I lootit doon to fes'n my spat wi' a bit twine. That an' coorse tyeuk 's up a fyou minits; an' fan we're settin' to the road again there comes up a bit gey kibble, fersell mannie, wi' blue claes an' a braid bonnet, gyaun at an unco flaucht. 'Weel, ye're for the hill-heid!' says he. 'Ou, ay. There'll be twa-three there the day——Is there to be ony din?' 'Gin there binna, nae thanks to them for 't,' says the mannie, meanin' the Presbytery like, an' wi' that he daccles a bit, an' keeps on wi' Gushets an' me. 'An' will they rnelly gae on till a sattlement wi' this Middleton?' says Gushets. 'An' they dinna their han'iwark winna be confeerin wi' their teels,' quo' he. 'Ye mean the Presbytery?' The mannie gi'es a lauch, 'Ay, the Presbytery's ill aneuch their leens. But bide ye still till we win up to the kirk. Gin ye dinna see a turn oot o' the ceevil poo'er the day 't the Garioch hisna seen the like o' 't i' the memory o' leevin' man, or aiven fae the days o' Black Jock o' Pittodrie, it's a ferlie to me. The

Shirra o' the coonty, Maister Murray, they tell me's been there sin' yesterday, an' the Fiscal, Maister Simpson, 's there; forbye Shirra Lumsdell, fae Pitcaple, an' I believe the Captain, fae Logie, tee. Of coorse, the Presbytery's legal awgent's up fae Cromwellside, an' they say anither lawvyer or twa. An' mair nor a' that, there's a batch o' that new rural constaabulary, as they ca' them, up the road, nae fyouer nor aboot foifteen o' them oon'er their captain, ane An'erson, a muckle blawn-up red-fac't-like chiel, wi' a besom o' black hair aboot 's mou', 't hed been i' the airmy, they say; an' fudder or no *he* said it, some o' them was lattin 't licht 't he did say 't he sud sattle the minaister to them at the point o' the baignet.' Isna that aboot the rinnins o' fat the Culsalmon' mannie taul 's, Gushets?"

"Ye 're weel within boun's, Hairry, man; an' fat we saw aifterhin clench't the feck o' 't to the ootside."

"Ye maun aye keep in min', my freen's," continued the Chairman, inspecting his MS., "that fan the Presbytery met on the twenty-aucht o' October to moderat the Call —an' a lang meetin' it was: fat wi' objections and interjections, they war aff an' on at it for aboot a haill roun' o' the knock—fan they met ye maun recolleck 't a' the names pitten to the Call in fawvour o' the presentee wus only forty-five; an' nae fyouer nor auchty-nine heids o' faimilies exercees't their veto against 'im. Thase were the circumstances oonder whuch the sattlement was forc't on wi' a' this mengyie o' shirras, an' lawvyers, an' constables.—It 's a vera stiff brae, an' ere we wan up to the kirk, it was gyaun upon eleyven o'clock. 'Hooever,' says the mannie, ' we 're in braw time; it 's twal ere the sattlement begin, an' I 'se warran they sanna apen the kirk doors till 's till than.' So we tak's a leuk roun' for ony kent fowk. They war stannin' aboot a' gate roun' aboot the kirk, in scores an' hunners, fowk fae a' the pairis'es roun' aboot, an' some fae hyne awa' as far doon 's Marnoch o' the tae han' an Kintore o' the tither, aw b'lieve; some war stampin' their feet an' slappin' their airms like the yauws o' a win'mill to keep them a-heat; puckles wus sittin' o' the kirkyard dyke, smokin' an' gyaun on wi' a kin' o' orra jaw aboot the minaisters, an' aye mair gedderin in aboot—it was thocht there wus weel on to twa thoosan' there ere a' was deen. An' aye a bit fudder was comin' up fae the manse aboot fat the Presbytery was deein —they war chaumer't there, ye see, wi' the lawvyers an' so on. 'Nyod, they maun be sattlin 'im i' the manse,' says ane; 'we 'll need 'a gae doon an' see gin we can win in.' 'Na, na,' says anither, 'a bit mair bather aboot their dissents an' appales bein' ta'en; muckle need they care, wi' sic a Presbytery, fat they try. But here's Johnny Florence, the bellman, at the lang length; I 'se be at the boddom o' fat they 're at noo.' An' wi' that he pints till a carlie comin' across the green, wi' a bit paper in 's han,' an' a gryte squad o' them 't hed been hingin' aboot the manse door at 's tail. 'Oo, it 's Johnny gyaun to read the edick,' cries a gey stoot chap, an' twa three o' them gya a roar o' a lauch. It seems Johnny's nae particular scholar, so the Presbytery hed been in some doots aboot the edick. 'Noo,' says they, 'ye 'll read that at the most patentest door o' the church—the wast door.' 'Yes,' says he. 'Can ye read vrite?' 'An' it be geyan plain,' says John; so the edick was read owre and owre again till 'im, an' Johnny harkenin' 's gin he uner'steed it —(We heard aboot a' this aifterhin, ye ken). But they gae 'im a gey time wi' 's readin' o' 't. Johnny was far fae clear upon 's lesson. 'Speak oot, min!' cries ane. 'I think ye mith pronounce some better nor that, Johnny,' says anither; an' they interrupit 'im fan he was tryin' to read wi' a' kin' o' haivers, takin' the words oot o' 's mou, an' makin' the uncoest styte o' 't 't cud be. 'Weel, hae ye ony speeshal objections to Maister Middleton?' cries Johnny, fairly dung wi' the paper. 'Haena we than! A hunner o' them, an' mair!' roars severals. Wi' ae put an' row, Johnny wan throu' the edick in 's nain fashion, an' syne cuts awa' back to the manse, wi' a lot o' them aifter 'im, leavin' 's faur we wus afore.—Sae far o' the edick," continued the Chairman, pausing to gather himself again. "Gin that was to be ca'd readin' 't, jeedge ye. Hooever, aw b'lieve the Presbytery wus content wi' the bellman's endeavour, and pat it upo' their beuks that 'objections were called for an' none offer't.' The multiteed wus tynin patience gey sair fan the sough gat up 't they war 'comin'!' The Shirra o' the coonty, Murray, Shirra Lumsdell, the Fiscal,—an' neen there hed a mair maroonjous face that day—Captain Da'rymple, an' this An'erson, the heid o' the constaabulary, cam up wi' them, ackin' as a body-guard appearandly, to defen' the shepherds fae the flock oon'er their chairge. An auncient poet hath said—

> The hurly burly noo began,
> Was richt weel worth the seein'.

An' gin it war lawfu' to be vyokie ower sairious maitters o' that kin', it's a rael true wye o' descryvin the thing. Oh, they war a roch an' richt set gey puckles o' them, and a sad ongae they made o' 't; only they war but ignorant kwintra fowk, an' little to be expeckit fae them, by'se fae the set o' leern't men 't hed ta'en 't upo' them to provoke them to mischief, tramplin' the richts o' the people oon'erneath their feet. They war makin' for the wast door; but several hunners hed congregat there, an' puckles at the tither door, a' ettlin for into the kirk fanever the doors sud be apen't. This Captain An'erson, wi' 's constaabulary, an' a fyou shirra's-offishers, triet to birze throu' an' mak' an apenin. 'Stan' back noo, my men: stan' back noo.' But, instead o' that, they 're jammin tee at their heels, wi' cairns o' them rinkin up upo' the dyke. The Presbytery wus stoitin here an' there: ane gat 's hat ca'd owre 's een, an' Maister Middleton, though the Shirra was takin' speeshal care o' his safe-aty, gat a bit clink or twa, it was said, wi' bits o' snaw ba's; an' there 's a story, though I sanna vooch for 't, that fan they war fairly stuck'n for a minit or twa, a lang airm was rax't owre atweesh the shou'ders o' twa three o' them, an' a han' that naebody kent fa 't belang't till gat a grip o' the nose o' ane o' the heid deesters an' gya 't sic a thraw that it didna tyne the purpie colour nor come back to the aul' set for a file. But the trowth o' the maitter was, naebody wud 'a kent sair fat was deein or fa was maist to blame. Some o' the ceevil authorities begood to repree an' thraten, but a chap or twa, naar grippit braid i' the crood themsel's, spak' back, 'Fat wye can we help it?' an' ithers, maybe nae owre weel inten'it, roar't, 'Fat are *we* deein?' 'We're nae touchin' naebody; we're nae brakin' the law;' an' some o' them 't cudna see speer't gin the 'police hed strucken yet?' But aw wat they keepit their temper byous weel: though it was said that some gey roch and win'y words pass't atween ane o' the heid deesters an' some orra chiels ere a' was deen. Hoosomever, ae chiel wi' the key wins at the door in coorse, an' apens 't, an' in they gaed, jist like the jaws o' the sea, cairryin minaisters, shirras, an' a', like as muckle wrack, alang wi' them. I tint sicht o' Gushets in a minit, an' hed muckle adee to haud o' my fit ava. An' fan I'm jist at the door cheek, fa sud be dirdit into the neuk fair afore me but Geordie Wobster, the shirra's offisher, fae Mel'rum. Ye'll min' upo' him, some o' ye, sin' the time 't he hed sic a pilgit huntin' up aul' Lindsay for stealin' bees. The raither him nor me, for he gat a yafu yark against the door cheek. Wobster gi'es a guller oot o' 'im, and some ane cries, 'Ye're killin' a man!' But fa cud help it? ye mith as weel try't to stop the north win' comin' throu' the Glens o' Foudland; an' in they gaed. Only the like o' 'im 's so weel ees't wi' sharries 't they're nae easy fell't—they say he gat a broken rib, or siclike. Aweel, in we gets to the kirk, an' I'se asseer ye I was blythe to edge into the first seat 't I cud win at. The shirras an' the fiscal manag't to win up to the laft, an' in o' the heritors' seat i' the forebreist; the Presbytery wus seatit at the fit o' the poopit. But sic a noise ye heard never in a kirk nor oot o' 't. Some ane said the moderawtor wud preach—that was Maister Peter, o' Kemnay, a weel-faur't young chap—but aw b'lieve he never wan in'o the poopit yet, nae mair nor he wud 'a heard 's nain word gin he hed wun. 'Keep 'im oot, the Tory!' cries ane; some wud 'a jokit wi' this Captain An'erson to 'gae up an' preach,' 'cause he wud 'dee 't better,' an' there was a gryte lauch that nane o' them hed brocht a Bible wi' them; and fan the shirras, first ane an' syne ane, deman'it quaetness, they only cried oot, 'Hoot, never min' 'im; keep up the din;' an' a' the time they war flingin' aboot bits o' skelbs o' stickies and siclike. Weel, this gaes on for I 'se warran' an oor, fan Captain Da'rymple —he's an el'er, aw b'lieve—he stan's up an' says, 'I noo claim the protection o' the shirra, the Presbytery being deforc't in its duty.' An' oot they forces the haill body o' them, awa' back to the manse, faur it was said a sermon was preach't fae the words, 'I have planted, and Apollos watered'—(a mannie says to me, 'Ay, he tyeuk the words oot o' Paul's mou', but Paul hed naething adee wi' sic plantin'; he sud 'a said *Peter* plantit at ance'—'t wusna that oonwutty o' the carlie). Weel, the din gaed on i' the kirk; oh, there was a set o' roch-like breets up aboot the poopit, an' ane in 't haudin a terrible hyse; an' aw b'lieve ere a' was deen they war singin' sangs an' smokin' their pipes intill 't. Ane cries oot o' 't, 'Will ye hae Culsalmon' psalms?' an' anither mak's answer, 'Gie 's Holy Willie's Prayer.' Of coorse the Presbytery an' the lawvyers concludit the sattlement i' the manse again' a' sponsible objections; an' syne they drappit aff hame ane an' ane, some ca'in i' their gigs, some ridin'; but though bourachs o' fowk wus stanin aboot the place, nae a tell wud they tell gin it was a' deen or no. The fowk i' the kirk bade still; some thocht they wud come back; some said that they be 't a pit the minaister throu' the kirk afore twal at nicht, or he wudna be richt sattl't; some said ae thing, some anither, but aye the reerie gaed on wi' a' kin' o' orra jaw. Fan it was beginnin' to gloam they war jowin' the bell like a' thing, an' declarin' they wud see the en' o' 't tho' 't sud be three o'clock i' the mornin'. An' aw b'lieve some o' them raelly bade till aboot midnicht an' nail't up the kirk doors ere they leeft; the gey feck o' the lozens i' the windows hed been broken ere that time; an' fa sud be brakin' amo' the lave but ane o' the bellman's ain loons— so they said. But we thocht it time to be stappin hamewuth afore we tint the daylicht a'thegither, an' that wye sawna the hin'er en' o' 't."

At this point the Chairman again paused; and gathering his MS., attempted an enforcement of the "moral reflections" to be drawn from what he had so fully stated. It will not be a very serious loss to omit this part. He then called upon Johnny Gibb to follow up his speech; and Johnny did so in a brief address, wherein he recounted how the Justices called a great meeting at Pitmachie, at which Sir Robert presided, and how the Captain reported, *ad longam*, all the horrors of the day at Culsalmond; and that not only windows were broken, and seats torn up, but that the "rioters" had made considerable progress towards toppling down the gallery, body bulk!—"Jist like 'im to tell that," exclaimed Johnny, with vehemence. And how the Justices gravely agreed that "a riot" *did* take place; that "a spirit of resistance to the law" had been gaining ground in that unhappy region; and that the Justices considered it their duty to intimate all this to "Her Majesty's Secretary of State for the Home Department," and a host of other high dignitaries, including the Lord Advocate; and to request that "such measures should immediately be taken as will lead to the detection and punishment of the offenders, and the effectual prevention of similar outrages in future; as otherwise, the powers and influence of the Magistrates will be completely set at defiance, and the expensive establishment of the rural police, into which the county has lately entered, will be rendered worse than useless." "An' that's the bonny upshot o' a meetin' o' a score o' Sirs, an' Generals, an' Captains, an' common lairds, heeld in Maister Cooper's on the thirti'et day o' November last past," said Johnny, throwing down a sadly chafed newspaper, from which he had been endeavouring to read. "A set o' brave birkies they are I'se asseer ye! Rinnin peeakin to the heid authorities o' the kwintra, like as mony chuckens 't hed tint their mither; an' a' for a bit stramash 't their nain deeins had brocht aboot. Jist jeedge ye noo fat kin' o' spiritooal guidance ye may expeck fae that quarter, fan ye see foo they ack wi' them that comes oon'er their merciment in ceevil maitters. Nae less nor five fowk 't was there that day wus ta'en to Edinboro', to gang afore the Lords, as ye 're a' weel awaar. Of coorse, they wudna miss oot Dr. Robison o' Williamston, he hed come owre sair forrat o' the non-intrusion side, but the ither four, they mith 'a as weel ta'en up Hairry or me, I suppose. An' aiven at the trial afore this Lord Joostice Clark, the doctor, as ye a' ken, was pruv't Not Guilty; the lads Walker and Spence wan aff unproven, an' the tither twa, they war fley't till try ava. That's the wye that yer joostices an' kirk pawtrons wud rowle the kwintra—a bonny set or than no. But fat syne; gin the law o' the lan' alloo 't, little to them wud jail ilka ane o' 's at their nain pleesour! That's nae maitter o' guess wark, but fairly pruv't by fat they 've deen ere this time. Noo afore we sin'er, I 've nae mair to say, but jist this, that it 's vera necessar' for ane an' a' o' 's to tak' a side, the side o' richt prenciple, an' be ready to mainteen 't till the Kirk o' Scotlan' establish her richts owre the croon o' 'er oppressors."

When Johnny Gibb had ended, there was a silence of some duration, till first Andrew Langchafts, and next Sandy Peterkin, expressed their sense of the high value of the speeches delivered. Very little more was said, and the meeting closed with the understanding that another would be called when circumstances seemed to demand it.

I may have occasion hereafter to note other results of this meeting. Meantime let me say that it served in reality as a sort of basis to such non-intrusion movement as distinguished the parish of Pyketillim. A few months previously the local newspapers had had the benefit of a very long advertisement, containing the names of a great many farmers in the Formartine district, and a few lairds, all zealous and godly churchmen, addressed in sympathetic terms to the noble brethren who formed the majority of the Presbytery of Strathbogie, and setting forth how the "Scripture" enjoins obedience to the law, and so on. Several of the leading men in Pyketillim, including Mains of Yawal and Teuchitsmyre, had thought it would be a creditable thing to follow this example; and they had spoken thereof to Jonathan Tawse. Jonathan, being in ill-temper at the time, gave them little audiscence, and so the thing fell flat. But now this whole section of the community seized the occasion of the Smiddyward public meeting to turn the public laugh and scorn, as far as might be, against those who had attended it. And, in particular, every individual who had been there, young or old, had attached to him or her the designation of a " Non," which, of course, signified non-intrusionist, but was understood to carry with it a deal of rustic wit or sarcasm, inasmuch as the Non was accepted as a sort of weak fanatic, whom it was right and proper to sneer at, or affect to pity, according to circumstances.

CHAPTER XIX.

MEG RAFFAN, THE HENWIFE.

ON the lands of Sir Simon Frissal it had been the practice from time immemorial to bind every tenant to pay yearly to the laird a "reek hen." In former days, however, the fowl in question had never been really exacted; it was merely a symbol of vassalage, as it were. But in the modernised form of lease to which the tenants who had renewed their tenure within a score of years bygone had been made subject, the figurative reek hen had, by the practical sagacity of Sir Simon's agents, been converted into half-a-dozen, nine, or a dozen "properly fed fowls," according to the size of the holding. These had to be paid over at the barn-yards in full tale; and when the damsels went thither with their arm-baskets, covered with such convenient piece of calico as they could fit on—the heads of the imprisoned birds bobbing up and down under the limp roof—it was seldom that Dawvid Hadden failed to be present to see their freights delivered. It was no part of Dawvid's duty to be there. Meg Raffan, the henwife, was quite fit to attend to her own business. But then Dawvid was a zealously diligent official; and a man's zeal may be expected to exhibit itself in the direction of that which is congenial to his nature. So it was that notwithstanding the uncomplimentary sneers of Meg Raffan, Dawvid would stand and not only count the fowls as they were discharged from the creels, but in so far as he could catch sight of them, scrutinise every separate fowl with the eye of a connoisseur. His observations on the birds were oftener of a disparaging sort than otherwise; and he had incurred the lasting enmity of Mrs. Birse, by remarking to her servant, on one occasion, in the audience of the henwife—" Nyod, lassie, the tae half o' that creatur's 's never seen meal's corn seerly sin' they war oot o' the egg shall; an' the lave, gin they ever laid ava, maun be poverees't wi' sax ouks clockin'; an' some o' them actually leuks as gin they hed been in Tod Lowrie's cleuks, an' wun awa' wi' the half o' their claes aff. We maun raelly tell the laird about that."

It was an insolent speech that of Dawvid, to be sure, though the last sentence was uttered in a half jocular tone; and when the servant damsel rehearsed it in the ears of Mrs. Birse, on her return to Clinkstyle, Mrs. Birse was naturally much incensed; but it readily occurred to her that Meg Raffan, the henwife, was a much higher authority on gallinaceous matters than Dawvid Hadden, and her communications with Meg had hitherto been of a friendly nature. So, as Lowrin Fair was at hand, when Peter Birse senior, Peter Birse junior, and others—including Dawvid Hadden himself—would naturally be drafted off to the market, why not have Meg Raffan down to tea in a quiet way, and at any rate take hostages against any possible hostile operations on the part of Dawvid? Only Miss Birse and herself would be privy to the transaction, and as secrecy was known to be an integral part of Meg's very nature, there was no risk of Clinkstyle gentility being tarnished by any sinister report going abroad; and then the possible advantages to be derived from the interview were obvious.

"Mrs. Birse's compliments," etc., and would Meg Raffan come to tea? Eh, Meg would be delighted; and Meg came accordingly.

How hospitable Mrs. Birse of Clinkstyle and her amiable and accomplished daughter were, it needs not my pen to set forth. The henwife felt, and declared it to be "rael affeckin;" and how could she but indignantly rebut the aforesaid vile insinuations of Dawvid Hadden? "Awat they war a'

K

richt snod, sizeable foolies," quoth Meg. "But he's jist a sneevlin, ill-fashion't creatur, 't maun be meddlin' wi' a'thing. 'Serve me, d' ye think 't the laird wud hear ony o' his ill-win' aboot respectable fowk; Sir Simon's mair o' a gentleman nor dee onything o' the kin'. Jist leuk sic an ongae's he's been haudin' aboot the Nons, an' that meetin' 't was doon i' the skweel at the Ward—aw 'm seer *that* was nane o' his bizziness."

"Weel, Mistress Raffan, fat kin' o' a conscience can he hae, fleein' i' the face o' the vera word o' Gweed?"

"The word o' Gweed! It's muckle 't he'll care for that, gin he cud get haud'n in wi' gryte fowk."

"Sir Seemon *hed* gi'en 'im orders to thraeten Sandy Peterkin, than?" suggested Mrs. Birse.

"Weel, aw 'm nae thinkin' 't he hed not mony orders, no. But the vera nicht aifter the meetin'—(aw div not believe but the creatur hed been lyin' at the back o' the dyke seein' them gedder)—faur's my gentleman awa' till, think ye?"

"Eh, but aw cudna say; ony wye but faur respectable fowk wud gae."

"Faur but dominie Tawse's! Ye see," continued Meg, attuning her voice to the very confidential pitch, "I gat a' this fae her hersel'. Eh, she has a sad life o' 't wi' 'im, the tyrannical, naisty, ill-livin' creatur; an' that vera nicht he cam' hame fae the dominie's bleezin—he's takin' sair to the drink, an' isna't a rael scunnerfu' thing to see the like o' Maister Tawse, a man o' leernin' an' pairts, colleagin wi' sic company?"

"Jonathan Tawse!—an aul' sneeshinie, drucken slype. Leernin' or than no!" said Mrs. Birse, scornfully. "It's jist sic mannie sic horsie atween the twa for that maitter."

"'Deed, awat an' ye never spak a truer word," answered Meg, bethinking herself. "I'm weel seer Maister Peterkin's a muckle mair discreet man to hae chairge o' onybody's bairns."

"He's seen a great deal more of the wordle; and been in better society than Tawse," interposed Miss Birse.

"Weel, 's aw was sayin'," continued Meg Raffan, "Mrs.

Hadden says to me at the time, says she, 'Dawvid was up b' cairts the streen, wusnin he?' 'But fan was Dawvid onything else wi' his tale?' says I. 'Gin we war to believe a' 't we hear, there's some fowk wud never mak' nor mell wi' naething less nor gentry.' I wudna lat 'er aff wi' och nor flee 't aw cud help; for they're *that* upsettin', baith o' them. 'Ay but,' says she, 'that was nane o' yer dog-dirders an' ostlers forgedderin to get a bit boose, fan they gat their maister oot o' the road.' This was lattin at me, ye ken, for inveetin the coachman an' the gamekeeper up bye, aifter Sir Simon gaed awa'; aw 'm seer decenter or mair neebourly fowk ye wudna get i' the seyven pairis'es. But, aw b'lieve, I hed 'er there no. 'Keep me, Kirsty,' says I, 'ye dinn mean to say 't Dawvid actually was fou at this braw pairty than? There was fowk 't ye ken weel i' the Lodge this vera nicht, 't wud 'a threepit owre me that they saw Dawvid stoiterin as he gaed hame the streen. But I wud *not* latt'n them say 't.' Gin that didna tak' the stiffin oot o' Kirsty' cockernony, I 'se lea'e 't."

"I 'm rael glaid 't ye chappit 'er in aboot the richt gate," said Mrs. Birse. "Settin' up their noses that wye, they wud need it—vulgar pack."

"Wi' that she pits 'er apron till 'er een, an' shak's 'er heid. 'Oh, Meggy,' says she, 'aw kent ye was aye my true freen; dinna mention 't to nae leevin. But Dawvid, though he was weel to live, was richt gweed company, an' was *not* nabal wi' me the streen.' 'It hed been a humoursome pairty, than, as weel 's a braw ane?' says I. 'Weel, an' it was a' that,' says she; 'an' Dawvid was that newsie aifter he cam' hame 't I thocht never to get 'im till 's bed.' An' foo that she sud say that Mains o' Yawal was there, an' Teuchitsmyre, an' severals o' the muckle fairmers."

"An' that was Dawvid's braw fowk—I wuss 'im luck o' sic mennerly company—Han' up the kyaak basket wi' the short-breid, Eliza," said Mrs. Birse.

"They're stupid and ignorant people," observed Miss Birse; "and if Jonathan Tawse were accustomed to good company, he wudna ask them till 's hoose."

"Na—nae mair, aw thank ye," quoth Meg. "I've deen byous weel. I'll jist drink oot my drap at leasure. The third cup sudna be the warst, ye ken; an' awat ye've gi'en 's 't richt gweed."

Meg Raffan paused; and, with the facts as they actually were, Mrs. Birse was too shrewd a woman not to comprehend the significance of the last remark.

"Noo, Mrs. Birse, ye *wull not* pit fusky in amo' my tae; na—nae the fu' o' that gryte muckle gless; ye wull mak' me licht-heidit gin ever a body was 't."

It was evidently worth doing, however; and, truth to say, Meg Raffan offered no very strenuous resistance to the emptying of the glass into her cup. Neither did the emptying of the cup itself seem to produce very much of the effect she had dreaded. Meg only got more talkative, and went on to describe fully how she had pumped out of Mrs. Dawvid Hadden all that had been transacted at Jonathan Tawse's party concerning which Dawvid had been so mightily uplifted. It appeared that in addition to Pyketillim people, there had been present Jonathan's friend, the younger Dr. Drogemweal, who had settled doon throu', so as to be beyond the limits of his father's sucken; and that Dawvid had enumerated to the company the entire list of those who had been present at the Smiddyward meeting, the result thus far being a sort of critical analysis of each individual's character and position. Johnny Gibb, the smith, and the souter, had been classed together as hopeless incorrigibles, compounded in pretty nearly equal parts of the fanatic and the radical; and it was deemed prudent to say little more about them. Sandy Peterkin was denounced very severely; and it seemed that Dawvid, in his elevation, had freely avowed his intention, and even boasted of the power he possessed, to "sort him, at ony rate." And not less was Dawvid incensed at that "fair-tongue't howffin, Hairry Muggart," by whom the zealous ground-officer all but confessed he had been fairly led on the ice, and on whom he declared his intention to be revenged. And then they had come nearer home.

"Noo, Mrs. Birse, aw wudna tell 't to my nain sister for warl's gear; but aw 'm seer she 'll never ken that it cam' fae me;" and Meg looked inquiringly toward Miss Birse, and next toward her mother, as much as to say, "Would it not be wise to remove her at any rate?"

"Eliza 's been taucht breedin' owre weel to cairry clypes," said Mrs. Birse, a little haughtily.

"Eh, forbid 't I sud mint at onything o' the kin', Mrs. Birse. She wudna be your dother to dee onything like that—weel the mair shame to them that sud speak aifter sic a fashion. 'An' hed they naething to say aboot the goodwife o' Clinkstyle?' says I to Kirsty, in a careless-like mainner. 'Weel, Meggy,' says she, speakin' aneth 'er breath—an' she gart my vera flesh creep fan she pat up 'er han' like a distrackit person—'I ken I can lippen onything to you,' says she, 'but Dawvid wud fell me gin he thocht 't I war to apen my lips aboot it to my nain mither—Maister Tawse sud say to Dawvid, "Weel, Davie, fat are ye to dee wi' that randy o' a wife o' Clinkstyle?"'—noo, Mrs. Birse, it's a Gweed's trowth 't aw 'm tellin' ye. Eh, he's a haiveless man; nae won'er nor ye was obleeg't to tak' yer innocent bairns awa' fae 's skweel."

"Mamma," exclaimed Miss Birse, in great excitement, "I wud gar papa prosecute him."

"'Liza, gae an' see that Betty's nae mislippenin' 'er jots i' the kitchie," said Mrs. Birse, addressing her daughter with unwonted peremptoriness. Miss Birse, with very evident reluctance, obeyed, so far, at any rate, as to leave the parlour; and her mother continued, "I'm nae su'pris't at onything 't that creatur wud say; but fowk maun hae regaird for the edification an' richt upfeshin o' their affspring, as Mr. Macrory taul 's weel-a-wat; an' I cudna lat the lassie sit an' hear 'er nain pawrents wilipen'it wi' the like o' 'im. Weel?"

"'Oh,' says Dawvid, 'aw 'm thinkin' nedder you nor Mr. Sleekaboot made yer plack a bawbee by tiggin wi' her. So I 'se lat sleepin' tykes lie there.' An' trow ye me, Dawvid thocht he hed gi'en them a gey clever cut wi' that

—impident smatchet that he is. An' maister Tawse sud 'a said some rael roch words, rebattin on 'im like. Eh, but aw cudna come owre them, Mrs. Birse, on nae accoont."

"Far be 't fae me to hear their coorse langige," said Mrs. Birse, "but it 's richt that fowk sud ken fat kin' o' characters they are."

"'Deed, awat that 's richt true; for as sair 's it is to mention 't. 'Weel,' says they, 'an' fat comes o' a' your blawin aboot fat ye cud dee 't nae ither man cud dee?' 'Oh,' says Dawvid, 'Peter 'imsel' 's a saft breet; he made oot to win free o' the meetin' by feingyin a drow. Jist bide ye still, fan the neist meetin' comes, gin I dinna mak' oot to fesh back 's drow till 'im as ill 's ever.' An' wi' that they hed haud'n the saddest hyse 't cud be. Tawse an' this young doctor—he was aye a weirdless blackguard—i' the lang rin o' 't, made o' Dawvid, an' swall't the creatur's heid, till he was as prood 's oor aul' turkey cock, an' blawin at the rate o' nae allooance aboot fat he cud and sud dee. An' I 'm seer, fae fat I gat oot o' Kirsty, that they hed eikit 'im up till as muckle mischief aboot this kirk wark 's they cud."

"I dinna doot that neen," said Mrs. Birse, with an air of grave self-satisfaction. "An' fat ither cud we expeck fae sic a weirdless mengyie makin' a teel o' an oonprencipl't drucken creatur?"

"Eh, he 's a coorse ill-gate't ablich," continued Meg. "Hooever, that 's the rinnin's o' the haill affair; an' aw 'm seer I cudna hed a licht conscience to keep it oot o' yer sicht; though—I was jist richt sair—owrecome—ere I cud mak' up—my min'—aboot tellin' ye 't."

Here Meg Raffan exhibited outward tokens of owrecomeness, for which, happily, Mrs. Birse knew the practical remedy, and applied it. And on the whole she concluded that her trouble as the entertainer had been tolerably well repaid by the henwife's visit. The glimpse of Jonathan Tawse's party, and the sort of estimate she had been enabled to form of Dawvid Hadden's position in relation to matters polemical, had put her in possession of information which she did not doubt of being able to use with good effect afterwards.

CHAPTER XX.

MRS. BIRSE AND HER OWN.

It was a fact incapable, I fear, of being successfully disputed, that Peter Birse senior had never profited as he ought by the exhortations of his wife, ably seconded of late years by her accomplished daughter, Miss Eliza Birse, in respect to the necessity of cultivating the virtue of gentility, and taking care to be select in the choice of his company. At any rate, had Peter been sufficiently perspicacious he would certainly not have given Mrs. Birse the too candid narrative he did of his ongoings at Lowrin Fair. Peter had gone to the Fair accompanied by his promising elder son. He had first visited the nowt market at the top of the brae, and cheapened several stirks; then he had come down to the fit market, and perambulated the same from Barreldykes to the Cross; and whereas he wanted a bandster for the harvest, he and Peter junior had, after due selection, set on to a regular haggle with an ancient-looking man, in threadbare blue, with a green head of oat-straw stuck within the band of his old stuff hat, signifying that he was a candidate for harvest-work. And by and by he had engaged the ancient man for thirty-two shillings and sixpence of fee, and given him a penny of arles. This done, Peter had no other business on hand; but he would, of course, have a look at the horse market, before he would go home, were it only to give Peter junior the opportunity of increasing his knowledge of the equine race, and of those who traffic therein.

It was then that Peter Birse met Dawvid Hadden, with whom he had long been on terms of somewhat close and confidential intimacy; and that Dawvid being in an uncommonly genial and hospitable humour, they two resolved to be social together, while Peter Birse junior forgathered with certain young men of his own age, and went off to see life for a little in the thick of men and animals.

But why should Peter Birse senior be so very soft as to tell out baldly to his wife, on the morning after the market, how Dawvid Hadden and he went away together into that canvas erection by the roadside, with the sign-board,

By DONALD M'GILL,
From GLENS OF FOUDLAND;

how Dawvid should have no sooner called out, "A half-mutchkin here, lassie," than they discovered Mains of Yawal and one or two acquaintances in a corner; and how they forthwith beckoned Mains over to bear them company, to which invitation Mains, who was settled down in the tent for the afternoon, affably responded? It was all very proper and necessary to tell Mrs. Birse, as he was in duty bound, about the character of the market and the terms of the engagement made with the bandster; but why not keep to safe generalities about his own movements thereafter? Of course Peter Birse wanted to bring out with impressive effect the gist of certain warnings delivered by Dawvid Hadden, in presence of Mains, as aforesaid, for behoof of all who were in danger of following divisive courses in kirk affairs at that juncture; but, poor man, he did not perceive that he was taking the very method to prevent his having the slightest chance of a respectful hearing.

"Man, aw div won'er to hear ye speak o' takin' drams fae the like o' that creatur!"

"Hoot, 'oman, ye wudna hed me to pay't mysel', wud ye?" said Peter.

"Peter Birse; will ye ever leern to conduck yersel' as ony weel-menner't person wud? Gin ye hae nae regaird for yersel', ye mith hae some for yer faimily, peer things."

"I wusna deein nae ill, I'm seer," replied Peter, in a bewildered way.

"Nae ill! gaen awa' sittin' doon drinkin' in a hovel o' a tent, wi' a leein', ill-win'et creatur like that, an' a drucken slype like Mains o' Yawal. A bonny example 't ye set to the risin' generation; an' your ain son tee—Faur was Patie a' the time 't ye was blebbin an' drinkin' at this rate?"

"Peter? Ou weel, he mitha been wi' 's an' he hed like't, but he gaed aff up the horse market fanever Dawvid an' me begood to speak."

"Mitha been wi' ye! A fine wye o' deein, leernin ony young creatur sic drucken haibits!—An' ye sat still there the feck o' the aifterneen?"

"Ou, na, we satna nae time. There was only the half-mutchkin 't Dawvid got, an' the boddom o' a gill 't Mains feish owre in 's han' i' the stoup. I wudna lat 'im ca' nae mair, though he threepit owre an' owre again 't he wud dee 't."

"Humph; an' ye never leukit owre yer shooder for Peter, to fesh him hame wi' ye, but cam' awa' wi' this low-life't creatur."

"Oh, 'oman, dinna speak that gate. Dawvid's a rael perjink, weel-leern't body; we 've been obleeg't till 'im mony a time, an' may be 't again; an' he has a gweed hantle o' poo'er fae the laird; I 'se asseer ye."

"Haud yer tongue, Peter Birse! Poo'er or than no—a grun-offisher glaid to gae aboot an' tell fowk fan to pay their hens to the laird; the thing that the vera flunkey wud scorn to dee. That's his poo'er; an' he mak's 'imsel' a muckle man meddlin' wi' the henwife's wark; an' syne comin' hame ilka ither nicht fae this an' the neist orra company as fou 's a piper."

"Weel, I never saw the man hae drink upon 'im, an' aw 'm seer he was freely sober o' the market nicht."

"Dinna ye tell me; the tae corbie winna pyke oot the tither's e'e. Fan fowk comes hame wi' a face like a Hallow-even fire, there 's rizzons for 't. Fat kin' o' a pawrent's hert can ye hae, to come oot o' a market wi' the like o' him, an' leave them 't 's sibbest t' ye to be prann't, or ill-guidet ony gate?"

"Keep me, 'oman, Peter's nae a littleane noo; fat wud come owre him?"

"Ay, ye may speer that noo. Gin ye hed been atten'in' till a fader's duty, ye wudna hed nae sic questions to speer. I suppose yer freen was needin' a' the help that ye cud gi'e 'im gin that time to get *him* hame."

"Forbye that, Dawvid an' me ca'd up an' doon the fit market for naar an 'oor leukin' for Peter—I 'se warran' he hedna been seekin' to come hame wi' 's."

"An' little won'er; nae gryte heartnin till 'im, peer man, to see 's nain fader takin' up wi' sic company."

Now, this last remark of Mrs. Birse was scarcely fair. For she very well knew what, she was fully aware, Peter Birse senior at that moment did not know, namely, that his eldest son, Peter Birse junior, had come home on the previous evening, not only at a late hour, but, furthermore, with a broken nose; which, on being caught by his mother as he was unobtrusively slipping away to bed without showing himself in the parlour, he accounted for by saying it had been caused by "something fleein up an' strikin' 's face" as he left the market. The rational theory on the subject was, that Peter had got into a quarrel, more or less, as young men of gallant and amatory disposition will sometimes do on such occasions, and that he bore the marks of his chivalrous daring on his countenance. A very few particulars in support of this theory were, with difficulty, extracted from him by his fond mother, when she had returned a second time to the charge; whereupon her reflections took this shape:—That, it being evident that Peter had got into a vulgar fight with two or three farm-servant lads, and all about a farm-servant girl whom Peter had desired, but had not been permitted, to accompany to her home, it was also evident that she must forthwith charge herself even more directly than hitherto with the duty of developing and directing the young man's matrimonial intentions. In her maternal solicitude she had not overlooked this part of her duty, and had, indeed, been fondly hoping that the little scheme of affection she had endeavoured to promote between Mrs. Gibb's niece, Mary Howie, and her own son, Peter, had been gradually ripening all this while. But the facts that had now partly emerged rather staggered her.

Mrs. Birse thought on the subject for days, with much frequency, turning it in her mind first in one shape, then in another. If she had known who the girl was, but this Peter stubbornly refused to tell—and, indeed, generally remained in a sulky state of mind—her feelings would certainly have carried her the length of seeking the damsel out on set purpose to upbraid and snub her for the audacious impertinence which, in such a sphere of life, could allow itself to be the object of admiration on the part of a wealthy and genteel farmer's son. Then would her thoughts revert, with a sort of angry feeling, to Peter Birse senior, as she remembered all his vulgarities; and I fear she sometimes audibly hinted at his baleful responsibility in this whole matter; and Peter slunk silently away to escape the heinous imputation. Towards Peter Birse junior her feelings had nothing of acrimony or heat in them. The notion of evil existing in her excellent son, otherwise than as it might have come by inevitable inheritance from his father, had not, in the least, entered her head. How, then, could she be angry with him?

The general result of these Lowrin Fair transactions then, was, first, to leave Mrs. Birse in a state of some dubiety about her son. That dubiety, however, she had made up her mind should be removed before long. Only a little more of explicitness on the part of Peter junior was needed to enable her to institute whatever proceedings the case might demand; and she knew a little time was required to allow the amiable young man to get over his present sullen mood. When he had so far relaxed, she knew it would require only a little tycein to induce him to pour forth all that was in his heart. So she would bide her time. Then, in so far as her husband was concerned, she had got, as she believed, most righteous cause for putting her ban on any

further intercourse of a friendly nature between him and
Dawvid Hadden. Peter had, as he imagined, been working
up to the point when he could, with telling practical effect,
bring in Dawvid Hadden's authority to impose a check on
the headlong course his wife seemed determined on following
in kirk matters. But, lo, his hopes were blasted at once
and conclusively; for, slow i' the uptak as Peter was, he
could not but feel that, after the recent morning's overhaul,
the quotation of Dawvid's name in support of his position
must be a good deal worse than useless. Poor Peter!
his state of mind was far from a comfortable one. How
willingly would he have given vent to his perplexities and
regrets to Mains of Yawal, to Mr. Sleekaboot, even to
Jonathan Tawse, or anybody who could sympathise in his
sentiments, and concurrently deplore with him what was
likely to happen if things went on in the direction in
which his non-intrusion neighbours were driving them.
But then the thought that Mrs. Birse might find it all out,
haunted him, and he could only obtain a solace for his
troubled mind by turning to his own servant, Tam Meerison,
now a staid married man, and, as opportunity offered, dis-
closing to Tam the burdened state of his feelings.

CHAPTER XXI.

PATIE'S PLUSH WAISTCOAT.

THE uniform and deep interest which Mrs. Birse of Clinkstyle manifested in the welfare of her family was clearly seen in her anxious desire to reach a full acquaintance with those causes that had led to her eldest son, Peter, coming home from Lowrin Fair slightly damaged in person, and considerably soured in spirit; and not less so in the course she adopted with a view to setting the young man up again, and inducing him to go on in the path chalked out for him by maternal wisdom and solicitude. In the first place, with a view to stimulate in Peter that sentiment of grateful confidence which was likely to lead to a full disclosure of the troubles that had been weighing on his spirit, she resolved to surprise him with a very handsome present. About that date, plush waistcoats were an object of strong desire with many young men of Peter's years and tastes: plush waistcoats, double-breasted, and with many pearl buttons on them. Such a waistcoat of blue plush was a garment of high attractions, but one of red plush fairly outdid it, and put its owner in a position of singular distinction. There was just a little doubt in Mrs. Birse's mind whether a plush vest was to be reckoned genteel. Miss Birse had pronounced it vulgar; but then it was well enough understood that the heart of Peter Birse junior was set upon having that very article of clothing, and it was not to be expected that Peter should change his mind for anything his sister might say; indeed, the contrary effect was certain to be produced. Therefore, to gratify his wish now was very much in the nature of making a virtue of necessity—not to speak of the object to be directly attained in so doing. Mrs. Birse went to the Kirktown, and ascertained through Jock Will, now promoted to the dignity of apprentice to Andrew Langchafts, that the merchan' had on his shelves a piece of red plush, which he might be concussed into selling on very reasonable terms, inasmuch as it had proved hitherto to be dead stock, being an article quite beyond the mark of the ordinary beaux of Pyketillim.

"The merchan' 's nae in, is he, laddie?" asked Mrs. Birse, turning over the pieces of plush on the counter.

"No, nae eenoo," was Jock's reply.

"But ye say the reid bit 's never been price't?"

"I heard 'im sayin' that."

"Weel, aw dinna won'er at it—lyin' tooshtin aboot there till it 's fooshtit and half ate'n wi' the mochs. Cut ye aff a yaird an' a finger-length than, an' gi'e me a dizzen o' pearl buttons, an' we'll sattle aboot the price wi' 'imsel' Na, Jock, but ye *are* a braw man noo," continued Mrs. Birse, as Jock went on to fulfil her orders in a business-like style. "Nae less nor cairryin a shears i' yer waistcoat pouch already; aw wudna won'er to see ye wi' a chop o' yer nain yet."

Jock laughed his own quiet laugh, and went on with his work.

The announcement of the red plush vest had a highly salutary effect upon Peter Birse junior. He now relaxed with a suddenness that made the muscles of his face feel the thaw almost uncomfortably; he would have desired that the severity of his countenance should have disappeared more gradually, but the sight of the red plush was too much for him—his mother had taken care to bring the unmade piece home with the pearl buttons to display them before his eyes.

It was in the parlour, and they two were alone by themselves.

"Noo, Patie, man," said Mrs. Birse, with affecting emphasis; "fa 'll dee as muckle for ye as yer nain mither? Gin her heid war caul i' the mools, aw doot there 's fyou wud leuk aifter ye as she wud dee."

Mrs. Birse endeavoured to look pathetic. Peter certainly did look sheepish for some minutes; and, in so far as he was able to distract his eye and his consciousness from the piece of red plush, he let his thoughts dwell next on what his mother had said, as he blurted out—"Hoot, fat 's the eese o' speakin' that gate?—I 'm sure I 'm nae af'en in an ill teen." And then Peter became confidential, and informed his mother how, failing to find his attentions duly reciprocated by Mary Howie, he had gone to Lowrin Fair in a somewhat desperate mood; how, at an advanced period of the fair, the determination had seized him to exhibit his gallantry independently, by walking home with a servant girl who was a mere casual acquaintance; so Peter said, the truth being that the girl was a former servant of Mrs. Birse's own; and how, as she happened to have another beau, certain little unpleasantnesses had occurred, and Peter, in addition to the slight amount of damage he had sustained, writhed greatly under the idea that he had been laughed at, —a sort of ordeal he greatly disliked.

"Ay weel, weel, Patie, man:—that 's jist a bit lesson to ye," said Mrs. Birse, who had now dismissed her charnel-house tone. "Them 't sets to coortin the lasses maun temper their nose to the east win' as weel 's the south."

"I wasna wuntin *her!*" quoth Peter, bluntly.

"Na, I 'm richt weel seer 't *ye* wud never leuk owre yer shooder at nae servan' quine. But, my laddie, min' ye 're nae to be bauch an' chucken-hertit though Mary Howie sud gie her heid a bit cast files at the first. That 's nae mark; she may be rael prood to be name't to ye. An' min' ye that Mary 's grown a strappin, weel-faur't lass : an' though she hisna the menners nor edication o' yer sister——"

"Hah! I dinna care a tinkler's curse for menners," exclaimed Peter, candidly, "gin aw cud get 'er."

"An' she 's a richt servan'," continued his mamma, not heeding the interruption; "an' fan the aul' fowk wears awa' ye wud be seer to get the muckle feck o' fat they hae gin ye play'd yer cairts the richt gate; for Gushets has nae near freens o' 's nain. An' ye mith aiven, in coorse o' naitur, come into Gushetneuk itsel', tee. It's a likeable spot, an' richt weel-in-hert kin'ly grun'ie."

"But fat wud aw dee wi' Gushetneuk? Aw thocht I was to get oor ain toon; amnin aw?"

"Seerly; but hear me oot. Ye cud manage baith pairts, brawly. Though fowk grows aul' in coorse o' time, yer fader an' me maun hae some gate to bide. An' wi' Robbie intill anither place, an' Benjie at 's buzness, *we* cud live there fine; awat it's a richt gweed hoose, gin it hed but a back chimley bigget; only there's little eese o' that as lang's the like o' Mr. an' Mrs. Gibb has 't. Your fader cud trock aboot at 's leasure on a placie like Gushetneuk; he wud be aye worth 's breid; an' lat you tak' chairge an' mak' market for baith places."

"Weel, that wud dee fine," said Peter Birse junior, brightening up at the brilliant prospect thus opened up to him. His countenance fell, however, as he added, "But I dinna ken gin she cares for 's ava."

"Care for ye? Fat wud pit that styte i' yer head?"

"Weel, at ony rate, ye ken, I bocht sweeties at St. Saar's Fair an' fuish till 'er——"

"Weel, an' didna she tak' them?"

"Ou ay, but I'm maist sure 't she hed taul' Jock Wull, for they war lauchin' at 's aboot the chop, upo' Saiterday's nicht."

"Lat them lauch that wins, Peter, man. Jock Wull wud need it. Fat's he—the sin o' a peer nace nyaukit beggar creatur, 't hisna passin' a gweed barrow load o' wardle's gear to bless 'ersel wi'! Set *himsel'* up wi' the like o' you, though ye warna my son! The impidence o' creaturs is a perfect scunner. But never ye min' Jock Wull; an' he gae far that road they'll seen get their sairin o' him, an' 's mither tee; an' little maitter, weel-a-wat.—Gin I hed bit kent that afore I gaed to the chop, no!" added Mrs. Birse, in a subdued key.

"But he gaes hame wi' 'er mony a time; an' fan I try't to get her to come hame wi' me fae the Ward at Yeel, she made fun o' 's a file, an' syne, aifter aw thocht she wud dee 't, gaed aff wi' aul' marriet fowk."

"'Fant hert never wan fair dame,' Peter," said Mrs. Birse, with a half scornful laugh. "That's been the gate wi' mair nor Mary Howie, as yer nain fader cud tell, an' he war willin'. Mony was the 'put an' row' wi' him ere he gat muckle audiscence, I can tell ye. But though *he* wusna the young man o' a braw fairm than, he made it oot at the lang len'th, by dent o' patience an' perseverance."

"Weel, but gin she like Jock Wull better," argued Peter, upon whom the green-eyed monster was operating so sensibly that the image of his, as he believed, more successful rival would not leave his mind.

"Gae 'wa' wi' ye!" exclaimed his mother, with some impatience. "Fear't at Jock Wull, an apprentice loon in a bit orra choppie, an' you as weel plenish't a fairmer's sin as there is i' the pairis'!—For shame to ye, Peter, man, 't ye hae so little spunk."

"Cudna ye fesh 't aboot nae wye to Mrs. Gibb than?" asked the gallant youth.

Mrs. Birse, after a moment's reflection, assented to this suggestion, and agreed to do her best with both Johnny and Mrs. Gibb, to pave the way more directly for Peter's matrimonial campaign. Meanwhile, she further exhorted Peter to pursue the same resolutely on his own account.

CHAPTER XXII.

MAINLY POLEMICAL.

To Johnny Gibb the summer of 1842 was a season of unusual mental activity. The great Kirk controversy was waxing hotter and hotter, and a crisis, in some shape, seemed certain at no distant date. The spring of that year had seen the settlement of a minister in a Strathbogie parish, in anticipation of which it had been deemed prudent, after what had occurred at Culsalmond, actually to have a company of soldiers conveyed from Aberdeen to the neighbourhood. The settlement took place quietly enough, but the fact that the moderatism of the Church had indicated its temper in this militant fashion could not fail to arouse still more deeply the belligerent element in a nature like that of Johnny Gibb. He declared that things could not stop short of a rebellion, which would put that of the Forty-five in the shade. Then, at the General Assembly, the deposed ministers of Strathbogie both presented commissions for those of their own number whom they chose to send up, and also offered at the bar of that right reverend house a Court of Session interdict against those of the minority of their brethren from the Presbytery, who had been elected commissioners, and who, according to the Assembly's own previous decision, were the only true representatives of the Presbytery. When the news of this had travelled north to Gushetneuk, through the medium, in the latter part of its journey, of a steady-going Aberdeen newspaper, which Johnny Gibb, notwithstanding that its opinions differed *toto cœlo* from his own, continued to peruse with regularity, Johnny hastened down in the gloamin to Smiddy-ward to relieve his overwrought mind by some conversation with the souter and the smith.

"I tell ye fat it is," said Johnny, "they winna halt till the earth open an' swallow up a batch o' them like Korah, Dathan, an' Abiram."

"Nae doot we're comin' upo' times o' trial," answered the souter, "but it chaets me sair gin a' this heemlin creen-gin to the Coort o' Session binna jist i' the wye o' plantin' a saplin' to grow the stick that'll brak their nain heids some day yet."

"That means 't punishment winna owretak' the Moderates in a han'-clap, as it cam' upo' Korah an' 's company," said the smith. "But hae the Stra'bogie Moderates actually been alloo't to tak' their seats i' the Assembly, you that's seen the papers?"

"Na, man: I hinna wull o' 't. Ill that we are, we're nae come to that yet," said Johnny. "But nae fyour nor eighty-five votit for them, an' twa hunner an' fifteen against; an' their enterdick to keep oot Maister Dewar, Maister Leith, an' this Mawjor Stewart, the rowlin el'er, was cas'n by a hunner an' seventy-three voters to seventy-sax."

"Gweed fair majorities that, Gushets; they're sair i' the backgrun, ye see."

"Ay, but leuk at oor parliamenters, the heid deesters amo' them ken so little aboot richt prenciples in kirk matters. This Graham's nae sair to ride the water on wi' that nor nae ither thing; an' Lord Aiberdeen's bit milk-and-water schaime 's far fae the richt thing."

"Jist like ither half-an'-half mizzours," said the souter. "It'll dee mair ill nor gweed i' the lang rin. Ye canna serve God an' mammon, aiven wi' a bull oot o' Parliament. But ye're comin' unco near 't there, Gushets. The fattal thing's nae that there's a camp o' Moderates to conten' against: lat them stan upo' their nain shee soles, an' they wud be scatter't like cauff afore the win'; but dinna ye see that they 're playin' into the han's o' a set o' men that hae poo'er o' their side, an' owre af'en but little o' the fear o' Gweed afore their een ?"

"The Government, ye mean?" said the smith.

"An' the Coort o' Session," added Johnny.

"Ay," continued the souter, "an' the pawtrons."

"True, true," interposed Johnny Gibb, "the thing's rotten, reet an' crap."

"Nae doot o' that; but leuk at this," and the souter took up a newspaper containing a report of the General Assembly, which he had carefully conned. "Here's the debate on pawtronage—' Mr. Cunningham moved that the Assembly resolve and declare that patronage is a grievance, has been attended with much injury to the cause of true religion in the Church and kingdom, is the main cause of the difficulties in which the Church is at present involved, and that it ought to be abolished;' that was sec-ondit by ane Mr. Buchan o' Kelloe, an extensive lan'it proprietor i' the Border coonty o' Berwickshire, Mr. Macrory taul' me. Foo cud ony richt-thinkin' man back-speak a motion like that noo?"

"I daursay Gushets winna dee't, but aw b'lieve him an' Maister Sleekaboot raither differs aboot the benefits o' pawtronage," said the smith, with a sly twinkle in his eye.

"I see ·brawly fat ye 're lattin at," answered Johnny. "An' nae thanks to Maister Sleekaboot to fawvour pawtronage, 't wud 'a never gotten a kirk ava haud awa' fae 't. But I 'se gae nae farrer nor 'imsel' for preef o' the evils o' that system; an ill-less, gweed-less creatur, ye may tell me, but nae mair fit to be minaister o' a pairis' nor a blin' man is to herd sheep. An' syne fat d' ye mak' o' sic ootrages as Marnoch an' Culsalmon', to keep near han' hame?"

"Weel, takin' a' that 's come an' gane intill accoont, fat sud actually happen noo, but that nae less nor a hunner an' forty-seyven members o' Assembly sud vote against Mr. Cunningham's motion; an' some nae far fae oor ain quarter spak' their warst against it?" said the souter.

"It was cairriet, though?" queried the smith.

"Ou ay, by a sma' majority: twa hunner and fifteen votit for 't. But see sic a han'le as that state o' maitters gi'es to them that's but owre weel-will't to be lords owre God's spiritual heritage, fan they can say, 'Oh, the tae half o' the kirk *wants* pawtronage.' But the rowle obteens throu' a'—'whatsoever a man soweth, that also shall he reap.' An' tak' ye my word for 't, the day 'll come yet that this pawtronage 'll be a bane that 'll stick i' the thrapple o' the Moderate pairty o' the Kirk o' Scotlan', seein' that they hed it in their poo'er to sweep it clean aff the face o' the lan', but refees't to len' their assistance. An' it's waefu' to see the num'er o' men that better things micht hae been expeckit o' takin' that time-sairin coorse. To them, also, may the words be appliet that oor freen sae af'en quotit:—

> 'The sons of Ephraim, who nor bows
> Nor other arms did lack;
> When as the day of battle was,
> They faintly turned back.'

Hooever, the Kirk's coorse has been made perfectly clear. Her 'Claim o' Rights,' mov't by Dr. Chalmers, an' sec-ondit by Dr. Gordon, 's been cairriet by twa hunner an' forty-one to a hunner an' ten; an' we'll see ane o' twa things—the true Kirk o' Scotlan' restor't till her richtfu' claims, or leavin' her manses, kirks, an' stipen's for the sake o' her spiritual liberties."

"It's a perfeck trowth, souter!" exclaimed Johnny Gibb. "Ye never spak' mair to the pint i' yer life. There'll be a winnowin' o' the cauff fae the corn yet, wi' a vengeance."

When Johnny Gibb took his yearly journey to the Wells at Macduff, he could not fail to visit his friend, Maister Saunders, at Marnoch, who gave him a spirit-stirring narrative of how the miniature Disruption there had been carried through; how they had worshipped in a quarry for a time; how about twelve months previous to the date of Johnny Gibb's visit they had commenced to build a church and manse, to cost, together, well on to £2000; and how subscriptions had come to them from east and west, from north and south, some even from across the Atlantic, insomuch that they had a goodly surplus, which they had trusted to invest as a partial endowment for their minister, who was now about to be inducted. On one point Johnny and Maister Saunders were quite clear—that there must now be a separation of the wheat from the chaff; that is to say, of the non-intrusion, or rather the evangelical, from the moderate element. Johnny returned, indeed, fully of opinion that the Kirk throughout would be rent in two, even after the manner of that which he had now seen with his own eyes on a small scale. "Lat it come," said Johnny; "onything to roose the countra fae the caul' morality o' a deid moderatism." Of course Johnny spoke strongly; but in that particular he was not singular; strong language was common on both sides. Even able editors on the side to which he was opposed, as Johnny heard and read, designated the leaders and clerical party in whom he believed by such choice designations as "Edinburgh popes," "Candlish & Co.," "highflyers," "wild men," "agitators," "reckless disturbers of the peace of the Church," and so on; and in point of warmth and "personality" the addresses of the fathers and brethren when they met were at times rather well worth hearing by those who relished anything in that vein. At the meeting of the Synod of Aberdeen, in October of this year, the moderate party had the upper hand—they carried their candidate for the moderatorship, Mr. Watt, Foveran, by 79 votes to 58 for Mr. Simpson, Trinity Church, Aberdeen, proposed by the other side; and also, after a fair amount of rather pointed talk, carried a resolution to admit to the sittings of the Synod the ministers of the Garioch Presbytery, who had been suspended for their part in the Culsalmond business. In a subsequent discussion one rev. brother observed that, "the blighting influence of moderatism had been thrown over all their institutions; and even its corrupting hand had been thrown over their colleges and universities, rendering them rather the schools of hell than of heaven ;" whereupon two other rev. brethren suggested whether the speaker's words should not be taken down, with a view to ulterior proceedings, while a third rather thought it might "be better to hear them with silent contempt."

CHAPTER XXIII.

JONATHAN TAWSE AND DAWVID HADDEN.

WITH the November "Convocation" of 1842, the ferment within the Kirk of Scotland reached about as great a pitch of intensity as it was possible for it to attain. While on the one hand the results of the gathering of over 400 ministers of the evangelical section in Edinburgh was held to give great encouragement to the non-intrusion party, it was predicted on the other "that the reign of fanaticism was near an end, and the triumph of moderatism and rational religion at hand." In a few weeks thereafter meetings began to be held here and there in the interest of the non-intrusion party, for the purpose of giving all who were desirous of receiving it, information "on the present state of the Church;" and affording to the people the opportunity of subscribing papers declaring their adherence to the resolutions of the Convocation. The attempt to hold such meetings in parishes where the ministers leant to the moderate side was denounced in language more vehement than polite. Jonathan Tawse was only re-echoing in a strictly literal way what he had read in very legible print in a Tory newspaper, when he characterised it as "a dirty and disgusting" proceeding. "But," added Jonathan, "the fanatics winna try that here—they'll never come this length."

"Cudna they be ta'en an order o' gin they war to dee't?" asked Mains of Yawal, to whom Jonathan had addressed the foregoing remark, as they walked amicably home, one Sunday afternoon, after counting the bawbees.

"Nae doot o' 't," answered Jonathan, promptly. "It's against baith ecclesiastical an' statute law."

"An' wud it be a fine or jilein, than?"

"That depen's o' the form o' trial; there micht be discipline, inferrin' censure, an' deprivation o' status an' privileges; or a process i' the ceevil coorts."

"An' filk o' them wud be warst likein?" inquired Mains, who was anxious to be informed, but rather bewildered by Jonathan's learned deliverance.

"Ou, that's jist as ye set maist store o' yer pride or yer purse; a bit canny joukin to lat the jaw gae owre's nae thrown awa' wi' presbyteries eeswally; nor heritors either," added Jonathan, with a slight tinge of bitterness, as he thought how scantily his own merits had been appreciated by that class.

"Weel, aw dinna ken: it's an unco time," said Mains, "'t peaceable fowk canna be latt'n aleen. I kenna fat they wud hae; there's been nae ane meddlin' wi' the kirk cep some o' that Edinboro' fowk, an' noo they're begun aboot Aiberdeen tee, they say."

The truth was that Mains had suffered one or two assaults from Johnny Gibb on this subject; when, being an elder, it was, of course, needful to be able to give a reason for the faith that was in him. There was no want of will on his part to do so, but while Mains's zeal in defence of rational religion had been growing, his stock of polemical argument had not correspondingly increased, so that he had felt a little hard pressed in the matter; and he therefore desired to avail himself as far as might be of the dominie's superior knowledge. Mains had now, as he believed, got such an insight into the law of the case as ought to stand him in some stead, if he could only bear in mind the phrases "ecclesiastical" and "statute" law. As his question indicated, he was not quite so confident as Jonathan that the "wild men" might not even invade Pyketillim, if they were not frightened off betimes; and he now articulately expressed his apprehensions on that head.

"Fat!" exclaimed Jonathan Tawse; "tell me that that

ettercap, Gushetneuk, 's been thraet'nin' that the faces o' some o' them 'll be seen here ere lang?"

"I'm nae biddin' ye tak' my word for 't, Maister Tawse, though he fell upo' me comin' oot o' An'ersmas Fair like a thoosan' o' divots, an' misca'd the minaister, an' said that he sud seen hae ane here that wud lat the fowk ken fat like he was; but speir ye at Dawvid Hadden."

"I'm nae misdootin yer word, Mains; he's a disaffeckit creatur, an' likes to be i' the heid o' things. An' fan the like o' 'im 's amo' them that canna keep 'im in aboot, they'll gae gryte len'ths."

The last remark was not exactly complimentary to Mains, who did not see its application clearly, however, but went on, "Ou weel, ye see, I wud 'a fun't wi' 'im a bit; only he wudna haud a word o' me; but was up i' my witters like a fechtin cock."

"Was Dawvid wi' ye?"

"Na, na; sin' ever that skweel meetin' i' the spring, Dawvid's been i' the black beuks wi' 'im, an' wudna gae within a rig-len'th o' Gushets an' he cud help it."

"Hoo cud he ken o' 's projecks than?"

"Weel, ye'll min' o' the cheelie that was wi' me fern-year was a year, that leern't to be a mole-catcher."

"Brawly——a settril, braid-fac't chappie."

"Ay, ay, jist that. He was at Gushetneuk a' hairst, an' 's been takin' moles i' the neebourheid throu' the en' o' the year. Weel, Gushet's pitten him as heich 's himsel' aboot this non-intrusion wark. He's aye eikin 'im up, an' Dawvid, fan he's on 's roun's, lats at him fanever they meet, aboot the kirk; an' syne Molie canna hae 't an' haud it, ye ken."

"Ou ay, an' Dawvid acks the moudiewort wi' *him!*"

"Weel, ye ken, Molie's a simple cheelie, an' Dawvid gets onything that's gyaun on wi' Gushets, aw b'lieve, seener throu' him nor he cud dee ony ither gate."

"Vera like Dawvid's sneck-drawin'; he was aye a straucht-oot-the-gate callant!" said Jonathan, with a very obvious sneer at the zealous ground-officer's proclivities.

But although Jonathan could be sarcastic about Dawvid Hadden in friendly conference with his brother elder, he was far from being averse to availing himself, as opportunity served, of Dawvid's gossip about the local feeling in kirk matters. Jonathan had, in fact, begun to regard himself as a sort of guardian of "rational religion" in the parish. The Rev. Andrew Sleekaboot held opinions more orthodox than his own, probably, anent the sacred rights of the patron, and the pernicious fanaticism which would question the powers of the Civil Court; but what then, if the Rev. Andrew Sleekaboot—with the exception of a quiet thrust from the pulpit occasionally—was rather studious to avoid collision, than desirous of enforcing his authority upon those of his parishioners who were manifesting a tendency to follow divisive courses? Mr. Sleekaboot believed in patient waiting; the spirit of fanaticism, he still said, would die out. But even although the whirligig of time might bring about a properly sobered state of mind among these people, the process was altogether too tedious for the Rev. Jonathan Tawse's temper. And he had become fully determined to strike a blow for Kirk and State, whenever and wherever occasion offered.

Therefore it was that, when, on a certain evening not many days after the occurrence of the foregoing conversation, Jonathan Tawse caught sight of Dawvid Hadden passing the end of the school homeward, he hailed him with the utmost frankness, and invited Dawvid in to take sneeshin and a drink of ale.

"An' fan saw ye Gushetneuk?" asked Jonathan.

"Weel, I foryet noo," said Dawvid, thoughtfully. "It's nae time syne; but I'm seein' sae mony daily day."

"Is he as keen o' the kirk sin' ye gae 'im sic a fleg aboot Hairry Muggart's meetin'?"

"Weel, they 've never daur't to try the like o' 't again; an' I gar't Hairry 'imsel' shak' in 's sheen aboot that at ony rate."

"An' Gushets—I 've nae doot he wud be o' the steel o repentance aboot it tee?"

"Hairry was a kin' o' heid deester there, ye see, an' it wusna worth *my* pains min'in' the lave."

"O-oh! I thocht ye gae Gushets up's fit—Fat's this 't he's been bullyraggin Mains aboot than; anither meetin' that he's to haud at the Ward wi' some o' the hightflyers?"

"I cud maybe tell ye that tee, Maister Tawse," said Dawvid with an air of some consequence.

"I dinna doot it, Dawvid; I dinna doot it. Ye've a gran' scent for fin'in' oot the like o' that, man."

"It maitters-na fat wye I fan 't oot; but I'm quite awaar 't they've set the nicht for a meetin' wi' ane o' the rovin' commission, doon at Peterkin's hole o' a skweel."

"So the mole-catcher creatur was sayin', I believe," remarked Jonathan, wickedly.

"Maybe," said Dawvid, in a half offended tone; "an' nae doot he wud tell ye a hantle mair nor the like o' me cud dee aboot it."

"Na, na; he only said that Gushets sud say that he was quite prepar't to set the laird's delegate, Dawvid Hadden, at defiance."

"An' did he tell ye fat authority the 'laird's delegate' hed fae Sir Simon 'imsel' to enterdick ony sic meetin', an' fat mizzours he hed ta'en ere noo to pit a stop till 't?" asked Dawvid, promptly.

These were points that Jonathan really desired to know definitely about, so he gave up the bantering tone, and by a little judicious flattery induced Dawvid to explain to him how, on the evening of next Friday, which was fixed for the meeting, he proposed being down with a body of men and some dogs absolutely to prevent the assembling of a non-intrusion meeting in the Smiddyward school. A letter he had received from Sir Simon gave him full authority to adopt that course (as Dawvid interpreted it); and Jonathan Tawse, who, as the conversation went on, had latterly waxed warm on the subject, not merely approved of the scheme, but declared he would be present himself, along with some of his trusty personal friends, to give what aid might be required.

"Friday nicht at seven o'clock—we'se gi'e Gushets an' 's non-intrusionists as snell a nizzen as they've gotten yet. Gweed nicht, Dawvid," said the dominie.

"Gweed nicht, sir: an' I'll be stappin," answered Dawvid.

And so they parted.

CHAPTER XXIV.

PREPARING FOR THE CONFLICT.

WHEN the Rev. Jonathan Tawse was to have a dinner party, the laddies at the school were sure to become quite aware of what was about to take place. The external symptoms of the coming event were visible in Jonathan's person and movements. He sowffed more to himself than usual, in an abstracted way, on these days; one or other of the lessons was sure to be curtailed, and more of them were slurred over, for Jonathan had to go out repeatedly to the kitchen through the middle door to confer with Baubie, his housekeeper; then, though we might be taken into school sharp at the end of the play hour, we knew that this would be more than made up by the promptitude with which we should be dismissed at a quarter after three, in place of an hour later. And above all—just as it was wont to be in the years before, on the days when Lord Kintore, and that great hero of our youthful imagination, Joe Grant, the huntsman, came round on a fox hunt—we knew perfectly well there would be no risk of lickin', unless for offences of the most outrageous kind.

On this side of it, Jonathan's character called forth my warmest admiration at the time; and, indeed, I don't know that I am called upon to qualify that admiration in any material degree even yet. At any rate, that he was a jovial and kindly host on those occasions was not to be doubted. It was testified by the very countenances of his visitors as they were sometimes seen by us assembling about the entry door, ere we began to take our loitering departure homeward.

It was on the afternoon of the Friday on which, as Dawvid Hadden had informed Jonathan Tawse, Johnny Gibb and his non-intrusion friends were to have their evening meeting, that Jonathan's pupils were set agog by symptoms of the nature of those referred to. Jonathan was fully bent on carrying out the resolution he had announced to Dawvid, of going down to Smiddyward school, and interposing an authoritative check to the proceedings of the fanatics, against whom his gorge had been gradually rising for many months. And he deemed it suitable to assemble a few of his friends, staunch and true champions of moderate religion, who should accompany him in the guise of faithful witnesses. The company included Mains of Yawal, Teuchitsmyre, and Braeside, who, of course, as his fellow-elders, could not be omitted, and Dr. Drogemweal junior, to whom he had written a note, specially explaining the object of the meeting. The doctor, as may be here said, was a great fleshy-looking fellow, about thirty, or a few years beyond it. He was not to be termed brilliant as a professional man. His grand characteristics seemed to be the enjoyment of robust animal health, and love of good fellowship, and his present zeal for the Kirk of Scotland was somewhat difficult to account for, seeing his attendance at church on Sundays did not average much over once in twelve months.

The dinner was a capital dinner, for Baubie's capabilities as a cook were unimpeachable, and she waited no less efficiently than she cooked. Her master spoke familiarly to her, and Baubie, in turn, spoke just as familiarly to the guests. And thus, as Braeside sat masticating, long and seriously, with his knife and fork in either hand, set in a perpendicular attitude on the table, she would coaxingly urge him to "see an' mak' a denner o' 't, noo ; an' nae min' fowk 't eats as gin they war on a waager ;" while to Drogemweal's mock profession of his sense of obligation to her for the numerous good dinners she had provided for him, she retorted promptly, "Oh, it 's weel kent that at'en maet 's ill to pay."

"Ye hae 'im there, Baubie, at ony rate," quoth the dominie. "If ye had been wise, doctor, ye wud 'a keepit by the aul' proverb that says, 'Dit your mou' wi' your meat.' Isna that the wye o' 't, Mains?"

Mains, who had been acting on the proverb by keeping perfect silence, and attending to his dinner, declared his belief that the dominie was quite right, and added something about Jonathan's "leernin" giving him such an advantage, in a wide comprehension of these "aul', aunctient byewords."

When the dinner was finished, they had their toddy. There were yet two hours to the time of meeting; and in the interval they would discuss the general aspect of affairs. So, after they had concocted the first tumbler, and duly pledged each other, Jonathan took up an Aberdeen newspaper, wherein were recorded certain of the proceedings of the evangelical ministers, who were visiting different parishes, for the purpose of holding meetings. First he put on his "specs," and next he selected and read out several paragraphs, with such headings as "THE SCHISMATICS IN A——;" "THE FIRE-RAISERS IN B——," and so on, winding up this part with the concluding words of one such paragraph, which were these—" So ended this compound of vain, false, and seditious statements on the position of the Church, and which must have been most offensive to every friend of truth, peace, or loyalty who heard it."

"I say Amen to ilka word o' that," said Dr. Drogemweal. "Sneevellin hypocrites. That's your non-intrusion meetin's. It concerns every loyal subject to hae them pitten doon."

"Here's fat the editor says in a weel-reason't, an vera calm an' temperate article," continued Jonathan—" he's speakin' o' the fire-raisers—'How much reliance could be placed on the kind of information communicated by these reverend gentlemen will be readily imagined by such of our readers as have read or listened to any of the harangues which the schismatics are so liberally dealing forth. If simple laymen, in pursuing objects of interest or ambition, were to be guilty of half the misrepresentation of facts and concealment of the truth which are now, it would seem, thought not unbecoming on the part of *Evangelical* ministers, they would be justly scouted from society.' That's fat I ca' sen'in' the airrow straucht to the mark."

"Seerly," interposed Mains, who had been listening with much gravity.

"A weel-feather't shaft tee," said Dr. Drogemweal.

"An' it's perfectly true, ilka word o''t. They're nae better o' the ae han' nor incendiaries, wan'erin' here an' there to raise strife amo' peaceable fowk; and syne their harangues—a clean perversion o' the constitutional law, an' veelint abuse o' the institutions o' the countra."

"Did ye hear sic a rouse as they hed wi' them doon in Fintray last week?" asked the doctor.

"No; the paper disna come till the morn," answered Jonathan.

"I wud 'a gi'en a bottle o' black strap till 'a been there; an' it was jist the barest chance that I didna hear o''t in time," said Dr. Drogemweal.

"Was there a row?"

"Row! ay was there. An' maugre the leather lungs o' them, the fowk roar't them doon whan they try't to get up a meetin' in a mannie Knicht's barn; an', fan they saw't it was like to be a case o' physical force, they war forc't to skulk oot o' the pairish, like as mony tykes wi' their tails atween their legs. That's the style for the non-intrusion fanatics, Mr. Tawse."

"Weel, I never thocht they wud be ill to beat at argument; but they dinna deserve a hearin', it maun be alloo't. They hinna a fit to stan' upon i' the licht o' logic and common sense, lat alane statute law."

"Na, na; a 'staffy-nevel job,' 's aul' Skinner has 't," exclaimed the doctor, with emphasis, refilling his tumbler. "Physical force is the argument for them."

Mains and his fellow-elders had been rather thrown out in this conversation, and while it still went on, Braeside, whose attitude had been purely that of a listener, now ventured to ask his neighbour, quietly, "Fat dis he mean, Mains, by aye speakin' o' 'feesikle force'—Is't ony kin' o' drogs?"

M

"Na, na," answered Mains, who was gratified to find himself in a position to give instruction on this occasion. "'Feesikle force' jist means to lay fae ye a' 't ye 're able."

"Keep 's an' guide 's," said Braeside, "that seerly canna be fat he means; there 's never been nae ill neepourheid amo' the fowk roon hereaboot."

"Weel, it 's their nain blame," answered Mains, vaguely.

"Fat is 't, boys?" shouted Drogemweal. "Keep the bottle gaen there—thank ye. Ye 'll need to lat the fanatics see that they winna come here for naething."

"We wus jist speakin' aboot 'feesikle force,' doctor," answered Mains, confidently.

"Ou ay; physical force, if it be necessary. Mr. Tawse 'll gi'e them jaw; an' I think for wecht at the ither style o' argument, 'we three' sud haud our ain. But they 're to hae nae meetin' here at ony rate."

"Dawvid Hadden 'll dee that pairt o' 't, dootless," said Jonathan, "if he be as gweed 's his word."

"Yon bit pernicketty wallydraggle! He'll dee some service, or than no."

"He 's airm't wi' poo'er fae the laird, though—so I b'lieve—to keep them oot o' their conventicle. But jist pit roun' the kettlie there, an' haud gaen. We 'll need to start in a few minutes."

"My certie, ye 're richt; it 's the quarter past six," said Dr. Drogemweal, looking up at Jonathan's eight-day clock. "We maun start at ance, or they may be a' gaither't afore we win there."

The doctor then gulped down the remaining contents of his tumbler, and Jonathan having given Baubie orders to have a haddock ready by the time Dr. Drogemweal and he should return, an hour and a half or so thereafter, the valiant Church defenders set out for Smiddyward school, Jonathan and the doctor marching in front, the latter with a big stick in his hand, and Mains, Teuchitsmyre, and Braeside, who had begun to be a little uncertain of the part they were expected to play, following behind.

CHAPTER XXV.

THE GUSHETNEUK MEETING.

WHILE Jonathan Tawse and his friends plodded down towards the hamlet of Smiddyward, they had, as I have indicated, separated into two groups, Jonathan and Dr. Drogemweal going in front, while Mains of Yawal and the other elders gradually fell behind, to the distance of about ten yards. It was a cloudy evening in February, though partial moonlight helped somewhat to lighten the darkness of the way. When they had reached to within about a furlong of the Ward, at the point where the road leading from the hamlet joined the kirk road, some one passed them going in the opposite direction.

"Eh, man!" exclaimed Braeside, after stopping and looking for a second or two in the direction in which the figure had gone, "an' that binna Dawvid Hadden, it's seerly his wraith."

"It canna be Dawvid," answered Mains, "for we ken't he'll be doon at the Ward skweel afore's."

"That's as lucky at ony rate," said Braeside, "for I'm nae jist vera keerious about that doctor's protticks, an' Dawvid's hed a hantle o' expairience — 'serve's, it wud be an unco thing to gar fowk get ill-willers amo' their neebours."

"Weel, but ye see they're brakin the staito law o' the kwintra," replied Mains; "speer ye at Maister Tawse an' he'll tell ye the same."

"It's a terrible daurin thing to gae on in sic a menner," said Teuchitsmyre.

"Ou, aw'm nae misdootin' 't; but it disna weel to mak' fash amo' kent fowk," replied Braeside.

In short, Braeside only deprecated conflict the more the nearer he and his friends came to the scene of action. They had passed Widow Will's cottage, and also the cottages of the smith and souter, where the lights were burning cheerily inside. They had met two or three more people, but there was no great appearance of a meeting gathering. When they got up to the school, the windows were quite dark, and the door still fastened.

"Owre early, ye see," said Jonathan. "We hed better step oot the loan a few yairds."

"Countra fowk's aye late," replied the doctor; "but faur 's your advanc't guard wi' 's dogs? He mitha been here at ony rate, by this time."

"Nae fear; he's owre croose o' the subject nae to be here in time," said Jonathan.

"Was that Dawvid Hadden?" inquired Mains, after a pause of some duration. "'Cause Braeside threepit owre hiz that yon was him 't we met at the glack o' the roads."

"Dawvid Hadden!" exclaimed the dominie, "Dawvid Hadden gyaun the conter gate?"

"I'm fell seer it was him, at ony rate," said Braeside.

"Ye've mista'en the hour; an' we're here afore the time," said Dr. Drogemweal. "What's to be done?"

"Mithna we speer some gate?" suggested Mains.

Sandy Peterkin's school remained suspiciously dark and silent, and so, for that matter, did Sandy's house, too; for when Dr. Drogemweal, who had gone off to ask about the meeting, came to the front of it, Sandy's modest window had the blind down, and there was no appearance of light within. The doctor rapped loudly on the door with his cudgel, and was in the act of rapping again, when "a fit" was heard coming down the loan, by the doctor's companions, who stood a little way back. The new arrival, who was walking rapidly, slackened his pace; and, as he approached the group, seemed to hesitate whether or not to stop. Stop he did, and a voice asked, "Is that you, Mains?"

"Ay," answered Mains, with that tone of dry reserve which a man adopts when he is in doubt about the identity or respectability of his questioner.

"Aw doot ye 're mista'en, as weel 's some mair."

"Ou, it 's you is 't, Molie," said Mains, in a mightily altered, and more human tone.

"Ay, it 's a' 't 's for me," answered our old friend the gudge, cheerfully. "Ye wud be gyaun to the meetin'?"

"Weel," replied Mains, speaking very slowly, "Weel, Maister Tawse an' ane or twa o' 's jist tyeuk a stap doon the howe i' the gloamin'—it 's a fine nicht."

"It *wus* till 'a been i' the skweel, but they cheeng't it, ye ken," said the simple-minded gudge, not heeding Mains's rather obvious attempt at *finesse*.

"Cheeng't it?" exclaimed Jonathan Tawse; "an' that creatur Hadden never to hint at sic a thing to me!"

"But aw doot Dawvid's gotten 's nain leg drawn a wee bittie;" and the gudge laughed quietly. "It was only the streen that the meetin' was cheeng't; an' I tyeuk a rin roun' to tell some o' the fowk aifter aw was laid bye for the day. Dawvid was doon in gran' time, aw b'lieve, as big 's the vera Sir 'imsel'—ye've seerly met 'im. He 's hame nae time syne in a terrible bung."

The gudge's information was rather more copious than palatable. But while Jonathan Tawse and his other friends were endeavouring to ruminate thereon, Dr. Drogemweal, who had returned from his ineffectual assault on Sandy Peterkin's door, asked, in a peremptory tone, "An' when 's the meetin' to be held, noo?"

"Ou, the nicht, the nicht," said the gudge.

"An' where 's it to be?"

"I' the barn at Gushetneuk. There cudna be a better place. Aw 'm seer ye ken, Mains, sic scouth 's there is i' the strae en' ahin the thrashin' mull. An' ye mitha seen 's fae yer nain toon biggin oot the strae i' the aifterneen." The gudge paused; and, there being no reply, he continued,

"Weel, I'll need to be stappin'; for aw hinna wull't aw war late, an' they're feckly a' up fae this side a filie syne. Aw'm sure it'll be a capital meetin'."

And the mole-catcher moved briskly on his way.

It was not altogether a pleasant predicament into which Jonathan Tawse and his friends had been led. The way in which things had taken the turn that had brought them into it was this. During the week, Dawvid Hadden had been unusually demonstrative not only in letting it be known what he was to do in the way of stopping the meeting, but also the authority by which he was to do it. Dawvid's object, of course, was to frighten the timid and wavering from showing face at the school. So far he had been successful, for not only was Peter Birse in a state of helpless agony, but even Hairry Muggart, when down at the Ward on some professional business, had left the impression on the souter and smith that there were really ground for Dawvid's boast that he had made Hairry "shak' in his sheen." The two friends, therefore, had begun to have some fears that the meeting might be spoilt in this way; and, moreover, the souter raised the question strongly whether it was altogether fair to Sandy Peterkin to make him voluntarily invite ejection from his school by holding the meeting there. He would go to Johnny Gibb, and suggest to him the propriety of transferring the meeting to his own barn. At first blush of the proposal Johnny got hot, and denounced it as mere truckling to petty tyranny, but he speedily saw the matter in a different light, and set zealously about reddin' up the barn as a place to meet in.

The change in the place of meeting had been intimated during the day as widely as possible, and probably none of the well-affected, who were likely to attend, had been left in ignorance of it. Nor was there any desire to keep others in the dark on the subject. Dawvid Hadden, even, had been indirectly informed very early in the afternoon; but unhappily for himself, Dawvid had concluded it to be a *ruse* to throw him off the scent; so Dawvid had observed that he was "owre aul' a sparrow to be ta'en wi' cauff."

THE GUSHETNEUK MEETING.

And the meeting in Johnny Gibb's barn was highly successful. Thither came the majority of the residenters at Smiddyward, including the souter, the smith, and Sandy Peterkin; Andrew Langchafts, the merchan,' was there, and his apprentice, Jock Will. And Mrs. Birse brought with her Miss Birse, along with Peter senior and Peter junior; Hairry Muggart, too, under the feeling that Dawvid Hadden was likely to keep at a respectable distance from Gushetneuk, also put in an appearance; and the zeal of the molecatcher had operated to the bringing out of a considerable number of farm servants, including his old rival Tam Meerison, so that the available space in the barn was fully occupied. It had been intended to reinstate Hairry Muggart in the chair, but Hairry being rather shy of the honour on this occasion, the smith proposed Johnny Gibb as the fittest person to be chairman in his own barn, and the proposal was "carried by acclamation."

This point had just been settled when the door was pushed open, and the head and shoulders of Dr. Drogemweal thrust in. "Come awa' an' tak' seats, we're jist gaen to begin," said the chairman in a somewhat emphatic tone. "Ou, that's you, Maister Tawse; a sicht o' you here's gweed for sair een. See, there's a bit bole ahin the shakker 'll haud you; ye're nae gryte bouk mair nor mysel'. Mains an' the lave o' ye'll get edge't in aboot the en' o' the furms."

After the mole-catcher had left the gentlemen just referred to, they had debated among themselves what was to be done. Jonathan Tawse, who had managed to get into a great rage, and did not know exactly upon whom to vent his anger, would have turned and gone home in disgust, and it need hardly be said that his fellow-elders would have been extremely happy to follow that example; but, as Mains of Yawal thereafter averred, Dr. Drogemweal "bann't feerious" at this proposal, and hinted that the zeal of the Pyketillim eldership must really be at a low ebb if it did not incite to pursuit of the fanatics wherever they went. In short, he persuaded Jonathan to go along with him to the meeting, albeit his temper continued in a ruffled state; and, on the whole, it was not improved by the reception he met with from Johnny Gibb on entering the barn.

The meeting was formally opened by singing part of a psalm, which Johnny Gibb precented, and prayer; a proceeding the like of which not a few of the rustics there assembled had not before dreamt of as possible in a barn; and they felt correspondingly queer in the circumstances. The chairman then abruptly announced that "We're to get addresses fae twa respeckit minaisters fae a distance, settin' forth the prenciples o' the evangelical pairty. As ye a' see, the skweelmaister o' the pairis' is here tee; an' he'll be waur nor's word an' he binna wuntin' to mak' a speech to defen' the Coort o' Session Kirk. We'll hae nae objection to gi'e 'im a hearin'; but lat me tell ye ane an' a', that I'll keep order i' my nain hoose; an' gin ony horse-coupin doctor, or ony ither ane, try to mak' disturbance here, we'll lat 'im see the bonny side o' the door raither seener nor he wud like maybe."

The chairman's remarks naturally drew rather more attention to Jonathan Tawse and Dr. Drogemweal than those gentlemen seemed to relish, but without allowing time for either of them to put in a word, he continued, "Noo, ye'll get an address fae the Rev. Mr. Nonem—come forret aside me here, sir." The platform consisted of a wooden threshing-floor, on which had been placed the chairman's seat and a small table with a lighted candle on it and a pair of snuffers. The rev. gentleman announced, at once commenced an earnest, though, perhaps, somewhat verbose address, wherein he dwelt at length on "the doctrine of the headship;" and then proceeded to expound the rights of the Christian people in the choice of their ministers, calling upon his auditors, with much emphasis, to say whether they were prepared to hand over their consciences to patrons who might be prelatists, or papists, or worse, and let the Judges of the Court of Session in the last resort decide all such questions for them, for that was the pass things were coming to now?

During the delivery of this address there was marked attention generally; the parishioners of Pyketillim had not yet learnt the mode of giving expression to their approval by "ruffing" with their feet, or otherwise, and the one demonstrative individual in that direction was the chairman, who once and again very audibly emphasised the sentiments of the speaker by such utterances as "Owre true, sir;" "We a' ken fat kin' o' caul' morality we get fae your law-made minaisters," and so on. It was evident that Dr. Drogemweal and Jonathan Tawse were on edge; and the doctor had once or twice attempted an interruption by such exclamations as "Not true, Nonem," and "Question;" but getting no support from the meeting, he had found himself uncomfortably individualised by the chairman's "Seelence, sir!" and "Wheesht, sir!" and had given up these attempts.

"Noo, Maister Tawse, we'll hear ye," exclaimed Johnny Gibb, "an' dinna deteen 's owre lang." Jonathan Tawse started to his feet, and curtly declared, "I did not want to speak." "Dinna dee 't, than," quoth the chairman, promptly. But Jonathan continued, "An there 's been vera little said here this nicht that deserves a reply." "Hear, hear," cried Dr. Drogemweal. What were they to think, Jonathan proceeded to ask, of men like those of the present deputation, who had vowed to uphold the Established Kirk, and were now trying to pull it down? What were they to think of men who had trampled an interdict of the Court of Session under foot? Could temerity further go? And why all this insensate hubbub about the interference of the civil magistrate? Had the civil magistrate ever sought to enter their pulpits,—he would like to know that? Had he ever done aught but his duty in controlling the actings of a set of hot-headed zealots, who set all law, civil and ecclesiastical, at defiance, whose language was seditious, and whose actings directly tended to anarchy and insurrection?

During his speech Jonathan not merely waxed warm himself; he also roused the feelings of the audience. The chairman once and again abruptly expressed himself in a fashion somewhat short of chairman-like calmness and impartiality; his excitement infected the mole-catcher, who also cried, "Keep to the pint;" "Nane o' yer ill-naitur'," and so on; and when Dr. Drogemweal cheered Jonathan on by thumping with his stick on the edge of the "furm" and shouting "Hear, hear," "Good," "That's it," and so forth, Andrew Langchafts, seconded by Sandy Peterkin, very audibly suggested to "Pit 'im oot!"

Jonathan finished abruptly, and, while the "steam" was still fully up, the second deputy rose, and endeavoured, by a few sensible words, to recall the audience to a state of calmness. It so happened that this gentleman had not only been an old college companion of Drogemweal, but the medical practitioner in question had for a short time been a parishioner of his. And so, Drogemweal's blood being now up, he forthwith commenced a somewhat coarse personal attack, charging the minister with habitually neglecting his own pastoral duties, while he, forsooth, had the presumption to invade the parishes of better men than himself. "I lived in his parish more than a year, and he never once visited me—that's the man to tell other men their duty!" exclaimed the doctor. "Yes, my friend," was the reply, "and there may be parishioners whose faces we have little chance of getting familiar with, except in the way of private inquiry." Dr. Drogemweal was about to attempt a retort, when Andrew Langchafts stood up and solemnly protested against any one being allowed to interrupt a speaker; and the chairman, with an emphatic shout, ordered "Seelence, sir, this moment, or I'll get ye pitten oot!" What might have happened in this way had not become apparent, when Jonathan Tawse got to his feet, hat in hand, and unceremoniously made for the door. Dr. Drogemweal, with a muttered malediction, and a great amount of noise, caused by his stick and feet, as he pushed past some of his neighbours, followed. Mains of Yawal and his brother elders looked as if they would have liked to go too; but, their presence of mind failing them at the moment, they had not moved when their friends were clean gone; and then, as they did not like to be conspicuous, they kept their seats.

"A gweed reddance; a gweed reddance, weel-a-wat," said the chairman, as he snuffed the candle beside him, after the barn door had been once more closed. "Noo, sir, we 'll tak' the lave o' yer discoorse." The speaker resumed accordingly, and spoke at length, and with a force and seriousness that evidently told on the more intelligent part of his audience, after which opportunity was given for persons present to signify adherence to non-intrusion principles, by signing their names to a paper to that effect.

Johnny Gibb was in his most exalted mood as he marshalled the forces to this part of the business, which seemed to him a process very nigh akin to signing the Solemn League and Covenant. Mains of Yawal and his brethren, who saw that the case was getting desperate, now rose and slipped to the door, while Johnny shouted, "Gweed nicht, men; we 're muckle obleeg't for your peaceable company." Some of the younger people had left while the preparations for signing were going on; but most of the prominent members of the meeting were still there, including Mrs. Birse, who now sat on the front form, with her husband close at hand.

"It 's nae a thing to be lichtly deen, sirs. Ye 're pittin your names till a dockiment that concerns oor ceevil an' religious liberty. Come awa', souter, ye 're weel fit to set 's a' an example; ye winna pit yer han' to the pleuch an' leuk back." The souter had no choice but do as he was bid, though the suggestion was made that the chairman's name ought to go first. "It 'll be lang to the day that I 'm fit to step afore Roderick M'Aul," said Johnny Gibb. Johnny had an appropriate word for each several adherent as he came up; and I don't think there was the least shade of conscious irony in the remark he addressed to Peter Birse, when Peter rose from his wife's side, and came slowly up to the table, "Come awa', Clinkstyle; I 'm glaid to see ye takin' pairt for defence o' the trowth set afore 's this nicht. I 'm weel seer ye 'll never see rizzon to be o' a different min' fae fat yer in cenoo, about fat yer deein here afore wutnesses."

Peter signed with very much of the feeling that might have been supposed to animate the traditional "John," when his wife desired him to put his neck into the mink to please the laird. Then Mrs. Birse, with a becomingly solemn countenance, rose, and after doing her best at a curtsey, and addressing an impressive "Good nicht, sir," to each of the deputies, left for home.

When men get into the position of public characters, they have, in some cases, as it appears to me, a considerable reluctance to allowing that aspect of their lives to get obscured, or be lost sight of. With Johnny Gibb this was not by any means the case; for although the barn meeting had brought Gushetneuk greatly more into prominence than before, while his handling of Jonathan Tawse and Dr. Drogemweal junior had made all Pyketillim "ring from side to side" with his fame as chairman, nothing more readily nettled Johnny than any allusion to the proceedings above narrated in the light of his own share in them. He was rather pleased that Dawvid Hadden had been, as it were, snuffed out for the time, and that the other two just named had been driven from the field, but the question before which they had succumbed was a question of great principles, in relation to which he, Johnny Gibb, was a mere entity of only the smallest dimensions, and not once to be named as a power in the case at all. In short, he was Johnny Gibb of Gushetneuk, as he had been for the last thirty and odd years; an inconsiderable person, speaking and acting as the impulse moved him, in accordance with what he believed at the time to be right. It was in Church affairs as it was in other things; Johnny followed his own path of duty, quite irrespective of the state of opinion round about him, and he was honestly unconscious of any claim to merit in so doing.

CHAPTER XXVI.

SANDY PETERKIN'S FORTUNE.

In the parish of Pyketillim the great event of the Disruption was not seen in any of its grand or striking features. Inasmuch as the Rev. Andrew Sleekaboot was a firm supporter of the authority of the powers that be, there was there no exodus from the Manse; the minister, for conscience' sake, leaving the comfortable home of bygone years, where his children had grown up about him; sending his family away many miles, and himself finding the home where he was to spend solitary months on months in a poor cottage, which afforded him the accommodation of only an indifferent but and ben. And, of course, if the entire body of the parishioners of Pyketillim would only have been guided by his advice, the Disruption, so far as Pyketillim was concerned, would have been a nonentity. It was curious to note how the three men of highest learning and position connected with the parish—viz., the Rev. Andrew Sleekaboot, the Rev. Jonathan Tawse, and Sir Simon Frissal—in their several ways, denounced the approaching event, or prophesied evil, and evil only, as its result, while they predicted disaster to all who might be aiding and abetting in bringing about its accomplishment. Nevertheless, I doubt very much whether it would have been for the advantage of Pyketillim, even at this day, that the event referred to had remained unaccomplished.

As it was, there was a small knot of the parishioners,

most of whom have been introduced to the reader, who had committed themselves definitely to the other side, on the question at issue. As to the varying degrees of intelligence and sincerity with which they had done so, I need not here speak; one thing is certain, that they had all more or less to learn from the circumstances under which they were placed; only we need not hastily call them slow in the uptak', for if I mistake not there are such singular examples in existence still, as people who took the same side as they did in 1843, and in 1870 have not more than half learnt the significance of the lesson taught by their own professed principles, and the stand they took twenty-seven years ago.

But to my story—It was on a Saturday afternoon in the last week of April 1843 that Dawvid Hadden came down to Smiddyward, evidently on business. He was accompanied by a man with bare cheeks, wearing a long-bodied waistcoat, and trousers tight about the ankles, betokening that his function lay in dealing with horses. Dawvid strode away past the smiddy without deigning to stop and converse with the smith, who was shovelling up a load of coals that had just been emptied for use. "Fine nicht, Dawvid," said the smith, and Dawvid gravely replied "Fine nicht," but did not "brak his pace." Of course, Dawvid did not hear the smith's semi-audible ejaculation, as he resumed his shovelling, "Fat's i' the creatur's noddle noo ava?"

Dawvid went straight up to Sandy Peterkin's, and without stopping to knock, thrust the door fully open. "Ony body here?" shouted Dawvid.

"Ou, ay, I'm here," answered Sandy Peterkin. Sandy lived mainly alone, the kindly matrons in the hamlet taking a general oversight of his domestic arrangements. He had been enjoying a quiet cup of tea by himself, and rose up to open his inner door, as he asked, "Is that you, Dawvid? Come awa' ben. I'm some tribble't wi' reek, but fan yer lootit doon it's nae sae ill."

"Na, na; I canna pit aff time, fan I've buzness adee."

"Hoot, ye mith jist tak' a seat a minit," said Sandy. "It's nae af'en 't we see you here."

Dawvid made no reply, but fumbled in his breast pocket for a bundle of papers.

"I'm owthereest, as awgent for Sir Simon Frissal, to summons you, 'Alexander Peterkin, residenter, furth of the dwelling-house and adjoining premises at Smiddyward, and to quit the same at the ensuing term of Whitsunday.'"

Dawvid held conspicuously in his hand an official-looking letter, with a seal upon it, and he read from another of his bundle of papers. And as Sandy stood and looked with an uncertain stare, he waved the letter toward him with a sort of flourish, and added, "Ye thocht-na muckle o' oor words, Saun'ers, man, fan we gya ye a bit warnin', but that's vreet upon 't noo; foo does that please ye?"

"Ou, weel, an' it come to that, I've haen to flit afore noo," said Sandy, complacently.

"Weel, ye'll tak' notice 't ye've been regular summons't i' the presence o' a lethal wutness, Peter M'Cabe, to remuv at the proper time. Ye may go noo, Peter," said Dawvid, turning to the horsey-looking man, whose company he did not seem to be desirous of having longer than duty required.

"I'm obleeg't to ye, Dawvid, for your great pains i' the maitter," replied Sandy Peterkin.

"Ay, Saun'ers, man, an' ye may be thankfu' that ye've gotten so lang warnin'. It wasna necessar' to gi'e a day's notice. Ye ocht to ken that ye've been at oor merciment ilka minit sin' ever ye sat doon here. Ye've nae proper possession o' the premises, accordin' to law; an' cud be turn't oot at ony time. But Sir Simon Frissal's mair o' a gentleman nor tak' advantage o' the vera peerest incomer on 's estates."

"Muckle obleeg't to Sir Simon; he'll nae doubt be turnin' the place till a better purpose ance he war redd o' 's."

"It maitters-na to you; he's entectl't to hae 's wull respeckit by them 't's behaud'n till 'im for a biel' to pit their heid in. An' nae less to see 't the premises on 's nain property sanna be ees't to herbour malcontents, an' gi'e encouragement to oonlawfu' gedderins. That's fat yer non-intrusion comes till; ye mitha leern't mair wut ere noo, man, an' ye cud a' ta'en a tellin' fae fowk wi' mair gumption nor yersel'."

"Oh, weel, gin Sir Simon be to clear aff a' the non-intrusionists upo' the place, I'll suffer in gweed company. Ye'll be gyaun owre bye to summons Gushets neist, nae doot?"

"Jist leern ye to keep a ceevil tongue i' yer heid, Saun'ers, man. That's nedder here nor there: but I've something ither adee nor waste time nyatterin on wi' the like o' you;" and with this the ground-officer turned and passed away, and Sandy Peterkin shut the door and proceeded to finish his tea.

On his homeward route Dawvid Hadden took care to make a call at the shop of Hairry Muggart, the wright; where, in an "overly" way, as Hairry said, he turned out the famous summons he had just professed to serve on Sandy Peterkin.

"An' will he raelly be pitten oot?" asked Hairry, with some earnestness.

"Pitten oot!" exclaimed Dawvid. "Div ye mean to say that Sir Simon Frissal wud mak' a feel o' 'imsel' or gae back o' 's word, aifter sen'in' 's nain awgent to summons ony ane oot? Ay, Hairry, man, that's but the beginnin' o' 't," said Dawvid, pocketing his papers. "The langest livers sees maist ferlies. Aw wudna won'er nor there may be mair summonses ere lang gyang."

On that very evening, after droppin' time, Hairry Muggart was away to Smiddyward to see the smith and the souter. Hairry's statement was the first intimation they had received of what Dawvid Hadden had really been about; and the question naturally enough arose what had become of Sandy himself that he had not been down with the intelligence. The readiest way to solve this question seemed to be to call on Sandy; and the trio accordingly went up to his house, where they found the honest dominie deeply engrossed in the perusal of a newspaper, which, he at once informed his visitors, contained a deal "o' vera interaistin" intelligence about current ecclesiastical affairs. It was this, in fact, that accounted for his not having got down to tell the souter and the smith of his fate. The proceedings recorded were of some length, and Sandy had read the speeches made by several popular divines with extraordinary satisfaction and edification, as he now proceeded to set forth. When he had got round to the less lofty but more practical subject of Dawvid Hadden's visit, he narrated the circumstances much as they have been set forth, and seemed rather pleased that he had been able to keep Dawvid tolerably well "in aboot" in the long run.

It was evident that Dawvid Hadden's visit was seriously meant. Sandy Peterkin's three friends felt it to be so; and I am verily persuaded, in full view of the somewhat awkward consequences it involved to him personally, Sandy was the least deeply concerned of the group. When Johnny Gibb had been told of it he stormed fiercely, and talked of employing a lawyer to set at defiance Dawvid Hadden's irregular summons. But of course this passed off, though Johnny retained his determination to give Sir Simon a few lines of his mind, so soon as he should return to the quarter. The settled conviction of the smith, in which the others concurred, was that the ejection of Sandy Peterkin was the joint performance of the Rev. Mr. Sleekaboot, Jonathan Tawse, and Dawvid Hadden; that is to say, their united wisdom had settled it as the judicious and proper thing to be done, with the view of striking terror into the fanatics, it being evident that things were coming to a head; and this once agreed upon, there was no difficulty in obtaining Sir Simon Frissal's authority for carrying it out in the fashion adopted by Dawvid Hadden.

The result was that, when Whitsunday came, the humble school door was locked for good and all. Sandy Peterkin's scholars took their several ways homeward, after a parting advice and much kindly clappin on his side, and not a few tears on theirs; and Sandy Peterkin was once more a gentleman at large in the world, a proposal to engage him as private tutor to his classical pupil, Benjie Birse, having fallen through, not because Sandy would have asked unreasonable terms, but because Mrs. Birse felt there was some force in Miss Birse's objection to admitting a person like him to the parlour society and parlour fare of Clinkstyle, while it would have been at the same time degrading to Benjie to have his tutor herding with the farm servants.

CHAPTER XXVII.

MAINS OF YAWAL AT THE SYNOD.

By the time that Sandy Peterkin had been summoned out of the school, Johnny Gibb was quite prepared for seeing the venerable Kirk of Scotland rent asunder. One thing that had strongly excited his feelings was the meeting of the Aberdeen Synod. Hitherto in the parish of Pyketillim, apart from the gathering and distribution of the offering, the office of the ruling elder, as already stated, had been very much of a sinecure. The Rev. Andrew Sleekaboot rode to the Presbytery meetings with great regularity, but he had not up to this time felt it necessary to have the intelligent laity of the parish represented in the rev. court. Now, however, great questions were at stake, and votes had come to be of importance. So, by the unanimous voice of the Session, Mains of Yawal was appointed ruling elder for Pyketillim. Mains went to a meeting of Presbytery, and sat out the affair in a wearied sort of way, but as the ait seed was just beginning, he loudly grudged the waste of time which his new dignity had entailed on him. The Synod met in the second week of April, and at the kirk next Sunday, Mains had an onset from the minister and the dominie, as to the absolute necessity of his accompanying the former to the meeting of Synod.

"Hoot, I haena been in Aiberdeen this three towmons; an' forbye, I cud be o' nae eese at Kirk maitters," urged Mains.

"Buff an' nonsense," said Jonathan Tawse. "Ye can seerly say 'Ay' or 'No,' whichever the minister bids ye."

"An' it's jist the heid hurry o' the sizzon; I've byous ill winnin awa'. Fegs, an' I hed kent, I sud 'a latt'n some ither ane be rowlin' el'yer, I can tell ye."

Mains's objections were speedily overborne; and the next point to settle was the mode of transit to Aberdeen. As the newspapers had just announced, the Aberdeenshire Canal was "again open for navigation," after some temporary stoppage, and Mains was decidedly favourable to going by the "swift gig boat," as the cheapest means of conveyance. So next day he had his old-fashioned gig a-yoke to convey himself and the minister to the "Canal Head," in time for the leaving of the boat for Aberdeen; one of Mains's lads had been sent on an hour before on foot to bring back the gig. Rev. Andrew Sleekaboot, as became his dignity, took his passage in the cabin of the "flyboat;" but this course his ruling elder resolutely declined to follow. He could save a shilling by going in the steerage, and why should he not do so? Then, as was his wont, the minister would put up at that well-reputed hostelry, the Lemon Tree. Mains demurred somewhat at the idea of going thither, being convinced that they might be accommodated at some stabler's at less cost. But, as his knowledge of "the City" had got rusted, he was unable to specify the particular inn where he would desire to take his ease, and, under a sort of protest, he agreed at last to go with the minister, provided Mr. Sleekaboot would undertake to devote part of next morning to assisting him in looking up certain shops where he wanted to make safe purchases, including that of Coutts, the cutler, in Gallowgate, who, as Mains believed, was unequalled in the production of a reliable pocket gullie.

The great question in which the services of Mains of Yawal and his lay brethren were called into requisition at the Synod was, whether the ministers of *quoad sacra* churches should be allowed to sit as members of the rev. court. There was long debate on the point, during which a well-known leader declared that he objected to the

General Assembly admitting the *quoad sacra* brethren to sit in the church courts, " not only on civil, but on religious grounds likewise;" and another less prominent member, no doubt feeling acutely where the shoe pinched him, observed that protesting against their admission " had cost him many a shilling." When the grand division was taken, it carried by 101 votes to 55, that the *quoad sacra* brethren should not be recognised as members of the Synod; whereat, amid no little noise and excitement, the whole evangelical party left the Synod House, viz. the West Kirk, and thereafter met in Melville Church. Of this sweeping majority, close upon one-half were elders, the Moderate party having succeeded in rallying a force of these zealous gentlemen from the country of rather more than double the number of elders who came up to vote for their opponents. As a very natural result, Mains of Yawal returned from the Synod somewhat elated at the part he had played. The ait seed had gone on favourably in his absence; he had furnished himself with a trusty Coutts' gullie, had hunted up, in inconceivable places, sundry remarkable bargains, including fully half a hundredweight of iron goods, consisting chiefly of a parcel of second-hand sells and thrammels, one or two back chynes, and similar chain work, got at a mere wanworth; all of which he brought with him by way of luggage. Above all, he had done his duty by Church and State, and for once had seen his name printed in the newspapers.

Mains had his weak points like other people; and though the least like it, of all men, there was not altogether wanting a slight touch of vanity in his composition. He had, some little time after his return, related his experiences of this his first grand ecclesiastical campaign to Braeside and Dawvid Hadden, and by both had been eulogised for his unflinching faithfulness, in as high terms as their respective natures allowed, Braeside remarking, " Goshie, man!" while Dawvid Hadden, with a proper allusion to his own recent doings, observed, " Weel, it's jist as I've aye said. Fowk 't's in a public an' 'sponsible wye maun tak' the lead an' ack o' their nain heids, but ithers canna be on-taen pairt accordin' to their capacity—ye sud be prood o' bein' alloo't to vote, Mains. I sanna foryet to mak' mention o' 't fan I vreet to Sir Simon." And fortified by all this, Mains felt that a man who had buckled on his armour and gone forth at the call of duty amid the gathered hosts, could afford to be aggressive in some degree against disaffected stragglers. It was with some dim notion of this sort that, when he was next down at the smiddy, he fell on to the smith with—

"Nyod, aw b'lieve we sortit yer Nons at the Seenit."

"Maybe that," said the smith, with great gravity. "An' fat did ye wi' them syne? Fowk canna believe a' 't they hear; far less a' 't they see i' the newspapers. But fan ye hed a han' in 't yersel', ye 'll be able to tell 's a' aboot it."

"Ou weel, it was jist to keep oot that *quod sacera* min-aisters—they 've nae bizzness there."

"Oh, aw thocht it wus the non-intrusionists 't ye wus settin' doon."

"Weel, an' arena they the vera warst kin' o' them?"

"Na, Mains; some o' them 's as gweed ' constitutional ' kirk men as yersel'."

"Hoot, dinna ye try to gar me believe that. Foo wud they be pitten oot, than? An' they *war* pitten oot, an' a bonny din yon Aiberdeen Nons made cryin' a' kin' o' orra jaw i' the vera kirk; stan'in' up o' the seats, an' aiven brakin' some o' the timmer wark."

"Ay, man, it 's a sairious case it 's like. But I was taul' that the day aifter ye had fleggit them awa', ane o' the Seenit inform't the meetin' that he hed that nicht offer't up his 'sincere prayers' for the misguidit fowk. Nae doot ye 've a' been as min'fu' at yer private devotions."

The smith spoke this very deliberately, and when he paused, Mains merely said, "Ou, ay, they heeld a prayer fan they met, an' the blessin' ere they brak up."

"Jist that; an' though we canna hae Seenits sittin' aye, fowk 't 's been there 'll be able to gi'e 's a word in sizzon as weel 's the benefit o' their prayers, gin we be lickly to gae owre the bows."

Mains did not altogether relish this train of remark, and

would not unwillingly have allowed kirk matters to drop again. But unhappily for him, Johnny Gibb entered the smiddy at that moment. It was not necessary for the smith to apply his match to the tinder in Johnny's breast; and Mains himself seemed to have an uncomfortable dread of an explosion. He tried, not very skilfully or successfully, to be cheery, and to lead a conversation on other subjects. The smith simply did not back him, and Johnny Gibb was something very like snappish. At last he put to Mains the rather unceremonious interrogation—

"Hae ye repentit o' that oonrichteous vote yet? Or is your conscience as sear't as though the smith hed scaum't it wi' that reid-het sock plate?"

"Hoot, Gushets, ye tak' a'thing owre sair in eernest," replied Mains, who was disposed rather to be amicable than the reverse.

"Owre muckle in eernest!" exclaimed Johnny, "owre muckle in eernest! An' you gyaun an' makin' a teel o' yersel' to sair the purposes o' a set o' carnal, wor'dly-minet rascals; gi'ein' your vote at the biddin' o' a peer seecophant, to deprive ten times better men nor him or the like o' him o' the preevileges that belang to them, gin there be ony trowth i' the Word o' Gweed, or ony vailue i' the conten'in's o' oor forefaders."

"Ou weel, it wunna hairm nae ane i' this pairt o' the kwintra, at ony rate," said Mains, with hardly an attempt to defend his position.

"Dinna tell me, min. It's accurs't, reet an' brainch. There's yersel', 't kens nae mair aboot the prenciples o' the struggle nor that turkis i' the smith's sheein box, gyaun awa' to Aiberdeen like a wull chucken, an' preten'in' to tak' pairt in decidin' the question, fan ye 're jist han'in' yersel' owre, sowl an' body, to dee mischief. That's the tae pairt o' 't; an' we see the tither fan that vicious, ill-gatet ablich, Hadden, mak's 'imsel' the willin' enstrument to cairry oot the tyranny o' yer kirk pawtrons an' moderate minaisters."

Mains had got very hot in the face and even angry

by the time Johnny had finished this extremely violent speech. He did not give any formal reply, however, but in a rather loud tone declared that he "wudna stan' that fae nae man."

"Stan''t or no's ye like, it's the trowth," said Johnny Gibb, as he turned away to direct the smith about some bit of work.

After this passage, the Kirk question was allowed to rest for the time being. But from that date onward Mains of Yawal entertained a pretty distinct grudge against his neighbour Gushetneuk.

A month thereafter the Disruption had occurred, and Johnny Gibb had, at no little expenditure of energy, got arrangements made for a Free Kirk service in his barn to be kept up, if not regularly, as frequently as "supply" could be obtained.

CHAPTER XXVIII.

THE FREE KIRK OF PYKETILLIM.

It was not Johnny Gibb's intention to be a Disruption leader, yet he had become so *de facto*. The small body of Pyketillim non-intrusionists not merely conceded that position to him, but without him it may be doubted whether they would have gathered into any compacted form at all. To say that he felt his leadership to be an onerous burden would not be true, because Johnny did not feel it in one way or another; did not indeed know that he was leader. When he prepared his barn as a place of meeting, when he travelled on foot six or seven weary miles to a Presbytery of the "Free Presbyterian Church of Scotland," to negotiate for a supply of preachers, and, to promote that, boldly undertook to raise a certain sum in contributions—though Johnny in all this was carrying out a work which very likely no one else among his friends could or would have carried out, he was simply doing what seemed to lie naturally to his hand to do. Of course Johnny had all the time the firmest possible conviction that he was doing what was right, while, perhaps, his patience was not very ample with those who had less decided opinions than his own. And I daresay it would have tended greatly to the comfort of Peter Birse senior if he could have been inspired with a tithe of Johnny's belief in, and fervency for, the "cause." Peter had, perforce, been riven away from the auld kirk; and, as he accompanied Mrs. Birse and family, Sabbath after

Sabbath, to "the conventicle," as Jonathan Tawse wittily called it, at Gushetneuk, many a wistful glance did he cast in the direction of the kirk road, along which the forms of his old familiar friends were to be seen wending in the distance. As a last despairing effort, Peter had pleaded—

"Keep 's, 'oman, it wud be a byous thing to brak' aff fae the hoose o' Gweed freely—mithna I gae up bye files?"

"To gae yer leen, no?"

"Weel, it wudna leuk sae glaurin like, ye ken."

"An' muckle better ye wud be o' that; it 'll be lang ere ye hear the Gospel there," said Mrs. Birse.

"Weel, but ye ken Hairry, 't was sic a han', 's been gyaun maist pairt sin' there was word o' Sir Seemon comin' hame."

"Humph, Hairry! He 's some mark, or than no. An' ye wud lat Dawvid Hadden fley *you* back to the hoose o' bondage neist?"

"Ou, it's nae him; but ye ken Hairry Muggart gaed a hantle forder a-len'th nor ever I did aboot that kirk wark."

"Ah, weel, ae turnkwite's aneuch," said Mrs. Birse, scornfully.

Peter's statement was mainly correct in point of fact. It was true that Hairry Muggart, in a sore strait how to carry out his convictions, and at the same time avoid calling down on his head the wrath of Sir Simon Frissal, had come to the conclusion that the Disruption was rather a hasty and ill-considered step. His principles? Oh yes, they were as staunchly held by as ever—so Hairry loudly averred—but why not keep within the walls of the national Zion, and at same time stoutly assail the citadel of Erastianism?—it would be gained "come time." So said Hairry: and I am not sure whether a similar proposal was not also mooted in much higher quarters, at the last meeting of the "Convocation," by some who have since laid claim to being distinctively the true representatives of Free Church principles. Besides, Hairry was an adept in theology, and those fledgling parsons of Johnny Gibb's, while he was pleased to hear the lads at a chance time doing their best, were hardly prepared to supply the strong meat that he desiderated. Accordingly, Hairry left it to be understood that he, in his own person, was a sort of concrete embodiment of the establishment principle combined with the theory of independent spiritual jurisdiction. So he generally countenanced the Rev. Andrew Sleekaboot at the delivery of his hebdomadal discourse, and then, in an unofficial way, would step quietly down to Gushetneuk to hear a sermon preached in the barn at such irregular hour as might happen, week-day or Sunday.

Johnny Gibb's other friends stuck together wonderfully; and thus it came to pass that after a summer of preaching in the barn, Johnny took it in his head that a permanent place of worship must be had. It was autumn; Sir Simon was now at home, and wherefore should he not be called upon to give a site? It was argued, in reply, that the man who had sanctioned the turning out of their teacher, because he was, in his estimation, a schismatic, was not in the least likely, in this practical way, to promote the establishment of a congregation of schismatics. "He ocht to be taul's duty at ony rate; an' lat *oor* consciences be clear't," said Johnny Gibb, and the sentiment was re-echoed by none more warmly than by the gudge, and Sandy Peterkin, whose season's labour, in default of anything in the pedagogue way, had consisted chiefly in hoeing turnips at Gushetneuk, and officiating as raker during harvest.

So Johnny Gibb and the souter were deputed to wait upon Sir Simon. This they did without loss of time, and were received by the stately baronet in his library, with great dignity.

"We're here, Sir Seemon, to see gin we can get a bit seet ony gate."

"A what, John?" asked Sir Simon, severely.

"A reed or twa o' grun to be a stance for a place o' worship," answered Johnny.

"John Gibb, let me tell you, once for all, that the course you have been following for some time past has my strongest disapprobation. I understand, on credible information, that you have been a ringleader in this most mischievous and schismatical movement———"

"It's been that craetur, Dawvid Hadden, 't's taul ye that, Sir Seemon. Only that's nedder here nor there."

"I'll allow no interruptions, sir! Disturbing the peace and good order of a quiet, well-conducted parish, by bringing a set of fanatics into it, to delude ignorant people."

"We've been deein fat we cud to get them taucht, Sir Seemon, baith in beuk leernin an' the prenciples o' the Gospel."

"You teach them!"

"Na, na; dinna tak' me up till I fa,' Sir Seemon," said Johnny, who was now fighting his way to a broader issue than he had at first meant to raise. "But we hed set up a gweed skweel; a thing that there was muckle need for, as a' the pairis' kens; though maybe naebody's been kin' aneuch to tell ye that; an' that aisp never haltit wi' 's ill win' an' 's clypes, till he gat the man turn't oot that was o' mair eese ten times owre nor the pairis' dominie ever was—speer at ony ane 't ye like."

"I cannot argue with you, sir, about the management of my property," said Sir Simon.

"Weel, weel; it's but richt 't ye sud ken the haill heids an' particulars for ance, fan we're at it. An' aw 'm thinkin' ye're nae lickly to get owre correct news fae them 't ye lippen maist till here."

"I suppose your business with me is at an end?" said Sir Simon, with dignity, rising as if to show his visitors, who had been standing in the library floor all the while, out.

"Deed, it doesna leuk like bein' weel begun, Sir Seemon," answered Johnny Gibb, in no way abashed. "We've gotten nae answer, mair or less."

"Answer to what, sir?"

"We made a ceevil request, Sir Seemon, for a stance at ony convainient spot to big a bit kirk upon."

"Build a church? What do you mean, sir? Do you suppose that I'll allow people following fanatical and divisive courses to erect a meeting-place within the parish?

I would as soon forfeit my allegiance to Her Majesty the Queen."

"Ou weel," answered Johnny Gibb, "there's aye been persecutors o' the trowth fae the days o' Herod an' afore 't. But it winna be pitten doon wi' you nor nae ither ane, ye needna think it, Sir Seemon. A good day."

And so Johnny and the souter—who had found no opportunity to open his lips during the interview—made their obeisance, which called forth no response whatever from Sir Simon Frissal, and withdrew.

The deputation had thus no favourable report to give; and it would have been a hopeless case with the Pyketillim non-intrusionists had it not so happened that at the very extreme corner of the parish there was a bit of land of no very great extent, but on which there were a few houses, that belonged to a laird of more plebeian extraction than Sir Simon, and who lived at some distance. The plebeian laird had at one time made advances to Sir Simon, and been snubbed for his pains. He therefore bore the baronet no great goodwill; and on learning the position of affairs, was not sorry to find that, by ceding to the Free Church folks a little bit of barren ground with some old buildings upon it, he could have the opportunity of materially annoying Sir Simon Frissal. It was not that he loved the Free Kirk more, but that he loved Sir Simon less, and therefore he gave the site on reasonable enough terms. Upon this very inconvenient spot, which was nearly two miles distant from Gushetneuk, it was resolved to build. Next spring the building was set about, the goodman of Gushetneuk devoting a deal of time and trouble to the completion of the kirk, the design of which was a good deal less elaborate and costly than has become usual since. The incidents of the kirk building were very much of the kind common at the time.

Sir Simon Frissal, the lord of the Manor, had again left the locality before it was known that a site had been got, and Dawvid Hadden naturally felt the responsibility that lay upon him of looking after the ongoings of the Nons. In the plenitude of his good nature, Braeside, though an elder of the national kirk, had gone to Gushetneuk, and offered to give a yokin of his horses and carts to assist in the heavy business of driving material: "For," said Braeside, "the fowk's been aye richt gweed neebours." And the offer had been accepted with great frankness by Johnny Gibb, who added, "I wudna won'er to see you in oor kirk yet, man," at which Braeside shrugged his shoulders and leuch. No sooner had Braeside's friendly deed become public, than Dawvid Hadden, rousing himself to a sense of duty in the matter, communicated with Mains of Yawal. Mains, who, from about the date of the Synod, had, as already mentioned, remained in a state of considerable sourness towards his Free Kirk neighbours, agreed that the act was extremely unprincipled on the part of Braeside, and readily undertook to speak about it quietly to his brother elder, Jonathan Tawse, who, he had no doubt, would "sort" Braeside in proper style for what he had been about. But the greatest explosion on Dawvid's part occurred when he discovered that Johnny Gibb's carting force was actually employed driving sand for the masons from a heap of that material, the accumulation of spates in the march burn between Sir Simon's property and that of the laird aforesaid. He now boldly went and ordered them to stop. It was Tam Meerison, who still remained Clinkstyle's foreman, who was loading his carts at the time; and Tam said—

"Na, sang aw, Dawvid. As lang's I've Gushetneuk's orders to full san', it's nae you 't'll stop me, nor a' the grunoffishers i' the kingdom."

It was in vain that Dawvid vapoured about an "enterdick." Tam said he might get a "dizzen o' enterdicks," if his taste lay that way, but he would take his loads of sand in the meantime. The result was that Dawvid at once wrote Sir Simon, and, as Jock Will, from his public position, was able to say, put on the outside of his letter the word "Hast!" Jock was observant, and could put this and that together pretty shrewdly, and his conclusion by-and-by was that the answer Dawvid received from Sir Simon was something in the nature of telling him to mind his own business, and not be perpetually meddling with what did not lie in his way. At any rate, nothing more was heard of Dawvid's interdict, and the new kirk was finished and occupied in due course, as will be noticed in its proper place.

CHAPTER XXIX.

A CHANGE OF TIME.

A PERIOD of three years had elapsed without bringing any very material alteration in the general aspect of affairs, although Pyketillim had seen one or two changes in its peaceful community. Our old acquaintance, Andrew Langchafts, had disappeared from the locality. The truth was that Andrew had not found the business of merchan' at the Kirktown altogether such a lucrative one as he had at one time anticipated it might be. Probably the people of the place were too staid and sober to appreciate the enlightened commercial principles on which his business was conducted, or to avail themselves sufficiently of the resources of his "entrepôt," though they had been in the habit, some of them, besides Mrs. Birse, of setting on somewhat resolutely on the leading articles which Andrew offered at a manifest "sacrifice." The misfortune was that he never succeeded in leading them far in that department of superior soft goods which he had endeavoured to cultivate. The primitive character of their wants, as well as their practical and economic habits, forbade it. And so this department came in course to be more replete than fashionable. Jock Will, too, who had reached the status of a fully matriculated shopman, had left Andrew, to push his way farther south, which was a great blow to the merchan', seeing Jock had acquired an aptitude for business considerably greater than his own. In short, Andrew Langchafts, finding that things did not meet his expectations, had been gradually tending to greater slovenliness in his habits. He took a deal of snuff, and, it was said, a little whisky sometimes, though nobody ever saw Andrew drunk; and he was apt to let the shop run out of this or the other commodity. Mrs. Birse, with her wonted sagacity, had a clear comprehension of the situation, and in a quiet communing with Miss Eliza Birse she expressed herself thus:—

"Ah, weel, they may say fat they like; but I'se warran' that loon Wull hed ta'en 's nain o' the peer stock afore he leeft 'im."

"Mamma! Fat makes ye think that?" asked Miss Birse.

"Speer at Widow Wull fat wye *she* paid for that braw French merino 't she 's been skyrin in this towmon noo; an' a velvet bonnet—she wud need it!"

"But he was shopman, an' would get them at prime cost."

"Weel, weel, I 'm seer he 's weel oot o' the road at ony rate; for that saft breet, Peter, wud 'a never made it oot wi' Mary Howie as lang 's he was i' the gate wi' 's sleekit tongue."

"Oh, mamma, don't be always speakin' of Peter in that manner."

"Lat that gang than. At ony rate, Meg Raffan taul me nae langer syne nor the nicht afore the streen that An'ro Langchafts was jist at the gae-lattin, and wud lickly need to gi'e up the chop a'thegither ere lang. Noo, ye ken, he has a hantle o' rael gweed claith upo' yon back skelfs; an' I 'se warran' gin a body war to gae in wi' a poun' note or twa i' their han' he sudna be that mealy mou't about the best that 's yon'er, gin he gat the offer o' siller."

"But fat wud be the use o' buyin' pieces o' cloth?"

"Ou, ye ken, yer breeders 's never oot o' the need o' new claes. There 's Benjie, noo that he 's livin' i' the toon, leernin a genteel buzness, maun hae a spare stan' or twa; an' forbye I 've been thinkin' 't that gray fer-nothing o' yer fader's, that the tailor docket the tails o' the ither year, 's

o

jist growin' some aul' fashion't, aiven for him; ye see **genteel fowk** notices the like o' that. Awat it's been **a** richt thrifty coat, for it was bocht the vera winter that Benjie was spean't; and though there's little eese o' a gweed thing for the like o' him **it's** jist eenoo 't fowk 's lickly **to** get a rug o' something that wud answer the purpose."

There is no reason to doubt that Mrs. Birse had at any rate attempted **to carry out** the proposal here outlined. But what took her, **as well as** sundry others **of the** people of Pyketillim by surprise, **was to** learn in a **few months** that Andrew Langchafts **had come to terms for his** whole stock-in-trade and the **goodwill** of his business, **the purchaser being none** other **than his old** apprentice, Jock **Will. And Jock,** something **smartened in** manner since he left **the** locality, but still retaining his undemonstrative aspect, **and** his quiet, soft chuckle as of old, was speedily settled **as** the merchan' of **the** Kirktown. How it was, nobody could have **told probably,** but from the day Jock Will commenced business and Andrew Langchafts retired, the shop had more **of the** aspect of business about it; and very soon the public **were** compelled to recognise in Jock, who **had** "flitted" **his** mother to the Kirktown as the head **of his** domestic **establishment,** a capable, obliging, **and thriving business man.**

At Gushetneuk, **too, some** changes **had taken** place. Willy M'Aul had acted **as Johnny** Gibb's principal servant for several years, and **then, as** Johnny averred, he had got to the stage that he "**wud nedder** haud nor bin' wi' tryin' new protticks," in the way **of farming** and farm implements.

"Ou, weel, **man,** an' foo **sudna he get an** iron pleuch as weel 's anither?" asked Mrs. Gibb.

"A timmer ane's sair't me for therty **year an' mair;** an' Hairry Muggart's as gweed a pleuch-vricht 's there is i' the kwintra side," replied Johnny.

"Ou ay, but it's the fashion, ye ken; an' Hairry an' you tee 's grown **some aul'** style, maybe."

"Weel, weel; **I'll** be naething **but deav't** aboot it," said Johnny; "**you an'** the lassie's **jist as ill 's he is.** It's

a keerious thing that ye sud baith tak' 's side to argue me oot o' 't."

This meant that Johnny had conceded the iron plough, just as he had been induced to concede other things under the same combined influence. But while Johnny would not yield a point in this way without something very like a grumble, he was secretly not ill-pleased to witness the spirit of enterprise manifested by his servant, who really conducted things very much according to his own mind. In due course, however, Willy M'Aul announced his intention of seeking enlarged experience in husbandry by obtaining an engagement with a leading farmer in another locality.

"An' fa 'll I get i' yer place, laddie?" asked Johnny Gibb.

"Ou, Tam, maybe?" said Willy M'Aul, tentatively.

"Tam Meerison, ye mean—wud he be willin' to come, noo?"

"Willin'! jist gi'e 'im the chance, an' ye 'll see."

"Weel, we've seen Tam saucy aneuch aboot bidin' here ere noo."

"Oh ay, but Tam's turn't owre anither leaf sin' him an' me sleepit i' the aul' chaumerie thegither, an' Jinse aboot the toon."

"Faur is he?" asked Johnny.

"Dargin, an' livin' in a bit hoosie near the fit o' the hill I 'll speak aboot it till 'im gin ye like."

Tam Meerison and Jinse, his wife, were liftit in no ordinary degree, at the prospect of Tam getting back to Gushetneuk, for which they were indebted to Tam's old tormentor. And thus the matter had been settled. Willy M'Aul had left on amicable terms to push his way in life, and his place had been supplied by Tam Meerison, who was now the father of a family of three. Tam was a really affectionate husband, and esteemed Jinse just as highly as the day she became his wife. Therefore it seemed to him to be in a measure Paradise regained, when he had the kind of work day by day which he liked and was fully competent to do, and when Johny Gibb not merely did not grudge his going once a week to see his family, but made Jinse Deans and her offspring heartily welcome to spend a day at Gushetneuk at all times when they chose to do so.

It came about after this that a certain portion of the tacks on Sir Simon Frissal's property ran out; and amongst these was the farm at Gushetneuk. Conjecture, therefore, was naturally rife on the subject of Johnny Gibb's haudin'. Some wondered whether Johnny Gibb would wish to retake it, some whether Johnny, in that case, would have the hardihood, after what had come and gone, to moot the subject to Sir Simon. At any rate, it did not seem likely that Sir Simon would have much difficulty, in the circumstances, in deciding how to deal with such a troublesome character.

CHAPTER XXX.

MEG RAFFAN ENTERTAINS DAWVID HADDEN.

To say that Mrs. Peter Birse was a careful and far-seeing matron is perhaps hardly necessary at this stage of affairs. Her capacity for management was felt to some extent in connection with the Free Kirk congregation of Pyketillim, for had she not once and again got the dog-cart sent from Clinkstyle to bring forward the preacher when they had only chance "supply;" had not certain of the supplies obtained been privileged to pass a night or more under her roof; and now that the congregation had the stated services of a promising and well-favoured young probationer, the Rev. Nathaniel MacCassock, was not Miss Birse, with the concurrence of her sagacious mother, the first to come forward and give her aid as a zealous lady collector? Mrs. Birse made much of Mr. MacCassock, the probationer, and failed not, as she felt moved thereto, to remind the people that they were highly privileged in having amongst them a man of such gifts. But it was in the more private or domestic phase of her life that Mrs. Birse's talent for diplomacy was best seen. It is known to the attentive reader, that she had some years ago contemplated a very judicious arrangement for the establishment in life of her eldest son, Peter, and, as subsidiary to that, the virtual retirement from active life of herself and her husband. The plan involved, too, the retirement of Johnny Gibb from his possession at Gushetneuk. And now that Johnny's lease was about to expire, the time to carry out the scheme was at hand.

So thought the goodwife of Clinkstyle, and she considered it right to take measures accordingly.

A little before the Lammas rent time, Meg Raffan had once again the pleasure of drinking a quiet cup of tea with Mrs. Birse, and on the evening of the day when the rents were intimated as payable, Dawvid Hadden, as he passed on his way homeward, found Meg's hospitality so cordial and pressing that, before he well knew what he was about, he occupied the rather unwonted position of guest to the henwife, sitting in the arm-chair in the farthest ben corner of her house, while Meg busied herself in ministering to his physical comfort.

"Yer health aw wuss, Dawvid," said Meg, when she had emptied a bottle of reaming home-brewed ale into a couple of tumblers, whereof she lifted one in her hand, having set the other handy for Dawvid Hadden; "aw 'm richt glaid to see ye. I'm seer ye hinna faul't yer fit i' my hoose this towmon," continued the henwife.

"Weel, it's but seldom that I gae ony gate cep faur buzness tak's me. Yer vera good health, Mrs. Raffan, an' luck to the fools. N-ay!" quoth Dawvid, after a goodly pull at the ale; "that's worth ca'in' ale—that gars a body's lugs crack."

"Weel, ye see, I can nedder dee wi' a jilp o' treacle bree, nor yet wi' that brewery stuff that some fowk mak's eese o'. There's naething like a starn gweed maut, maskit i' yer nain bowie, an' a bunchie o' wormit to gi'e 't a bit grip—tak' oot yer drap noo. Aw'm seer ye maun be thristy as weel's tir't toitin aboot amo' that rent fowk a' day. Ye raelly wud need a bit shalt to cairry you no."

"It's nae little traivel that tak's a body owre the grun, I 'se asseer ye," said Dawvid. "I've nae fyouer nor twaan'-foorty entimations to gi'e ilka time."

"Eh, ay; that's weel min'et," replied the henwife, "an' foo mony o' yer tacks rins oot at this turn?"

"Lat me see—a'thegither there's only aboot half-a-dizzen, encloodin' Hairry Muggart's craft an' the smith's an' souter's."

" Dear me, aw thocht the crafts hedna tacks, but jist gaed on superannuat like ? "

" Ay, but that's oon'er nae lethal obligation," answered Dawvid, drily.

" An' fat 'll ye be deein wi' the bodie Gibb's placie at Gushetneuk ? " pursued Meg. " It's oot, aw b'lieve."

" Weel, I hinna jist leuket at the maitter vera particular yet, I've hed so muckle on han'. But an the crap war aff o' the grun, I 'll need 'a be at the road wi' the chyne to mizzour aff some o' that bits o' placies, an' lat Sir Simon ken fat to dee."

" It's sic a noughty little bit haudin'. Sudna ye jist pit it tee to the like o' Clinkstyle, an' mak' a richt fairm at ance ? "

" Weel, ov coorse there 'll *be* a cheenge at it at ony rate —but there's a fyou year o' Clinkstyle to rin yet ; an' fat eese wud Peter Birse hae for mair grun ? The man's lang past's best."

" Keep me, Dawvid, ye 're foryettin that he has twa strappin' lads o' sins at hame."

" Ou, weel, lat them leuk oot some ither gate. To tell the trowth, Meg, though I ees't to think Peter Birse a saft, weel-dispos't breet—an' wud 'a been owre bye to hae a newse wi' 'im ilka ither gloamin—that wife o' his has sic a swye owre 'im an' 's so contermin't, that I hinna been naar the place for years, cep fan my buzness tyeuk me."

" Na, Dawvid, to hear ye say 't ! " exclaimed Meg Raffan, shaking her head with much solemnity. " That's the wye that ill-will begins. Dear me; didna I jist hear her the tither nicht oot o' 'er nain mou' speakin' about you, and remorsin sair that they sud never see ye owre bye. ' Ay,' says she, ' he's a richt able creatur, Maister Hadden, an' a richt humoursome. There's fyou o' yer beuk-leern't fowk like him,' says she. An' fa's a better jeedge, Dawvid, nor Mrs. Birse—ye winna say that black's the fite o' *her* e'e."

" Ou weel," said Dawvid, whose vanity was visibly flattered, " I never hed nae ill-wull at the 'oman. But ye ken foo they gaed on aboot that non-intrusion—— "

"Hoot, Dawvid, fowk sudna keep up um'rage. 'Them that buys beef buys banes,' as the aul' by-word says."

"Ou ay; but I'm perfeckly seer Sir Simon 'll gi'e nae fawvour to nane o' that Free Kirk fowk. Ye ken foo he order't that creatur Peterkin to be turn't aff, 't 's been gaen aboot like a supplicant sin' syne; an' there's severals 'll hae to gae yet; lat me tell ye that; or than my name's nae Hadden."

"Hear ye me, Dawvid Hadden," said the henwife, with the air of one who has something important to communicate, and drawing a little nearer as she spoke. "Ye maunna lat licht that I taul ye. But it's true that ye say that Peter Birse's growin' an aul' fail't stock. Noo, Mrs. Birse mintit to me as muckle 's that they sud be thinkin' o gi'en owre the place to the aul'est sin, Peter—yon stoot chap, wi' the fite fuskers—an' themsel's gyaun to some lesser wye o' deein, or a genteel hoose wi' a bit craft, for easedom i' their aul' age. 'Awat, fat needs fowk forfecht themsel's fan they hae plenty?' says she. An' for that maitter, the sin's nae a Free Kirker ava."

"Ou nae!" exclaimed Dawvid, incredulously.

"Na, weel-a-wat no. He's never been a commeenicant at nae kirk, though the Miss is a gryte Non, an' 's said to be weel on wi' that fair-hair't chappie, MacCassock, that preaches to them."

"Ou yea; a bonny bargain the like o' 'im wud be. Better till 'er tak' ane o' 'er fader's pleughmen."

"Weel, weel, Dawvid. Ye ken 'an 'oman's wut 's in her foreheid,'" said Meg, jocularly. "Ye maunna be owre hard on 's; we're a' feelish mair or less fan men fowk comes i' the wye;" and Meg bridled up like any other interesting female.

When Dawvid Hadden had left for his home, Meg Raffan thought with herself that she had succeeded in serving the ends of her friend, Mrs. Birse, pretty fairly. She had not, perhaps, convinced Dawvid of the propriety of attaching the possession of Gushetneuk to the farm of Clinkstyle, but she had a shrewd notion that she had brought Dawvid into that state of mind in which he was not unlikely to yield himself to the furtherance of Mrs. Birse's design so soon as that astute matron might have opportunity of more directly operating upon him, and that she would in due season find such opportunity there was not the least reason to doubt.

Meanwhile, Johnny Gibb plodded on in his wonted style, unconscious of the arrangement that was in contemplation to relieve him from the cares of active life as farmer of Gushetneuk.

CHAPTER XXXI.

THE ELECTION OF ELDERS.

WHEN the Free Kirk congregation of Pyketillim had got in a measure consolidated, and had begun to think of calling a pastor, it was considered desirable to form a regular kirk-session, for hitherto they had merely had the services of two elders as occasion required, one of these being the souter, Roderick M'Aul, who had been ordained at a bygone time before he came to Pyketillim, and whose "orders" had quite safely been accepted as "indelible," and another elder belonging to a neighbouring parish, who had turned Free Churchman. So Mr. MacCassock, the probationer, exchanged pulpits for a Sunday with the moderator of the Free Presbytery, who read "the edict" for the election of three new elders and five deacons, and invited the congregation to meet on the succeeding evening to nominate fit and proper persons.

The election was a new experience in the quarter, and it caused a good deal of speculation. Jonathan Tawse declared that it would be a very ludicrous farce if it were not that the thing so nearly bordered on profanity, and his friend, Dr. Drogemweal, swore at this aspect of it even in presence of the Rev. Mr. Sleekaboot, under whose hospitable roof the two friends were at the time. Nevertheless, there was a goodly turn-out of the congregation at the nomination meeting, females as well as males. Mrs. Birse was there, and Peter Birse senior along with her. There had evidently been some pains bestowed on Peter's toilet; he was arrayed in what was understood to be ecclesiastical black, and, in particular, the upper part of his person was uncommonly carefully done up, with a shirt "neck" of formidable dimensions and stiffness threatening his ears, and his hair combed into a sort of clerical flatness very different from its ordinary ragged state. The only other member of the Clinkstyle family present was the second son, Rob Birse, who has simply been mentioned in this history previously. Indeed, it would be difficult to say anything more of Rob than simply mention his existence. He was a lad who was content to vegetate on in an entirely undemonstrative way at Clinkstyle—a sort of new and somewhat duller edition of his father, so far as he had hitherto exhibited any character whatever. He was rarely stirred into anything like mental activity, except it might be through the aggressive action of his mother and sister. It was by their orders that he came to the congregational meeting, grumbling somewhat at the hardship of being obliged to do so.

Mrs. Birse maintained a demonstratively devout attitude during the opening exercises. She and her husband sat in a pew well to the front, and behind them sat Hairry Muggart—who had come up to the meeting in their company—and the mole-catcher.

The Moderator, in opening the business, pointed out the duties required of the elders, and the qualities that fit a man for that office, and then asked the meeting to nominate such as they deemed suitable. Forthwith, the smith rose and nominated Johnny Gibb, then somebody nominated the smith himself, and both the nominations were duly seconded. Then there was a pause; and the Moderator invited further nominations of men of known piety and zeal, and of unblemished life, no matter how poor they might be, or how humble their station. Another pause; and Mrs. Birse sighed with impressive solemnity, and laid her head on one side. Then the mole-catcher started up, and with a preliminary "hem," said—"Maister Moderawtor, there's ane that I think 't we canna pass owre fae eleckin to be an el'yer. He's vera weel kent to a' here present; an' weel-wordy o' siccan a office though he's nae ane that wud pit 'imsel forrit. But my opingan is that he's been aye owre bauch in 's nain beheef." (Here Mrs. Birse kicked Peter, who had been looking very uneasy, in the ribs with her elbow, making him sit upright and show himself.) " But ae wye or ither," pursued the mole-catcher, " though he hasna ta'en muckle direck pairt, he's been a great freen to the cause in this neebourheid." (Mrs. Birse modestly looked to the floor, and shook her head.) " Moderawtor, aw 'm sure I needna mak' a speech, though aw cud dee 't; ye a' ken Maister Peterkin as weel 's me—I beg till propose Maister Alexir Peterkin."

At this announcement Mrs. Birse drew herself up with a severity approaching to violence, and Peter, who had kept watching her movements with the " tail " of his eye, looked more uncomfortable than before. The general audience signified their approbation of the mole-catcher's proposal, and Johnny Gibb starting to his feet said, " I sec-ond the motion."

Then there was another pause; and the Moderator reminded the meeting that though the number of elders absolutely required had now been nominated, yet it was quite open to anybody to propose one or more additional candidates; and he had no doubt there were other members of the congregation well qualified to discharge the duties of the eldership. Upon this, Hairry Muggart, who for some short space back had evidently been meditating a speech, swung himself to his feet by the aid of the pew desk, and said :—
"Maister Moderawtor, I perfeckly agree wi' your opingan that there ocht to be ane or twa owre an' abeen, to wale amon'; or else fat 's the eese o' the prenciples o' spiritooal oondependence, whuch I 've aye mainteen't an' for whuch oor forefaders conten'it? Moderawtor, I beg hereby to exerceese the preevilege wherewith you have inveetit every one present to be a partaker; an' in doin' so I have to bring one oonder the fawvourable attention o' this meetin'; for the vaeluable service render't to this congregation, which

speaks for itsel'; an' also his excellent partner in life." Hairry, who had found it more difficult than he had expected to face his rather unsympathetic audience, and speak, ended abruptly with, "I will add no more at present, but muv that Maister Peter Birse, fairmer at Clinkstyle, be eleckit."

They waited a little, but nobody seconded. But the Moderator said this was not necessary; so the name of Peter Birse was added to the list of elders elect. The next business was to nominate deacons, which was speedily done, the name of Jock Will coming first, and that of the mole-catcher second in order; and in all some seven or eight, chiefly of the younger men, were named. When all this was done, the meeting was brought to a close in the usual way, after the Moderator had conducted another "exercise," in which the souter, who at his request took part, prayed earnestly that He who knew the hearts of all might show them which of these men He had chosen; and that there might be close dealing with conscience on the part of the elders elect, to make sure that the carnal man had no place in moving them toward this spiritual office.

"An' that's yer meetin' no!" exclaimed Mrs. Birse, addressing Hairry Muggart, who had kept as close by her as his ponderous style of locomotion would allow whilst the goodwife flung through the people as they loiteringly dispersed from the door of the place of meeting. "I wud like to ken fat kin' o' a moderawtor he is; or foo they sud 'a pitten him into Maister MacCassock's place. A man that kens nae ane there fae the orraest creatur i' the congregation!"

"Weel," said Hairry, "aw b'lieve they maun hae ane't 's been ordeen't to be moderawtor, accordin' to the rowles o' the Kirk. But he's nae gryte deykn at it, weel-a-wat."

"Humph! deykn at it! It was seerly his duty as a minaister o' the gospel to warn them to leuk oot for fowk o' respectable character, instead o' gaen oot o' 's gate to tell them that they mith eleck ony wil' ranegill, or ca'd aboot ne'er-do-weel, though he hinna three bawbees i' the wardle to bless 'imsel' wi'."

"Nae doot," said Hairry, "nae doot. But ye ken they're nae eleckit yet. Fan the votin' comes that'll turn the guise wi' them, or than I won'er at it. Ye see I hed it weel i' my min' till objeck to Sandy Peterkin, an' request the meetin' to exerceese the veto on 'im at ance. But, as I was sayin', fan ye cam' owre the streen i' the gloamin to see *her*, an spak' aboot it, I hed my nain doots futher or no aw wud be latt'n nominat' Peter—Maister Birse, ye ken. An' it was jist as weel 't the moderawtor didna ken 't aw wasna a regular maimber; but gin I hed latt'n at Sandy, Gushets or the souter wud 'a been seer to hae their horn i' my hip, an' they mith 'a refees't 's a hearin' a'thegither syne, ye see."

"Weel, seerly Gushetneuk mith 'a latt'n aleen there no; fan he hedna the menners to apen 's mou' for 's nearest neebour nor nane belangin' 'im—fowk 't 's lickly to be near conneckit wi' 'imsel'—I kenna fat he hed adee speakin' for ony ane."

"I thocht Gushets unco dry the nicht," replied Hairry.

"An' a bonny smiddy they wud mak' o' 't," continued Mrs. Birse. "Mak' an el'yer o' the like o' Sandy Peterkin, 't 's livin' fae han' to mou' o' the wull o' Providence, an' a deacon o' that peer simple vulgar creatur o' a mole-catcher; it 's really nae fair to Maister MacCassock to bid 'im sit doon wi' the like o' them."

"Weel, no," said Hairry. "The like o' the merchan', Jock Wull, mith dee, but——"

"An' aw wud like to ken fat Jock Wull 's deen to gi'e *him* ony preevilege," exclaimed Mrs. Birse. "Aw 'm seer Gushetneuk kens weel that oor Robbie hed a muckle better richt to be nominat', oot o' regaird for fat 's sister 's deen. Peer thing, mony a sair fit has she traivell't for the gweed o' the Free Kirk, and that 's fowk's thank."

Hairry could only express concurrence in this sentiment. But as he and Mrs. Birse had now reached the point where their roads separated, they pulled up to wait for Peter Birse senior, who had fallen some little way into the rear, he having actually stayed to converse for a minute or two with the mole-catcher and some of his friends. When he came

up, Hairry assumed the jocular vein, and begged to congratulate Peter on his personal appearance in his "stan' o' blacks," so very suitable to the new dignity that awaited him.

"Ah, aw dinna ken, Hairry," said Peter, glancing towards his wife. "The lave 's seer to be eleckit, an' Sandy Peterkin may aiven be pitten on afore me."

"Hoot, Clinkies, that winna bide a hearin', man," said Hairry, confidently.

"Bless me, man, keep yer han's oot o' yer breek pouches; dinna ye see 't yer rivin' that black claith doon the seam? There 's naething would leern ye menners," said Mrs. Birse.

Peter withdrew his hands from the pockets of his ecclesiastical unmentionables accordingly. Then they bade each other good night, and went on their separate ways homewards.

CHAPTER XXXII.

DAWVID HADDEN VISITS AT CLINKSTYLE.

In the autumn of 1846 Dawvid Hadden was laboriously at work on certain parts of the lands of Sir Simon Frissal, with his measuring chain and sundry poles, one of which had a small bit of square board nailed on the top of it. A rough-looking gurk ov a loon carried the end of the chain, and fulfilled Dawvid's orders in running here and there as Dawvid took a sight over the square-headed pole, and then shouted and waved his hand to the loon. This process was what Dawvid called "layin' aff the awcres." The results, it was understood, were all to be laid before Sir Simon; but in what particular shape it might be hazardous to guess, for there is reason to believe that Dawvid could do nothing whatever in the way of making a plan, and though he was great at "castin up" the contents of a piece of land, that operation did not seem of very essential importance in the reletting of the farms, seeing Sir Simon had their various sizes all carefully booked already. However, it was enough that Dawvid deemed the layin aff of consequence.

His operations at this time included, of course, the farm of Gushetneuk, and on the day that Dawvid was expected to be at work there, Mrs. Birse addressed her husband in this wise :—

"Noo, man, ye'll jist mak' an erran' owre bye to the smiddy, an' cast yersel' in Dawvid's road fan he's aboot the heid o' the faul'ies; an' see an' get 'im to come owre edder till 's denner, or than afore he lowse."

"I was jist gyaun awa' to tirr that bit huickie that we wus takin' into the barn to thrash," said Peter, not over anxious to undertake the mission. "Cudnin some o' the boys gae?"

"Peter Birse, will ye dee 's ye 're bidden? A het invitation that wud be to ony ane ackin oon'er yer laird. Sen' a laddie, an' you gyaun aboot the toon the neist thing to han' idle!"

"Weel, gin Dawvid 'll come. But we 're nae needin' the smiddy. I was there the streen. I 'll raither gae owre to Gushets wi' the probang that we hed the tither nicht fan the yalla feeder worriet on a neep. Aw 'se warran' the fowk 'll be needin' 't."

"Geyan lickly gae to Gushets! As muckle 's ye wud gi'e Dawvid to oon'erstan' that we 're as gryte 's creel heids wi' them. Some eese o' seekin' 'im at that rate. Fan will ye leern rumgumption, man?"

Peter did not see it clearly even yet. Only he knew it was needless to maintain further debate. So he went away and searched out a hayfork that had got lamed of one prong, and started for the smiddy. It was only after he had been there and was on his way home again that he found Dawvid Hadden at a point where he could be conveniently approached. Rather to Peter's surprise, Dawvid proved to be affable in a high degree. Mrs. Birse could have given Peter a probable reason for this; but it was not to be expected that Mrs. Birse would feel it in the least necessary to do anything of the sort. Dawvid could not by any "menner o' means" come to Clinkstyle that day; for he had got to finish his layin' aff, and then go home and write Sir Simon; and he even hinted that that might not exhaust the buzness before him; but Peter was authorised to give Mrs. Birse assurance that he would be "athort the morn's gloamin," without fail.

Dawvid Hadden was essentially a man of his word in so far as fulfilment of his engagements was concerned, and accordingly he duly made appearance at Clinkstyle as he had promised. I rather think that Mrs. Birse was not disappointed at his putting the visit off for a day. It gave her leisure to mature things more fully. It was just a fortnight after the meeting for the nomination of elders; the election had taken place in the *interim*, and Peter Birse senior had stood at the bottom of the poll. On this occasion (it was on a Wednesday evening) Peter, who had no clerical character now to maintain, had been instructed to wash his face and shave (which he sometimes did, if anything happened to be going, when the week was only half run), and then to put on his gray journey claes, and step up the loan and meet Dawvid. All this he did, and then he, with due ceremony, conducted the ground-officer round by the "entry" door and into the best parlour. The room in question was finished much in the usual style, the front wall carrying oil portraits of the master and mistress of the house, done at a former date by an itinerating artist, when Peter Birse was assumed to be a sprightly young man, given to sticking his hand into the breast of his black vest, and Mrs. Birse, a blushing beauty, who manipulated a rose in her slender fingers; the other pictorial decorations of the parlour were the framed print of a man who was either Sir William Wallace or Rob Roy, attitudinising with a sword and shield, and the traditional sampler. It was laid out for tea. An enormous old-fashioned urn, which lay under the disadvantage of leaking so badly as to compel its presence there to be purely ornamental, occupied the centre of the table, while the multiplicity of crockery of all sorts surrounding it was enough to bewilder any ordinary mortal. Mrs. Birse was dressed in her black silk, with a collar spreading over her shoulders, and a most formidable black lace cap, perfectly ablaze with branches of "gum-flowers" of very pronounced colours and uncertain botanical character. She met Dawvid Hadden at the half-opened parlour door with a gracious, yet not too familiar, "I howp yer weel the nicht, Maister Hadden. Jist leave yer hat i' the lobby an' step in—alloo me." When Dawvid had stepped in he *was* a little taken aback, and would perhaps have felt slightly embarrassed, as Peter Birse, who had shuffled in at his heels, had stopped his discourse, and seemed to feel the need of walking gingerly till the introduction should be over; but Mrs. Birse came to the rescue.

"My daachter; Maister Hadden, an aul' freen."

Miss Eliza Birse, who had sat stiffly in the corner of the room till that moment, rose, and, with the air of a polished lady, bowed to Dawvid Hadden. "Glad to see you," said Miss Birse.

Dawvid Hadden was not easily put out; but he did not expect all this, so much in advance of what he had been wont to see aforetime at Clinkstyle; and by the time that he had been duly introduced to Miss Birse, and had got seated on the chair placed for him, he almost fancied that his face did manifest a slight tendency toward perspiration. Dawvid had not quite understood that he came there to tea, but tea was ordered in at once. The want of a bell to call the servant was a great defect in the appurtenances of the house at Clinkstyle, against which Miss Birse had repeatedly protested. Mrs. Birse's device in lieu of the bell was to open the parlour door half-way, cough in an incidental sort of tone, and then shut the door with a sharp snap. To "cry ben" was so horribly vulgar that it could not be once thought of.

So the damsel brought the tea in a huge, ancient, china tea-pot. Miss Birse dispensed it with infinite grace, and Mrs. Birse showed no end of attentions to her guest. Even Peter Birse had latterly got to be demonstrative in that way, and urged Dawvid to take several more of the small biscuits, for the reason that "ane o' that's but a bite, man," at the un-gentility of which saying Miss Birse looked shocked; only her father was too pleasantly occupied at the time to observe this very particularly.

When tea was over, Miss Birse, according to arrangement or otherwise, left the party, as she had to go and make some visits.

"Ye see she's jist like yersel' there, Maister Hadden—

though there be a gryte differ atween a man o' lang expairience an' a lassie—for she has aye some bizziness or anider on han'. Oor youngest laddie, Benjie, 's been i' the toon, 's ye 've maybe heard, for several year?"

"I wusna awaar," said Dawvid.

"Ou ay; he 's wi' a Maister Pettiphog, ane o' the heid lawvyers o' Aiberdeen—I 've nae doot ye 'll ken him?"

"Weel, no, aw cud hardly say that—we 're jist speakable acquant."

"Aweel, at ony rate he 's an aul' servan' o' my uncle's that was the lawvyer, and has a braw bizziness o' 's nain noo. An' Benjie 's been wi' 'im for mair nor twa year, leernin the law; an' aw 'm seer aw canna but think that he lippens owre muckle till sic a young creatur—actooally vreetin o' dockiments an' fat they ca' progresses. Fat was that 't he said, man, fan we hed him and Mrs. Pettiphog oot here veesitin for an ouk fernyear? Ou ay, says he, 'Lat ye Maister Benjamin alone; it 's a sharp client that 'll tak' mair nor the worth o' 's siller oot o' him.' Weel, as aw was sayin', Maister Pettiphog hed gotten chairge o' that peer breet An'ro Langchafts' maitters; an' ye wud raelly won'er, Dawvid. An'ro hed len'it oot triffles here an there 't 's nae paid till this day's date."

"Ye dinna mean siller o' 's nain?"

"*So* it wud appear; though a'body thocht vera different. An' fat does Maister Pettiphog dee, but get Benjie to vrite oot here to mak' inquaries."

"Ye see he thocht we mith 'a kent something aboot it," observed Peter Birse.

"Noo dinna ye begin to speak aboot things 't ye ken naething aboot, man," said Mrs. Birse. "Ye see, though we be tellin' Maister Hadden, 't 's sic an aul' freen, a' this, fat 's deein in a lawyer's office mauna be claickit aboot to ilka body. So 'Liza wudna pit aff nae langer, but jist vrote back to Benjie the nicht, an' nae doot we 'll hear mair aboot it."

Dawvid Hadden's curiosity, it must be owned, was not a little aroused by the dose of information so judiciously and skilfully administered by Mrs. Birse, and which seemed to give good promise of something more yet to come. From the point now gained, the conversation flowed on easily and naturally to a discussion of the character and credit of the neighbourhood generally. Johnny Gibb came in for some notice, Mrs. Birse purposely letting fall the remark that Johnny had not treated them altogether in the way they were entitled to expect. "He's jist owre bitter no," said the goodwife, "an' I'm thinkin' that oor nain Patie's nae sae far wrang," added she, with a laugh. "It's a pity that he's nae at hame the nicht; but he's sic a bricht fairmer that he's aye o' the ootleuk for bargains, an' he's awa' at the Hawkha' market, faur he bocht a byous chape coo fernyear, an' half-a-dizzen o' stirks—for he has af'en naar dooble the beasts 't oor boun's 'll keep. Patie's a stainch Aul' Kirk man, ye ken, an' says he till's sister, 'Ah, Lizzie,' says he, 'the Free Kirk may dee for women creaturs, but ye needna think that mony men, at ony rate young chaps, wi' ony spunk i' them, wud thole yer psalmin' lang.' Peer 'Liza tyeuk it unco het, but fient a flee care't Patie."

When Mrs. Birse had repeated these sentiments of her son approvingly, Peter Birse senior brightened up, and showed some disposition to pursue the same line of thought on his own account, but his better half promptly and adroitly turned the conversation, and the rest of the evening was passed chiefly in the narration of examples of the prudence, sagacity, and administrative capability of Peter Birse junior, his father, Peter Birse senior, being freely used in illustration as a sort of foil to set off the young man's merits. At parting, Mrs. Birse ventured to say, "Weel, weel, Maister Hadden; it's a gryte feast to see you for an evenin'; an' ye maun come back shortly an' see Patie, for he's to be at ye to gi'e 'im mair grun noo, fan some o' yer tacks is oot. Him an' you can sattl't atween ye. We sanna enterfere—aul' fowk, ye see, maun gae oot o' the gate o' the young. It's their pairt to be thinkin' aboot ither things."

"Aweel, I'll be thinkin' aboot the new arreengements, an' aw'll lat ye ken fat a''s to be done vera shortly," said Dawvid Hadden.

CHAPTER XXXIII.

THE MERCHANT'S SHOP.

JOCK WILL'S career as merchant in the Kirktown of Pyketillim, although every way creditable to Jock himself as a man of enterprise and business habits, furnished in so far an illustration of the saying that a prophet has no honour in his own country. There were people in Pyketillim who had not been able to make up their minds as to the how and wherefore of Jock's position, and who manifested a disposition to treat him in his mercantile capacity accordingly. They had failed quite in finding out how Jock Will obtained the pecuniary means that had enabled him to become successor to Andrew Langchafts; and it was a natural solace to hint a doubt now and then as to the *bona fides* of particular transactions, or the soundness of the footing on which his business was conducted generally. No matter though Jock was steady, pushing, and obliging to all; what business had *he* to be reticent on what concerned himself, and did not concern other people? And if he would have his own way of it, he must not take it amiss if some of those whose natural curiosity he chose so unfeelingly to baffle should also use his shop simply in the way of a secondary convenience; that when they had a pretty large order they should go to "the Broch" or elsewhere for it, and apply at the Kirktown shop only in a casual way, for any temporary eke that was needed to complete their supplies. And all under the implied belief that Jock's goods were not exactly of the highest character; or else that his prices were open to question. It was somewhat in this way that Mains of Yawal had been affected when taking in his stock of spring seeds. Jock had advertised the neighbourhood of his readiness to supply all these of guaranteed quality at the best prices going, and had solicited early orders to enable him to select his quantities. "Na—na," quoth Mains, "aw 'm nae keerious aboot lippenin muckle to the like o' 'im—Fa kens but he may be at the gae-lattin? We'll maybe get a starn clivver seed to mak' up, gin we rin oot, for convainience; but we 'll get better an' chaeper seed fae ither fowk." And Mains did run out; and he came to Jock Will's shop and not merely insisted on having his deficiency in clover seed supplied, much to Jock's inconvenience, who feared falling short of the quantity that customers of a less suspicious turn had ordered, but threepit hard to induce Jock to let him have it at a halfpenny per pound less than he had paid for his stock elsewhere.

Mrs. Birse, it must be owned, had never been quite at ease on the subject of the inner history of Jock Will's start in business; and the letter from her son Benjie, to which reference has been made, seemed unexpectedly to open the way to light on the subject. She instructed Miss Birse how to frame a reply to her brother, the young lawyer, accordingly; and the epistle addressed to Benjamin took the following shape:—

"DEAR BROTHER—Your welcome letter was duly received, and we are glad to hear that you are quite well. This leaves us all the same at present. Your letter is very interesting, particularly about Andrew Langchafts' money, which he loaned to Dr. Drogemweal, by signing a bill for him, and getting it to pay. Mamma bids you tell Mr. Pettiphog that he is always in a bag of debt, and always promises to pay his debt, and never does it. So there is no use of craving him, she says, except a sheriff-officer do it, and *reest* his horse, which he cannot want, having so long roads to travel. Mamma would like if you can tell us more about anybody that has not paid; and the most particular, to know if Mr. Will got all the shop things on credit, and has paid any of them yet. Mamma thinks he is in debt, because he had no money at the first; and I would like to know as well as her. Don't tell Mr. Pettiphog that we was asking this. But the shop is so nice now, and everbody says that Mr. Will is a good business man.

"Father was not elected an elder, but Mr. Will was the highest among the deacons. Mamma was very angry when father lost; but says he has himself to thank for it. Last Sabbath, Peter and him was both at the parish church. Mamma said he could go, but I was grieved. She thinks we must not offend Sir Simon too much, and it is father's own conscience that will accuse him if he does not do right. But she would not give him a halfpenny to give to the brod, because the Established Kirk has no right to that now, when it is Erastian.

"Just fancy—they elected Sandy Peterkin to be an elder; and him is not doing nothing but living mostly upon charity! Mr. Mac-Cassock *could* not be pleased about it. He is to be called for our minister soon.

"With kind love from all
"Your affectionate sister,
"ELIZA BIRSE.

"P.S.—Write soon, and tell me all the Aberdeen news, and especially if you have got any new acquaintances, and been at any parties."

With this note in her bag, Miss Birse, leaving the "party" at which Dawvid Hadden was guest, had set out to make some calls as collector, and to post the note at Jock Will's shop at Kirktown of Pyketillim.

To the news-gizzened rustic, a lounge about the merchant's shop door of a gloamin, as he purchases his ounce of tobacco, or other needful commodity, is inexpressibly grateful. He can see and hear as much as will furnish topics to keep himself and his cronies newsin for several days. And thus it was that when Miss Birse got to the post-office, she found good part of the available space in Jock Will's shop occupied by customers of the class of farm servants, and amongst them Tam Meerison, Gushetneuk's man and ex-foreman at Clinkstyle. She could have posted the letter at the customary slit in the window, but Miss

Birse chose to take it inside. At the counter was Jock himself, with bland countenance, attending to the more important orders, while the apprentice, dight in an ample white apron, measured out tobacco, whipcord, and siclike. And— could she believe it—at the desk sat Sandy Peterkin, pen in hand, and with a long narrow day-book before him ! Miss Birse tripped through the parting group of rustics, and, with extended arm, gracefully dropped the note from between the tips of her gloved fingers into Mr. Will's hand.

" D' ye do to-night ?" asked Miss Birse, with an engaging smile.

" Vera weel, thank ye: hoo d' ye do ? " answered the merchant, politely.

Then she asked particularly after the welfare of his " mamma ; " and then she seemed at a loss whether she should recognise Sandy Peterkin or not ; but Sandy put an end to the dilemma, thus far, by nodding familiarly to her as he lifted down the merchant's big ledger. He could not speak at the moment, because he held the quill pen with which he had been writing in his lips in a horizontal position. Miss Birse smiled graciously in return to Sandy's nod. Jock Will invited her into his dwelling to see his mother and as the apprentice was adequate to any business now going, he opened the counter gateway, stepped out, and gallantly escorted her from the shop to the house.

" She disna ken you nor me the nicht, Tam," said a red-haired chap with a very freckled face, and an enormously ample sleeved moleskin waistcoat, as soon as Miss Birse and the merchant had gone out.

" Na, na, Archie," answered Tam ; " fat wye cud a leddy ken a Jock Muck like you ?"

" Weel, weel, Tam, you an' me tee kens fat kin' o' gentry bides at Clinkstyle ; an' faur 'll ye get a rocher, coorser breet nor young Peter, 'er breeder ? "

" Sang, ye may say 't," answered Tam. " Div ye min', fan we wus aboot the toon thegither there, twa year syne, oor needin' to fesh 'im hame ae nicht late, that drunk that he didna ken faur he was ?"

"Ou, ay; that was the nicht was 't, 't we fell in wi' 'im stoitin aboot o' the road atween this an' Clinkstyle, plaister't wi' dubs to the vera croon o' 's heid. Weel, man, I thocht aw wud rive my yirnin lauchin at 'im that nicht, fan he begood an' grat an' taul 's aboot that deemie that they said hed the bairn till 'im."

"Weel; it was keerious. He hed aye a terrible notion o' you, Archie; an' leet ye win farrer ben wi' 'im aboot 's lasses nor ony o' the lave o' 's."

"Ou, ay," said our red-haired friend; "ye see the wye 't I was orra man, I wasna never fess't wi' beasts at even; an' cud tak' a roun' amo' the deems ony nicht; an' I ees't to lat 'im gae wi' 's files. Mony a roun' han' did the jauds play 'im—he 's a saft gype—but Peter was jist as redd to gae back 's ever for a' that."

"Noo lads, noo lads, min' ye that 's nae discoorse to yoke till here," interposed Sandy Peterkin, suspending his operations at the ledger for a moment, and trying to look severe.

"Hoot, never ye min', Sandy," answered Archie, "though ye be made a el'yer ye maunna be owre snappus wi' fowk. —Weel, man, he was an awfu' munsie that nicht. We hed to lay 'im doon upon a puckle strae i' the chaum'er for a file, an' skirp water in 's face till he cam' some till 'imsel'."

"Ay, an' d' ye min' foo fear't he was 't we sud tell ony o' the neepours sic a feel 's he hed made o' 'imsel'."

"Weel, it wasna the first time, though he was never freely so ill 's that nicht. But they say he 's gyaun to get your maiden yon'er, and that Gushetneuk 's to be pitten tee to Clinkstyle to mak' a richt fairm to them."

"Aw dinna believe a word o' 't," said Tam, decisively.

"Divnin ye?" asked Archie. "Man, ye wudna ken. She 's a terrible wife yon."

"Ay, she 's a coorse ane," interjected another of the group.

"Coorse!" exclaimed Archie. "That 's a' that ye ken aboot it, min. An' ye hed been wi' 'er, like Tam an' me, ye wudna not till 'a been taul' that there's nae the marrow o' 'er atween this an' Tamintoul, for an unhang't limmer, wi' a' kin' o' greed, an' twa-fac't chaetry."

Sandy Peterkin looked up again with a remonstrating look, but, not heeding this, Archie went on—

"An' yon peer, simple idiot o' a man o' hers; she canna haud fae ill-guidin' an' makin' a feel o' 'im afore fowk's faces, though for that maitter he's far owre gweed for 'er."

"The dother's nae far ahin the mither in some things," said Tam Meerison.

"Ho, there she goes!" said Archie, as he happened to glance outside. "My certie, the merchan' 'll better tak' care o' 'imsel' wi' 'er—Weel, are ye gyaun to be stappin, boys?"

These last words were uttered as Jock Will re-entered the shop. Jock bade his customers good-night very affably as they left, and then proceeded to arrange for closing his place of business.

The reader has not been informed how it came to pass that Sandy Peterkin had come to occupy a position in Jock Will's establishment. It came about very simply in this wise. That Sandy Peterkin was in need of some suitable employment was a fact patent to anybody, and it weighed particularly on the minds of his three friends, the souter, the smith, and Johnny Gibb. Johnny even declared that the idea of a man of Sandy's pairts an' leernin hoeing neeps, or raikin in hairst to him, was degraadin, which Sandy did not in the least seem to feel, but did the work contentedly. They did not, like Job's friends and others, proceed to comfort him in a critical way, but having met and considered his case—"Weel," said the smith, "I canna think o' onything better nor tryin' the merchan' to set him to dee his clarkin; he has owre muckle adee till 'imsel', an' Sandy winna be ill to say till wi' the waages."

"Man, that's the vera thing; aw'm seerly dottl't or I wud 'a thocht o' that ere noo," exclaimed Johnny Gibb.

"He vreets a bonny han'," said the souter.

"Bonny! its like the vera copper-plate," added Johnny Gibb.

Johnny at once undertook to see Jock Will in Sandy Peterkin's interest. Jock, like a sensible man, readily fell in with the proposal of his seniors, and Sandy was forthwith put on trial as clerk, much to his own satisfaction, and with no disappointment to the expectations of his friends.

CHAPTER XXXIV.

DAWVID HADDEN REPORTS TO SIR SIMON.

If Johnny Gibb's farm of Gushetneuk was to be reft from him, and he, Johnny, sent adrift from the lands of Sir Simon Frissal, as an incorrigible disturber of the peace, civil and ecclesiastical, it was very evident that the prospect before him gave Johnny no manner of trouble or anxiety whatever. When Dawvid Hadden, in the plenitude of his power as ground-officer, had deliberately stalked about for a day or two on the possession of Gushetneuk, climbing over fences, and sten'in through turnip and potato drills, or kicking up hillocks among new girse stibbles as he went on layin' aff the awcres, it had seemed to Dawvid a settled matter that the obstinate bodie would feel the necessity of making up to him in a somewhat more deferential spirit than that which had marked their later intercourse about the date of the Disruption. But in this Dawvid was disappointed. Johnny was to be seen jogging leisurely about, snodding up the corn yard, turning out his young stock to pick up the natur' girse by the margins of the now cleared fields, or directing the operations of Tam Meerison and the orra man as they laid on a substantial coat of top-dressing on the old lea that was to be broken up; but he heeded Dawvid just as much and no more than if Dawvid had been some insignificant interloper whom it was not worth while to turn off the land.

"Fat 's that preen-heidit ablich deein there, Tam ?" said

Johnny Gibb, as he saw Dawvid Hadden cross the fence, with his attendant carrying the measuring chain.

"Ou, he 's been at it yesterday an' the day baith, layin' aff the grun," answered Tam Meerison.

"Humph!" quoth Johnny, as he turned away homeward, "a bonny layin' aff, or than no; he mith 'a sav't himsel' that tribble at ony rate."

"The maister has a richt ill-wull at that mannie," said the orra man, when Johnny Gibb had got beyond earshot.

"Ill-wull!" answered Tam Meerison. "Man, he disna think 'im worth haein an ill-wull at: peer win'y smatchet, gyaun aboot preten'in that he's Sir Seemon's awgent. Little to me wud set the dog at 'im: ye wud shortly see foo he wud tak' owre the dyke, chyne an' a' thegither."

Tam did not set on the dog, however, but pursued his labour.

"Nabal vratch," soliloquised Dawvid Hadden within himself. It was not that he had heard the sentiments uttered by Johnny Gibb, for the two were a couple of hundred yards distant from each other at the time that Johnny had spoken; but, as Dawvid fixed his squaring pole, he had allowed the "tail" of one eye to wander toward Johnny in the hope that, in place of going away in contemptuous disregard of his, Dawvid's, presence, he would come towards him, if not in a supplicating, then in a bellicose spirit; and Dawvid flattered himself that he knew the precise attitude which, as a man in authority, it was becoming to assume in either case. Johnny simply turned in the other direction to attend to some trifling concern affecting the temporary convenience of his stirks. "Nabal vratch; hooever, they gae far aboot that disna meet ae day—Fat can he mean cairnin on the tap-dressin' that gate? He winna get the gweed o' that in ae crap, nor twa.—Ou weel, it 'll pit the grun in gweed hert for somebody, ony wye."

In this mood had Dawvid Hadden begun his layin' aff: in this mood he continued it. It has been already narrated how Dawvid paid a friendly visit to Clinkstyle, and what communings took place on that occasion. Thereafter, the ground-officer set about the onerous duty of reporting to Sir Simon Frissal the result of his land-surveying labours. The statement was fully more verbose than lucid; yet Dawvid contrived to make it abundantly apparent what he conceived should be done with the farm of Gushetneuk, at least. Of it Dawvid reported thus :—

"The pleace is two small and John Gibb has not led it owt according to plan which is allways very disrespectfull to supperiors and obstinat small farms is bad for increasing pauppers under the new poor law i have been applied too by severals but told them the new plan had not been decided which it was likely you would not need no new tenant when you could get quiet well behaved people among the old tenants the supperficies off the new farm is 173 acres arrable encloodin the commodation road and the smal belt which is not more nor an acre and a half. the fire howse at Gushetneuk would stand and with improvements which they is willing to do at their own coast would be shootable for Mr. and Mrs. Birse. there sun which is also called Peter is to be the farmer and is a remarkable good marketman and steady and is much respected by Mr. Sleekaboot and considers him one of the best disposed young men that comes to the parish church and never a sunday out of it. I also noes off tenants for the smith's and shoemaker's crofts. no more at present."

To the ground-officer's laboured production Sir Simon's reply was brief; and these were its terms :—

"DAVID—I intend coming home per mail coach on 23d inst. Please give the gardener your assistance in making the approach tidy and clearing it of dead leaves and rubbish. Also intimate to the people whose holdings are out, that Mr. Greenspex, my agent, and I will meet them on 25th. John Gibb, the smith, and shoemaker, are to wait on me the previous night. S. FRISSAL.
"October 10th."

With the contents of this note Dawvid Hadden was highly pleased. It was now past doubt that his plan of re-letting was approved, and he carried in his pocket a warrant of expatriation, as it were, against the three men, who of all Sir Simon's tenantry had set most lightly by his authority. Yet Dawvid was not void of magnanimity.

"Weel, Hairry, man," said he, addressing our friend the wright, "I'm a kin' o' sorry for the souter an' the smith—the smith in particular—he's a gweed tradesman, an' a humoursome chiel—though he hae a gey sharp tongue in 's heid files—but ye see they hedna ither till expeck. I warn't them weel fat it wud come till lang syne."

"Ou ay; they war baith owre heidie, ye see. Prenciple's ae thing, but jist to rin yersel' clean intill a snorl disna dee."

"Ye was a wise man that drew in yer horns a bit, aw can tell ye, Hairry."

"Weel, weel," said Hairry, with a somewhat forced laugh, "it disna dee to bide at Room, an' strive wi' the Pape. An' I'm a kin' o' mair oonder the Sir nor aiven the like o' them."

"Be thankfu' 't ye are 's ye are, Hairry; for Sir Simon was onything but pleas't aboot you gaen aboot makin' speeches at some o' that non-intrusion meetin's, I can tell ye. An' though I say 't mysel', that maybe sudna say 't, it wud 'a requar't only twa scraips o' the pen fae me fan aw was makin' oot my report to gar Sir Simon tak' a vizzy backar't; an' syne I wudna gi'en a goupenfu' o' sheelocks for yer chance."

"Muckle obleeg't to ye, Dawvid," said Hairry, in a tone indicative of earnestness, not unmixed with anxiety. "It's nae fae you 't I've kent sae lang 't I wud 'a dreadit an ill turn, though I ken weel ye 've a hantle i' yer poo'er."

"Ay," continued Dawvid, quite observant of Hairry's state of feeling, "fan ye was gaen clampin doon to that bit hole o' a skweel ilka ither nicht, an jawin awa' amo' yer nons, Sir Simon says to me, 'Dawvid,' says he, 'do you know that that fellow Muggart's been repeatedly down haranguin thaese poor ignorant fanatics?' 'I'm not awaar hoo af'en, sir,' says I, tryin' to mak' as licht o' 't 's aw cud. 'Well,' says he, 'keep your eye upon him, an' let me k-now.'"

"Eh, did he raelly say that, Dawvid? Weel ye ken, I never tyeuk nae active pairt, 'cepin twice. I was in fawvour o' the prenciple, ye see; but the like o' Gushetneuk an' them carrie't things owre gryte a len'th."

"Weel, weel, Hairry, ye better lat sleepin' tykes lie noo. The places is to be set aboot the twenty-foift, so ye'll need-a be owre by. My plan's been afore Sir Simon this aucht days, an' I hed 's letter the streen, fully approvin' o' 't; so there'll be little adee but get the lawyer to tak' oor enstructions, and vreet oot the dockiments."

"An' *will* there be ony cheenge than, Dawvid, forbye fat ye 've mention't?" asked Hairry.

"Ye'll see; ye'll see. We maunna cairry clypes oot o' the skweel. Hooever, aw'm gaen up to the Manse to call upo' Maister Sleekaboot, an' converse wi' 'im aboot ane that he was recommen'in' to me. Gweed nicht wi' ye."

Dawvid went on to the Manse accordingly, and knocked at the front door.

"Ou, jist say it's Maister Hadden that wunts 'im for a minute," said Dawvid, in answer to the inquiry of the damsel who opened the door to him. Mr. Sleekaboot came down from his study, and found Dawvid seated in the parlour, dangling his hat between his knees.

"I'm glad to see you, David; your wife is quite well, I hope; and the children?" said Mr. Sleekaboot.

"We're a' vera muckle aboot the ordinar', sir," answered Dawvid. "Gweed be thankit. I've call't up aboot yon that ye mention't—the settin' o' the crafts, ye ken."

"Oh! Sir Simon returns this month?"

"We 've arreeng't things jist is I taul ye, an' ye can lat me ken whuch craft, the smith's or the souter's, it would be maist agreeable to get for this person that ye're interaistit in."

"Indeed!" exclaimed Mr. Sleekaboot. "I'm really much obliged to you, David."

"Dinna mention 't, sir."

"It's not that I would desire to dispossess any man; far from it; but as you said Sir Simon could not allow these people to remain after what had come and gone, I thought I might as well recommend a most respectable man to you—a most *respectable* man."

"Fat's his name, sir? aw'll better book it at once," said Dawvid, putting down his hat on the carpet, and pulling out a crumpled book of the penny diary order, together with a bit of black lead pencil, the point of which he dipped into his mouth, in preparation for writing.

Mr. Sleekaboot gave Dawvid the name of some unknown person, a sister's daughter's husband of Jonathan Tawse, and Dawvid booked it in proper style. "It will be a particular favour," added the minister, "and he will be entirely indebted to yourself for it, David."

"Ou, I'm aye willin' to dee a fawvour to them that's enteetl't till onything o' the kin'. Ye'll maybe adverteese 'im to leuk in aboot upo' me at's convainience."

"And don't mention my name, you know, David, in connection with the matter; being of a secular nature, my motives might be misunderstood."

"I un'erstan' ye perfeckly, sir," said Dawvid; then he again put up his diary and black lead pencil; and soon thereafter bade the minister a formal good night, and went away home.

CHAPTER XXXV.

THE SETTLEMENT OF MR. MACCASSOCK.

The settlement of the Rev. Nathaniel MacCassock, as Free Kirk Minister at Pyketillim, was an event that afforded an altogether new experience in the place. To the younger people the placin of a minister was something which they had never witnessed in any shape. Their seniors could remember the time when Mr. Sleekaboot was ordained as minister of the parish. But that was a different style of thing altogether. Sir Simon Frissal had, of his own good will and pleasure, "presented" the Rev. Andrew Sleekaboot, without consulting any individual more or less; and the Presbytery had mainly carried the matter through, without anybody in the parish being a bit the wiser. When the ordination "trials" were completed, and the settlement was to take place, they fixed it, as the use and wont is, for a week day, whereat certain of the parishioners grumbled, because the Presbytery had been unmindful of the fact that the neeps were pressing for hoeing at the time. And one or two doubted whether a week-day service was constitutional.

"Aw 'm fell dootfu' aboot gyaun naar them ava, fader," said Mains of Yawal, then a promising young man, addressing his male parent; "the neeps is spin'lin' up till they 'll be connach't; an' they 've nae poo'er to gar fowk gae to the kirk on ouk days, 'cepin o' the fast-day."

"It 'll be siccarer to gae, loon," said the judicious senior

"Ye wudna ken fat mith happen. Sir Seemon 'll be there 'imsel', an' the factor wi' 'im, nae doot, an' they wud seen see gin oor seat war freely teem. Tak' ye a stap owre bye an' see fat like a birk he is. As the aul' by-word says, 'It 's aye gweed to hae yer cog oot fan it dings on kail.'"

Like an obedient son, Mains of Yawal had obeyed his father's injunctions, and patiently witnessed the ordination services. Then the Presbytery had the ordination dinner, from which, it was said, every individual member of the reverend court departed in a more or less "glorious" state. Mains of Yawal did not say this, but on that very evening he had occasion to witness a part of the tail of the ordination programme for which he had not bargained. The old man, as his custom was, before retiring to rest, went out in the quiet summer gloamin to the hillock at the western end of his cosy stob-thacket house, and cast his eyes abroad over as much of the farm of Mains of Yawal as they could take in from that point of vantage. He gazed and gazed again in the direction of the lower part of the farm, past which the road from the Kirktown of Pyketillim led.

"Jamie!" cried he, "fat's that makin' sic a reerie amo' the stirks doon i' the Shallhowe? Seerly the tod, or a set o' cairds rinkin aboot the pumphel. Rin awa' doon, man, an' see fat 's oonsattlin the beasts fae their lair."

He was a notionate old fellow the elder Mains of Yawal, and would be obeyed. So when Jamie went down till he had full command of a point a little beyond where his father could see to, what should he behold but a gentleman in white neckcloth, with his hat far back on his head, and seated on horseback, completely locked into the corner of the lower field among the growing corn. He had deliberately ridden off the road, in at the yett; there could be no doubt that the rider was responsible for that aberration and not the horse; and after traversing the field in various directions to the infinite astonishment of Mains of Yawal's stirks, which had some dim notion, evidently, that the proceeding was not in proper ecclesiastical form, he had got, as it were, jammed into the neuk of the field. There the rider, who, on finding further progress impossible, had been thrown back on the previous proceedings, was hilariously reciting part of a speech he had delivered in the manse that day, and the horse was occupying his time by nibbling grass off the top of the feal-dyke. Our young farmer, who knew perfectly well the name and local habitation of the reverend brother of the Presbytery who had been caught straying in this odd fashion, was naturally incensed, and rated his obfuscated reverence severely for "blaudin the corn" in such an unwarrantable fashion. And his reverence, in tones of serene contentment, replied, "Ho-ot, man, hoot; jist lead ye my horsie oot; I'll pay all damages. We hae-na or-dination dinner every day, min' ye."

I fear this digression is hardly to be justified; only let the indulgent reader bear in mind that the habits of Pyketillim are to me of perennial interest, whether the date be a quarter or half a century ago, or more.

Well, while the scheme, of which the reader knows, relative to the possession of Gushetneuk had been maturing, the subject that specially occupied Johnny Gibb's thoughts was not the renewal of his lease, but the settlement of Mr. MacCassock. Johnny had been at pains to stir up the people of the Free Kirk to a sense of their privilege in electing a minister; and he had had the satisfaction of seeing a full meeting present on the day of election, when Mr. MacCassock was unanimously chosen. Then Mr. MacCassock had his "trials," and, albeit the souter was Presbytery elder at the time, Johnny felt it incumbent upon him too to travel to the Presbytery's place of meeting, and sit through a five hours' "sederunt," in order that he might lose nothing in the procedure that was fitted to edify. Some parts of the exercises to which Mr. MacCassock was subjected were confessedly beyond Johnny Gibb's intelligent comprehension; yet he and the souter returned from the Presbytery with the steadfast conviction that he was a "gran' scholar," and "poo'erfu' i' the original langiges;" and the congregation readily accepted their report on this point. That Mr. MacCassock was an able preacher they all knew of their own knowledge. Mr. MacCassock had now passed his "trials" with approbation, and following on that they had next settled the details of the ordination. They did not reckon brevity the soul of wit, nor attribute to it any desirable character whatever in such a matter, and so Johnny Gibb and the souter, who had got a remit on this head from the congregation, had pleaded it almost on the ground of a personal favour that three of the fathers and brethren should take part in the services; the moderator to preach the sermon, then one brother to "address the newly-ordained pastor," and another to "address the people." This was all agreed to, and the 23d of October was fixed for the ordination.

"The vera day 't Sir Seemon comes hame!" exclaimed Mrs. Birse, addressing her daughter, who had just returned from some piece of visiting. "I' the face o' fortune fa said that, 'Liza?"

"I heard it at the shop."

"The chop! Fowk 'll get a' ca'd aboot clypes there; I think they mith get something ither adee nor turnin' owre a' the claicks i' the kwintra."

"Well, mamma, if it please ye any better, it was Mr. Gibb himself that told me."

"Gushetneuk 'imsel'? It wud set him better to bide at hame, an' leuk aifter that sweer fangs o' servan' chiels o' his."

"An' he bade me say that there 'll be a great turnoot, for the ablest speakers i' the Presbytery 's all to tak' part; an' he wud expect to see every one o' us there that day."

"To see 's a' there! Weel, weel! Easy till 'im that has naething to loss or win. But it 's jist aye the gate wi' them 't hisna faimilies o' their nain; there 's nae en' to their selfitness. Fat wye cud ye expeck Patie an' yer fader there fan the tacks is to be set immedantly aifter?"

"Well, mamma, ye know well aneuch that if Peter offen' Mr. Gibb, he needna think to get Mary Howie to be 's wife. An' ye 've helpit a' 't ye cud to get 'er till 'im yourself."

"Peter! Peer man, aw doot he hisna sol't 's beets wi' 's

transack amo' the lasses. But an' he war goodman o' 'Newtoon,' 's Dawvid ca's 't, an' Mary Howie needin' to gae awa' to the frem't, she maybe winna be sae saucy, aiven though an inhaudin, unedicat taupie chiel in a kwintra chop sud be garrin 'er troo that he 's wuntin' 'er—Fat sorra wud he wunt 'er for but to get 's han's o' the siller that Gushet 's len'it 'im, or I 'm sair mista'en?"

"Mamma!" exclaimed Miss Birse, with vehement emotion. "That 's not a proper way to speak of Mr. Will; and him one o' the deacons too. I 'm sure he don't deserve that fae no one belongin' to the Free Church," and Miss Birse flung herself on the parlour couch in a state midway between sobbing and sulking.

"Hoot, 'Liza," said Mrs. Birse, in a cooler tone, " I wasna meanin' to lichtlifie him—Gweed forbid. We a' ken weel fat kin' o' an upfeshin he gat; an' gin he be able to hae a chop noo it 's the mair till 's credit; only, ye ken, the like o' 'im canna hae the same respeck 's a man o' edication like Maister MacCassock, 't 's been weel brocht up a' 's days, an' gane throu' the College, like yer nain broder, Benjamin. But aw *was* provokit at that bodie Gushets gaen on that gate, 's gin he war enteetl't to rowle the roast owre a'body."

"He only wantit 's a' to be there, because there 'll be gran' preachers; and Gushets' ain people 'll hae some strangers wi' them," said Miss Birse.

"Weel, ye ken, Patie has a gryte prefairrance for the Pairis' Kirk, an' it winna dee to swye nae creatur's conscience, 'Liza, ye ken that yersel'. An' yer fader is *not* stoot. I was thinkin' 'im leukin jist rael wainish't-like aboot the queets the tither day; it 's raelly a gryte harassment to the like o' 'im to be gar't shave au' cheenge his claes on an ouk day."

Of course Mrs. Birse had it her own way; although, with the exception of Peter Birse senior and Peter Birse junior, the members of the family at Clinkstyle did attend the ordination services. The Free Kirk of Pyketillim was crammed on the occasion; and Johnny Gibb looked altogether like one who reckoned it a high day. There had been a promise of long standing on the part of his friend "Maister Saun'ers" at Marnoch to pay him a visit, and now Johnny had pressed fulfilment of the promise. Mrs. Gibb was not improved in pedestrian powers, so Johnny made Tam Meerison yoke the cart, and in that useful vehicle Mrs. Gibb, himself, Maister Saun'ers, and Jock Will's mother, rode pleasantly enough to the Free Kirk. The merchan', carefully done up in a stan o' blacks, came on behind in the company of Mrs. Gibb's niece, Mary Howie, who was also escorted by Willy M'Aul, whose muscular frame, and ruddy, open face, formed a good contrast to the merchant's careful style and semi-demure air. Willy, who had been for a time a stranger in Pyketillim, was there to hit at least two dogs with one bone, if he might, by visiting his home, and at the same time attending the ordination services. And if one might judge, it was no unpleasant experience for him again to meet certain of his old acquaintances, in whose company he now found himself. He had moreover been specially invited to take tea at Gushetneuk with his old master and mistress, and in company with the perspicacious Maister Saun'ers from Marnoch.

It is needless to say how impressive the ordination services were; how closely, for three long hours, they were listened to by a crowded congregation; and how the psalmody swelled up beyond its wonted volume. It was the mole-catcher who now occupied the precentor's desk, but the mole-catcher was a modest man, and on great occasions he would always have Johnny Gibb in the lateran also, to give him assurance, for Johnny's presence of mind never deserted him. And Johnny's voice had a grip in it. At the points in the metre he could ring out with a penetrating "birr" that set straggling elements in the general body of sound at defiance, and when occasion required, overbore in its prolonged twang even the shrill piercing note of the principal female voice. When the service had ended, and Mr. MacCassock had received the usual "cordial welcome," the congregation betook themselves to their several homes. Mr. MacCassock having as yet no manse, and

THE SETTLEMENT OF MR. MACCASSOCK.

there being no other suitable accommodation available, it had been found necessary, reluctantly, to give up for the present the idea of "entertaining" the brethren of the Presbytery.

As the congregation were in process of gradual dispersion by the various routes leading to and from the Kirk, the carriage of Sir Simon Frissal came along the highway with that dignified baronet, who had just arrived on his autumn visit to the locality, in the interior. Johnny Gibb's mare, Jess, which was already under way, manifested an evident disposition to keep pace with Sir Simon's fleeter steeds as they passed, and Johnny, who was in command of Jess at the time, did his best simultaneously to check the vivacity of the animal, and accord the customary recognition to his laird by lifting his hat. Whether Sir Simon deigned to return the salute of the tenant of Gushetneuk was not clearly determinable; at any rate, Jess by her capers made very sure that the baronet should not pass without having his special attention fixed on her master.

CHAPTER XXXVI.

THE SETTIN' OF GUSHETNEUK.

It was an honourable feature in the policy of the Frissal family that within the memory of living man or woman no old tenant had ever been turned off the property. No matter that adverse fortune had overtaken a man, nor even that his own sloth or mismanagement had reduced him to straits; if unable to continue in his existing haudin, some smaller place, or at least a bield to put his head in, was found for him, and he was allowed to end his days with the centre of his wonted orbit as little disturbed as might be. Though Sir Simon had been from his youth upward what would have been rightly described as a "hard-up" laird, and though the more industrious of his tenants evidently made a very comfortable living, the rents remained easy, and no foreign influences had hitherto been permitted to inflame them. Perhaps the system had its drawbacks. I recollect one or two tenants, for example, of a type that could certainly never be developed under the more modern system, by which the lands, erstwhile of Sir Simon, as well as other properties, are now regulated. Their laziness and capability of mismanagement were positively of the nature of genius—at anyrate in so far as genius can achieve results without effort. Here was Ga'in Tamson now—Who could have told from Ga'in's pastures that Italian ryegrass was a plant known to the British farmer; or said with certainty from his green crop that the turnip was other than an exotic of doubtful growth in our severe climate? In point of fact, Ga'in allowed a large screed oftener than once, to "lay" itself "out," without his troubling it with anything in the shape of clover or grass seeds; and he objected to "bone manure" on principle. His patches of corn bloomed a bright yellow with the ancient skellach, and the aspect of his kine and of his old "brown" mare did not belie the fare on which it was their fortune to be sustained. Ga'in was a "fine stock," with a fluent and compendious power of newsin; yet he got into difficulties, and latterly ceased to pay rent. But even Ga'in Tamson was not sent adrift. He merely roupit aff at Claybogs, and being transferred to a croft near by, placidly cultivated the same, or refrained from cultivating it, as he had a mind, for the remaining period of his life. Well; if Sir Simon's system had its drawbacks, I am not sure that the system which has succeeded it is quite faultless.

Anyhow, things being thus, the report that Johnny Gibb, the souter, and the smith were to be turned off, caused no little sensation in the neighbourhood, as the 25th October 1846, being the day of letting, approached.

"Na; but it's keerious no, that Dawvid sudna been owre bye ere this time to gi'e 's the rinnins o' the maitter."

The speaker was Mrs. Birse, and she addressed her husband and her eldest son, Peter, when they had finished their breakfast on the morning in question.

"Hooever, he has sae mony things to deteen 'im; ye'll baith rank yersel's eenoo an' be ready in richt time to gae up to the Hoose."

"Fat wud be the cese o' that? we'll be in gweed time this twa 'oors," quoth Peter junior, rising and making his way towards the parlour door. "Aw'm gyaun awa' to lat oot the stirks an' ca' them to the Backhill, faur Mains's orra man's reddin oot the mairch stank, till aw see foo he's gettin' on."

"Noo, Patie, fat eese has the like o' you to be gyaun treeshin an' ca'in' aboot at nowte beasts eenoo?"

Peter went, however; and, as Mrs. Birse could do no

better, she called after him, "Min', noo, and nae bide owre lang. Ye ken Sir Seemon's vera punctooal, an' 's nain words to Dawvid wus to bid 'every one be there by twel' o'clock.' —Na, man, but aw mitha bidden *you* pit on yer claith breeks i' the mornin'! There ye hae them skaikit wi' skirps o' sharn bree to the vera waistban'."

"Hoot, 'oman, it's neathing o' the kin'; ye ken they've hed that marks o' them this three towmons," and Peter Birse senior wetted his thumb and proceeded to rub at certain spots on the rather shrivelled-looking rusty-black unmentionables in which the lower part of his person was enclosed.

"Noo, min' yer nae to gae throu' yer gremmar gin Sir Seemon speer onything aboot the Free Kirk at ye, fan ye 're sattlin aboot Gushetneuk; as it's nait'ral that he will."

"Weel, gin he speer, aw maun jist tell 'im the trowth; ye ken brawly that I never was a weel-wuller till gyaun awa' fae the Pairis' Kirk."

"There's mair wyes o' tellin' the trowth nor ane, man; ye 're seerly aul' aneuch to ken that ere noo. Sir Seemon kens fae ithers nor you that Maister MacCassock's come o' genteel, respectable, weel-livin' fowk, an' that he's vera intimat' in oor faimily. An' gin he speer aboot ony ither transack that there's been, there's nae occasion for you to say ocht or flee, but jist, 'Weel, Sir Seemon, the best wye's joost to refar ye to yer nown awgent, Maister Hadden.'"

"But foo sud aw dee that?"

"Foo sud ye dee that! Foo sudna ye dee 't fan yer bidden?"

"Dawvid hisna naething adee wi' 't."

"An' fat for hisna Dawvid naething adee wi' 't? He gya *you* a braw fleg aboot it af'ener nor ance. Jist hear ye fat I say—'It wusna for naething that the cat licket the stane,' 's the fowk says; an' aw think it wud be ill Dawvid Hadden's pairt nae to dee a' that he cud for them that's coontenanc't him as we've deen."

"Hoot, but ye lippen owre muckle to Dawvid," argued Peter; but Mrs. Birse, who had begun to give her attention to some household matters, did not think it worth while to keep up the discussion, knowing, as she did, that though Peter was disposed to regard the occasion as one on which he might not inopportunely remind Mrs. Birse, in a friendly way, of his own safe instincts in matters ecclesiastical, he would undoubtedly fall in with, and act according to his instructions.

In due course, Messrs. Birse, senior and junior, set forth on their important errand. I rather think there had been some slight qualms of conscience in the case of the former; else he need not have proposed to his son that, in place of taking the straight road, they should go along the dykeside through the field, and round by the Backhill, so as to steer quite clear of Gushetneuk. At any rate, they reached the precincts of the great house in good time. Then they were puzzled somewhat. The prefatorial part, as it were, had been solely intrusted to Dawvid Hadden, and Dawvid they had not seen; and notwithstanding they had hung about where it seemed likely they might catch the vigilant ground-officer's eye, there had been no sign of his appearing. So they would go past his house. Oh! that very morning Dawvid had had to leave post haste for "doon throu'," on business of Sir Simon's. There was nothing for it then but walk up to the Hoose alone. And when they had done so the butler told them that Sir Simon and Mr. Greenspex had been going on for a while.

"The parson's been here, no less, for the last half-hour," quoth the functionary aforesaid.

"We wus expeckin to see Dawvid Hadden; will there be ony chance o''s bein' in aboot shortly?" asked Peter Birse senior.

"Davie?" said the butler. "Not if he's a wise man; there's been a awful kick-up about some promise he had made to his reverence to give the smith's croft to a *prodigee* of his."

"Raelly!" answered Peter.

"And the upshot's like to be to unship poor Muggart."

"Eh, fat wye, man?"

"Well, you see," said the butler, who was a not much less important official in his own way than Dawvid Hadden,—" so far as I gather, Sir Simon, at the preliminary audience last night, settled to give both the smith and shoemaker their crofts—so I gathered from the conversation of the agent when we had a glass of wine together. Sir Simon put on his most severest look—and he can do it in style—when he heckled them about the Free Church. But, as you Scotch say, he gave them ' the bit and the buffet with it '—and quite right, quite right, they 're both very good tradesmen. Ah! but his reverence comes up with this *prodigee* of his; a parson's not to be denied, you know; besides, Sir Simon was very angry at Muggart for making such a botch of that new gate at the bottom of the lawn; and I gather that Hairry's to get the sack to make way for this person."

"Isnin that byous!" said Peter Birse senior. "Ye see we cam' up aboot Gushetneuk."

"Gushetnook! what about it?" said the butler.

"Weel, we wus thinkin' o' takin' *it* tee to oor pairt for *him* here;" and Clinkstyle canted his hat half-way over in the direction of his son.

"Takin' Gushetnook! Bless your 'art, didn't you hear that it's took already? Old Gibb was here last night; sich a row wi' Sir Simon and he; might 'a heard them half-way down the lawn—not Sir Simon, of course, he's too much of a gentleman to speak loud. But Gushetnook's let—not to old Gibb, mind ye, but to some friend o' his, I didn't gather who. Excuse me, gentlemen," continued the butler, who was also discharging the office of footman. "His reverence is just going."

The butler went to open the door, and Peter Birse senior looked at Peter Birse junior uneasily.

"Nyod, I dinna think 't we sud bide langer, laddie."

"Please yersel'," said Peter Birse junior. "Fat 'll my mither say to ye, gin ye gae hame onseen the laird?"

"We canna be nae better o' seein' 'im noo, fan it's ta'en oot amo' oor vera fingers."

THE SETTIN' OF GUSHETNEUK.

"This way, gentlemen—leave your hats," said the butler, returning with a pompous swing.

"Weel, we wusna thinkin' o' tribblin' Sir Seemon aifter fat ye 've taul 's," said Peter Birse senior.

"I 've announced you—please don't keep Sir Simon waiting," was the response, uttered with some sharpness.

So the Messrs. Birse were ushered into the presence of Sir Simon Frissal and Mr. Greenspex. The interview was not a long one, yet Peter Birse senior, I am sure, could have honestly said he did not want it further protracted. He had only endeavoured to perform his "boo," in answer to Sir Simon's "Well, Birse, what do you wish?" and got a sentence or two muttered to the effect that "We wus gaen to speer aifter Gushetneuk," when the lawyer interposed, "Oh, yes, yes; supposing that it might be in the market. Very natural. Anything about your own farm? No; that 's right. Well, I suppose this finishes—allow me"—and Mr. Greenspex opened the door to give him the opportunity of whispering to Peter Birse, "That 's another piece of Dawvid Hadden's han'iwork, I presume. Oh, Dawvid, Dawvid! Ye may thank your stars that I 've ta'en you oot without wakenin' the old gentleman's wrath again. Good day."

When the tenant of Clinkstyle and his son left the Hoose, after a voluble good-bye from their friend the butler, there was an aspect of considerable blankness on both their faces; and had the senior of the two been asked at that moment in what shape he was to report proceedings to his wife, I do believe that he would have been a good deal at a loss for a reply.

CHAPTER XXXVII.

CLINKSTYLE AGAIN.

As Messrs. Birse, senior and junior, pursued their way homeward to Clinkstyle, the conversation between them could hardly be described as animated. The elder Peter moralised in his own way on the " keeriousness " of the whole thing: how it should have come about that Dawvid Hadden's plan so elaborately got up should have gone for nothing; how Dawvid himself should have been to seek of all times at the very time that the possessions which he had so laboriously laid out were a-letting; and how, above all things, Gushetneuk could have been let to any friend of Johnny Gibb—a man of such unconstitutional opinions. Peter junior was not less sulky than his wont in addressing his father; so he merely said—

"Humph! ye was near as ill's him yersel'."

"Ou na, Peter, man, I never votit against the laird," said Peter Birse senior.

"Hoot, that's lang syne; an' aw'm seer ye jist conter't 'im as muckle aboot the kirk, though ye dinna mak' oot to be pitten on for a Free Kirk el'yer."

"Weel, Peter, it was maybe as lucky for's a' 't yer mither didna get 'er nain gate there. It's cost me mony an 'oor's sleep that wark."

"Ye'll needa get a pairt till's some wye at ony rate," said Peter Birse junior.

"A pairt? Ye ken ye'll get oor nain pairt in coorse

but it wud 'a made a hantle better a place gin Dawvid's plan hed been carrie't oot—There wud 'a been richt scouth for the sax shift gin we hed hed a swype across a' the braes, an' doon to the burn side yon'er."

"That's nae fat I'm speakin' aboot, ony wye."

"Ou, weel, ye ken, your name'll be in'o the neist tack o' Clinkstyle; and that's only four year come the time."

"Ye needna think that I'll wyte the half o' that time," replied the amiable Peter junior.

Peter Birse senior looked at his son inquiringly. He would have liked to get at the young man's mind with a little more of definiteness; but was far from clear about the proper method of reaching that end. The thought, however, occurred to him that if Johnny Gibb himself was to leave Gushetneuk, the lassie, Mary Howie, Peter's future wife, would have to leave it too, and naturally enough Peter's chivalrous nature might lead him to desire that his marriage and settlement in life should be then, so that Mary might be saved the hardship of going to the frem't, which had been hinted at in a quarter not unknown to Peter, as a possibility. Peter Birse senior regarded this conception of his brain as an unusually happy inspiration; and he answered with spirit—

"Weel, weel, Patie, man, we'll see fat yer mither says; only I wud *not* like to be chaumer't up in a toon.—Eh, man—fa'll that be gyaun aboot wi' Gushets there at the back faul'ies?" and Peter Birse senior put his hand over his brow to get a better view of three figures who were discernible in one of Johnny Gibb's fields.

"Fa cud ken fowk mair nor half a mile awa'?" inquired Peter Birse junior.

"Weel, but I'll waager something it's that mannie fae Marnoch—ane o' them—wud he hae onything adee wi' the takin' o' the place?"

"Lickly aneuch. Fat ither wud he be wuntin here, trailin' a' the road fae that."

"Fa *cud* that tither ane be ava?" said Peter Birse senior, stopping to fix his eyes as steadily as possible on the objects of his scrutiny. In this his example was followed by Peter Birse junior, who incontinently exclaimed, with a sort of sneer, "Hah! it's Willy M'Aul, the souter's sin. He's doon here eenoo, an' preten's till hae leern't fairmin' at some o' that muckle places 't he's been sairin aboot."

"An' wud this new man raelly be takin''s advice b' wye o'?" queried Peter Birse senior.

The father and son passed on, till Clinkstyle was full in view, when the former suggested—

"Nyod, Peter, ye mith jist gae in aboot, an' tell yer mither siclike speed 's we 've come; an' aw 'll gae roon an' see Hairry Muggart, peer stock; he's lickly heard some sleumin o' fa it is that *has* raelly gotten Gushetneuk—tell 'er 't aw 'll be hame in nae time."

There is no reason to doubt that Peter Birse senior looked upon this as a happy mode, so far as he was concerned, of getting the news broken to Mrs. Birse.

When Peter Birse junior had reached home he was met at the door by his mamma, who was in the mood described as "vokie."

"Weel, Newtoon," exclaimed Mrs. Birse, with affable jocularity, "fat's the rent o' yer fairm no?"

"Stoit, mither; fat needs ye aye gae on that gate?" answered Peter Birse junior, with some emphasis.

"Noo, noo, Patie, that winna dee to be so short i' the trot. Gin ance ye war mairriet, an' hed a muckle chairge o' yer heid, as ye 'll seen hae, ye 'll need 'a leern to hae mair patience wi' fowk."

"Weel, aw hinna gotten Gushetneuk, ony wye."

"Hinna gotten 't! Fat d' ye mean?"

"It 's ta'en till some freen o' Gushets's nain."

"Freen o' Gushets's nain! Fat wye o' the face o' the wardle's earth's that? Did yer fader speak in a discreet menner till Sir Seemon?"

"He didna say hardly naething ava."

"Tchuck-tchuck! Was ever an 'oman triet this gate? I mitha socht till arreenge things an' expeck that he wudna ca 't a' to the gowff i' the hin'er en'! Faur is he?"

Peter Birse junior had just answered this question, and informed his mother of the position Hairry Muggart stood in, when that gentleman and Mr. Birse senior passed the window outside. As they came in, Peter Birse junior stalked away out to attend to his "beasts," merely remarking to Hairry Muggart, "Weel, Hairry, aw b'lieve ye're oot o' the craftie."

A fellow feeling makes us wondrous kind, 'tis said; and it so happened that while Peter Birse senior was on his way to seek out Hairry Muggart for the purpose of mutual condolence, Hairry was pursuing his way to Clinkstyle with the like object in view; and so they had met midway.

"Come awa', Maister Muggart, aw'm vera glaid to see ye—foo's yer goodwife the nicht?" said Mrs. Birse.

"Thank ye, muckle aboot the ordinar'," said Hairry.

"Isna this fine apen weather?"

"Raelly, it is so."

"It lats fowk get the young beasts keepit thereoot; an' that's an unco hainin o' the strae at the beginnin' o' the sizzon." After a pause, during which Hairry sat in a pensive attitude with his hands on his knees, Mrs. Birse went on in a calm and cheerful tone, "Ay; an fat's the news aboot your gate en', no?"

"Nae muckle 't 's gweed," said Hairry. "There's some o' 's gettin' the bag, aw b'lieve."

"Eh!" exclaimed Mrs. Birse, "an wusnin Patie jist tellin' me something that he hed heard aboot that—aw never was mair vex't i' my life nor to hear 't ye was to be oot o' yer craft."

"We've a' been—sair't oot o' the same caup—" Peter Birse was about to say, in a half dolorous tone; but Mrs. Birse, by a glance which Peter sufficiently comprehended, checked the sentence, and herself went on—

"Raelly, Maister Muggart, it's a heemlin thing to think fat wye fowk sud be pitten upon in sic a menner. There was that bodie Hadden trailin' here ilka ither nicht aboot the time 't they were plannin' oot the grun; an' he never haltit till he sud say that we would be willin' to tak' tee

Gushetneuk till oor place. Aw b'lieve I begood funnin' wi' 'im aboot it mysel' first—fowk wud needa tak' care o' the frivolousest word that they speak to the like o' 'im, weel-a-wat. Aweel, this fares on, till Dawvid sud come here an' tell *them* that Sir Seemon hed sattl't to gi'e them't; an' disna they gae up to the Hoose the day; but my lad's awa' fae hame, an' nae a cheep aboot Gushetneuk."

"Weel," said Hairry, "I never thocht Dawvid Hadden a man o' prenciple, but aw did not expeck this o' 'im."

"Ah, weel," replied the goodwife, "it was only *their* traivel. Forbid 't it sud be said that we socht to pit ony ane oot o' their pairt."

"But Gushets is lea'in 't ony wye," said Peter Birse senior.

"Ay," added Hairry, "that's the keerious pairt o' 't. Depen' ye upon 't there's been mair joukry-pawkry wi' Dawvid nor ye're awaar o'."

"An' fa's gettin' 't syne?" asked the goodwife.

"Weel," answered Hairry, "some say it'll be that mannie 't's been wi' them fae Marnoch. I cudna say."

"Fat ither," said Mrs. Birse, with a complacent nod. "Ah, weel, weel, I'll hae a craw to pluck wi' Maister Hadden for this, noo. Trystin' fowk to tak 's places to fawvour him, an' syne lea'in them wuntin hae or haud-again." She said this with a forced laugh; and then recollecting the impropriety of merriment in Hairry's depressed circumstances, she continued, "But aw'm richt sorry, Hairry, man, to think aboot sic a gweed neebour's yersel' bein' pitten aboot—fa's been hertless aneuch to tak' your craft owre yer heid?"

"Some ane 't the minaister recommen'it, we wus taul," blurted out Peter Birse senior, without reflecting on the implications of the remark.

"Ou ay!" said Mrs. Birse in an impressive tone. "This wordle has an unco haud faur there's an Erastian speerit."

Neither Hairry nor Peter Birse senior had any observation to offer on this statement of a principle; and the interview ended with little beyond a general condemnation of Dawvid Hadden, whose conduct it was unanimously agreed called loudly for explanation.

Peter Birse junior had gone away in the gloamin to discuss the question with his old friend the red-haired orra man, at this time in service at Mains of Yawal; and his doubts about the new tenant of Gushetneuk were solved forthwith.

"Gosh-be-here, man," said the red-haired orra man, "Tam Meerison taul hiz the streen that it was ta'en to the chap M'Aul—ye mitha been seer he wasna there for naething."

"Dozen 't, min, I never thocht o' that," said Peter Birse junior. "Fat ither but that's fesh'n 'im here? But the like o' 'im 'll never be able to pay the inveetor, forbye to pit a cover upo' the place."

CHAPTER XXXVIII.

MEG RAFFAN GOES TO THE SHOP.

"Dawvid Hadden—Fat's come o' 'im, said ye? Ou, didna ye hear that Dawvid's been a perfect laimiter wi' a sair fit, sin ever the day that the tacks wus settin'?"

It was Meg Raffan who spoke. She had gone across to the Kirktown to do some needful business at the shop, and was in conversation with Sandy Peterkin, who had asked how it came to pass that Dawvid, who was wont to be a frequent caller, had not been seen there for over a week.

"That's nae sae gweed," said Sandy. "Fat's come owre's fit? naething sairious, I houp?"

"Dear only kens," answered Meg; "aw sudna won'er nor it'll be a fit till 'im a' 's days!"

"Hoot, fye!"

"Ou ay!" answered the waggish henwife. "But fat better cud ye expeck? Fat's this that you Free Kirk fowk's been deein till 'im, aifter he hed ye a' pitten oot o' the lan'?"

"Weel," said Sandy, "he ettl't sair to get some o' 's awa'. But aw'm seer I wuss 'im weel."

"The mair credit to ye, Sandy, man. But, weel-a-wat, it sair't 'im richt, puchil, upsettin' smatchet, 't things sud gae the gate 't they've gane."

"Was 't a hurt; or fat?"

"Auch! A hurt or than no! Gin a' bools hed row't richt wi' 'im we wud 'a never heard a word o' a' this scronach aboot a strain't queet, an' him nae able to gae fae hame."

"We wus missin' 'im, ye see; he af'en calls for the letters, fan the dog-dirder chappie's occupiet," said Sandy Peterkin.

"Ay, ay; but ye see gin he cam' this len'th he beed 'a be thocht unco saucy gin he didna ca' on 's freen's at Clinkstyle i' the bye gaein," said Meg, with a cackling laugh. "An' Mrs. Birse mithna be jist sae couthy eenoo 's gin Dawvid's gryte promises hed come true, an' a' ither thing gane richt wi' 'er, peer 'oman. The best fun wi' Dawvid was wi' Sir Simon 'imsel' the tither day. He sees Dawvid comin' for 's orders, clenchin awa' wi' a bit staffie in 's han'. Sir Simon was o' the Greens at the side o' the braid walk —an' says he, 'What's the matter now, Hadden?' says he. 'Ou, sir,' says Dawvid, 'I've strained my quiyte. 'Your what?' says Sir Simon. 'Oné o' my cootes,' says Dawvid, turnin' up the side o' 's fit. 'Oh,' says Sir Simon, 'sprained your ankle—How did that come about?' 'Weel, sir,' says Dawvid, 'I cudna richtly tell; it was the day 't aw was doon throu', it cam' o' me a' at ance—jist a kin' o' income'. 'I wanted to send you some errands, but I must get some one else—you 'll not be able to go.' 'I mith manage, keep 'aff o' braes an' kittle road, siclike 's owre by the Kirktoon,' says Dawvid; an' fan my lad kent that it was to the Broch disna he set oot like a five-year-aul'; nae word o' the straint, queet syne, fan he cud win awa' doon an' get a boose wi' some o' 's cronies."

It was the temporary absence of Jock Will himself from the shop, and the fact that Meg was being served by the 'prentice, aided by Sandy Peterkin, that had given her full scope for indulging in all this pleasant gossip.

"Is that a' noo?" asked Sandy, in the usual business way.

"Weel, I dinna min' upo' naething mair, but my puckle preens, an' a stan' o' wheelin' weer; the lang evenin's 's drawin' on noo, an' it 's tiresome nae to hae a bit shank to tak' i' yer han' files. An' I've a pair or twa o' stoot moggans 't aw think 'll be worth fittin."

Meg got her preens gratis, and closed a bargain about the stan' o' wires accordingly. This concluded her purchases, but she was not quite spent of talk, and as no other customer had happened to come in, she held the good-natured Sandy Peterkin a little longer with her tongue.

"Ay," said Meg, "leanin" herself leisurely "doon" on a seat by the side of the counter, "an' •so ye'll be haein' nae ordinar' o' mairriages amo' ye in a han'-clap."

"Aw dinna ken," said Sandy Peterkin, blandly.

"Dinna ken! Hoot, fye. Ye *are* a peer set, you an' the merchan' baith. Fat sud 'a gar't him lat the chappie M'Aul rin awa' wi' Mrs. Gibb's lassie? Aw'm seer there's nae a blyther, better-leukin lass i' the pairis'."

"I'm weel seer o' that, Mistress Raffan; an' gin she get Willy M'Aul she'll get a richt clever, weel-deein lad, an' a weel-faurt."

"Ou, aw dinna misdoot that; an' he'll get a braw doonsit at Gushetneuk—likely Maister Gibb'll be lea'in 't an' biggin a bit cottage till himsel' aboot the Broch, or siclike. But wudna 't 'a been unco handy for Johnny Wull to get her, an' the bit clossach that'll come fan 'er aunt wears awa'?"

"It was raither thocht that young Peter Birse was to get Mary, wasna 't?" said Sandy in his own simple way.

"Na, Sandy Peterkin, man," exclaimed Meg Raffan lifting both her hands; "an' that's a' that ye ken aboot it! We expeck to get the news fan we come to the merchan's chop; ye mith lea' 't to the like o' me to be speerin aboot Peter Birse—he's wun intill a bonny snorl, aw doot, peer stock."

"Hoot awa'; his fowk'll be vex't aboot that."

"Weel, ye may jist say that, Sandy. His mither hed inveetit me owre by to get the news, the gloamin aifter a' the places wus set. She's a byous aul' acquantance o' mine, ye see; an' awat I've been aye vera fawvourable till 'er, an' never loot on aboot 'er fools, though she's sent them, owre an' owre again, half-nyaukit, stairv't creaturs, 't ye wudna fin' i' yer han', forbye to sen' them in to Tibby, the kyeuk, for the table. Aweel, nae wottin o' fat hed been brewin', though I was weel awaar that Dawvid hen gi'en them a' a begeck, I steps my wa's up by to Clinkstyle. The goodman 'imsel' was pirlin aboot the byre doors wi' a bit graipie in 's han', an' 's breeks row't up, and cryin' at the men. He was unco dry like, fan I leet at 'im in a menner, nae meanin' nae ill, ye ken, 'Na, Clinkies, ye 've seerly younger fowk,' says I, ' to leuk aifter the beasts—fat needs ye be aye hingin i' the heid o' things?' Wi' that he mum'l't oot something aboot fowk makin' themsel's eesefu' as lang 's they not the bit an' the dud. Only he was aye a sauchen, saurless breet; an' I thocht little o' that, but gaed awa into the hoose, an' meets hersel at the vera door. 'Weel, Mistress Raffan,' says she, ' I 'm glaid to see ye ; na, but foo the ouks rins by, I didna think that it was near the time o' gi'ein' in the fools; ye 'll be hacin' mair company wi' the laird bein' at hame.' 'Deed no, Mistress Birse,' says I, ' it 's nae upo' that precunnance 't I cam' here the nicht, at ony rate; I 'm nae sae dottl't 's that, though some fowk's memories is nae vera gweed.' 'Keep me, Marget,' quo' she, ' fat am aw speakin' aboot? my heid 's in a creel, seerly; come awa' in an' rest ye.' An' wi' that she tak's me awa' ben to their hole o' a parlour; they 've gotten a secont-han' rickle o' a piano in o' 't noo for Miss Birse, an' twa three bits o' beuks laid doon here an' there. The dother was there 'ersel', a vera proper Miss, nae doot. 'Will ye take a seat, please?' says she, an' wi' that her mither says, ' 'Liza, wud ye gae to the kitchie an' tell Eppie'—that wud be the servan' lass, nae doot—' to pit in jist a jimp full o' the timmer ladle o' yesterday's mornin's milk an' a starn meal amo' the kail to the men's sipper —I canna win ben eenoo.' Wi' a' this, no, I notices brawly that the quine hed been greetin'. An' thinks I, for as sharp 's ye are, ye hinna hodd'n that, no. Aweel, Mrs. Birse begood wi' a fraise aboot foo aw hed been keepin', an' this an' that,' sittin' as stiff 's a clockin hen upon a dizzen o' turkey's eggs. But brawly kent I that a' this was but a scoug to keep some ither thing oot o' sicht. Aw cudna think that the lossin' o' Gushetneuk was the occasion o' 't a'; but she was nae mair like fat she hed been afore nor caul' sowens is like het aleberry. Hooever, thinks I, 'Madam, I'se be at the boddom o' this, no.' I sits awa' a fyou minutes, nae to leuk oonceevil like for a' this—I hed lows't the strings o' my mutch an' ta'en the preen oot o' my shawl. 'Ye're het,' says she. 'Deed awat, I *am* that,' says I, 'it's jist a feerious fortiggan road atween oor place an' this.' But, wud ye believe 't, Sandy Peterkin, an' 't hedna been 't aw socht a drink o' water, I wud 'a gaen oot o' that hoose on-been bidden kiss a caup! 'Eh,' says she, 'aw'm richt sorry 't oor ale is *not* drinkable, it's jist new aff o' the barm.' 'Ou, weel, Mistress Birse,' says I, 'we're nae ill aff wi' a drap clean water. We've kent ither fowk ere noo 't hedna mony choises.' Wi' that she gya 'er heid a bit cast. 'We're nae jist come to that yet, no,' quo' she; an' oot wi' twa three o' that bits o' braid-boddom't bottlies fae the aumry—their sideboard, nae less —an' pooers a drap in'o a wee shall o' a glessie. 'This is a vera nice cordial, recommen'it by Maister Pettiphog, that's a streck teetotaller an' a byous gweed man,' says she. Aweel, aw cudna but drink it for ceevility's sake—a jilp o' fushionless, tasteless trash; it is *not* gweed for a body's inside, they may say fat they like aboot it. Hooever, there wasna as muckle o' 't 's dee naebody gryte skaith; an' I tribbletna them wi' lang o' my company, aw can tell ye."

Meg Raffan had gone on all this while with only a barely audible ejaculation now and again from Sandy, who on the whole felt rather embarrassed at being made the depository of her narrative, and flitted backward and forward in the short space between his desk and the counter; while the apprentice, with his elbows on the counter, his cheeks and chin resting on the palms of his hands, and his check-sleeved forearms forming a support between, hung rather than stood, a fixed and interested auditor. After a pause Meg proceeded—

"Weel, weel, I gat it a' gin four-an-twenty 'oors, no."

"Raelly," said Sandy Peterkin, vaguely.

"She's idolees't that faimily o' hers aneuch to fesh a jeedgment o' them. Aw'm seer for a file back it was aye 'oor Patie's' this; an' 'oor Patie's' that, till it wud 'a scunner't a tyke; but she'll maybe hae less to braig aboot Patie for the neist towmon."

"Has Patie deen ony ill?" queried Sandy.

"Ou, na, na; naething but fat was to be expeckit o' 'im. He's been aye a naisty lowlif't kin' o' a slype, wi' a' 's fader's gawketness, an' a gey gweed share o' 's mither's greed. Ye've heard, nae doot, that a creatur o' a deemie that was wi' them twa three year syne hed a bairn till 'im?"

"Eh, but it seerly wasna true!" exclaimed Sandy. "It wasna heard o' hardly."

"True! 'Wa' wi' ye! Gin 't hed been a peer servan' lad, a' the pairis' wud 'a kent o' 't in an ouk's time. That's the wye 't your walthy fairmers an' fairmers' sins keeps their bastards oot o' sicht—sen' the mithers o' them 'awa' oot o' the pairt; an' you that's el'yers never sees *their* faces i' the session: till aifter-hin, fan they've marriet i' their nain set, an' grow douce el'yers themsel's, like aneuch!"

Sandy Peterkin could not stand this, and protested eloquently against the Free Kirk being chargeable with any such laxity of discipline.

"Ah weel, we'll see," said Meg Raffan. "Hooever, Mrs. Birse's Patie's throu' 't again. The same deemie's i' the faimily wye till 'im ance mair. Patie, it wud appear, made oot to keep it a' quaet, expeckin' to get Gushetneuk, an' pit 's fader an' mither there to lat 'im mairry the creatur. Fan that gaed owre them, he grew as sulky's a wil' bear; the pooder was oot immedantly; an' Patie bann't 's sister fat was her bizness; the creatur o' a deemie has an unco poo'er owre 'im, it seems, an' they're to be marriet at the term."

"An' fat's the lassie's fowk?"

"Weel, but aw canna tell ye that," answered Meg; "only aw ken that the aul' cadger mannie that ees't to ca' fish up this gate fae Collieston, wi' a gray horsie an' a cover't cairtie was 'er gran'fader, an' fuish 'er up feckly. So ye may guess that the gentry o' Clinkstyle winna be jist owre prood o' their new freens."

That any formal assurance should be necessary to certify the accuracy of the intelligence conveyed to Sandy Peterkin by Meg Raffan was not once to be thought of. Meg had an incisive and unerring instinct in such matters. Where, or how, she obtained the information which formed the subject matter of her gossip it would often have been in vain to inquire; but on this you might rely, that in matters of domestic history in the neighbourhood, and particularly if the subject approached the borders of scandal, Meg was certain to be informed; and, moreover, if you were pleased to accept a statement of the case in hand *more Raffanico*, you obtained a narrative with such collateral references as carrried its authenticity home to the weakest capacity. Poor Sandy Peterkin was at a loss what to think about it. He doubted whether he should have allowed Meg to go on, and after she had left the shop he began to wonder whether it was favourable to the morals of Jock Will's apprentice that he had been allowed to stand by and hear Meg gossiping away as she had done. But it was past and gone now; the apprentice did not seem, personally, to have either compunctions or apprehensions on the subject, and he certainly failed to show the like interest in the region of polemics into which Sandy, with a view to fortify his mind, endeavoured incontinently to lead him by an easy transition.

Sandy Peterkin took the subject of the two marriages to *avizandum*. In three days after it was noised abroad in the general community of Pyketillim that Willy M'Aul, the son of the humble souter, was to marry Mary Howie, and be farmer of Gushetneuk, *vice* Johnny Gibb; as also that Peter Birse junior, farmer's son, Clinkstyle, was to be married to the granddaughter of a fish cadger, and that the aid of Mr. Pettiphog, the celebrated lawyer, had been invoked to get a settlement legally made, whereby the said Peter Birse junior would be deprived of his right as heir of the tack of Clinkstyle, and sent adrift to somewhere undetermined, to follow fortune on his own account, with his low-caste wife.

CHAPTER XXXIX.

PATIE'S WEDDING.

It was a natural enough result of the maternal policy adopted in his case that Peter Birse junior should, in a sort of reckless wudden dream, determine that his marriage should not pass over otherwise than in the form of a regular out-and-out demonstration. The news fell on Mrs. Birse with a shock that made her hardy frame vibrate from head to heel. She had hoped that it might be smuggled through in a way that would hardly admit of its attaining the dimensions of a public event at all. But to be told that Peter and his bride had actually invited a company of fully thirty persons, consisting chiefly of farm servants, male and female, and residents in the Kirktown, whose gentility was more than questionable; and that, of all places in the world, the marriage was to come off at the house of Samuel Pikshule, the bellman of Pyketillim, was more than the heart-broken mother could well be expected to bear up under.

Peter was deaf to all entreaty, however. In the matter of the recent settlement, forced on by his mother, he had shown himself a man of safe instincts, inasmuch as, despite the legal acumen of Mr. Pettiphog, he had stubbornly refused to sign a renunciation of the lease of Clinkstyle until he had got formally awarded to him what he considered a sufficient equivalent in the shape of a good round sum of money. With the capital thus provided in store, Peter felt as independent and confident as a man would naturally do in the circumstances, his purpose being, as his father phrased it, "to lay moyen for a placie come time; an' gin naething dinna turn up ere simmer, tak' a girse parkie or twa, an' trock aboot amo' nowte beasts." And as the marriage festivities were frowned down and ignored at Clinkstyle, what more appropriate than that they should receive their legitimate development under the hospitable roof of Samie Pikshule, who had been discovered to be a remote relative of the bride, and had accordingly readily given her a sheltering bield when he heard of her excellent prospects.

In carrying out his arrangements, Peter Birse junior went to work in quite a business-like style True, he was a little perplexed as to form; but in this Samuel Pikshule was able to post him up in a very satisfactory measure; and Peter had called on Tam Meerison, in a friendly way, with a "Hoot, min, ye 've gaen throu' 't a' yersel' nae lang syne; an' you an' Jinse maun come an' help 's to keep up the spree." The invitation was not to be resisted, and the mole-catcher was pressed into the service, it being left to him and the red-haired orra man, who has been mentioned as an old friend of Peter's, to settle who should be best, and who warst young man; and they drew cuts, whereby it was decided that the mole-catcher was not to have the higher post of honour. Peter had gone to Jonathan Tawse with his best young man on the beukin nicht, and got the publication of banns duly arranged. Jonathan, to encourage him, had remarked, "Ye 'll better come an' get yersel's session't the Sunday aifter the marriage." Peter did not seem to see the propriety of this, and demurred, whereat the dominie went on to say, "Ah-wa, man, it winna hin'er ye lang. Fan ance fowk 's pitten their necks aneth the yoke thegither, fat 's the eese o' a lang say-awa'. I wat I 'm muckle o' aul' Mr. Keith's wye o' thinkin'. Mony was the pair that cam' up to him to be rebukit that he made man an' wife afore they wan owre the kirk door again, though they had nae mair thocht o' mairryin fan they cam' there nor I hae o' gaen to Botany Bay the morn. She 'll be an uncommon suitable wife, an yer faimily 'll be weel at the road shortly, Peter, man."

The bridegroom's party mainly assembled at Hairry Muggart's. Clinkstyle was forbidden; yet Hairry lent the occasion his countenance on the calculation that Mrs. Birse would in due course soften down, and it would then be a pleasing recollection to have befriended Peter in his need. Peter Birse senior had been absolutely forbidden to attend the marriage; but Rob, who had so recently become, as it were, heir-apparent, and who had been taking counsel with the red-haired orra man, sadly to the disgust of Mrs. and Miss Birse, was not only determined to attend the marriage, but highly up in spirits at the thought of it. And lucky it was that this proved to be the case. For, as it turned out, the unsophisticated mole-catcher had failed altogether to realise the extent of the responsibilities laid upon him as warst young man. When the red-haired orra man called him quietly aside at the end of Hairry's peat-stack to arrange for the proper performance of their duties, it was found that Molie had made no provision for doing anything beyond the part of a simple layman on the occasion.

"Bleezes, min!" exclaimed the red-haired orra man, "wasnin ye never at a mairriage i' yer life? Nae fusky, nor a pistill nedderin!"

The red-haired orra man hitched half-way round, and exhibited the necks of a couple of quart bottles; one peeping from under the ample flap of each of his goodly coat pouches; and he dragged from the interior of the same garment a formidable flintlock horse pistol, considerably the worse for wear, which he not quite accurately designated his "holster." The mole-catcher, whose sole attention had been given to the decoration of his own person, and who did not feel quite at ease in his high shirt neck and long hat, looked foolish, and said—

"But I never cud sheet neen ony wye."

"Buff an' nonsense, min! Aw say, Rob!" shouted the red-haired orra man, stretching forward, and addressing Rob Birse round the corner of the peat-stack; "man, ye'll need-a gi'e Molie yon bottle 't I gied you to cairry; he hisna fesh'n a drap wi' 'im!"

Rob did not seem quite willing to comply with this suggestion; and the mole-catcher by a happy thought at once extricated them from all difficulty.

"Mithna *he* dee 't 'imsel'?"

"Ay wull aw," said Rob, brightening up and fumbling in his pocket to show that he was not behind in the matter of firearms.

"Dozen 't; it lea'es us terrible bare o' the stuff," said the best young man.

Now the red-haired orra man had given Rob the third bottle to carry simply as a reserve for him, seeing he had not three available pouches. So the thought was a natural one. But he was a man of prompt action.

"Weel, weel, we canna better dee, aw suppose. Come on, Rob;" and away they went full swing, leaving the mole-catcher alone at the stack mou'.

Ten minutes after, and the party was marshalled, Peter Birse junior being consigned *pro tem.* to the care of a couple of sturdy bridesmaids, set out in the loudest rustic fashion.

"Noo, heelie, till we wun awa' twa-three rig-len'ths at ony rate," said the red-haired orra man. And he and Rob set off in the character of sen's to Samie Pikshule's, duly to inquire if there was a bride here. "Are ye load?" queried the orra man. "We needna pit in primin' till we hear some o' them sheetin." They were directly opposite Clinkstyle at the moment, and just heaving in sight of Mains of Yawal. Mains's "boys" had determined to give them a regular fusilade, and the words had scarcely escaped the red-haired orra man's lips when a faint crack was heard in that direction. The orra man stopped, pulled the powder horn from his breek pouch, seized the cork in his teeth, primed his holster, and handed the horn to Rob, with a nod to follow his example quickly. Then they fired; then they marched again, reloading as they went.

"Sang, we winna lat them far awa' wi' 't," said the red-haired orra man, and Rob, with a loud laugh, declared it was "first-rate."

Had they been in the interior of the parlour at Clinkstyle at that moment, they would have heard these words faintly uttered—

"Ah, 'Liza, 'Liza, that sheetin *will* be the deeth o' me. Mony's the trial 't we maun endure fan we're i' the path o' duty. Maister MacCassock never spak' a truer word."

"My certie, hiv aw tint my gless?" exclaimed the red-haired orra man. "Na, na; it's here i' my oxter pouch. Tak' care an' nae brak yours: we're seer to meet somebody in a han'-clap; an' 't wud never dee nae to be ready wi' the leems for oor first fit. An' some o' Mains's boys's sure to be within cry."

The orra man was perfectly right in his forecast; for they had not gone over a hundred yards farther, when, turning a corner, whom should they encounter but the excellent henwife, proceeding homeward from the Kirktown.

"Hilloa, Meg!" roared the red-haired orra man. "Heth, that's capital. Fa wud 'a thocht it! Oh, Meg, Meg, aw *thocht* you an' me wud mak' something o' 't aye."

"'Serve me—the sen's!" exclaimed Meg, lifting her hands very high.

"Haud my holster here noo, Rob," said the best young man, in a thoroughly business key. He pulled out one of his bottles; then drew the glass from the recesses of his oxter pouch, and after shaking out the débris of dust and cauff that had lodged therein, and blowing into the interior to insure its being perfectly clean, poured out till the whisky ran over the edge and over his fingers.

Meg wished them "muckle joy," primly kissed the glass, and offered it back.

"*Oot* wi' 't!" shouted both the sen's.

"Eh, my laddies; it wud gar me tine my feet a'thegither —I wud seen be o' my braid back amo' the gutters."

"Feint a fears o' ye," said the red-haired orra man. "Wheep it oot; yer garrin hiz loss time."

"Weel, aw 'm seer I wuss ye a' weel," said Meg, as she

s

demurely returned the glass to her lips and took it empty away.

"See, I kent ye wudna thraw yer face at it," said our energetic friend.

Then they made Meg promise, as first fit, to turn and walk back a space when she met the marriage party, which Meg assured them she would do. The sen's hurried on; and, after the next volley, they made a detour through a bit of red lan' to meet Mains of Yawal's men half-way, and give them their dram. The orra man did not do things by halves, and not a single wayfarer that they met but had the hospitalities of the bottle thrust on him or her; and in very few instances would less than emptying the glass, as in Meg Raffan's case, suffice. No wonder if the orra man should say, "We'll need-a see an' get a drap mair at the Kir'ton; aw never was naarer nicket i' my life nor wi' that creatur, Molie. It disna maitter, we're a hantle better wuntin 'im."

And thus they went on to Samie Pikshule's.

Meg Raffan pursued her onward way, passing the marriage party with many hilarious exclamations on both sides.

"Na, Hairry, but ye are a feel aul' breet," said Meg to our friend the wright, who was bringing up the rear in his own ponderous style, with a blooming young damsel by his side. "Aw thocht your daft days wus deen as weel's mine. Ye've leeft Mistress Muggart at hame, no. But bide ye still, gin I dinna tell 'er fat wye ye cairry on fan ye win awa' oot aboot amo' the young lasses!"

In point of fact, Meg had already made up her mind to be across next night, and have a hyse with Hairry on the subject generally, when she would, without the least trouble get the full details of the wedding at first hand.

CHAPTER XL.

THE NEWS OF THE MARRIAGE.

"Ou ay, Hairry, man! This is a bonny wye o' gyaun on! Dinna ye gar me troo 't ye wasna dancin' the hielan' walloch the streen. Fa wud 'a thocht 't ye wud 'a been needin' a file o' an aul' day to rest yer banes aifter the mairriage?"

Such was the form of salutation adopted by Meg Raffan as she entered the dwelling of Hairry Muggart early in the afternoon of the day after Patie's wedding, and found Hairry stretched at full length on the deece.

"Deed, an' ye may jist say 't, Hennie," answered Hairry Muggart's wife. "Come awa' ben an' lean ye doon. Fat time, think ye, came he hame, noo?"

"Weel, but it's a lang road atween this an' the Broch, min' ye," said Hairry. "An' ye cudna expeck fowk hame fae a mairriage afore it war weel gloam't."

"Weel gloam't!" exclaimed Mrs. Muggart. "I 'se jist haud my tongue, than. Better to ye speak o' gray daylicht i' the mornin'."

"Hoot, fye!" answered Hairry. "The souter's lamp wasna oot at Smiddyward fan I cam' in'o sicht o' 't fae the toll road."

"Ou, weel-a-wat, ye 've deen won'erfu', Hairry," said the henwife. "Ye hed been hame ere cock-craw at ony rate. An' nae doot it wud be throu' the aifterneen afore ye gat them made siccar an' wan awa' fae the Kir'ton."

"Ay, an' dennerin' an' ae thing or ither."

"Hoot, noo; aw mith 'a min'et upo' that. An' coorse the like o' young Peter Birse wudna pit 's fowk aff wi' naething shabby. Hed they a set denner, said ye?"

"Weel, an they hedna, I'se haud my tongue. Aw b'lieve Samie's wife was fell sweer to fash wi' the kyeukin o' 't. Jist fan they war i' the deid thraw aboot it the tither day, I chanc't to leuk in. 'Weel, I'se pit it to you, Hairry,' says she. 'Fan Samie an' me was mairriet there was a byowtifu' brakfist set doon—sax-an'-therty blue-lippet plates (as many plates as mony fowk) nately full't o' milk pottage wi' a braw dossie of gweed broon succar i' the middle o' ilka dish, an' as protty horn speens as ever Caird Young turn't oot o' 's caums lyin' aside the plates, ready for the fowk to fa' tee. Eh, but it was a bonny sicht; I min' 't as weel 's gin it hed been fernyear. An' the denner! fan my lucky deddy fell't a hielan' sheep, an' ilka ane o' the bucks cam' there wi' 's knife in 's pouch to cut an ha'ver the roast an' boil't, an' han' 't roun' amo' the pairty. *He* was a walthy up-throu' fairmer, but fat need the like o' that young loon gae sic len'ths?' says she. 'Ou, never ye min', Mrs. Pikshule,' says I, 'gin there be a sheep a-gyaun, it'll be hard gin ye dinna get a shank o' 't—It'll only be the borrowin' o' a muckle kail pot to gae o' the tither en' o' yer rantle-tree.'"

"Na, there would be a richt denner—Nelly Pikshule wasna far wrang, it wudna be easy gettin' knives an' forks for sic a multiteed."

"N—, weel, ye see, puckles o' the young fowk wudna kent sair foo to mak' eese o' them, though they hed hed them. Samie 'imsel' cuttit feckly, bit aifter bit, on a muckle ashet wi' 's fir gullie, 't I pat an edge on till 'im for the vera purpose; ithers o' 's han't it roun'; an' they cam' a braw speed, weel-a-wat, twa three o' them files at the same plate, an' feint a flee but their fingers—a tatie i' the tae han' an' something to kitchie 't wi' i' the tither."

"Eh, wasnin 't a pity that the bridegreem's mither an' 's sister wusna there to see the enterteenment," said Meg, rather wickedly. "Weel, ye wud start for the Broch syne?"

"Aifter we hed gotten a dram; an' wuss't them luck. But jist as we wus settin' to the road, sic a reerie's gat up ye heard never i' yer born days! Aw 'm seer an' there was ane sheetin' there was a score—wi' pistills an' guns o' a' kin kin'. The young men hed been oot gi'ein draps o' drams; an' *they* hed their pistills, an' severals forbye; an' the tae side was sheetin, an' the tither sheetin back upo' them, till it was for a' the earth like a vera battle; an' syne they begood fungin' an' throwin' aul sheen, ding-dang, like a shoo'er o' hailstanes."

"Na, sirs; but ye hed been merry. Sic a pity that ye hedna meesic. Gin ye hed hed Piper Huljets at the heid o' ye, ye wud 'a been fairly in order."

"Hoot, Meg, fat are ye speakin' aboot? Isna Samie Pikshule 'imsel' jist a preuciple han' at the pipes fan he likes? Aweel, it was arreeng't that Samie sud ride upon 's bit gray shaltie, an' play the pipes a' the road, a wee bittie afore—he 's ill at gyaun, ye ken, an' eeswally rides upon a bit timmer kin' o' a saiddlie wi' an aul' saick in aneth 't. But aul' an' crazy though the beastie be, I 'se asseer ye it was aweers o' foalin' Samie i' the gutters, pipes an a', fan a chap fires his pistill—crack!—roun' the nyeuk o' the hoose —a gryte, blunt shot, fair afore the shaltie's niz! Samie hed jist begun to blaw, an' ye cud 'a heard the drones gruntin' awa', fan the shaltie gya a swarve to the tae side, the blower skytit oot o' Samie's mou', an' he hed muckle adee to keep fae coupin owre 'imsel'."

"Na; but that wusna canny!" exclaimed both Hairry's auditors simultaneously.

"Samie was fell ill-pleas't, I can tell ye," continued Hairry Muggart. "'Seelence that shottin this moment!' says he, 'or I 'll not play anoder stroke for no man livin'.'"

"Eh, but it wusna mowse," said Mrs. Muggart.

"Awat Samie was on 's maijesty. 'Ye seerly don't k-now the danger o' fat ye 're aboot,' says he. 'It 's the merest chance i' the wordle that that shot didna rive my chanter wi' the reboon o' 't.' An' wi' that he thooms the chanter a' up an' doon, an' leuks at it wi' 's heid to the tae side. 'Ye

dinna seem to be awaar o' fat ye 're aboot. I once got as
gweed a stan' o' pipes as ony man ever tyeuk in 's oxter
clean connacht the vera same gate,' says Samie."

"Weel?" queried Meg.

"Hoot! Fa sud hin'er Samie to hae the pipes a' fine
muntit wi' red an' blue ribbons. An' ov coorse it was naitral
that he sud like to be ta'en some notice o'. Nae fear o' rivin
the chanter. Weel, awa' we gaes wi' Samie o' the shaltie,
noddle-noddlin aneth 'im, 's feet naar doon at the grun' an'
the pipes scraichin like onything. For a wee filie the chaps
keepit fell weel in order; jist gi'ein a bit 'hooch,' an' a caper
o' a dance ahin Samie's they cud win at it for their pairtners;
for ye see the muckle feck o' the young chaps hed lasses, an'
wus gyaun airm-in-airm. But aw b'lieve ere we wan to
the fit o' the Kirktoon rigs they war brakin' oot an' at the
sheetin again. Mains's chiels wus lowst gin that time, an'
we wus nae seener clear o' the Kirktoon nor they war at it
bleezin awa'; an' forbye guns, fat hed the nickums deen but
pitten naar a pun' o' blastin' pooder in'o the bush o' an aul'
cairt wheel, syne culf't it, an' laid it doon aneth the briggie
at the fit o' the Clinkstyle road, wi' a match at it. Owre
the briggie we gaes wi' Samie's pipes skirlin' at the heid o'
's, an pistills crackin' awa' hyne back ahin, fan the terriblest
platoon gaes aff, garrin the vera road shak' aneth oor feet!'

"Keep 's and guide 's!" said Meg. "Aw houp there
wasna naebody hurtit."

"Ou, feint ane; only Samie's shaltie snappert an' pat 'im
in a byous ill teen again. But I 'm seer ye mitha heard the
noise o' 's sheetin an' pipin', lat aleen the blast, naar three
mile awa'."

"Weel, aw was jist comin' up i' the early gloamin' fae
lockin' my bits o' doories, an' seein' that neen o' the creaturs
wasna reestin the furth, fan aw heard a feerious lood rum'le
an 't hed been Whitsunday as it's Mairti'mas aw wud a raelly
said it was thunner. But wi' that there comes up o' the
win' a squallachin o' fowk by ordinar', an' the skirl o' the
pipes abeen a'. *That* was the marriage—Heard you! Awat,
aw heard ye!"

"Oh, but fan they wan geylies oot o' kent boun's they war vera quate—only it disna dee nae to be cheery at a mairriage, ye ken."

"An' fat time wan ye there?"

"Weel, it was gyaun upo' seyven o'clock."

"An' ye wud a' be yap aneuch gin than!"

"Nyod, I was freely hungry, ony wye. But awat there was a gran' tae wytin's. An aunt o' the bride's was there to welcome the fowk; a richt jellie wife in a close mutch, but unco braid spoken; aw 'm thinkin' she maun be fae the coast side, i' the Collieston wan, or some wye. The tables wus jist heapit at ony rate; an' as mony yalla fish set doon as wud 'a full't a box barrow, onlee't."

"An' was Peter 'imsel' ony hearty, noo?"

"Wusnin 'e jist! Aw wuss ye hed seen 'im; an' Rob his breeder tee, fan the dancin' begood. It wudna dee to say 't, ye ken, but Robbie hed been tastin' draps, as weel 's some o' the lave, an' nae doot the gless o' punch 't they gat o' the back o' their tae hed ta'en o' the loon; but an *he* didna tak' it oot o' twa three o' the lasses, forbye the aul' fishwife, 't was bobbin awa' anent 'im b' wye o' pairtner, wi' 'er han's in 'er sides an' the strings o' 'er mutch fleein' lowse. It 's but a little placie, a kin' o' a but an' a ben, an' it wusna lang till it grew feerious het. I 'se asseer ye dancin' wusna jeestie to them that try't it."

"Weel, Mistress Muggart, isna yer man a feel aul' breet to be cairryin on that gate amon' a puckle daft young fowk?"

"Deed is 'e, Hennie; but as the sayin' is, 'there 's nae feel like an aul' feel.'"

"Ou, but ye wud 'a baith been blythe to be there, noo," said Hairry, "an' wud 'a danc't brawly gin ye hed been bidden."

"An' Samie ga'e ye the meesic?"

"Maist pairt. They got a haud o' a fiddle—there was a cheelie there 't cud play some—but the treble string brak, so that wudna dee. An' files, fan they were takin' a kin' o' breathin', he wud sowff a spring to twa three o' them; or

bess till 'imsel' singin', wi' the fiddle, siclike as it was.
Only Samie ceswally sat i' the tither en' to be oot o' their
road, an' mak' mair room for the dancers, an' dirl't up the
pipes wi' a fyou o' 's that wusna carin' aboot the steer takin'
a smoke aside 'im."

"Na, but ye hed been makin' yersel's richt comfortable.
Hedna ye the sweetie wives?"

"Hoot ay; hoot ay; till they war forc't to gi'e them
maet an' drink an' get them packit awa'—that was aboot
ten o'clock. An' gin than," continued Hairry, "I was
beginnin' to min' 't I hed a bit traivel afore me. Aw
kent there was nae eese o' wytin for the young fowk to be
company till 's, for they wud be seer to dance on for a file,
an' than there wud lickly be a ploy i' the hin'er en' at the
beddin' o' the new-marriet fowk; so Tam Meerison an' me
forgaither't and crap awa' oot, sin'ry like, aifter sayin' good
nicht to the bride in a quate wye—Peter was gey noisy gin
that time, so we loot him be. We made 's gin we hed been
wuntin a gluff o' the caller air; but wi' that, fan ance we
wus thereoot, we tyeuk the road hame thegither like gweed
billies."

CHAPTER XLI.

THE MANSE SCHEME.

LIKE most events of a similar character, the marriage of Peter Birse junior served as a nine days' wonder to the people of Pyketillim—neither more nor less than that. Yet to the diplomatic mind of Mrs. Birse, the nine days had not expired, when it seemed good that means should be taken to certify the world of the fact that, despite the untowardness of recent events, the family of Clinkstyle had suffered neither in social status nor ecclesiastical character. It was not very long before this that that "big beggar man," the Rev. Thomas Guthrie, had perambulated Scotland in behalf of the Free Church Manse Scheme. In the course of his travels he had visited the Broch, and addressed a public meeting in the recently erected Free Kirk there. To that meeting Johnny Gibb, the souter, and the smith had tramped all the way from Pyketillim. They had listened with profound interest to the speaker's graphic story of parish kirks in the Highlands, where the scant handful of worshippers sat "like crows in the mist;" kirks through which at their fullest you might not merely fire a cannon ball, as some one had said, but "a cart-load of whins," without hurting anybody. Their indignation had burned keenly as there was set before them the picture of the minister's family forced to leave the comfortable manse, the pleasant home of many years, and go away, the mother and children to the distant town, while the persecuted minister himself was fain to take up his abode in some miserable out-of-the-way hut that the laird had no power to keep him out of; a hut so miserable that summer rains and winter frosts and snows alike visited him through the roof and sides, till the poor man had almost, or altogether, sunk physically under the discomforts of his cheerless abode. After all this, set forth with mingled humour and pathos, while the deep, eloquent tones of the speaker told with hardly greater force on the ear than the gleam of his singularly expressive face did on the eye, it needed but the faintest indication in the way of direct appeal to make Johnny Gibb determine to put down his name as a subscriber of £5 to the Manse Fund. The subscriptions asked were payable in one year, or in five yearly instalments, and Johnny Gibb said, "Ou, we 'se pay't aff at the nail; fa kens fat may happen ere five year come an' gae?"

It was not that Johnny made a boast of his subscription to the Manse Fund; far from it. As he knew that the souter and smith had other claims which emphatically forbade their following his example, he was at pains to make it appear to them that the sum he gave was in a manner a representative contribution from the Free Kirk in Pyketillim.

"Ye see we 'll need a manse oorsel's," said Johnny. "Nae doot we 'll get it a' back, an' mair wi' 't; an' still an' on there 'll be a hantle adee till 's a'. But fa cud hear the like o' yon onbeen roos't to the vera itmost? Oh, but he 's a gran' speaker, Maister Guthrie; keepin' awa' fae 's droll stories, he 's like some o' the aul' ancient woorthies 't we read o'; an' aw was vera glaid to hear 'im crackin wi' oor nain minaister, an' speerin aboot the kirk an' siclike."

Nevertheless, Johnny Gibb's subscription to the great Manse Scheme became the subject of talk among the Free Kirk folks in Pyketillim, and of laudatory talk, too; inasmuch as it was deemed a very liberal act, following on sundry other very liberal acts done by Johnny in the building of the kirk. Would any one else do the like? was the question asked by various people at various other people; and these latter doubted it, although they could give no conclusive reply.

A few days after the events recorded in the last two chapters, Miss Birse had raised the question with her mother, when Mrs. Birse took occasion to enlarge on the merits of Mr. MacCassock, and not less on the zealous services already rendered in the interest of the Free Kirk and that of the minister by the family at Clinkstyle. A manse Mr. MacCassock should have; but, while anybody might gain a certain *eclât* by a "supperscription till an Edinboro Fond," Mrs. Birse desired to give her valuable services in the shape of a social meeting to be held at Clinkstyle, in direct promotion of the local Manse Scheme.

The proposal was one that, on the whole, commended itself to Miss Birse. Both mother and daughter felt that the intended soiree, to give it the correct designation, could not fail, from its novelty and splendour, to excite attention, and dazzle the intellect of Pyketillim in a way that would tend, among other things, to wipe out all recollection of Patie's unhappy wedding.

The success of the soiree for inauguration of the proposal to erect a manse to the Rev. Mr. MacCassock was, on the whole, gratifying. The persons invited to attend it included Johnny Gibb, the souter, the smith, the merchan', and Sandy Peterkin, even. The mole-catcher was not asked. It was necessary to stop somewhere in the social scale, and Mrs. Birse resolved to draw the line just over the head of the mole-catcher.

"It's nae 't we wud wuss to lichtlifie the creatur," said Mrs. Birse. "He's gweed aneuch in 's nain place; an' sma' blame till 'im though he ken little aboot menners; fowk wud need to min' 't 's upfeshin wasna vera lordlifu'—Willna we seek Hairry Muggart? Deed, we 'll dee naething o' the kin', 'Liza. That's jist like ane o' yer fader's senseless projecks. He may be never so aul' a neebour, an' never so weel-will't to mak' 'imsel' eesefu' noo; but yer fader sud ken brawly that he hisna been gryte spyauck for him ony wye. He's jist been a rael oonstable man, though he has aye a fair tongue in 's heid; an *he's* been owre ready to be goy't owre wi' 'im—little won'er nor he was defate o' bein'

made an el'yer. The fowk kent owre weel fa it was't was
proposin him; a man't hed made 'imsel' sae kenspeckle at
the first ootset, an' syne for love o' the wordle turn 't aside
in sic a Judas-like menner."

In point of fact, Hairry Muggart had no claim to an
invitation to the soiree on the ground of principle; and
although Hairry, after he knew his fate in so far as his croft
was concerned, had once more pronounced himself an
adherent of the Free Kirk, it was a weak thing in Peter
Birse to suggest that he should be invited. Peter, for his
own part, would have felt Hairry's presence comforting, and
he urged that his friend was a "gran' speaker." He was
reminded that his chief care ought to be to improve the
occasion in the way of re-establishing his own somewhat
obscured ecclesiastical reputation.

The exclusion of Hairry Muggart was unlucky in this
wise. Our old friend Dawvid Hadden, in returning from
one of his business journeys in the late gloamin, and in
excellent spirits, had observed the unusual brilliancy of the
lights at Clinkstyle, and jalousin that something must be
going on, Dawvid, as he passed the henwife's door, with a
levity of tone meant to arouse sore recollections in the henwife's breast, but which he speedily had reason to repent,
cried in—

"Fat's been adee wi' yer braw bohsom freen the wife o'
Clinkstyle, the nicht ava?—Is she gettin' 'er dother marriet
neist?"

"Dear be here, Dawvid, fat wud gar the like o' you
speer a question o' that kin'?" said Meg Raffan.

"Ou," answered Dawvid, "ilka window o' their hoose
is bleezin o' licht like a new gless booet. There maun 'a
been fowk there."

"Fowk there!" exclaimed Meg. "Weel, an' there hinna
been that, ye're nae mark. Oh, Dawvid, Dawvid, it's a
gweed thing for some o' 's to hae the markness o' nicht to
fesh us hame files. Nae doot fan fowk meets in wi' company moderate things is exkeesable, but seerly it's gyaun
owre the bows to foryet faur ye've been."

"Fat div ye mean?" said Dawvid, sharply; "I wasna there, I tell you, woman!"

"Hoot, noo," answered Meg, with provoking persistency, "I'm nae reflcckin o' ye, Dawvid, man; mony ane plays waur mistak's, an' lies doon i' the gutters, or tynes their road a'thegither, comin' fae their freen's hoose."

"They're no freens o' mine; an' I'm not i' the haibit o' goin' there," said Dawvid, with rising dignity.

"Dinna be sayin' 't noo, Dawvid. Fa sud be inveetit to Clinkstyle but Maister Hadden, Sir Simon's awgent; fan fairms has to be mizzour't aff an' arreeng't for them 't 's to get them, fa can dee 't but him? Wow, sirs—wasna there!"

"It's a lie, I tell ye!" roared Dawvid, and as he roared he marched abruptly off, shutting Meg Raffan's door with a snap.

"There maun hae been something or ither gyaun on, that's seer aneuch; the creatur *has* a drap in, or he wudna been tiggin wi' 's. But he's nae sae far on but he wud 'a notic't onything oot o' the ordinar' as he cam' bye." So mused Meg Raffan with herself. And Meg resolved to find out all about it on the morrow. Her first movement was to catch Hairry Muggart as he went past in the morning to his work, but all Hairry could tell was that there had been a "pairty—some kin' o' a kirk affair," whereupon Meg suggested that, all things considered, it was extreme ill-usage to Hairry to have failed to invite him; and Hairry hardly denied that he was disappointed, seeing he had some services to speak of, not the least considerable of which were the friendly lift he had endeavoured, against his better judgment, to give Peter Birse senior when he wanted to be made an elder; and the element of respectability thrown into the initial stage of Peter Birse junior's wedded life by his presence at his marriage. However, Hairry bore it with what resignation he could.

The same afternoon found Meg Raffan at the Kirktown shop. Her object this time was to gather news, not to distribute. It did not tend to promote success in this operation that Jock Will was in the shop along with Sandy Peterkin.

Had Sandy been alone, Meg felt confident she could have pumped him to the extent of his knowledge. With Jock Will present, Sandy was not accessible, and to pump Jock himself was a different matter. Jock was bland and civil, and his replies to Meg were candid and literal; but he could not be drawn out by leading questions, and as little would indirect thrusts in a bantering style serve to betray him into inadvertent admissions. Meg was somewhat nonplussed. She had got very little beyond the point to which Hairry had been able to advance her, and now, with her artillery almost exhausted, and Jock Will giving distinct indication that his time and patience also were exhausted, she felt the difficulty of hanging on longer.

"An' yer mither *is* keepin' middlin' stoot?" asked Meg, as she made to leave, with an emphasis indicative of special concern for Mrs. Will's state of health.

"Ou, she's fine," answered Jock, who was unaware of any cause that Meg had to doubt a previous assurance she had got on entering that Mrs. Will was "vera weel, thank ye."

"I thocht she was leukin warsh like fan I got a went o' 'er the tither ouk; but 't 's so seldom 't we see ither noo-a-days."

Meg's drift thus far was obvious; and Jock Will could not do less than invite her in to see his mother. Once into the house, Meg leant her doon for a crack. The merchan' naturally had to return to his business, and so soon as he was gone the henwife came to the point at once, with the exclamation—

"Ou, they war tellin' 's there was a feerious interaistin meetin' about the kirk at Clinkstyle the tither nicht. An' it 's nae ca'd aboot clypes, Mistress Wull, fan aw say 't yer nain sin was richt muckle thocht o', an' 'll seen be ane o' the heid deesters. Awat he needna wunt the maiden of Clinkstyle, an' he wulls to tak' 'er."

With this preface, Meg speedily got out of the unsuspecting widow every particular that she knew about the Clinkstyle manse meeting, and had asked several searching questions bearing on the subject collaterally, to which Mrs. Will had been unable to give any answer whatever, when Jock, who had been scarcely ten minutes absent, looked in again.

"*Noo,* merchan'," exclaimed Meg, with an air of perfect satisfaction, " ye 're fear't that we sit owre lang gin ance we begin an' clatter aboot oor nain transacks. But we 're aul' acquantances, min' ye, an mony 's the cheenge 't we 've seen sin' we kent ither. I was jist o' my fit fan ye cam' in—Eh na, aw cudna bide langer; nae the nicht."

That same gloamin, as Hairry Muggart plodded on his way homeward, after finishing his day's work for Sir Simon, Meg Raffan, by the purest accident, turned up in his way, as he passed between the offices and the Lodge gate. Dawvid Hadden was walking alongside Hairry, newsin, the two being now, as Hairry put it, only "freens fae the teeth outwuth." Hairry stopped at once to converse with Meg, and Dawvid made a sort of broken halt too, though his disposition evidently was to step on.

"Na, Dawvid," said Meg, "ye gaed aff in a bung the streen fan I wuntit ye to tell 's aboot yer pairty at Clinkstyle. Fa wud 'a thocht it o' ye, noo?—a braw new hoose to be biggit for a manse till this lad MacCassock. Nae word o' enterdickin them noo. Na, na; they 'll be gettin' a stance for 't at the boddom o' the Greens, gin they like, a' throu' fawvour, an' hacin a freen i' the coort. That *is* cheeng't wardles."

Dawvid was taken aback by the audacity of Meg's address; but in the presence of Hairry Muggart it was necessary to assume an air of *nonchalant* knowingness, and so Dawvid replied—

"Weel, Meg, ye 're the ae best han' at gedderin a' the claicks o' the kwintra side 't I ken. Fat for sudna the man get a manse, gin 's fowk be willin' to big it till 'im? That 's nae buzness o' yours nor mine nedderin, seerly?"

"Keep 's an' guide 's, Dawvid, ye 're dottlin a'thegither. Hinna we a' seen fowk lang ere noo rinnin aboot preten'in' to hae buzness, layin' doon the law to a' kin' o' kirk fowk, bun' an' Free alike?"

"Is Sir Simon raelly gi'ein a stance than?" asked Hairry, with a good deal of earnestness.

"Speer at Dawvid there," said Meg. "He's aye the fountain-heid o' buzness."

Dawvid looked somewhat embarrassed, when Hairry turned to him inquiringly; but recovering his composure and dignity, he said, with some asperity, "Gin ye be edder to gi'e heid to a' the idle jaw 't ye hear, Hairry, or till imawgine that I've naething adee but reel aff to you aboot fat Sir Simon inten's to do; an' mair sae gin ye think that I wud dee onything o' the kin' withoot ony regaird to fa mith be in oor company at the time, ye maun be sair leeft to yersel', man; that's a' that I 'se say aboot it."

"Ou, dinna be sae sanshach, Dawvid," said Meg, with great equanimity. "Hairry disna need me to tell 'im aboot the begeck that the guidwife o' Clinkstyle gat aboot the fairm o' 'Newtoon;' an' nedder o' 's wud coont 'er sic a saunt as to think that she cud a forgi'en you for that yet; forbye 't it leet the haill kwintra ken foo kin' she was to be, leukin oot for some o' 'er neebours; only 't they war raither farrer ben wi' the laird nor some fowk 't we ken wus awaar o'. Hooever, she's managin' to coort the fawvour o' this minaister lad wi' makin' a fraise aboot a manse till 'im. An' fat think ye has she garr't Peter dee, but pit 's han' i' the moggan, an' gi'e a five poun' note, nae to be ahin your freens, Gushetneuk an' the merchan'. An' the Miss is to be at it colleckin amo' them, to gi'e something a' owre heid. Jist bide ye still noo, an' gin ye dinna see a manse biggit ere this time towmon, an' the minaister lad waddit till the quine Birse or some ither ane, my name's nae Raffan.

Good part of this was certainly meant to be heard by Dawvid Hadden, but by the time the last sentence was uttered, Dawvid had gradually moved on till he was almost beyond earshot, when Meg, lowering her key, and in a considerably altered tone, said—

"Ye see we canna dee ither nor lat at 'im files; an' there's naething nettles Dawvid waur nor to be lickened wi' the wife o' Clinkstyle—*Was* he there? Ah-wa', Hairry.

As seen speak o' 'im bein' socht to dine wi' Sir Simon. Na, na; they 've hed their sairin o' ither—an' chaep o' them. But awat ye loss't-na muckle yersel' o' nae bein' there. It's a gweed thing fan near-b'gyaunness an' gentility rins thegither; but aw 'm thinkin' Gushetneuk hedna miss't 'er for settin' the fowk 't she inveetit doon a' roun 'the parlour' —fat ither—like as mony born dummies. The wife 'ersel' was bleezin' in a mutch an' gum floo'ers, makin' oot the tae, in gryte style, an' the Miss sailin' aboot like a vera duchess amo' them. Aul' Peter hed been set on to mak' a speech; but did little, peer stock, but swat an' pech't, till some o' the lave tyeuk up the sticks. Hooever, a manse they 're to hae; that 's the short an' the lang o' 't.—Noo be toddlin, Hairry, for Dawvid 's wytein ye oot at the yett there; nae doot he 'll be sayin' we 're speakin' aboot 'im—Gweed nicht."

CHAPTER XLII.

SIR SIMON INSTRUCTS DAWVID HADDEN.

WHEN Sir Simon Frissal was about to leave his ancestral seat at Glensnicker for a two months' sojourn in Edinburgh, during the dead of winter, he called for his ground-officer, Dawvid Hadden, to give him such instructions as he considered needful for the guidance of that zealous functionary during his absence. The footman had carried down the message that Sir Simon wished to see him next morning at ten o'clock, and Dawvid manifested his wonted enlarged desire to fulfil his patron's behests.

"Aw 'm sayin', 'oman, ye 've seerly been lattin that bairns lay tee their han' to my vreetin dask: that 'll never do. There's the cork o' the ink-bottle oot; an' aw div not believe but the lid o' the penner 's been amo' the aise, an' my vera memorandum book blottit oot o' ken. Ye sud be awaar gin this time that I'm nae responsible to gae afore Sir Simon onhed my papers upo' me."

Dawvid Hadden's wife had heard similar addresses before; and, despite the pleasing haze which connubial fidelity interposes between the wife and her husband in such cases, was able to apprehend, with tolerable distinctness, what it all meant. Dawvid, it was clear, was too well pleased with himself meanwhile to be really angry; so she did not even think it necessary to express regret for the raid made on the dask by the band of junior Haddens, but said, "Weel, man, I canna hae the bairns aye preen't to my tail."

Dawvid got the memorandum book stowed away in his oxter pouch, after duly scanning the more recent part of its contents and gravely adding one or two pencil jottings. Then he started for the appointed interview with Sir Simon Frissal.

"You are quite aware, then, Hadden, of the changes that take place during the ensuing season among tenants?" said Sir Simon.

"They're a' vrote doon here, sir," answered Dawvid, tapping the board of his memorandum book.

"There—What do you mean by that?"

"My book, sir; they're reg'lar enter't."

"H—m. There's a change in the occupation of Gushetneuk, and a new tenant comes to the wright's croft. Then the old house, occupied as a side school at Smiddyward, is still vacant?"

"They're all here, sir; with the full heids an' particulars," said Dawvid, again tapping the memorandum book.

"That is the only vacant cottage at the hamlet?"

"The only one 't can be said to be clean vawcant. There's been nobody there sin' the creatur Peterkin was turn't oot. Hooever, there's only a fairm servan', John Gibb's ploughman, i' the hoose that Widow Will hed—he needna stan' i' the road gif the place be wuntit for anoder."

"I wish you to bear in mind, with respect to the farm and croft, that you will get written instructions hereafter from the factor, Mr. Greenspex, about getting some reliable person to take all necessary measurements of the extent of land in new grass, and other things; but I want you, in the first place, to attend to one or two other matters. Have you seen Birse at Clinkstyle recently?"

"No, sir; but I was hearin', on gweed authority, that he's fairly owre to the non-intrusions noo, as weel's his wife an' daachter. They're proposin' byuldin a hoose for a manse to the Free Kirk minaister chappie."

"Who told you that?"

"It was a vera parteeclar acquantance 't hed it fae some o' themsel's."

"I want you then to ascertain certain particulars without any loss of time."

"I do k-now a good dale already, sir; but nae jist sae authentic maybe as gin it war a maitter o' buzness—but I 'm quite awaar hoo I can get first-han' information."

"Taking the house first——"

"I 'll jist mak' a' bit memorandum at once," said Dawvid, pulling out his black-lead pencil.

"Put that aside—your memory may serve for once," said Sir Simon, in a tone that made Dawvid look blank. "The labour and expense of putting a fresh roof on this school-cottage and other repairs, were borne, you told me at the time, by John Gibb.—Is that so?"

"Ou, certaintly, sir, certaintly," answered Dawvid in a perplexed sort of way.

"Well, as it seems very likely the house will be required for occupation again; you'll go and ascertain from Gibb what he would consider an equivalent for his outlay—get it from himself personally."

"Yes, sir. An' wud it need to be shortly?"

"At once. The other matter, about which you have to see Birse, is the march at the lower end of his farm between Clinkstyle and Gushetneuk. The old bauk there is very crooked and runs off from the Clinkstyle side with a long point into the other farm, does it not?"

"You 're quite richt, sir," said Dawvid, brightening up at the idea of his topographical knowledge being consulted. "I k-now the spot perfeckly; Clinkstyle's wastmost intoon shift rins in wi' a lang nib, an' a gushetie o' finer lan' there is *not* upo' the place."

"The extent, I am told, is about an acre and a half?"

"Fully that, sir, fully that. I never pat the chyne till 't, but b' guess o' e'e I 'm sure it 's aboot an awcre an' three reed, forbye the bit o' naitur girss at the burnside."

"Well, it 's very awkward to have a pendicle of that sort belonging to one farm and lying into another—it goes against good husbandry. And now, when a new lease is to be entered on, I intend to have the march straightened—you will inform Birse of this."

"An' wud ye gi'e 'm an excamb like? I doot he winna be keen aboot lossin' the grip o' that piece for the same breid farrer up the brae."

"He'll get an equivalent reduction of rent, fixed by competent valuers—tell him so. Mr. Greenspex agrees with myself in holding that the march ought to be straightened, and as Gushetneuk is the smaller farm of the two, it is advantageous otherwise to make the addition to it."

"Weel, sir," said Dawvid, who was beginning to see rather more than he desired of somewhat unpleasant work cut out for him, "I wud hae raither a different idea aboot the squarin' aff o' that nyeuk——"

"I daresay," answered Sir Simon, drily.

"An' wudna it be better to pit aff for a little, till it cud be gotten mizzour't, afore ye proceedit feenally? I cud——"

"It may be measured as well after as before. Go you to Birse, and tell him my mind, and make sure that you adhere literally to your instructions—tell him the valuation will be fairly made for this acre and a half or two acres that are to be cut off his farm, and put to Gushetneuk, and that he will be allowed a deduction of rent per acre according to valuation."

"Will Mr. Greenspex vrite 'im to that effeck, sir?"

"No; certainly not, at this stage. Attend to what I say—I want you to go first, without loss of time, and inform him of my wish, and get his formal consent. Then Mr. Greenspex will carry out the arrangement. You understand, then, that what you have to do is to ascertain from John Gibb the amount of his outlay on this house, and then to get Birse's consent to cede this bit of ground?"

"Perfeckly weel, sir," said Dawvid, in a slightly dubious tone.

"Well, see that you lose no time about it. You may go now. If I've got anything else to say, I'll leave a message for you with Piggles the butler."

There were various thoughts coming and going in the mind of Dawvid Hadden when he left the presence of Sir Simon Frissal, at the close of the interview briefly narrated. He asked himself what in the name of wonder Sir Simon intended to do with Sandy Peterkin's old cottage and school? He did not half relish the idea of going to Johnny Gibb even for the purpose of offering him the prospect of payment for his outlay on these structures. He felt morally certain that Johnny would not omit calling up reminiscences of his, Dawvid's, previous connection with the school buildings, and that not for the purpose of complimenting him on the part he had taken. And then Dawvid saw for the first time that he had committed a strategic mistake when he got Sandy Peterkin turned out, in not also getting his premises levelled with the ground. But the most ticklish business was that of the Clinkstyle march. It is known to the reader how Dawvid contrived to plan a notable addition to the farm of Clinkstyle; how that scheme gained him high favour and repute with Mrs. Birse and her husband; how it disastrously fell through; and how Dawvid had, since that date, fought shy of Clinkstyle, and those who dwelt there. And now here was an imperative command to face Peter Birse—Dawvid would have been glad if he could have felt assured that facing Peter would be all—with a direct proposal not to enlarge, but to curtail, his farm. Dawvid was very keenly alive to all the difficulties and adverse contingencies of the case. He came at once to the conclusion that the hand of Mr. Greenspex was to be traced in it all, and the indignation to which the thought of the lawyer's unwarranted intrusion on what he felt to be his own domain gave rise, afforded a temporary diversion to his feelings. But the reflection soon came up again that in any case, Sir Simon's instructions must be carried out. And because, when he returned to his home, he found his eldest son employed quite harmlessly sketching a flight of crows on the slate on which he used to cast up land-measuring operations, and siclike, he gave the lad a very vigorously laid-on sclaffert on " the side o' the heid."

"Canna ye haud the han's o' ye?" said Dawvid. "It's a keerious thing that creaturs winna keep fae meddlin' wi' fat disna lie i' their gate. Aw think aw wud need-a get every article belangin' me lockit up fanever aw gae owre the door."

CHAPTER XLIII.

DAWVID HADDEN CONSULTS THE HENWIFE.

SIR SIMON FRISSAL's instructions were a subject of engrossing cogitation with Dawvid Hadden, or rather the adverse reception he was likely to meet in carrying them out was so. "But," thought Dawvid with himself, "it's joost fat we maun expeck. There's naebody that's in a public wye need think to please a' body. Upo' the tae han' we're nae accoontable gin we dinna tak' an order wi' them that's owre-gyaun the laws o' the lan', an fleein' i' the vera face o' Parliament itsel', lat aleen the grytest nobility i' the kwintra; an' syne the best that is canna dee mair nor they may. Sir Simon may prefar the advice o' an Aiberdeen lawvyer, that never tyeuk a squarin' pole in 's han', aboot the layin' oot o' 's lan', to the advice o' them that k-nows the contents o' every feedle upo' the estate, ta'en aff wi' 's nown chyne, but he'll maybe ken i' the lang rin fa's cawpable o' layin' oot a place in a gatefarran wye an' fa's nae."

Thus far of Dawvid's cogitations; but though Dawvid knew perfectly that under a broad and enlightened view it would be found that his sagacity and prudence had been unimpeachable, and his principles of action unassailable, he knew also, that it behoved him to proceed without loss of time to carry out Sir Simon's orders. And he could not get rid of the reflection that the petty details of the thing would, it was more than likely, turn out to be a little annoying. In the case of Johnny Gibb of Gushetneuk, it was true Dawvid had nothing in the shape of unpalatable proposals to make, yet he could not avoid having a slightly uncomfortable feeling at the thought of the explosion that might occur when he took up the subject of the old schoolhouse. However, the offer of an addition to the farm of Gushetneuk could hardly fail, as Dawvid Hadden sought to persuade himself, of mollifying Johnny Gibb's temper, and the happy idea occurred to Dawvid of smoothing his way by playing that card first. And on the whole he felt rather pleased at the prospect in this case. With the Birses of Clinkstyle his task was entirely different. What he had to communicate there would undoubtedly awaken feelings the reverse of pleasant; and in the remembrance of what had occurred so recently in connection with his plan for remodelling the farm of Clinkstyle, Dawvid was to be excused if he did not see clearly how he was to get through the business comfortably. While Dawvid was perplexing himself by turning the question over and over in his mind, he felt a very strong tendency to get confidential on the subject with Meg Raffan. They had had their small encounters; but Dawvid knew that Meg meanwhile was really incensed against her friend, Mrs. Birse, and he somehow felt that her sympathy was worth having.

"Aweel, Dawvid," said Meg, cheerfully, when she had got the ground-officer's gloss on the matter in hand, "we 've baith been weel aneuch ta'en in-owre wi' that carline o' a wife o' Clinkstyle; but ye hae the chance o' bein' upsides wi' 'er this time at ony rate. Na, sirs, but she will be in a rampauge fan she hears Sir Simon's projeck aboot takin' aff a piece o' their grun. Aw wauger onything she 'll come doon upo' aul' Peter's heid aboot it; as gin he cud help it, peer gype. Noo, dinna be mealy mou't, Dawvid, man, fan ye tell them. Aw declare aw wud gi'e my best brodmil o' Mairch chuckens naarhan' to be aside an' hear foo she 'll brak oot aboot it wi' that rauchle tongue o' hers."

Dawvid thought within himself that he could forego this coveted opportunity for a slighter consideration than that mentioned by Meg; yet, under the inspiriting words of the henwife, he felt his courage sensibly rising, as he said, "Ou, weel, I winna flench a hair's breid for nedder man nor 'oman; that's ae thing seer aneuch. I've stan't mony a roch hotter afore noo i' the wye o' duty, as ye ken brawly, Meg."

"Weel-a-wat ye never spak' a truer word, Dawvid. Mony's the body that's hed their gullie i' ye aboot yer bits o' transacks; but gin' I war you I sud set up my bonnet a hack fan I gaed owre to Clinkstyle this time."

"Ou, weel, aw'm seer she's been at your merciment as weel's mine, mony a day ere noo," said Dawvid.

"Nae doot aboot it," said Meg. "An fowk hed wuntit to sclaive 'er throu' the kwintra they wud 'a not nae mair nor the wye 't she's been gyaun on wi' that peer simple minaister lad to get 'im insnorl't wi' 'er dother. An' fat sud be upo' go noo, but a braw new 'viackle,' 's she was ca'in 't—we sanna say fa till. But it's order't fae the coachmakker's, no—jist bide ye still till the spring day comes in again, gin ye dinna see a braivity at Clinkstyle that hardly beseems fowk 't 's sib to fish cadgers an' siclike! Eh, but she has muckle need o' something to lay the pride o' 'er the richt gate!"

"An' dinna ye min' o' the fools?" interjected Dawvid. "Fat like trag she's sent here owre an' owre again. Awat, she was ill deservin' o' oor leenity for that."

"Ay, but bide ye still, I hae the hank i' my nain han' for that maybe."

"Hae ye gotten this sizzon's hens yet?"

"Feint a feather, no; though the time's lang owre-gane; an' aw was *that* ill aff ere the laird gaed awa' that I hed to fell some bonny yearocks 't aw was keepin', an' 't wud 'a been layin' haill on the feck o' the winter."

"I must see aboot that, though," said Dawvid, in a lofty and half magisterial tone of voice.

"Weel, will ye jist gi'e 'er my remem'rances," added Meg, "an' say 't though we canna be but sair obleeg't to them that tak's sic lang pains feedin' the laird's fools, I'm raelly fley't that they may rin 'er oot o' black dist an' potawto skins? I wud be unco fain to pit my thooms across their craps—an' gin they binna freely at the point o' perfection, I'll sen' them back till 'er for a fortnicht o' her raffy keep wi' the grytest pleesour."

"Weel, Meg, it does raelly set ye to speak," said Dawvid, blythely.

It was after he had been thus instructed and fortified that Dawvid Hadden set out on his important mission of carrying out the orders of Sir Simon Frissal at Gushetneuk and Clinkstyle.

CHAPTER XLIV.

JOHNNY GIBB DISCUSSES THE SITUATION.

To Johnny Gibb, the autumn of 1847 had been a season of varied and engrossing business. There was first the erection of Mr. MacCassock's new manse. So long as the project had remained a matter merely to be talked about and resolved upon, there had been no lack of people to express their ideas and give their advice, but when it had assumed the practical aspect of settling contracts for the building, some of those who had talked most fluently became remarkably vague, and did not seem in haste to commit themselves to any specific action. Johnny Gibb's course was precisely the reverse of this; the erection of the manse was not his proposal, but once it had been resolved upon, Johnny declared that it must be carried out forthwith. "We maun hae the wa's up an' the reef on immedantly, an' lat 'im get marriet, an' win in till 't fan simmer comes roon again." Everybody admitted that this was expedient and desirable, and everybody felt how naturally it fell to Johnny Gibb to push the necessary operations on. And Johnny pushed them accordingly, taking no end of pains in getting materials driven, and kept to the hands of the workmen. Then there were the private arrangements at Gushetneuk, in view of Johnny Gibb ceasing to be tacksman. The general belief was that Johnny would flit down to the Broch, buy half-a-dozen acres of the unfeued land, and settle down in a sort of permanent attitude as a small laird, cultivating his own land. Johnny meditated much on the point but said little, until one day, addressing his wife on the question of their future arrangements, he ran over one or two points that had come up to him, and, without indicating any opinion, abruptly finished with the query, "Fat think ye, 'oman ?"

"Hoot, man," replied Mrs. Gibb, "fat need ye speer at me? I've toitit aboot wi' you upo' this place naar foorty year noo, an' never tribbl't my heid the day aboot fat ye micht think it richt to dee the morn; an' aw sanna begin to mislippen ye noo at the tail o' the day."

"Weel," said Johnny, with an air of more than his ordinary gravity, "I've been thinkin' 't owre a' up an' doon. It's a queer thing fan ye begin to leuk back owre a' the time byegane. The Apos'le speaks o' the life o' man as a 'vawpour that appeareth for a little, and than vainisheth awa';' an' seerly there cudna be a mair nait'ral resem'lance. Fan we begood the pilget here thegither, wi' three stirks, an' a bran'it coo, 't cam' wi' your providin', the tae side o' the place was ta'en up wi' breem busses an' heather knaps half doon the faul'ies, an' the tither was feckly a quaakin' bog, growin' little but sprots an' rashes. It leuks like yesterday fan we hed the new hooses biggit, an' the grun a' oon'er the pleuch, though that's a gweed therty year syne. I min' as bricht's a paintet pictur' fat like ilka knablich an' ilka sheugh an' en' rig was."

"An' ye weel may, man, for there's hardly a cannas breid upo' the place but's been lawbour't wi' yer nain han's owre an' owre again to mak' it."

"That's fat aw was comin' till. Takin' 't as it is, there's been grun made oot o' fat wasna grun ava; an' there it is, growin' craps for the eese o' man an' beast—Ou ay, aw ken we've made weel aneuch oot upon 't; but it's nae i' the naitur' o' man to gyang on year aifter year plewin, an' del'in', an' earin, an' shearin the bits o' howes an' knowes, seein' the vera yird, obaidient till's care, takin' shape, an' sen'in' up the bonny caller blade in its sizzon, an' aifter that the 'fu' corn i' the ear,' as the Scriptur' says, onbeen a kin' o' thirl't to the vera rigs themsel's."

"Weel, a bodie *is* wae tae think o' lea'in' 't."

"Ay, ay; but that's nae a'. Gin fowk war tae leuk at things ae gate we wud be wae to pairt wi' onything 't we hae i' the wardle. But here's oorsel's noo 't 's toil't awa' upo' this place fae youth-heid to aul' age, an' wi' the lawbour o' oor nain han's made it 's ye may say—Gushetneuk the day's nae mair fat Gushetneuk was fan we cam' here nor my fit 's a han' saw. Sir Seemon ca's 'imsel' laird o' 't; but Sir Seemon's deen nae mair to the place nor the man o' France. Noo, you an' me can gae roun' an' roun' aboot it, an' wi' a' honesty say o' this an' that—'Here's the fruit o' oor lawbour—that 'll bide upo' the face o' the earth for the eese o' ithers aifter we're deid an' gane.' Noo, this is fat I canna win at the boddom o' ava. I'm weel seer it was never the arreengement o' Providence that the man that tills the grun an' spen's the strength o' 's days upon 't sud be at the merciment o' a man that never laid a han' till 't, nor hardly wair't a shillin' upon 't, to bid 'im bide or gyang."

"Hoot, man, ye're foryettin seerly 't Sir Seemon gae ye an offer o' the tack yersel', an' that it's ta'en to oor young fowk," said Mrs. Gibb.

"Vera true," answered Johnny. "Sir Seemon, peer man, 's made little o' 't, ae gate nor anither. He's jist as sair in wunt o' siller the day as he was fan the aul' factor gat the first hunner poun' 't ever we scraipit thegither to len' till 'im in a quate wye. But it's nae oorsel's nor Sir Seemon 't aw 'm compleenin aboot in particular. It's the general run o' the thing. Fat for sudna lawbourin the rigs in an honest wye for beheef o' the countra at lairge gi'e a man a richt to sit still an' keep the grip, raither nor lat the hail poo'er o' traffikein wi' the grun, for gweed or ill, be leeft wi' a set o' men that nae only never laid a han' till 't, but maybe never hardly leet their een see 't?"

"Is that the lairds?"

"Ay, ay."

"Eh, but ye ken they gat it fae their forebears."

"An' fat aboot it? Fa gya 't to their forebears, aw wud

like to ken? A set o' reivin' scoonrels that tyeuk it wi'
the strong han', and syne preten't to han' 't doon fae ane till
anither, an' buy 't and sell 't wi' lawvyers' vreetin on a bit
sheep's skin. Na, na; there's something clean vrang at
the boddom o' 't. We're taul that the 'earth is for the use
o' all; the king 'imsel' is served by the field.' The Government o' the countra sud tak' the thing i' their nain han' an'
see richt deen; an' the best teetle to the grun sud be the
man's willin'ness to lawbour 't, and grow corn an' cattle for
the susteenance o' man."

In this high flight Mrs. Gibb did not attempt to follow
Johnny. She merely smiled and said, "Weel, aw'm seer,
man, ye div tak' unco notions i' yer heid. Hairry Muggart
wud be naething to ye for a politician."

"Ou, weel, aw daursay Hairry wudna differ wi' me aboot
that. But that's nedder here nor there. Fowk canna
mak' owre seer that there's a richt an' a vrang in a'thing;
an' lang eesage 'll never gar oonjustice be right nae mair
nor it'll mak' black fite, say fat they like. Only we wus
speakin' aboot oor nain sma' affair—I div not think that
there would be muckle thrift in you an' me gyaun awa'
buyin' a twa three rigs o' grun' an' sittin' doon wi' a'thing,
unco aboot 's to fecht upon 't for a fyou years. Fan ance
fowk 's at oor time o' life they sud be willin' to lat the
theets slack a bit; an' gin they've ta'en up their yokin'
straucht an' fair, they can leuk back wi' a kin' o' contentment upo' the wark that's deen, min'in' a' the time that
ithers sud be layin' their shooders to the draucht, raither nor
themsel's hingin' i' the heid o' things as gin this wardle
wud laist only as lang as they keepit fit wi' 't. Noo, I'm
fell sweer to think o' a cheenge fae this place, an' I'll tell
ye foo."

"Loshtie man, ye're seerly gyaun gyte——"

"Na, na. I see fat ye're ettlin at. I'm nae foryettin 't
the place is set to the young fowk, 's ye ca' them; nedder
wud I wunt to stan' i' their road a single hair's-breid, nor
to meddle wi' them ae gate nor anither. For ance *they're*
waddit *we're* supperannuat, that 's a doonlaid rowle. But

there sudna be nae gryte diffeekwalty aboot gettin' hooseroom for twa aul' fowk. The hoose is a byous size for len'th; an' yer neebour 'oman, ye ken, 's taul ye a dizzen o' times owre that it wud be a spawcious hoose for a genteel faimily gin it hed a back kitchie wi' a lang chimley biggit. It winna be in oor day that Willy M'Aul an' the lassie 'll be so far up b' cairts as be needin' a castell to haud their braw company, an' wi' little contrivance an' nae muckle biggin' we mith get a snod aneuch beil' by partitionin' aff the wast en' an' makin' a sin'ry door to oorsel's."

"Weel, fa wud 'a minet upo' that but yersel', noo?" exclaimed Mrs. Gibb, lost in admiration of her husband's inventive genius. She was not in the habit of ever seriously disputing his will, yet Johnny was evidently gratified to find that his project was not merely acceptable to Mrs. Gibb, but that the prospect it opened up, as the good woman phrased it, "liftit a birn aff o' her min'," and would, she was sure, be welcomed by all concerned.

"Weel, we 'll see," said Johnny; "we maun jist a' leern to ken that the wardle can dee wuntin 's. We a' get oor day, an' oor day's wark; the time slips by like the mist creepin' seelently up the howe. 'What thy hand findeth to do, do with thy might,' is the lesson we ocht aye to bear in min', though we af'en, af'en foryet it; an' fan we leuk back fae a point like this o' the lang track o' years streetchin into the saft mornin' licht o' oor days, an' a' croon't wi' blessin's, it 's like a dream, but a pleasant dream tee, an' foreshaidowin' a better time to come to them that 's faithfu' to their trust. But, ye ken, an aul' tree disna seen tak' reet again, nor yet haud the grun weel fan it 's liftit. An' aw 'm thinkin' gin they 're to get ony mair gweed o' me, they 'll hae maist chance o' 't by lattin' 's stick faur we are. An' though Sir Seemon may ca' the rigs o' Gushetneuk his, I 'm maistly seer, gin the rigs themsel's cud speak, they wud ca' me maister raither nor him. But it mak's na muckle back or fore. They 'll be mine to the sicht o' my een maybe as lang 's I 'm able to see the sproutin' blade or the yalla corn sheaf; an' Sir Seemon's lairdskip canna gie 'im mair."

I think Johnny Gibb had about finished his moralising, but he had scarcely ceased speaking when the lassie, Mary Howie, opened the room door, in which Johnny and Mrs. Gibb had been seated all the while, and, under the impression apparently that she had interrupted their conference, asked, " Was ye speakin', uncle ? "

" Ou ay, lassie, but never heed. Fat was ye needin' ? " asked Johnny.

" Naething," said Mary, with a comical side glance toward her aunt. " It's only Dawvid Hadden that's wuntin to speak to ye."

" Faur is he ? " asked Johnny, with a hard, abrupt sort of snap that contrasted very oddly with his previous tone of voice.

" Oh, he's at the door, but he canna come in on nae accoont ; he's in a hurry—he has ' more calls to mak'.' "

Johnny Gibb rose with a kind of half grunt, and went away toward the door to speak with Dawvid Hadden.

CHAPTER XLV.

DAWVID HADDEN MAKES TWO BUSINESS CALLS.

"There's a fine nicht, Maister Gibb," said Dawvid Hadden, in a tone of much affability, on Johnny Gibb showing himself at the door of the house of Gushetneuk at the time already mentioned. "No—aw canna bide to come in. I've forder to gae, ye see. Aw was jist wuntin a fyou minutes' discoorse on a maitter o' buzness."

"Weel, ye'll jist sit as chaep's stan'," said Johnny, sententiously. "But please yersel'."

"A—y," exclaimed Dawvid, with a prolonged sound, and searching his breast pocket deep down. "That's vera keerious. Aw thocht aw hed a' my material here. Hooever, ye can maybe gi'e's pen an' ink gin we requar't—an' as ye say, Maister Gibb, we'll sit as chaep's stan'."

With this Dawvid went inside without more ado. After graciously saluting Mrs. Gibb, and making some further demonstrations in the way of professing to produce papers, Dawvid said—

"Weel, I joost cam' owre bye as seen's aw cud get some oder things arreeng't aifter Sir Simon leeft, to forquant ye that we had resolv't to straucht the mairch atween you an' Clinkstyle, clippin aff that lang heugh an' the bit burnside fae him, an' pittin 't tee to Gushetneuk. There's jist—lat me see, I hae 't here till an ell—twa awcre an' aboot half a reed—It's prime intoon grun, ye ken."

Dawvid had not been so definite about the measurement

with Sir Simon; but it would not do to indicate weakness on that point to a mere tenant. He would have gone on to descant on the advantages that would accrue to the farmer of Gushetneuk from the proposed addition, but at this stage, Johnny Gibb, who had been a little taciturn hitherto, broke in—

"An' ye 're nae tir't yet meddlin' wi' fat ye ca' the layin' oot o' fowk's grun? I thocht ye hed gotten aboot as muckle, short syne, as wud 'a sair't maist fowk at that trade. Hoo-ever, it maksna futher ye be leein' or tellin' the trowth this time; a' that I hae to say is, that I 'm nae tacksman langer nor the term, an' hae naething adee wi' 't. An' I 'se only tell ye that ye mith be a hantle better employ't nor makin' dispeace amo' neebour fowk—feint ane 'll thank ye for cheengin the mairch."

Dawvid evidently had not expected this style of retort. He was put out accordingly, and only managed to blurt out—

"It 's Sir Simon's enstructions to me at ony rate."

"Maybe," said Johnny, curtly. "We 've heard fowk speak o' 'Sir Seemon's enstructions' lang ere noo, fan Sir Seemon beheev't to be haud'n on the ill gate that he was gyaun b' them that ackit the pairt o' mere seecophants till 'im, or tyeuk a pride in rinnin Sawtan's erran's onbidden."

"Weel, Maister Gibb," said Dawvid, with a forced attempt at hilarity, "we sanna cast oot aboot aul' scores; fowk sudna keep up um'rage aifter things is ance past, ye ken. Sir Simon 's mair o' a gentleman——"

"It 's nae Sir Seemon 't we 're speakin' aboot eenoo," interjected Johnny, abruptly.

"Weel, Gushets, I 'm only Sir Seemon's—servan'," pursued Dawvid, in a nonplussed sort of way.

"I 'm weel awaar o' that; an' gin ye hed been aye content to dee an honest servan's pairt ye wud 'a been a muckle mair respeckit man nor ye are this day."

Whether it was in accordance with proper etiquette in Johnny Gibb to invite Dawvid Hadden into his house, and then heckle him after this fashion, I shall not pretend to say; but of this I am certain, that the proceeding was in entire accordance with the whole tenor of Johnny's general procedure, and could not be construed into anything of the nature of intentional rudeness. That it was rudeness at all could be admitted only on the principle that it is rude in a man to utter his honest opinion in plain words. Anyhow, the collapse on Dawvid Hadden's part was somewhat marked. Fairly dismounted from his high horse, he found refuge for once in the literal truth.

"I'm nae here o' wull, I 'se asseer ye; but to cairry oot Sir Simon's doon-laid orders. He wuntit to ken immedantly fat was auchtin you for fat ye laid oot upo' that—place at the Ward."

"Fat place? The skweel? Little won'er nor ye think shame to mak' mention o' 't, man. Haud'n you an' the like o' ye awa', it mith 'a been a blessin' to the pairt at this day, an' for generations to come. Tell Sir Seemon that it stan's there the reproach o' 's estate, an' 'll rise up in jeedgment yet against them 't has the swick o' makin' 't a desolation."

"I must go, ony wye," said Dawvid, rising to his feet, and taking out his memorandum book. "Will ye obleege b' jist gi'en 's the figure o' fat ye laid oot on 't?"

"I nedder can nor wull," replied Johnny, in a decisive tone. "Fan ye carriet things 's ye did, the black gate, that 's a sma' affair, an' the tow may gae wi' the bucket. It 'll be time aneuch to speak o' that fan anither tenan' comes till 't."

"There 'll be no oder tenan' there; it 'll be knockit doon; but Sir Simon wunts to vrang no man o' 's money—ye better mention a soom."

"I 'll dee naething o' the kin'. Gin ye gi'e Sir Seemon a true accoont o' fat I 've said to ye this minit, I 'se be content."

When Dawvid Hadden had left Gushetneuk, and had got time to glance calmly at the situation, the temper of mind in which he found himself was the reverse of amiable. He had an uncomfortable impression that the representative of law and authority had after all come off not exactly first best in the interview that had just ended, and then what was he to report to Sir Simon? That Johnny Gibb had snubbed him, and sent him away without any proper answer to the inquiry that had brought him there? Dawvid felt irritated in a high degree; and I daresay there was a certain advantage in this, after all, for as he toddled across the fields towards Clinkstyle, the feeling of irritation merged into a sort of savage resolution to march right on, and fearlessly beard the Birses in their own den. This thought carried Dawvid on rather briskly for a space; yet I think he was on the whole somewhat relieved mentally when he suddenly stumbled upon Peter Birse senior stalking along the end rig of one of his fields, at the distance of nearly a couple of hundred yards from the steading. Dawvid strode firmly up to Peter, with the intention of at once announcing Sir Simon's proposal, and securing Clinkstyle's assent to it.

"There's a mochie nicht, Clinkies," said Dawvid, gravely.

"A mochie nicht, Dawvid," answered Peter, in an uncertain kind of tone.

"I've gotten a bit dockiment here to get yer percurrence till, than," continued Dawvid, thrusting his hand into his pocket.

"I houp it's nae neen o' that duty papers—aboot rinnin horse, coach kin' o' viackles, nor naething?" asked Peter Birse, uneasily.

"No, no," said Dawvid. "I dinna interfere wi' fat's nae buzness o' mine.—I've to do only wi' the lan'. Sir Simon's resolv't to rectify the boundary atween you an' Gushetneuk. Leuk here (and he pointed down the brae), takin' a swype clean doon fae that bit elbuck at the back o' your infeedle, to the burn side, an' cuttin' aff twa awcre odds o' the lang point."

"Nae the ootwuth nyeuk o' fat we ca' the Pardes park—we hinna grun like it upo' the place?"

"That's the spot," said Dawvid, decisively.

"An' fat wud he be gi'ein's b' wye o' excamb like?"

"Nothing, nothing," said Dawvid. "Ov coorse there'll be an allooance ta'en aff o' the rent fan we get it calculat."

"Man, that's sair," exclaimed Peter Birse, in a pitiful voice.

"Weel, it's not my arreengement, ye k-now," said Dawvid Hadden, "but that's fat I've to get yer consent till. So ye'll better jist say that ye're agreeable at ance, an' nae deteen me nae langer."

"Na—na; aw cudna dee 't upon nae accoont," and Peter began to move away as he spoke. "Ye wud need to come in aboot to the toon at ony rate, Dawvid, man, afore we cud speak aboot onything o' the kin'."

"Oh, I've nothing ado gaen to yer toon," said Dawvid, as he slowly followed his retreating interlocutor. "It's you that I hae to sattle wi' as fairmer o' the place, that's the short an' the lang o' 't.—Fat am I to say to Sir Simon, than?" added Dawvid, in a louder and more imperious tone.

"She's jist at han'; it winna hin'er ye nae time," replied Peter, moving on rather faster than before.

Dawvid Hadden knew perfectly well what it all meant; only if Mrs. Birse had to be faced—why he was just the man to do it. "It's a keerious thing," said Dawvid, "that some fowk cudna ca' the niz o' their face their nain withoot speerin leave."

To this sarcasm Peter Birse made no reply.

Mrs. Birse had happily observed the approach of her husband and Dawvid Hadden from the parlour window, and it was but the work of a moment to call her servant maid and say, "Gae to the door there, an' gar yer maister tak' that—person—to the kitchie!"

It was in the kitchie, then, that the present interview between Dawvid Hadden and Mrs. Birse took place. When the lady was sent for she sailed majestically ben to that apartment, took her stand near the door, and with a becoming toss of the head, uttered the monosyllable "Weel?"

Dawvid Hadden had succeeded this time in restraining his impulse to mention the state of the weather; and in so doing, left himself barren of a topic for the moment.

"Noo, ye better jist say awa', Dawvid, an' tell *her* fat ye was speakin' aboot," remarked Peter Birse.

With a sort of bravado air, Dawvid then repeated Sir Simon's proposed "rectification of the frontier" of Clinkstyle.

"Onything mair, no?" asked Mrs. Birse, with a look that would like enough have withered Dawvid, had that process not been pretty effectively performed on his hard skinny person previously. "Ye're seerly owre modest the nicht i' yer thiggin !"

"Gin there's onything mair ye 'll lickly hear o' 't in 't's nain time," answered Dawvid, sharply. "Lat the thing that we cam' here aboot be sattl't i' the first place."

"Indeed! I sud think I ken my place better nor be forespoken by ony oon'er—servan'—at ony rate."

"I dinna k-now fa ye refar till," said Dawvid; "but gin ye gae muckle forder a-len'th ye 'll maybe gar me lowse o' ye the richt gate; that 's a'."

"Noo—noo, dinna come to heich words, sirs," interposed Peter Birse.

"I 'm only wuntin a plain, ceevil answer till a vera legible question to tak' back to my maister," continued Dawvid, "an' that I 'll hae."

"My compliments to yer maister, than," said Mrs. Birse, "an' tell him that there's people that k-nows their richts, an' foo far the law o' the lan' 'll cairry him or the like o' 'im; or than the best lawvyers in Aiberdeen 'll be sair mista'en. We 're nae at that yet that we 're needin' to be trampit upon aiven b' them that ca' themsel's nobility."

Having uttered this speech, Mrs. Birse turned and sailed away to the parlour again in even a more stately style than before. Dawvid, who had just been getting up steam, and who felt that, with the hints afforded him by Meg Raffan, he would speedily get into good trim for sustaining a continued onset with Mrs. Birse, was thus suddenly left high and dry, with only Peter Birse senior in a powerless, half-frightened state before him. He could get no approach to a definite reply, of course, from Peter, who was able only in a faint way to deplore and deprecate a rupture with the laird, which seemed so imminent. And Dawvid departed with the terrible threat to Peter Birse senior, "Weel, weel, ye 'll jist hae to stan' the consequences," but otherwise little enough satisfied with the results of his visit, and slightly at a loss as to the terms in which he was to report to Sir Simon.

It was in vain that Dawvid Hadden, on his way home, bothered his brains to devise a mode of avoiding Meg Raffan till the events of his afternoon's journey should be stale news, or at least until he had fully collected his thoughts on the subject. What mattered it that he stole quietly up to his house through the old fir-trees, so as to steer clear of the Lodge where Meg dwelt? He had barely been five minutes under his own roof when Meg, with leisurely step, entered, conscious of her right on this occasion to get the news in full tale. And Dawvid, when fairly put to it, gave a narrative, the distinguishing characteristic of which, as Meg Raffan herself would have expressed it, was the disposition indicated to "mak' a' face that wud be face."

"H——m, weel, Gushets was fell nabal at the ootset—mair sae nor ye wud 'a leukit for, aw daursay. But i' the lang rin, aifter I hed latt'n 'im get oot's breath a bittie, he cam' tee won'erfu'; an' fan I cam' to the prencipal thing—fat was yawin 'im for the reef o' the skweel, he ackit like a gentleman. 'Naething, Dawvid,' says he, 'naething; mak' yer best o' 't.' Nothing, cud be mair rizzonable in a menner nor that.—Na, 's ye say, 't 's nae lang till Gushets gi'e ye edder alms or answer. Ou, weel, Birse was jist like 'imsel'. I hed hardly apen't my mou' till 'im, fan we forgedder't at the fit o' the loan, till he was hingin' 's lugs like ony supplicant. To the hoose he wud be, an' to the hoose he gaed. No, no, it was i' the kitchie 't I saw 'er—I wasna wuntin naar their parlour, I 'se asseer ye. Weel, gin she wasna ensolent, my name 's nae Dawvid Hadden. Hooever, 't 's Sir Simon 't she 'll hae to be answerable till for that. But gin I didna grip 'er in aboot, I did naething to the purpose, that 's a'. Aw b'lieve she sochtna lang o' my company, at ony rate."

Meg's advice to Dawvid was to report very adversely of the Birses to Sir Simon Frissal, and Dawvid was nothing loth, merely adding the remark that of course one could not give so full and effective a narrative as might be wished in a "vrutten dockiment."

CHAPTER XLVI.

HAIRRY MUGGART GOES TO THE TOON.

WHEN "the spring day" came round, it found Johnny Gibb still occupied in attending to the completion of the fabric of Mr. MacCassock's new manse; and then he had begun to carry out his idea of preparing a separate habitation for himself at Gushetneuk. It had been suggested to Johnny that this operation would be in good time, as he need not be disturbed in his occupancy of the whole house as tenant till Whitsunday. Johnny's reply was that "the thing that 's deen the day winna be adee the morn, an' I may be deid an' buriet gin Whitsunday." In short, Johnny had resolved to push forward the arrangements connected with his quitting the position of tenant.

Hairry Muggart was architect-in-chief in the adjustment of Johnny Gibb's residence. It was Hairry's practice to season the dry details of labour with abundance of wholesome discourse, and he accordingly expatiated amply to both Johnny and Mrs. Gibb on the various conveniences that might be combined in their new dwelling. And then Hairry's thoughts reverted to his own pitiful prospect of being out of his house and croft at Whitsunday.

"Man, gin I could get but the four wa's an' a bit reef ony wye i' the neibourheid!" said Hairry.

"An' fat sud hin'er ye?" asked Johnny Gibb. "There's the aul' skweel roun at the Ward 's stan't teem till a gweed hoose 'll be connach't."

"Ou, but they wudna gie 't to nae ane, Gushets. It 's gyaun to be dung doon."

"Fa taul ye that, Hairry?"

"Weel, it 's nae ca'ed aboot story," answered Hairry. "It was jist Dawvid Hadden 'imsel'."

"An' foo muckle dee ye b'lieve o' fat he says?" said Johnny. "Win'y, leein' bodie."

"Weel, I hae kent Dawvid slide a bittie files. An' aw'm seer I'm neen obleeg't till him."

"Slide, Hairry, man! It's i' the vera natur o' 'im to lee b' word o' mou', an' haudin' 'imsel' oot to be fat he 's nae—dinna ye think the tane jist as ill 's the tither?"

The result of Johnny Gibb's advice was that Hairry Muggart took coach next morning for Aberdeen to see Mr. Greenspex, the factor. And Hairry returned in great spirits, inasmuch as the factor, without once mentioning the name of Dawvid Hadden, had said if Johnny Gibb, the only man who had any claim on the fabric of the old schoolhouse, agreed to the arrangement, Hairry was at full liberty to occupy it from Whitsunday onward; indeed his acceptance of it would fall in opportunely with a proposal of Mr. Greenspex's own, and would relieve both the factor and Sir Simon from the uncomfortable thought of turning an old tenant off the estate. Then Hairry had a perfect budget of general news to unfold; but as Johnny Gibb was not a patient listener, except on certain subjects, he did not get his "crap" fully cleared until a favourable opportunity occurred when Johnny was absent. With Mrs. Gibb and Mary Howie for his auditors, Hairry, who had set himself down on the deece for a rest, proceeded—

"Ay, but I wauger ye winna guess, Mary, fa I met i' the toon, the vera first kent face? Na, it wasna the minaister, though I gat a went o' him tee—Weel, it was jist aul' Peter Birse, o' Clinkstyle. As I cam' up the Green, fa sud be stannin there gowpin an' leukin at the antic mannie o' the Wall, but Peter. 'Loshtie me, Hairry, man,' says he, 'fan cam' ye in?' 'Jist fan the coach lichtit,' says I—'Fan cam ye?' Ou weel, Peter begood to tell 's that they hed

been in sin' the streen. 'Is the goodwife wi' ye?' says I.
'Ou ay, an' they 're awa' eenoo leukin aboot some furniture
an' things.' I didna like to catecheese 'im forder, 'cause aw
saw 't he was some bauch kin' o' the subjeck. Hooever,
him an' me staps aboot i' the market a filie, an' syne I tyeuk
'im in an' gya 'im the half o' a bottle o' ale, an' he grew a
gweed hantle crackier. 'We 're in aboot a new viackle kin'
o' a thing, Hairry,' says Peter. 'Oor aul' gig was some sair
awa' wi' 't, an' noo fan the creaturs is growin' up an' ae thing
or anither, she thocht it wud be better to get it niffer't for a
kin' o' box't-in concern—ye mith come up to the coachmakkers an' see 't.' So awa' we goes, an' jist 's we cam' up
to Union Street fa sud we meet fair i' the chafts, but Mrs.
Birse paraudin awa', an' an aul' doowager wi' 'er, haudin a
curryborum 's gin they hed been sisters—awat she was
stickin' to the doowager; an' a wee bittie awa I sees the
loon Benjie Birse, dress't like a laird, hingin' in to Maister
MacCassock, airm-in-airm wi' 'im. Peter gya a kin' o' skair't
glent, an' daccl't, an' says he, 'Na, that 's her an' oor Benjie,
tee—they hinna notic't 's.' 'Nae lickly,' says I, but wi'
that I saw brawly that Madam was takin' a vizzy o' Peter
an' me wi' the tail o' 'er e'e a' the time—Ou na, aw daursay
the minaister sawna 's; the loon Birse 't was atweesh him
an' hiz strade past 's fader an' me like a bubblyjock wi' 's
tail up, onwinkit 's e'e. Hooever, aw got oot o' Peter that
this doowager sud be some aunt, or siclike, o' the minaister's
't bides i' the toon; an' 'her an' her,' 's Peter said, wus
wylin furniture to Mr. MacCassock. Awa' up we gaes to
the coachmakkers an' sees the new 'viackle.'—Fat like is 't?
Weel, Mary, it wud bleck an unctioneer to tell you that.
It 's a kin' o' muckle box-barrow i' the boddom pairt, set on
upo' four wheels, an' syne it has a closin'-in heid-piece concern that min's me, for a' the earth, upon a mutch that my
wife hed ance wi' a byous muckle squar' kell—awat it 's a
close carriage, wi' a dickey for the driver. Jist bide ye noo,
fan there 's nae ither body to ca', aul' Peter 'imsel' 'll be set
up o' the dickey. Oh, it 's nae new, an' the man hed ta'en
back the aul' gig for pairt paymen'. 'It cost a gey penny,

I can tell ye,' says Peter. 'Ay, but ye see fat it is to be braw i' yer aul' age,' says I. Peter an' me toddl't aboot a lang time; an', at len'th, fan we wus wearin' up the wye o' the stabler's, i' the Back Wynd, up comes Mrs. Birse wi' a byous fraise—'Keep me Hairry,' says she, 'fa wud 'a expeckit to see you in Aiberdeen?' 'Weel, we're nae vera easy seen files, though we're nae jist a mote a'thegither,' says I. 'I'm jist worn aff o' my feet gyaun o' the hard stanes,' says she. 'Ye see we tint *him* there i' the foraneen, an' I've been seekin' 'im this file, an' was growin' rael eargh aboot 'im, Hairry; for there's sae mony mishanters 't we hear o' happenin' wi' the like o' 'im 't 's kent to be fae the kwintra, wi' ill company an' that, gowin' them owre, an' takin' siller aff o' them.' An' wi' this she cheenges her key —Ou ay, the loon Benjie was wi' 'er, an' as frank's frank, noo. Ye see we wus aff o' the prencipal street wi' the braw fowk on 't, an' naebody but a fyou ostlers an' cabmen, an' a man wi' a san' cairt seein' 's. 'Weel, Maister Muggart,' says she, 'it's not an easy thing to hae the upfeshin o' a faimily fan fowk tries to dee their duty an' get them sattl't i' the wordle—Oh, it's nae you Benjamin, your buzness requares a muckle ootlay—(the loon hed scowl't at her, ye ken)—but though I say 't mysel', Hairry, his nain maister says he wudna pairt wi' 'im for goold. It's 'Liza, peer thing, that I was mintin at; she'll hae a solemn chairge on 'er heid, nae doot. But ye winna differ wi' me, Hairry, fan aw say 't wudna 'a leukit weel to lat *her* come in eenoo. An' fan Maister MacCassock loot licht that he was thinkin' o' buyin' the furniture to the manse, I cudna dee less nor offer to come wi' 'im.' This was as muckle's lattin oot the pooder aboot the mairriage to me, ye see; so I tak's 'er up, an' says I, 'Aw'm vera glaid 't yer dother's gettin' sic a bargain; we wus leukin at the new viackle; it'll jist be ooncommon weel confeerin to the new connection.' —Foo cud aw say that? Gae awa' wi' ye, Mary, 'oman; yer nain waddin 'll be here in a crack, an' aw'm seer ye wudna like to hae neen o' the bucklin's mislippen't. 'Weel, Hairry, it's been a muckle thocht to me,' says she. 'For ye see it's a Gweed's trowth that we 're nae the rowlers o' oor nain acks oon'er Providence; an' fan fowk 's call't till occupee a parteeclar spear ('s we 've been af'en taul oot o' the poolpit) they maun tak' the responsibility alang wi' 't; aiven though they sud become a mark for the envious speeches o' the people o' this wordle.' 'Vera true, Mrs. Birse,' says I, ' but that 's a spawcious machine; an' I 'll be boun' Sir Seemon 'imsel' canna turn oot ane wi' a mair jinniprous heid-piece.' So she gya a bit keckle o' a lauch, an' says she, ' Ah weel, Hairry, it beheeves ither fowk to ken fat belangs them as weel 's Sir Seemon.' By this it was vera naar coach time, so I staps awa' doon, nae to loss my seat. Peter an' her tee wud 'a fain made oot fat I was deein' i' the toon; but aw b'lieve I made-na them muckle wiser. Ou weel, aw dinna doot nor they 'll be come hame i' the new viackle by this time. An' jist bide ye still, gin ye dinna see a turn-oot worth the pains I sanna bid ye believe my word again."

It was not long before Hairry Muggart had permitted his journey to Aberdeen to become publicly known in its main features. What had previously been little more than vague conjecture concerning the marriage of Mr. MacCassock to Miss Birse, seemed then to have grown into a matter of certainty, and the community of Pyketillim speculated and criticised accordingly.

CHAPTER XLVII.

JOHNNY GIBB MAKES HIS WILL.

The new domiciliary arrangements at Gushetneuk had barely been completed when Johnny Gibb's health began to give way. For many years Johnny had not had a single day's sickness, but now he had, to use his own expression, "grown as dwebble an' fushionless as a wallant leaf." What the precise nature of his complaint was nobody knew; unless the doctor did, which was doubtful; but certain it was that Johnny was not thriving physically, and he felt it his duty to put his house fully in order. He hastened on the marriage of his wife's niece, Mary Howie, to enable him to quit the active management of the farm of Gushetneuk; and he then set about the settlement of his worldly affairs generally.

"Ou, we winna dee a single day seener o' haein' ony bit tes'ment that we're needin' made," said Johnny, in discussing the point with Mrs. Gibb. "Ye'll get the souter an' the smith owre bye—an' Sandy Peterkin. Sandy's gweed at the pen; an' they'll be the executors—Hoot, 'ooman, dinna be snifterin that gate, aw'm nae awa' yet. But there's nane o''s has a siccar tack o' life, ye ken; an' aw'm seer it's a gryte comfort to you an' me tee, to hae fowk so weel wordy o' bein' lippen't till in oor sma' affairs."

"An' the merchan'," suggested Mrs. Gibb, who found some difficulty in maintaining her composure, as Johnny wished her, "wudnin he be ta'en in?"

"Ye're forycttin the triffle that's lyin' wi' 'im," said Johnny. "There's him an' Willy M'Aul baith weel aneuch fit to be trustit. But it's aye best to keep clear accoonts, aiven wi' yer nearest freens. Noo, ye ken, the tae half o' the savin's o' oor time's lyin' oot wi' the merchan' an' Willy."

"But ye wudna seek to tak' it up!"

"Never, never. Fat better eese cud ye mak' o' 't? But nedder the tane nor the tither o' them wud wunt to be trustee owre fat 's i' their nain han'."

"An' ye wud need the minaister tee."

"The minaister!" exclaimed Johnny Gibb. "Aw' won 'er to hear ye, 'oman. Only fat need aw say that? It's the thing that we wus a' brocht up wi'. The minaister to mak' yer tes'ment an' 'say a prayer,' fan it comes to the push an' ye canna better dee. An' syne tak' an oonwillin' fareweel o' the wardle. That min's me upo' aul' Sprottie, fan he was makin' 's will; tes'mentin' this, an' tes'mentin' that, 'an' syne there's the twal-owsen pleuch;' but aye he pat aff sayin' fa wud get it—sweer to think aboot pairtin wi' 't. An' at the lang len'th, fan a'thing else was will't awa', an' the minaister speer't again, 'Weel, there's the ploo now?' an' says Sprottie, 'Ou weel, Doctor, aw think aw'll keep the pleuchie to mysel' aifter a'.'"

"Hoot man," said Mrs. Gibb, half shocked at Johnny's apparent levity in the circumstances.

"Weel, weel, a body canna help a bit idle thocht rinnin i' their heid. There's nae ill o' speakin' o' the aul' man— peer ignorant stock. He's awa' mony a day sin' syne; but there's mony ane jist as oonwillin to tyne the grip 's him, till this day. Hooever, that's nedder here nor there, we're nae to coontenance settin' the minaister on to ony sic thing. He's oor spiritooal guide, an' ochtna to be made a mere convainience for the sattlement o' oor war'dly affairs. Fat cud that be but tryin' to entangle him wi' the things o' this life —wastin' 's time, that sud be gi'en to the office o' the minaistry? I won'er fat the Apos'le Paul wud hae said to be socht to dee the buzness o' a screevener or lawvyer, vreetin oot papers fa was to get this an' fa was to get the **tither thing?** **Wudnin he taul** the man that spak' o' sic a thing **that his ministry o' the** gospel deman'it ither things o' 'im? Ah, **weel, weel, I** daursay there's twa three points o' difference **atween Paul** an' a time-servin' moderate like Maister Sleek-aboot; an' a body cud **weel** believe **that** the like o' oor pairis' minaister **wud be the best han'** o' the twa to seek in aboot fan a puckle **gear hed to be tes'mentit."**

Johnny Gibb **then had his own way in the** making of his will. Sandy Peterkin, who modestly **rated his** legal knowledge and clerkly capabilities a good **deal lower than** Johnny did, was diffident of undertaking **the duty asked of** him; but Johnny would have **no na-say.** So the will **was made out,** Johnny taking **care** to make Mrs. Gibb's comfort **secure in the** first place. He then did by **every** relative **he had** according to his own idea of justice; and in every case Johnny took into account the use that had been **made of** such previous assistance as he had given them. "It's nae eese to gi'e siller till a man gin **it be** only to gar 'im **grow** lazier; or gae awa' an' mak' ill bargains," said Johnny. "We sud try to keep **it rinnin faur it 'll be paymen'** for honest, eesefu' wark, an' gi'e industrious fowk **the means o'** makin' **a** liveliheid; aye **keepin' in min'** the **claims o'** charity **an' the** gospel." And on these principles Johnny Gibb based the ultimate settlement of his worldly affairs, the Free Church of Pyketillim being set down for a future special **donation; as well as the general** funds of the Free Church.

The making of Johnny Gibb's **will** was an event that **cast a** sombre shade over **the small** community amongst whom Johnny moved; **and all** the more that after it **had** been done, Johnny's state of health worsened considerably, **so that** he was unable to make his appearance at church, or indeed leave his home at Gushetneuk to go **anywhere.**

"Eh, but he'll be a sair-miss't man, Maister Peterkin," said Meg Raffan, addressing our old friend, whom she had **been fortunate enough** to catch in Mr. Will's shop alone. "Fat he's deen for your Free Kirk ae gate or anither! An' nae doot a gweed man like him winna foryet ye i' the tes'ment."

"He 's been a vera upricht, honest man, an' an eesefu'," replied Sandy. "There 's fyou like 'im, I can tell ye, Mistress Raffan."

"Fowk *will* speak, ye ken," pursued Meg, "an' there was that bodie Dawvid Hadden gabbin awa', as though he sud ken that Gushets 's lost sae muckle wi' len'in trifles to peer kin' o' fowk, an' muckler sooms to them that it wudna be easy to uplift it fae again, that the goodwife 'll be leeft a hantle barer nor fowk wud think. But though I be sayin' that to you, Maister Peterkin, aw wudna for the wardle turn owre a word that mith pass atween 's ootside o' this chop door;—Eh, forbid it! but I was jist richt ill pay't to hear onything o' the kin' gyaun aboot fowk 't aw respeckit sae weel."

"Ou na, it wudna dee to speak aboot ither fowk's affairs," said Sandy, with the utmost simplicity. "We've naething adee wi' that, ye ken, ava."

"Na, but aw wudna mention't it till a leevin creatur but yersel', that Gushets hed aye sic a reliance till."

"I 'm muckle obleeg't; but I was ill wordy o' bein' lippen't till b' sic a man—It 'll be a sair loss to the pairt fan it losses John Gibb."

"Weel, weel, that 's the stories that 's gyaun," said Meg, baffled in her purpose of drawing information from Sandy Peterkin. "But aw 'm richt glaid to hear ye say that the goodwife 's stan'in oot sae weel; for I was byous anxious to hear aboot 'er, aifter aw kent that Gushets was thocht to be wearin' awa'."

CHAPTER XLVIII.

THE CLIMAX OF GENTILITY.

When Peter Birse senior went down to the Broch at the January market, in 1848, it being a sort of feeing-market, and Peter being in want of a man to fill a vacancy in his staff of servants, caused by a recent quarrel and dismissal, he had received this instruction—

"Noo, ye'll see an' get a smairt, genteel lad; an' tell 'im that he'll be expeckit, gin the spring day war in, to drive a fawmily convaiyance to the kirk every Sabbath; an' to be providit wi' a silk hat o' 's nain, an' claith breeks; he'll get glives an' a licht neckcloth fae 's employers."

In short, Mrs. Birse, acting with her usual foresight, wished to arrange, by anticipation, for the proper driving of the new vehicle. What she aimed at was a servant set out in a sort of subdued livery.

Peter Birse diligently endeavoured to carry out his wife's behest, but received from several likely-looking chaps whom he sounded an unceremonious rebuff. "Na, sang; gin we work sax days i' the ouk we dee brawly; ye can ca' yersel' to the kirk, laird. Ye'll need-a try some ither ane to be a flunkey to ye; we're nae come to that yet freely." So said number one; and numbers two and three repeated it with slight variations. The day was wearing on, and Peter getting the reverse of hopeful, when he encountered the red-haired orra man who had officiated as best young man at the marriage of Peter Birse junior. The red-haired orra man, who had been offering himself to fee in a free and easy sort of way, but had not encountered anybody who met his terms, was approaching the state known as "bleezin." Peter Birse senior averred that he, personally, was "chilpy stan'in' aboot amo' the gutters," whereupon the red-haired orra man declared they ought to go inside, and they did so. As they sat in Kirkie's tent, and refreshed themselves with the gill which the orra man had called, Peter proceeded to lay out the difficulties of the mission he had presently in hand. It was not that he thought of asking the red-haired orra man to undertake the duties of the situation, but that the latter, in his somewhat elevated condition, conceived the notion that it would be a good "rig" to engage himself to Peter as the genteel lad wanted. Peter Birse senior had some hazy doubts, which, however, a second gill dispelled, and the red-haired orra man was engaged to return once again to Clinkstyle, and there to officiate as coachman as required.

Naturally the announcement that Peter Birse senior had to make as to the result of his efforts in the market ensured for him a somewhat snell reception on his return. However, there was no use in declaiming against accomplished facts. All that could be done was to make the best of things as they were. And Mrs. Birse was fully determined that this should be done.

She had made sundry tentative excursions here and there in the new viackle, but it was only when Sir Simon Frissal had returned to the locality in the beginning of the month of April that she resolved to turn out in full style. Sir Simon, as was well known, drove along to the parish kirk at the same hour precisely, every Sabbath day that he was at home and in health; and the modest scheme devised was to time the departure of the Clinkstyle carriage, so as that it should at any rate cross Sir Simon's carriage at a favourable spot, if it were not found possible even to drive half alongside the laird a little space where the two kirk routes concurred. To accomplish all this Mrs. Birse judiciously coaxed and flattered the red-haired orra man, giving him assurance how well he looked when properly "cleaned," and his coat buttoned. She would fain have had a sight of his Sunday wardrobe, but had to be content with the general statement that it was " spleet new fae the nap o' the bonnet to the point o' the taebit." Sunday came, the carriage was trundled out, and it was with a kind of dignified satisfaction that Mrs. Birse saw the red-haired orra man bustling about, minus his coat and hat, yokin' the carriage horse. The family had taken their seats, not without a kind of protest from Miss Birse, who, to her mother's great disappointment, had as yet failed to exhibit any symptoms of satisfaction with the carriage scheme. They were ready to start, when Mrs. Birse was horrified by seeing the red-haired orra man mount the dickey with an unmistakable sample of the broad blue bonnet on his head. It was one of those substantial bonnets that were wont to be manufactured on big knitting wires, and the nap, or top, was formed of a huge bunch of worsted, wrought up right in the centre of the bonnet. The orra man spoke truly in saying it was " spleet new," for the bonnet had evidently been purchased for that very occasion, as its extraordinary circumference and bulk testified. Mrs. Birse started indignantly, and uttered an exclamation which was a sort of half protest against the orra man, and half reproach to Peter Birse senior, who had crammed himself into one of the back corners of the viackle, and wore an extremely uncomfortable look. But the carriage was already in motion, and the driver seemed noway disposed to interrupt his progress for any mere incidental utterance. He rattled on mercilessly over the roughly-causewayed road leading out from the steading of Clinkstyle to the highway proper. Then in a trice they were into the head of the stream of kirk-going people, many of whom the red-haired orra man saluted with great familiarity, nodding his portentous bonnet, and flourishing his whip, while once and again he called out to an old cronie, " Hilloa, lad ; there's the style for you !" Attempts at remonstrating and checking this reckless course were, it need not be said, utterly out of the question in the circumstances. Mrs. Birse strove hard to cover her wrath with an air of sanctimonious resignation, while Peter Birse, who timidly watched her face with a lively apprehension of the after consequences, looked increasingly ill at ease, and Miss Birse and her brother Rob, in so far as they could make themselves heard, concurred, though on different grounds, in the folly of ever setting a fellow like the red-haired orra man to drive. Rob, who kept his equanimity better than any of the others, seized the opportunity of reminding his mother that he had been perfectly willing to act as driver, adding, with a feeling of satisfaction, that he "kent a hantle better aboot ca'in' horse nor that gype did. An' here's the laird's carriage," added Rob, as sure enough it was. And the orra man rattled on. To cross Sir Simon's carriage in proper style had been Mrs. Birse's highest ambition. But the vision of that horrible braid bonnet, with its big nap passing in view of the dignified baronet lying back on his velvet cushion was enough to make one faint away, without the addition of those deplorable vulgarities on the part of the red-haired orra man in cracking his whip, and shouting to Sir Simon's coachman to "Ca' awa', min, or gae oot o' ither fowk's road."

Mrs. Birse did not faint away; but when the viackle reached the church, and pulled up in the midst of many loitering, eagerly-gazing onlookers, she threw open the door and preceded her daughter into the church with a severely devotional air.

Next day the duty devolved on Peter Birse of informing the red-haired orra man that his services were no longer required at Clinkstyle. The orra man did not much mind. He swore a little, and demanded wages for the time he had laboured, which was conceded, and Peter Birse, in filling his place, was not asked to look out for another coachman.

"Eh, but that was a precious discoorse 't we got on Sabbath," said Mrs. Birse, addressing her daughter two days after the incidents last recorded. "There's naething to be leukit for in this wordle but cheenges an' disappointments. Sic a blessin' 's it is to be near conneckit wi' a man like Maister MacCassock. Aw cud not 'a been onmin'et upo'

Gushetneuk, peer man, fan he spak' so edifyin aboot foo little wor'dly riches cud dee for 's fan the day o' affliction or the oor o' deeth cam'."

"Mr. Gibb's not dyin', he's some better," said Miss Birse.

"Eh, 'Liza, fat cud gar ye think that?—the man's been gi'en owre this aucht days near. An' forbye that, didna ye hear 'im pray't for wi' yer nain—ears?"

"Weel; the minister pray't for his recovery.

"Oh, 'Liza, 'oman, fan did ever ye hear a person pray't for that wusna dyin'; tell me that?"

Miss Birse was evidently unconvinced of the futility of prayer for the sick except when the subject of it was, as the doctors say, *in articulo mortis*, or certainly entering on that state. As little was her mother to be shaken in her belief on the point, which, indeed, was the popular belief in Pyketillim. But Mrs. Birse had a lingering suspicion of the quarter from which her daughter's information had come, and she had just put the question, "Did ye see Mrs. Wull i' yer roun's the streen?" when the servant girl knocked at the parlour door, and handed in a letter, with the remark, "That's a letter to the Mistress, 't the merchan's laddie fuish jist eenoo."

"Letter to me, 'Liza! It's fae yer nown broder Benjamin. Foo i' the wordle hisna he vrutten to you as eeswal. I houp he's weel aneuch—See read it, there—I hinna my glesses."

The latter sentence was a sort of euphemism which, literally explained, would have helped to account for Benjamin Birse ordinarily addressing his sister directly in place of his mother. Miss Birse broke open the note, and read as follows :—

DEAR MOTHER—I hope father and you will open this—not Eliza. What a precious ass you've made of me, saying that MacCassock was to marry Eliza; and me going toadying them like this till yesterday, when his aunt offered to introduce me to a Miss Catchbands, "her nephew's intended wife." The old hag says it's all settled to be in a month.

That's what I call doing the greenhorn, and no mistake. However, it's easy enough to cut them here; and just shave my head if you catch me at Clinkstyle, till this idiotic affair blows over.

Your affectionate son,
BN. BIRSE.

P.S.—MacCassock's not a goose—no more than the rest of your parsons—she has plenty of tin.

Mrs. Birse managed somehow to hear out Master Benjamin's note to the last word. She then expanded her arms, and with a huge screech went off in what was meant for hysterics.

CHAPTER XLIX.

THE CONCLUSION.

The first thought struggling in the mind of Mrs. Birse was, whether etiquette demanded that she should faint and give way to utter unconsciousness under the blow which Benjie's letter had inflicted upon her, or whether grief, in a more demonstrative form, could be properly exhibited. But human nature quickly asserted its sway, and, rising to the occasion at once, she exclaimed—

"The Judas-like person! Fa in this wordle cud 'a believ't onything o' the kin'. Eh, but it's aneuch to fesh the vera jeedgment o' Gweed upo' the place. Aifter fat we've deen for 'im, late an' ear'! An' you, my peer innocent lamb! But I'll gar 'im swate for 't no, as lang's there's gweed lawvyers in Aiberdeen. Get your vritein dask, this minute, 'Liza."

Miss Birse, who had maintained her equanimity in a wonderful manner, obeyed her mother's injunction without uttering a single word.

"Noo, ye'll jist vreet aff at ance to your broder, Benjamin, an' tell him to forquant Maister Pettiphog wi' a' the haill rinnins o' the maitter; an' I'm sair mista'en gin he binna as weel up to the quirks o' the law as can vreet a letter that'll gi'e 'im a fleg that he hisna gotten the like o' sin' he leeft's mither's awpron-strings."

To Mrs. Birse's utter surprise, her daughter, with perfect composure and equal explicitness, answered, "No, mother, I'll do nothing o' the kin'."

"'Liza! are ye i' yer senses?" exclaimed Mrs. Birse.

"Mr. MacCassock never asked me to marry him; an' though he had I didna want him. It's all been a plan o' your own. I am sure he was not wantin' to deceive you."

The explosion that ensued was violent, and the sound of Mrs. Birse's voice could be heard even outside the parlour in a higher key than well accorded with the rules of genteel society. It was soon over, however, and at the close Miss Birse had retreated to her bedroom in tears, but without having written, or consented to write, the letter to her lawyer brother. Mrs. Birse stalked out of the parlour and to the kitchen with a face that spoke of combustion, and a sensation in her breast of groping after the proper object on which she might expend her feelings. "Fat's come o' yer maister?" said she, addressing the servant girl. "That was his fit that aw heard nae mony minutes syne."

"Ou, he cam' into the kitchie, an' aifter hoverin' a minute makin' to gae ben, turn't, rael swyppirt, an' said he wud awa' to the back faul's an' see foo the mole-catcher was comin' on."

Peter's instinct was quite correct; but the reader, who should imagine that this sudden elopement saved him his full share in the stormy ebullition that followed the collapse of the MacCassock matrimonial project, would have formed even yet but an imperfect idea of his astute spouse's character and views of duty. Those who have really understood that amiable matron, as she lived and moved, will have no difficulty whatever in realising for themselves the agonising ordeal through which Peter Birse senior had to pass on this subject.

It was even as Mr. Benjamin Birse had written; and Mr. MacCassock's marriage had speedily to be numbered among accomplished events. Who could wonder that the succeeding Sabbath should see the Clinkstyle viackle on its way to the Free Kirk at the Broch, and not to the Free Kirk of Pyketillim? It was occupied by Mrs. Birse and Peter Birse senior, and Rob Birse was the driver. For several succeeding Sabbaths the viackle pursued the same route.

"Aw div not won'er nor ye canna be edifiet wi' sic a man," said Meg Raffan, on whom Mrs. Birse had conferred the unexpected honour of a visit at the Lodge. But Meg Raffan checked her utterance, for she had an impression that Mrs. Birse and her daughter were not of one mind on this question. Therefore Meg confined herself to the safe ground of a moral and social dissection of the newly-arrived Mrs. MacCassock, and to discreetly answering the leading questions put by Mrs. Birse with a view to find out what was being said of herself in connection with recent events. "Eh, Mrs. Birse, ye needna gi'e yersel' twa thochts aboot that," said Meg; "ye're owre weel kent i' the pairt. It's nae orra claicks that'll blaud your character."

But Meg Raffan was rather at a loss now for news concerning the Free Kirk and sundry other matters. Whitsunday had come and gone, and Hairry Muggart, who had flittit down to Smiddyward, was no longer available as a regular medium, seeing he had ceased to be the laird's vricht. and had no occasion to pass the Wast Lodge statedly. The claims of her feathered charge at that season—multiplied in number by a succession of brodmils of young turkeys, ducks, and other poultry—absolutely prevented Meg leaving home for more than a very short space of time. Yet when one is gizzen't for want of news some shift must be made, and she had at last taken a rin owre to see Hairry Muggart in his new abode.

"Ou ay," said Hairry, who was in the highest spirits on the subject of his change of residence. "We live here like prences, wi' oor kailyard for a kingdom. Gin we wunt the rigs, we're free o' the cost an' tribble o' earin' them. Hoot, fye! is Dawvid gyaun throu''t wi' the new vricht already? Weel, weel, lat 'im drink 's he 's brew't; gin the man binna cawpable o' 's wark the laird 'll ken fa he's obleeg't till."

"Weel-a-wat, Dawvid an' him was at the knag an' the wuddie ere he was an ouk there; an' Dawvid keest up till 'im that he was only an incomer, a peer freen o' the dominie's, an' mair nor muckle obleeg't to the minaister for winnin there ava—aw div not believe but they 'll hae the creatur afore the session for 's ill win'. 'But,' says Dawvid, 'ye 'll k-now that, dominie or no dominie, it 's only at my merciment gin ye be lang here.'"

"Aye the aul' man, Hennie," said Hairry. "He hed been roun' aboot the Kirktoon, it wud seem, lattin licht foo that he sud be instrucket to 'lay aff' Clinkstyle in coorse afore the tack rin oot, 'cause Sir Seemon 's to pit Peter Birse awa'."

"Weel, weel; lat them b'lieve 'im that 's nae better employ't," said Meg; "but fat 's this that you Free Kirkers 's been deein' mairryin yer minaister by the maiden o' Clinkstyle?"

"Keep me, Meg; an' that 's a' 't ye ken aboot it. That 's piper's news! Speer at Lucky Birse hersel' fat gar't the Miss leave the toon last ouk aifter a throu'-the-muir that dreeve aul' Peter naarhan' dementit, an' refeese ever to lat 'er face be seen there again oonless the viackle—saw ye ever sic a moniment o' a thing, Meg?—sud be sent back faur it cam' fae, or pittin o' the hen-reist, never to be ta'en doon again."

"Na, Hairry, but ye dee gar me ferlie; an' me hed 'er in aboot at the Lodge nae passin' aucht days syne. 'Fat neist?' thinks I. 'The gryte goodwife callin o' oorsel', a peer indwaller i' the hirehouse!' Hooever, she camna wuntin' 'er erran'. She thocht to get me to tak' half-a-dizzen o' peer stilperts o' cock chuckens at the price o' grown fools; but I beheeld 'er; an' than she lows't the richt gate aboot the minaister an' a' 's ation. But wi' a' 'er ootbearin' an' pride, aw cud see 't she was jist a kin' o' made like, an' wud 'a unco fain hed a bodie's 'sempathy,' 's yer freen Dawvid, wi' 's muckle words, wud say. But the Miss daurin' to flee in 'er mither's witters that gate! Na, sirs!"

"Ah," said Hairry, with a sage smile. "It 's a' a maitter o' sympathy, Meg; nae doot ye 'll oon'erstan' 't perfeckly. Your mither's wull wud be a law to ye sae lang, i' yer bairnheid; but fan ye cam' fae lassie to lass, maybe ye wud come to hae a bit o' a saftness an' a drawin' oot to some ither ane nor yer mammy, an' a wull fae the tither side o' the hoose wud begin to hae swye wi' ye.—Ou, ye needna leuk, 'oman," said Hairry, addressing his wife.

"For shame to ye, Hairry Muggart," exclaimed Meg Raffan, assuming as much of the affronted-maiden air as she could.

"Deed, ye may say 't; isnin he a feel aul' man, Hennie?" said Mrs. Muggart, in her usual fashion.

"That's mair nor lickly," answered Hairry, with great composure. "Hooever, the Miss's oot o' 'er mither's leadin-strings, aw' doot; an' it chaets me sair gin the peer lassie hedna a man body wi' a wull o' 's nain at the back o' 't, ere she cud mak' it a doon-laid rowle that the curricle sud be disabolish't. There's to be nae mair ca'in' awa' to hyne awa' kirks; an' forby that, 'er fader's to be latt'n gae to see his gweed-dother—young Peter's wife, ye ken—an' 'er bairns o' the market days."

"Na, sirs, an' the Miss's gotten some ane to help 'er to coup the creels o' the aul' 'oman?"

"Aw sudna won'er," said Hairry, with a half-careless, half-mysterious air.

"Cud it be the merchan', no?" asked the henwife, with growing interest.

"Weel, I've seen fowk blater at guessin, Meg," answered Hairry; "we'll see, come time."

"Na, but didna I tell 's nain mither that, near twa towmons syne?" said Meg Raffan.

"Noo, man," said Mrs. Muggart, putting in her word with something of decision in her tone, "ye winna need to sit there a' aifterneen lyaugin wi' fowk, an' negleckin yer erran'. It's time that ye war owreby to meet Gushet-neuk."

"Eh, but that's weel min'et," said Meg. "Peer man; an' Gushets's aye to the fore, is he? Aw was dreamin' aboot 'im the tither nicht richt sair."

"Ye live at the back o' the wardle, seerly, noo, Meg. Dinna ye ken that Johnny Gibb 's fairly cantl't up again?"

"Eh, but aw'm richt blythe to hear 't. Aw heard that he was feerious far gane in a swarf the tither day, an' hardly expeckit to come a-list again? But he's winnin to the gate a bittie?"

"Hoot; he was able to be doon at the kirk last Sunday, on 's nain feet, an' I 'm jist gyaun awa' owrebye that gate to see 'im aboot some jots o' wark at the Manse offices, that 's been lyin' owre sin' he fell bye; and nae ither ane cud gi'e me orders aboot them.—Ou ay, he 's gotten a bit o' a shak'; but he 's nae that oonfersell again growin'. He has a free han' noo, like the lave o' 's, an' young fowk aboot him as prood o' atten'in' 's comman's as gin he war the laird. Na, na, Gushets is courin up fine; an' him an' the goodwife 's makin' ready to gae doon to the Walls for an aucht days or siclike; an' that 's a hantle better for the constiteetion nor a' the doctor's drogs that ye can pit in'o yer inside."

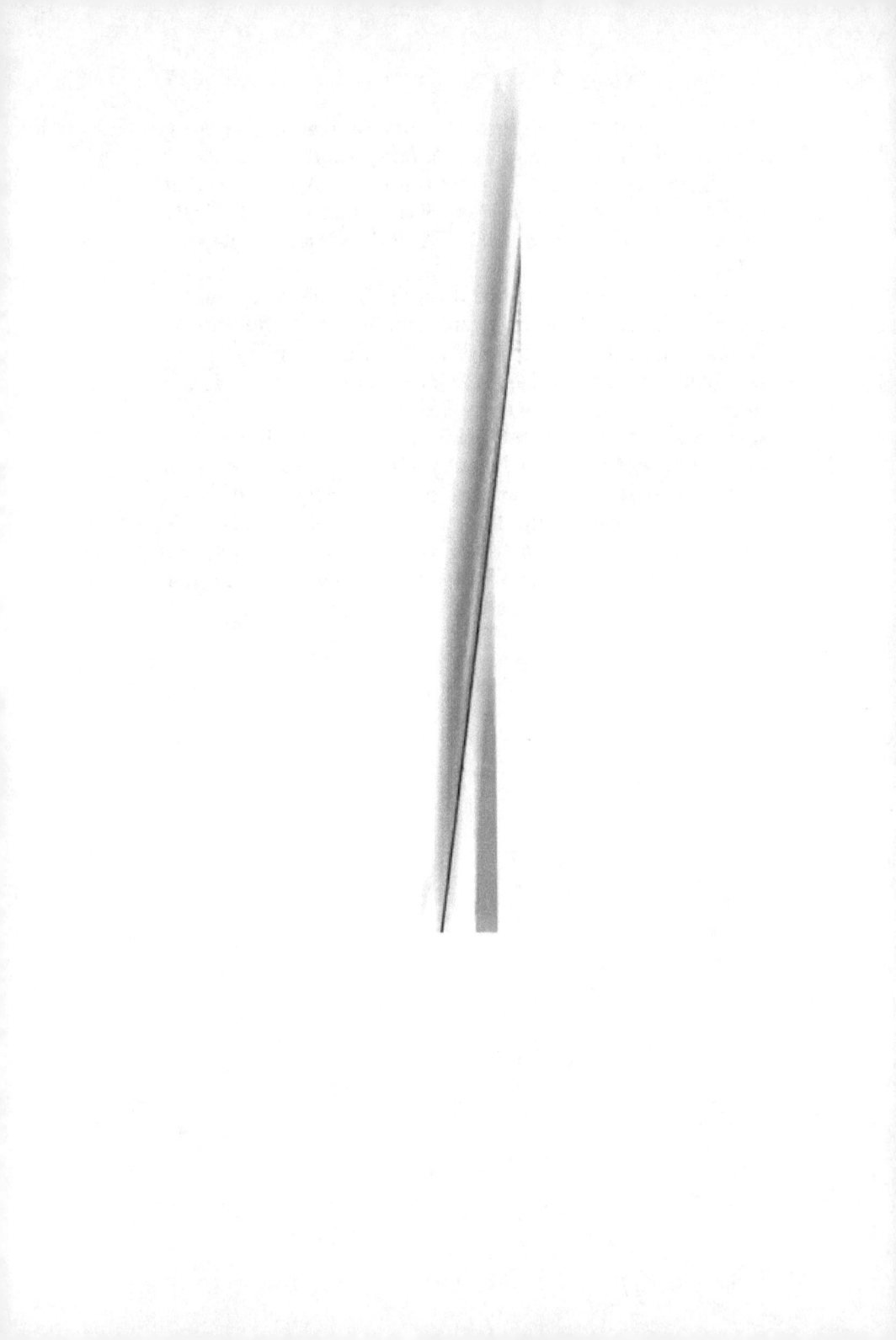

GLOSSARY.

[THE purpose of a Glossary being simply to facilitate intelligent reading, it has not been sought either to trace the words explained below to their etymological sources, or to give *all* the meanings that may be attached to some of them.

The dialect of Aberdeenshire is so peculiar that many of its words will hardly be intelligible even to the inhabitant of the southern and western districts of Scotland. It is, however, tolerably consistent in its peculiarities; and, therefore, while the Glossary presents the *meanings*, a remark or two may be allowed with the view of enabling the reader to arrive at the *pronunciation* of the words.

In certain present participles, and participial nouns, **the** only **difference between** them and the same words in English is the dropping of the **terminal** *g*; thus, *workin'* for *working;* and therefore **it** has not been thought necessary **to** cumber the Glossary by the insertion of such words. In many of the words the digraph *ch* has been substituted for *gh* in the spelling, in order to indicate the guttural sound; thus, *nicht* for *night*. *Wh* is changed into *f*, to express the **actual pronunciation**; thus, *wha* (who), *fa ; whip, fup.*

Oo **in** the south **of** Scotland has the sound of the French *u ;* as, **in** *shoon*, *moon*, *spoon*, but, by the time he has crossed the Dee, the philologist will find **the** *oo* changed into *ee*, sounded precisely **as** in the name of that beautiful river, **and thus we** get *sheen, meen, speen.* There are, however, various exceptions to **this** rule ; *look*, for example, becomes *leuk*, **not** *leek ;* and *book, beuk*, not *beek*. *Th* gets changed into *d ;* as *fader* for *father ; breeder* for *brother*, **and so on.** The change of *wh* into *f*, and of *th* into *d*, both find illustration in **one word**, *fudder* (sometimes *futher*), *whether*.

Diminutives, in which Aberdeenshire **Scotch** is peculiarly rich, are generally formed by adding *ie* to **the** noun, as **lass, lassie ;** *dog, doggie.* *Ock*, supposed by some to represent the **Gaelic** *og*, young, **is not**, however, uncommon, as *lass, lassock*. And, frequently, **as** indicating a **still greater** degree of diminution, both are employed, thus : *lass, lassock, lassockie.* **But, not** satisfied with this, the natives carry the diminution yet farther, by two or **three** degrees. And so we have a *bit lassockie,* a *wee bit lassockie ;* and lastly, a *little wee bit lassockie*, in **the** fifth degree of comparison. Examples of such **kindly diminution** occur in the lines—

> There was a *wee bit wifockie,* an' she gaed to the fair,
> She gat a *wee bit drappockie* that bred her muckle care.

D, t, **and** *l* at the end of words are often dropped: thus, *respect* becomes *respeck ; wind, win' ;* and *wall, wa'.* **The** omission of final *d* after *l* is uniform, and distinguishes the dialect from classical Scottish. Thus *aul, baul, faul,* (pl. *fauls*), for *auld, bauld, fauld ;* English old, etc. *V* is also frequently omitted wherever it occurs: thus *have* becomes *hae*, and *harvest, hairst*.

320 GLOSSARY.

[In the spelling of certain words *y* or *e* has been introduced to indicate, as near as might be, the veritable pronunciation; as *gyaun*, *neuk*, *leuk*. *G* and *k* are always pronounced before *n*, as in German, thus *g*nash, *g*nap, *k*nife.

The greater part of the words will be found in Jamieson's *Scottish Dictionary*, though by no means the whole. It has not been thought necessary to adhere to Jamieson's spelling, the author taking it upon him to believe that neither in Jamieson nor elsewhere is authoritative or perfectly satisfactory guidance to be got in determining the correct orthography of the Aberdeenshire dialect. In the circumstances, while taking care to make his characters speak with idiomatical accuracy in the text, he has endeavoured there and in the Glossary to present their speech to the eye with as little departure from relative Saxon or other forms as might be, and yet with such regard to phonetic considerations as seemed likely to give a measure of guidance in pronunciation.]

A

Ablich or *ablach*, an insignificant person.
Aboot, about.
Adee, ado.
Aff, off.
Ahin, behind.
Aifter, after.
Aifterneen, **afternoon.**
Ain, own.
Airm, arm.
Airt, quarter of the heaven; point of the compass.
Aise, ashes.
Aise-backet, a box for ashes.
Aisp, asp.
Aiven, even.
Aleberry, oatmeal boiled in beer and sweetened with sugar.
Aleen, alone.
Amnin aw? am not I?
Amo', among.
Anersmas, St. Andrew's Day, the last day of November.
Aneth, beneath.
Aneuch, enough.
Anidder, another.
Antrin, occasional; accidental.
Argle-bargle, to chaffer; to haggle.
Arles, the earnest given in striking a bargain.
Arreenge, to arrange.
Asseer, to assure.
Aten, eaten.
A'thegither, altogether.
Athort, athwart.
Ation, generation; family connections.
Atween, between.
Aucht, property.
Aucht, to owe; *auchtin*, due.
Aucht nor *oucht*, nothing at all; neither one thing nor the other.
Audiscence, audience; encouragement to speak; a hearing.
Aught, eight.
Aul, old; *aul'er*, older.
Aumry, cupboard; ambry.
Ava, at all.
Aw, I.
Awa, away.
Awat, I wot.
Awcre, acre.
Aweel, well!
Aweers o', on the point of.

B

Back, to address a letter.
Back-chap, back-stroke; **to haud in** [interpose] *a back-chap;* **to back one.**
Backin, the address on a letter.
Bairn, child.
Bairnheid, childhood.
Bandster, one who **binds sheaves.**
Basketie, small basket.
Bather, trouble; **teasing conduct.**
Bauch, sheepish; backward through bashfulness.
Bauk, balk; (1) uncultivated strip of land between fields; (2) cross beam uniting the rafters of a roof.
Baul, bold.
Bawbee, a halfpenny.
Behaud'n, beholding or beholden; *behaud'n to*, beholden to; under obligation to.
Beheef, behoof.
Bess, to play or sing bass (in music).
Be't, behoved.
Beetikin, bootikin; half-boot.
Beetle, to beat clothes with a heavy wooden mallet.
Beetlin-stane, the stone on which clothes are beetled.
Begeck, disappointment; to disappoint. [Comp. English *geck*, a dupe.]
Begood, began; pret. of begin.

GLOSSARY.

Ben and *but*, the two ends of a cottage [see *But-bed*].
Bestial, cattle.
Beuk, book.
Beukin'-nicht, **the** night on which the **names** of the persons about to be married **are** booked, or given in to the Session-Clerk to have the *banns* proclaimed.
Bield, shelter ; a house.
Billie, a companion ; comrade.
Bing, a heap.
Binna, be not.
Birkie, a smart roguish fellow.
Birn, a burden.
Birr, force ; energy.
Birsle, to toast ; *birslin*, **toasting** ; completely dry so as **to** be **rustling.**
Birst, to burst.
Birze, to press ; to push forward as in an opposing crowd ; the southern form is *Brizz*, *e.g.*, *We'll* **brizz** *yont;* a phrase attributed to the titled owner of an extensive Highland property, when remonstrated with on the apparent folly of building his castle at a point closely touching the marches of certain feebler neighbours.
Blaewort, the blue-bell.
Blaik, to blacken.
Blate, sheepish ; bashful.
Blaud, to spoil ; to deteriorate.
Blaw, to boast ; to speak ostentatiously.
Bleb, to sip freely or continuously ; to tipple.
Bleck, to puzzle ; to surpass.
Bleed, blood.
Bleezes, blazes ! used as an expletive.
Bleezin (literally), blazing ; conventionally) hilariously tipsy.
Blythe, glad ; cheerful ; happy.
Boddom, bottom.
Bowet, a lantern.
Bools, bowls.
Boose, a bout of drinking ; to drink freely.
Boun's, bounds ; limits.
Bourach, knot or group as of people.
Bow, an arch ; the part of the harness bent under the neck of the draught-ox in the old-fashioned team to fasten the yoke : *owre the bows* signifies acting in **an** obstreperous or irregular manner.
Bowie, a **cask.**
Brae, sloping ground ; acclivity.
Braig, to brag ; to boast.
Braivity, show ; splendour ; **finery.**

Brakfist, breakfast.
Braw, fine ; elegant : **in** *braw time,* **in** good time.
Brawly, bravely ; **finely ;** prosperously.
Breeder, brother.
Breeks, breeches.
Breem, broom.
Breet, brute ; wonderfully attenuated in signification when applied to a person : *peer breet*, poor fellow.
Breid, bread ; breadth.
Britchen, breeching ; harness on breech of horses.
Broch, burgh ; *the Broch*, emphatically applied to the nearest burgh.
Brocht, **brought.**
Brod, **the collecting-box in church ; the** ladle.
Brodmil, brood of **chickens.**
Bruik, broke.
Bubblyjock, turkey cock.
Buckies, univalve whorled shells.
Bucklin's, marriage paraphernalia, **or** other outfit.
Buff, idle talk ; **nonsense.**
Bull, bill.
Bullyrag, to treat in a bullying manner.
Bun, bound : *bun-bed*, a wooden bed shut in with folding or sliding doors.
Bunchie, dim. of bunch ; a small quantity.
Bung, ill-humour ; pet ; huff.
Burn, a small stream : dim. *burnie.*
But-bed, a cottage is divided into two apartments, the *but* and the *ben*, properly the outer and inner rooms ; the *but bed*, therefore, is the bed in the *but*, or semi-parlour end.
Byous, out of the common ; **extra**ordinary ; exceedingly.
Byoutifu, beautiful.
Byre, a cow-house.
By'se, besides.

C

Cairnin', laying **on in cairns or heaps ;** spreading thickly.
Cairt, cart.
Caller, cool ; **fresh.**
Can'lesmas, Candlemas.
Canna, can't ; cannot.
Cannas, canvas ; especially that used in winnowing grain : *cannas breid*, the breadth or size of such a piece of canvas.
Canny, prudent ; cautious ; sly ; skilful.
Cantle-up, to brighten up, as on regaining health.

Y

Carle, churl : dim. *carlie*.
Carline, fem. of *carl* ; a rough, vociferous woman.
Catechis, Catechism.
Cauf, calf ; dim. *caufie*.
Cauff, chaff.
Caums, moulds for balls, horn spoons, etc.
Caup, a bowl turned out of a single piece of wood.
Cept, or *cep*, except.
Chack, blue and white chequered linen or calico cloth.
Chafts, chops ; jaws (used contemptuously).
Chanter, the flute-like part of the bagpipes on which the tune is played.
Chap, a young fellow ; to knock ; to strike with a hammer.
Chaep, cheap.
Chaum'er, a chamber, applied to sleeping place for farm servants in outhouses ; to shut up in a chamber.
Cheenge, to change.
Cheer, chair.
Chiel, a proper fellow ; dim. *chielie*.
Chimley, chimney.
Chop, shop.
Chuckens, chickens.
Chyne, chain.
Claer, correct ; distinct ; ready.
Claes, clothes.
Claikit, idly tattled.
Claiks, clacks ; gossip.
Clampin, walking noisily, as with hobnailed shoes.
Clench, to limp
Cleuk, a claw or talon ; the hand (contemptuously).
Clivver, clover.
Clossach, a mass ; sum of hoarded money.
Clype, to carry tales.
Clypes, tattle ; tell-tale gossip.
Coblie, dim. of *coble* ; a wayside watering-place.
Cockernony, the starched *kell* or crown of a woman's cap.
Confeerin, suitable ; corresponding.
Connach, to spoil ; to destroy.
Conter, contrary ; to oppose.
Contermin't, counterminded ; contradictory.
Coont, to count.
Coontin, arithmetic.
Coorse, coarse ; harsh ; course.
Coort, court.
Coup, to upset ; to tilt up ; to overturn : *to coup the creels*, meta., completely to upset a plan or project.

Cour, to recover (said of health).
Cowshus, cautious.
Crackie, talkative ; **pleasingly communicative**.
Craft, croft ; dim. *craftie*.
Crap, crop, particularly of cereals ; dim. *crappie* ; also the crop of a bird.
Craw, to crow : *to craw in your crap*, to prove indigestible, used meta. of what will give trouble afterwards.
Creelie, dim. of *creel*, an osier basket.
Creengin, cringing ; obsequious.
Cronies, familiar companions.
Croon, crown.
Cudna, couldn't ; could not.
Culph, *culph't*, to drive home the wadding, or culphin.
Curryborum, confidential conversation, of a quiet, earnest, and semi-gossiping sort.

D

Daar, dear ; expensive.
Daccle, to slacken one's pace.
Daily-day, every day ; continually.
Dargin, working as a day labourer.
Daumer't, stunned ; stupefied.
Daurin, daring.
Daursay, daresay.
Dawtie, a pet.
Deave, to deafen ; to annoy by importunity.
Dee, to do ; to die.
Deece, a long wooden seat in the form of a sofa, with panelled back, and no padding.
Deed, indeed.
Deem, dame ; lass : dim. *deemie*.
Deen, done ; used in a secondary sense, thus : *nae that deen ill*, not so very ill.
Deesters, doers ; actors ; promoters ; agents.
Deeth, death.
Deid, dead.
Del'in, delving ; cultivating with the spade.
Dementit, mad ; unreasonable.
Dennerin, providing or serving dinner.
Descryve, to describe.
Deval, to cease.
Deykn, deacon ; one who excels in his profession.
Didnin, didn't ; did not.
Diffeekwalty, difficulty, accented on the second syllable.
Dilse, dulse.

Ding-on, to rain or snow.
Dinna, don't ; do not.
Dird, to drive or cast violently.
Disabolish, to abolish.
Discoont, discount.
Disjeest, digest.
Dist, dust ; the pollen of oats detached in grinding, used for feeding poultry, etc.
Dit, to close ; to fill.
Div, do ; *fan div ye gae?* when do you go ?
Divnin, do not ?
Divot, a flat turf.
Dizzen, dozen.
Dog-dirder, whipper-in ; kennel attendant.
Dog-oil, oil extracted from **the livers** of dog-fish.
Doitit, stupid ; stupefied.
Dominie, a schoolmaster (from *domine*).
Dook, **to** bathe.
Dooker, **one** who ducks, **or bathes.**
Doon, down.
Doosht, **a soft** heavy blow.
Doot, doubt : *nae doot*, no **doubt.**
Dossie, a small quantity in **the form** of **a** knot or cluster.
Dother, daughter.
Dottl't, forgetful (chiefly through age) : *dottlin*, becoming stupid or forgetful.
Dozen't, exclamation equivalent to con-**found** it ! stupefy it !
Drap, **drop** : dim. *drappie.*
Dreeve, drove.
Drogs, drugs.
Drow, fit of sickness.
Dud, cloth : *duds*, clothes.
Dummie, one who is dumb ; a mute.
Dunt, to knock ; strike with **a** hollow sound : *to dunt it oot*, to settle a dispute by a stand-up encounter.
Dwelble, feeble ; bending with **weak-**ness.
Dyker, a builder of rough **stone fences** or dykes.

E

Ear or **air**, early.
Eargh, **frightened** ; superstitiously afraid.
Easelom, **ease** ; relief.
Edder, either.
Edick, an edict.
Een, eyes.
Eenoo, even now ; just now.
Eese, use ; to use.

Eesefu' useful.
Eeswal, usual : *war nor eeswal*, worse than usual.
Eident, industrious ; diligent.
Eik, to make **an** addition : *to eik him up*, to egg him on.
El'ers or *elyers*, elders **(in the Presby-**terian Church).
Erran', errand ; message.
Ettercap, a poisonous spider ; a person of a crabbed and troublesome or irritable disposition.
Ettle, to endeavour ; to aim at.
Excamb, one piece of ground exchanged for another.
Exkeesable, excusable.
Expeckit, expected.
Expoon, expound.

F

Fa, who.
Fa', **fall.**
Fader, father.
Fae, from.
Fan, when.
Fangs, louts ; **lumpish fellows.**
Fant, faint.
Fash, trouble.
Fat, what.
Fatsomever, whatsoever.
Faugh, to plough stubble land in **wide,** shallow furrows.
Faul', fold : *to faul your fit*, to sit **down.**
Faulies, dim. of *faulds* ; orig. folds for cattle or sheep, applied to the fields where these had been.
Faur, where.
Favvour, favour.
Feal-dyke, a fence made of turf.
Feck, the greater part ; the majority.
Feckly, chiefly ; for the most part.
Fedder, feather.
Feedle, field.
Feelish, foolish ; thoughtless.
Feerious, furious ; but used in a curiously softened sense, as *feerious het*, exceedingly or very hot ; *feerious gweed natur't*, very good-natured.
Fegs, a minced oath, presumably for *faith!*
Feingyin, feigning.
Feint, exclusively used in strong negatives : *feint ane*, never a one.
Ferlie, wonder ; oddity.
Fer-nothing, fear-nothing ; dreadnought.

Fernyear, last year.
Fersell, forceful; energetic.
Fesh, to fetch.
Fess't, fast; **engaged**.
File, while: dim. *filie*, a little while.
Filk, which!
First-fit, the first person that meets a marriage party or other procession.
Fit, foot; *to give one up his fit*, to reprove one.
Fite, white.
Flaucht, flight; hurried **walk** or **run**.
Flee, fly: *nae a flee*, not a particle.
Fleerish, a steel for striking fire from flint, by which *match*, or touch **paper** is kindled.
Fleg, to frighten.
Fley, to frighten.
Foifteen, fifteen.
Folla, fellow.
Fond, fund.
Fools, fowls: dim. *foolies*.
Foort, fourth.
Fooshtit, fusted.
Foraneen, forenoon.
Forbears, or *forebears*, ancestors.
Forder, further.
Forebreist, front **of** a church or other gallery; front **of** a cart.
Forfecht, overdo; **overtask**.
Forgather, to meet together.
Forhoo, forsake; spoken of a mother bird deserting its **nest** during incubation.
Forquant, to acquaint; **to intimate**.
Forrit, forward.
Fortiggan, fatiguing; **tiresome**.
Foryet, to forget.
Fou, full; drunk.
Foumart, polecat.
Fowk, folk; people.
Fozy, spongy (as a turnip); hollow (as a laugh).
Fraise, to use *phrases*; to speak flatteringly, with a desire to ingratiate.
Frem't, strangers; those not related by blood.
Freely, very: *freely fine*, very or remarkably fine.
Fudder, whether; also *futher*.
Fuish, pret. of *fesh*, fetched; brought; *I fuish*, I brought.
Full, to fill.
Fung, to throw with a jerking motion.
Fup, whip.
Furm, form, a long seat or bench without a back.
Fusion, power; strength.
Fusionless, powerless; weak.

Fuskers, whiskers.
Fusky, whisky.
Futher, whether.
Fyou, few: comp. *fyouer*.

G

Gae, gave; pret. of *gie*.
Gue, to go; pr. part. *gyauin* (going), or *gaen*.
Gae-lattin, letting go; meta. *at the gae-lattin*, on the eve of bankruptcy.
Ga'in, **Gavin**, proper name.
Gang, to go; to walk.
Gar, to force; oblige.
Gast, fright; what takes one suddenly aback.
Gatefarrin, presentable; fit to be seen on the road.
Gawkie, a silly, loutish person.
Gawkitness, uncouth silliness.
Gedder, to gather; to collect.
Gey, considerable.
Geyan, rather; somewhat: *geyan stoot*, rather stout.
Geylies, pretty well.
Gie, to give: *giein*, giving.
Gin, if.
Girss, grass.
Gizzen't, shrunk through drought.
Glack, ravine; point where two **ways** separate or branch off.
Glaid, glad; happy.
Glaiket, idle; thoughtless.
Glives, gloves.
Gloamin, evening twilight.
Gluff, a sudden gust of air; sensation experienced on plunging into cold water.
Gnap, a morsel of anything eatable.
Go-och, oh!
Goshie, an **expression of surprise**.
Goupenfu', the fill of the two hands hollowed and placed side by side.
Gow, to talk **over**; **to gull**; **to decoy**.
Goweff, ruin; destruction.
Graip, three-pronged **dung fork**.
Graith, harness.
Grain, groan.
Grat, wept.
Greet, **to cry**; **to weep**.
Grieve, **farm** overseer.
Grippie, inclined to greed; also dim. of *grip*: *a grippie o' yird*, bending the point of the *sock* slightly to the *yird* or earth.
Gruesome, frightful; horrible.
Grun, ground; land: *grunie*, dim. of *grun*.

Gryte, great.
Gudge, a stout, thick-set fellow.
Guller, sound in the throat, as of choking.
Gullie, knife, commonly of large size.
Gumption, common-sense.
Gurk, stout lad.
Gushet, anything shaped like a gusset; triangular bit of land.
Gweed, good; God.
Gweed-breeder, good-brother; brother-in-law.
Gweeshtens, exclamation expressive of surprise.
Gya, gave.
Gyana, gave not.
Gyaun, going.
Gype, simpleton; a stupid fellow.
Gyte, mad; demented.

H

Hack, a notch.
Hae, to have; imperative, *hae*, take it.
Haill, whole.
Hain, to save; **to husband.**
Hairst, harvest.
Haiveless, unmannerly; reckless.
Haiver, to talk foolishly, incoherently, or nonsensically.
Haivril, a person that talks foolishly; half-witted (from *haiver*).
Hallach, light-witted and noisy.
Hamewuth, homeward.
Han'fu', handful.
Hantle, a considerable quantity or number; a deal.
Harassment, fatigue.
Harns, brains; *harn pan*, the skull.
Haud, hold.
Haudin, holding; possession.
Haugh, alluvial ground on the margin of a stream.
Haumer, to walk **clumsily.**
Ha'ver, to halve; **to lay open.**
Hay-soo, haystack.
Heeld, held.
Heely, cautiously; used as an exclamation, it is equivalent to Stop! take care! *Heely, heely, Tam!* Stop, stop, Tam!
Heemlin, humbling; fitted to humble.
Heich, high: comp. *heicher*, higher.
Heid, head.
Heidie, headstrong; opinionative.
Heidy-peers, persons of equal height.
Helpener, minister's assistant.
Hennie, familiar appellation for henwife.

Henwife, woman who **has** charge of poultry.
Herrial, **means of harrying; ruin :** *perfect herrial*, perfectly ruinous.
Het, hot.
Heth, exclamation equivalent to *faith!*
Heugh, a crag; a rugged steep.
Hillockie, dim. of *hillock*: an instance of double formation — hill, hillock, hillockie.
Hin', at the end, or behind.
Hinna, have not.
Hirehoose, place of servitude.
Hirsle, to draw oneself along **as on a seat**, without rising: *hirsle yont*, move a little farther off.
Hir't (lit. hired), seasoned, made palatable **by the** addition of butter, etc. *weel hir't*, **well** seasoned.
Hisna, **has not.**
Hiz, us.
Hizzie, hussy.
Hodd'n, hid **or hidden.**
Hoo, how.
Hoose, house.
Hoosewifeskip, housewifery.
Hoot, interj. expressive of surprise, irritation, or sometimes doubt; also implying remonstrance: *Hoot, min!* Why, man!
Horsie, dim. of *horse*.
Hotter, a rough shake.
Hoven, heaved, swollen.
Howffin, a clumsy, senseless fellow.
Howp, hope.
Huddry, towsy; disordered.
Huickie, small rick or stack.
Humoursome, affably disposed; **merry.**
Hunner, hundred.
Hurb, clumsy, awkward person.
Hurl, to be driven in any sort **of** carriage; also to drive.
Hyne, afar: *hyne awa'*, far off.
Hyse, banter; boisterous play or frolic.

I

Ilka, each; every.
Ill-win', coarse or abusive language.
Immedantly, immediately.
Income, an ailment whose cause is unknown.
Induck, to induct.
Insnorl, to entrap.
Intill't, into it.
Intoon, originally the land nearest adjoining the *toon* or farm-house; the best land on the farm.

Inveetor, inventory; value of goods inventoried.
Isnin't, is not it? or, is it not?
Ither, other.
Itmost, utmost; to the greatest degree.

J

Jalouse, to suspect; to surmise.
Jaud, jade.
Jaw, a wave; pert, or ill-considered and abusive talk; to talk continuously and idly.
Jeedge, to judge.
Jeesty, matter for jest; used ordinarily in the negative form *it's nae jeesty*, it is not to be trifled with.
Jelly, jolly; buxom.
Jilin', jailing; putting into jail.
Jilp, an indefinite small quantity of any liquid, applied contemptuously, *e.g.* to inferior liquor.
Jinniprous, ingenious; natty.
Jinse, Janet.
Jist, just; merely.
Jouk, to stoop; *to jouk an' lat the jaw gae owre*, to yield to circumstances.
Joukry-pawkry, underhand dealing; trickery; deception.
Jow, to move from side to side; to ring (said of a bell).
Juggie, dim. of *jug*.

K

Kail, colewort (greens).
Kaim, to comb; a comb.
Kebbuck, a cheese: dim. *kebbuckie*.
Keepit, kept.
Keerious, curious; strange.
Keest, cast.
Kell, caul; the puckered part of a woman's *mutch* that rises over the back part of the head.
Ken, to know; to recognise; *kenna*, know not.
Kenspeckle, easily recognisable.
Kettlie, dim. of *kettle*.
Kibble, strong and active; compactly formed.
Kirktoon, hamlet near or around the parish church.
Kiss a caup, lit. to put a vessel with drink to the lips: *onbeen bidden kiss a caup*, without being asked to take liquid refreshment.

Kist, chest.
Kitchie, kitchen; whatever seasons bread.
Kittle, difficult; critical.
Klyack, the conclusion of reaping: *klyack supper*, the harvest-home feast.
Knablich, an irregularly-formed loose stone.
Knag, a knob or pin.
Kneevlick, a roundish piece of anything that may be cut or broken, as cheese.
Kneggum, sharp or disagreeable smell or flavour.
Kneif, well in health; intimate.
Knoweheid, top of a hillock.
Korter, quarter of an oat cake.
Kwintra, country.
Kwite, coat.
Kyaaks, oatmeal cakes.
Kye, cows.
Kyeuk, cook.

L

Laddie, dim. of *lad*; a boy.
Ladle (kirk ladle), small oblong box attached to a long handle for the purpose of collecting the offering; otherwise the *brod*.
Laft, the gallery in a church.
Laimiter, one who has been lamed; a cripple.
Lair, place of repose; bed; grave.
Laird, squire; proprietor of land.
Lairdskip, lordship; right as proprietor.
Lairstane, table or altar-shaped gravestone.
Lane or *leen*, lone; alone: *yer leen*, by yourself.
Lang, long.
Langheidit, long-headed; knowing; shrewd.
Langiges, languages.
Lanstells, parapets of a bridge.
Lant, to jeer or taunt.
Lassie, dim. of *lass*; a girl.
Lat, to let; to permit.
Lave, the rest; the remainder.
Lawvyers, lawyers.
Lee, a lie; to lie.
Leeft, left.
Leems, implements; apparatus; also any kind of vessel over a somewhat wide range, *e.g.* the jovial laird of Balnamoon, *We maun hae a leem*

GLOSSARY. 327

't'll haud in, spoken of his carriage after he had been unluckily spilt therefrom.

Leern, to learn; also to teach.

Leernin, learning: *leern't*, learned.

Leet, let; allowed: *leet at him*, struck or assailed him.

Leevin, living (being); a person.

Legible, intelligible, according to Dawvid Hadden.

Lethal, legal. Dawvid misapplies the word in the display of his learning.

Leuch, laughed.

Leuk or *luik*, to look.

Licht, to alight.

Lichtlifie, to undervalue.

Lickly, likely; probably.

Liftit, elevated; overjoyed.

Likein, like as; for example.

Limmer, a worthless woman; a term of reproach.

Lippen, to trust; to pūt confidence in.

Lippie, the quarter of a peck.

Littleanes, little ones; children: *little littleanes*, small children.

Liveliheid, livelihood.

Loan, a piece of uncultivated land about a town or homestead.

Locker, a small compartment in the end of a chest.

Loon, a lad; a boy.

Loot, let; to stoop.

Lordifu', lordly; bountiful to lavishness.

Loshie, interj. expressive of wonder.

Loss, to lose.

Loup, to leap; to jump.

Lowrin Fair, Lawrence Fair; the annual fair referred to in the ballad where the fates of a hapless maiden's two lovers are described:

"The tane was killed in a Lowrin Fair,
An' the tither was droont in Dee."

Lowse, to loose or **loosen; to leave** off work.

Lozen, pane of glass.

Luggie, a small wooden vessel for table use, with *lugs* or handles on the sides.

Lugs, the ears; handles.

Lyaug, to talk idly and copiously.

Lythe, shelter; sheltered.

M

Maet, meat; victuals.

Mainteen, to maintain.

Mair, more.

Mairch, march; boundary.

Maister, master.

Maitters, matters; affairs.

Maksna, makes not; matters not.

Mammy, mamma; mother.

Mannie, dim. of *man*: sic **mannie sic** *horsie*, like master like man.

Maronjus, harshly stern.

Marrow, equal; companion.

Mask, to infuse.

Maugre, despite: *i' maugre o' my neck*, in spite of all I could do.

Mealy-mou't, **nice; squeamish**.

Mear, mare.

Meesic, music.

Mell, to meddle.

Mengyie, a multitude; a huddled mass.

Menners, **manners**.

Merciment, mercy; **tolerance**.

Mertyreese, to torture one as a martyr.

Milkness, the business of caring for and preparing milk; milk.

Min', to mind; **to care for; to remember**.

Min, man; used **chiefly** in the vocative.

Minit, minute.

Mink, a noose; **the noose of** a hangman's halter.

Mint, to endeavour feebly; to insinuate; to allude to.

Misca', to miscall; to vilify.

Misdoot, distrust; doubt: apparently intensified by *mis*.

Mishanter, accident: **contracted form of** misadventure.

Mislippen, to neglect.

Missionar, missionary: derisively applied to the early congregational preachers and their followers.

Mith, might: **mithna, might not**.

Mither, mother.

Mithnin, might **not**?

Mixter-maxter, confusion; a **confused** mass.

Mizzour, measure.

Mochie, misty, the idea of **moistness and** warmth being implied.

Mochs, moths.

Moderate. Prior to and at the Disruption **the two** parties in the Church of Scotland were known as Moderates and Evangelicals. In the Presbyterian Church, *to moderate in a call* is to hold a meeting of Presbytery, at which the congregation sign the call to a preacher to become their minister.

Moggans, stockings without feet.

Molie, familiar designation of mole-catcher.
Moniment, anything conspicuous by its oddity.
Mools, moulds; earth cast out of a grave.
Morn, the, to-morrow.
Mou', mouth.
Moudiewort, mole.
Moufu' mouthful.
Mows, jests; but used in the negative form: *nae mows*, that may not be treated jestingly; dangerous.
Moyen, influence; means: *to lay moyen*, to use means.
Muckle-boukit, large-sized.
Multiteed, multitude.
Munsie, one who has been made, or has made himself, a spectacle, as by ill-treatment.
Mutch, a woman's cap.
Mutchkin, a liquid measure of four gills.

N

Na, no; nay: direct negative.
Nabal, ill-natured; churlish (1 Sam. xxv.)
Nace, destitute; threadbare.
Nae, no: as *nae sense*, no sense.
Naething, nothing.
Nain, own: *nown* is an ostensibly more refined pronunciation.
Naitral, natural.
Naitur-girss, natural herbage.
Na-say, nay-say; refusal.
Near-b'gyaunness, niggardliness.
Nedder, Nedderin, neither.
Neen, none.
Neeps, turnips.
Negleck, to neglect. *negleckit*, neglected.
Neibourheid, neighbourhood.
Neist, next.
Nervish, nervous.
Neuk or *nyeuk*, nook; corner.
Newse, to talk or gossip.
Newsie, full of news; communicative.
Nicket, disappointed; put in a dilemma.
Nickum, mischievous or roystering boy.
Nievefu', handful.
Niffer, to exchange.
Niz, nose.
Nizzin, nosing; a sharp reception; a drubbing.
No, now, at the end of sentences, especially when interrogative.

Non-intrusion, not intruding a minister on a reclaiming congregation.
Noo, now.
Nor, than (after a comparative).
Not, needed; required.
Notionate, opinionative; obstinate.
Nowte, nolt; cattle.
Nyatter, to talk peevishly; to grumble.
Nyod, semi-profane exclamation, equivalent to *ods* or *od*, with the characteristic negative prefixed.

O

Ochtna, ought not.
On-been, without being.
On-cairry, ongoing.
Ondeemas, enormous; extraordinary.
Onfeelin', unfeeling.
Ongaens, ongoings; transactions; proceedings.
Ongrutt'n, lit. uncried; without shedding tears: *cudna been ongrutt'n*, could not have refrained from crying.
Oo', wool: *a' ae oo'*, all one wool.
Ooncanny, uncanny; mischievous; dangerous.
Oor, our: *oor nain*, our own.
'Oor, hour.
Oorlich, shivering with cold and rain: *oorlich nicht*, a cold, raw night.
Ootfeedles, outfields.
Ootgang, outgo; excess over weight or measure.
Ootwuth, outwardly; fully.
Opingan, opinion.
Ordeen, to ordain.
Orpiet, peevish; querulous.
Orra, unappropriated: *orra man*, one who does odd jobs not appropriated to the other servants.
Ouk, week.
Overly, incidental; incidentally.
Owdience, audience.
Owre, over.
Owsen, oxen; applied specially to those trained for the draught.
Oxter, the arm-pit; the bosom.

P

Pairis', parish.
Pairts, parts; abilities.
Pape, the Pope.
Parkie, dim. of *park*; a small enclosed field.
Partan, crab.

GLOSSARY.

Pass, passage.
Pech, forcible emission of the breath; something between a sigh and a groan.
Peeuk, to complain peevishly; to cry like a chicken.
Peer, poor.
Penner, penholder; cylindrical wooden or tin case for holding quill pens.
Percurrence. Dawvid meant concurrence.
Perfink, precise.
Pernickity, precise; fastidious.
Piece, a bit of oatcake, etc., given as extemporised lunch.
Pig, a jar.
Pilgit, contest; struggle.
Pirl, to stir gently; to move anything from its place by slow degrees.
Pit, to put: *pitten*, put.
Place, the laird's residence, by eminence.
Placie, dim. of place; a small farm, croft, etc.
Plaids, blankets.
Pleuch, plough; dim. *pleuchie*.
Plype, to plump, or fall into water; to dabble in any liquid.
Points, shoe-strings or shoe-ties.
Poleetics, politics: *politician* is applied to one given to discussion or the expression of opinion, whether political or not.
Pooder, powder: *lattin' oot the pooder*, divulging the secret.
Poo'er, power; *poo'er o' pot an' gallows*, the old feudal power to hang or drown.
Poopit, pulpit.
Pow, poll; head; *wag his pow in a poopit*, periphrasis for to preach.
Pran, to crush; to hurt.
Preceesely, precisely; exactly.
Precent, to lead the psalmody in a Presbyterian kirk.
Precunnance, footing; understood conditions; *upo' that precunnance*, upon that footing or understanding.
Preen, pin.
Preen-heidit, pin-headed; of diminutive mental calibre.
Prent, print.
Progresses, processes; Mrs. Birse meant the legal means of bringing the defendant into court.
Protticks, rash or idle experiments.
Puchil, self-important; consequential; *a puchil mannie*, a conceited little man.

Puckle, a quantity or number: dim. *pucklie*.
Pumphel, enclosure or pen for cattle; the laird's seat being "boxed in," by the greater elevation of the panelling, suggested the comparison to "irreverent youth."
Pun' and *poun'*, a pound; when used for weight, pronounced *pun'*, but for money *poun'*.
Put an' row (*wi' a*), with difficulty: possibly from *putting* the stone, where the goal is reached only by the stone *rolling* after it falls.
Purpie, purple.

Q

Quaetness, quietness; peace.
Queetikins, gaiters.
Queets, ankles.
Quine, quean; sometimes implying moral delinquency, and sometimes not.

R

Raffy, abundant; liberal; generous.
Raik, to reck; to care: *what raiks?* what does it signify?
Raith, quarter of a year.
Raither, rather.
Rampauge, fury; rage.
Ramsh, hasty; rash.
Ramshackle, thoughtless; also loose-jointed or crazy, as applied to any kind of framework.
Randy, a scold; a loose-tongued woman.
Ranigill, renegade.
Rantletree, the beam across the chimney from which the *crook* is suspended.
Rape, a rope, especially one made of straw.
Rauchle, noisy; clamorous.
Rave, pret. of *rive*; synon. with *rieve*.
Reamin', creaming; mantling; foaming.
Rebat, to retort; to speak again.
Redd, to clear out; *redd up*, to put in order.
Reed, rood; land measure.
Reef, roof.
Reek, smoke; to give one his *kail through the reek*, is to punish him, as by fisticuffs.

Reek-hen, a hen exacted for every *reeking* chimney or inhabited house; later, hens were exacted in proportion to rent of farm.
Reerie, uproar; clamour.
Reest, to arrest; to put an arrest upon; to roost.
Reet, root.
Refeese, to refuse.
Reive, pret. of *rive*; tore.
Remorsin', expressing regret.
Reproe, to reprove.
Requair, to require.
Richt, to right; *richtet*, righted.
Rickle, a structure put loosely together, or getting dilapidated.
Rig, a ridge; a practical joke or frolic.
Rin, to run; *rinnin'*, running.
Rink, to scramble, as over a fence.
Rinnins, outlines; principal points; heads.
Robbie, dim. of Robert.
Roch, rough; coarse.
Roon, round.
Roose, to rouse; to stir up.
Row, to roll.
Rowle, rule.
Royt, wild; full of rough frolic.
Ruck, a corn-stack; dim. *ruckie*.
Rug, to pull.
Rumgumption, common-sense; mother-wit.
Ryn, rein.

S

Sae, so.
Saick, sack.
Sair, to serve; *sairin*, serving.
Sair, sore; painful; oppressive.
Sang, expletive, possibly from *sanguis*, blood.
Sanna, shall not.
Sanshach, saucy; disdainful.
Sattle, to settle; *sattl't*, settled.
Sauchen, still and unsociable in manner.
Saun'ers, Alexander.
Saurless, tasteless, or spiritless.
Saut, salt.
Sauter, salter; one who can do sharp or severe things.
Sawna, saw not.
Sax, six.
Scaad, scald.
Scabbit, scabbed.
Scaum, to scorch; to burn or heat slightly.
Scaup, hard, thin soil.

Sclaffert, a stroke with the palm of the hand.
Sclaittie, dim. of *sclate*, a slate.
Sclaive, to proclaim sinister reports open-mouthed.
Scoon'rel, scoundrel.
Scoug, a shelter; a pretence.
Scouth, room; accommodation.
Scraichin', screaming; screeching.
Scronach, a querulous outcry.
Scry, to cry; to proclaim as an advertisement.
Scunner, disgust.
Scunnerfu', disgusting; loathsome.
Seelent, silent.
Seen, soon: *seener*, sooner.
Seenit, Synod.
Seerly, surely.
Seet, site; ground on which to build.
Seetivation, situation.
Selfitness, selfishness.
Sells an' thrammels, the fastenings of cattle. The *sell* goes round the neck. The *thrammel* is a chain with swivel in it for attaching the *sell* to the stake.
Sen's, those sent as forerunners.
'Serve's, contraction of *preserve us*.
Settril, slightly stunted in growth.
Seyven, seven.
Shall, shell: *shally*, shelly, abounding in shells.
Shalt, a pony.
Shakker, the part of a threshing-mill which shakes out the straw.
Shank, a stocking in process of being knitted; the leg.
Sharger, one who is stunted in growth.
Sharnie, besmeared with sharn or cow's dung.
Sharries, contentions; quarrels.
Sheelocks, the shells or husks of ground oats.
Sheen, shoes.
Sheet, to shoot.
Shelvins, slipboards to put on the topsides of a cart.
Sheugh, a ditch; a small ravine.
Shirra, sheriff.
Shoo'er, shower.
Shou'ders or *shooders*, shoulders.
Shrood, shroud.
Sib, allied by blood.
Sic, such.
Siccan, such.
Siccar, sure; secure.
Siclike, such-like.
Siller, silver; money in general.
Simmer, summer.

GLOSSARY. 331

Sin', since.
Sindoon, sundown.
Sin'er, to sunder; **to separate.**
Sin'ry, separate; apart.
Sinsyne, since that time.
Sipper, supper.
Sizzon, season.
Skaikit, bedaubed; besmeared.
Skail, to break up or dismiss, as a congregation.
Skaillie, slate-pencil.
Skair't, frightened.
Skance, glance; cursory examination.
Skelbs, splinters; broken pieces.
Skelf, shelf.
Skellack, charlock, **wild mustard.**
Skirp, to splash; **to throw water,** or any liquid **matter, in drops or** small quantities: *skirpit*, **splashed.**
Skouff, to quaff; **to drink off.**
Skweel, school.
Skyrin, **shining glaringly, obtrusively,** or ostentatiously.
Sleicht, sleight.
Slewmin, hint; surmise; faint intimation.
Slichts, slights.
Slype, contemptible fellow; a peculiarly opprobrious epithet.
Smatchet, a wilful or impertinent child; a pert and insignificant person.
Smeddum, shrewdness; intelligence.
Snapper, to stumble, as a horse.
Snappus, snappish.
Sneeshinie, snuffy: from *sneeshin*, snuff.
Snell, keen; piercing.
Snifterin, drawing air through the nose; breathing **in a** lachrymose manner.
Snippet, having **a white streak** down the face.
Snod, neat.
Snorl, a difficulty; **a scrape.**
Soo, sow.
Sook, suck.
Sorra, sorrow; the devil in semi-profane exclamations, as, *Sorra tak' you*.
Sough, an indistinct sound; **a** rumour.
Soun', sound; in religion, orthodox.
Souter, shoemaker.
Sowens, oatmeal flummery.
Spats, abbreviation of spatterdashes; gaiters.
Spean, to wean.
Speer, to ask; to question.
Spin'lin', to spindle; to grow up **as** a spindle.
Sprots, coarse grass.
Spull, spill.

Spyauck, example; guide.
Squallachin, clamorous noise; squealing.
Staffy-nevel, staff-in-hand; *staffy-nevel job*, fight with cudgels.
Stainch, staunch.
Staito, statue.
Stamack, **stomach**: dim. *stamackie*.
Stan, a set.
Stance, **a** station, or site.
Stane, *steen*, stone.
Stank, a ditch.
Starn, a star; a very small quantity.
Starshie, uproar; quarrel.
Stappin', stepping.
Steadin', farm-house and **its appurtenances.**
Stech, to cram; to satiate; to gorge; also **to fill** any given space uncomfortably, as with hot or bad air.
Steel, stool.
Sten'in, **standing;** walking with long strides.
Stibble, stubble.
Sticket, stuck; unsuccessful; *sticket minister*, one who, after a certain extent of study, has failed to get licence as a preacher.
Stickie, dim. of *stick*, a piece of wood.
Stiffen, stiffening; starch.
Stilperts, stilts; meagre, long-legged chickens.
Stob-thacket, thatched by driving in **the** straw with a *stob*.
Stock, a good-natured fellow.
Stoit, or *styte*, nonsense: *stoit*, **to walk** jerkingly or staggeringly.
Stoot, stout; healthy.
Stoups, props; supports; the two pieces of the frame of a cart that project beyond the body, and support it when tilted up.
Stramash, disorder; broil.
Strae, **straw.**
Strap, **to** bind as with an iron plate.
Strappin, tall, handsome, and agile.
Straucht, straight; to straighten.
Stravaig, to wander about idly.
Streck, strict.
Streek, to stretch: *streekit*, stretched; begun, applied primarily to ploughing.
Streen, yesternight.
Streetch, to stretch.
Strunge, sour; surly.
Stur, stir: *sturrin*, stirring.
Succar, sugar.
Sucken, the district *thirled* to a mill; generally the district in which anyone carries on business.

Superannual, annually, **according to** Mrs. Raffan.
Suppit, eaten with a spoon.
Supplicant, a beggar.
Swarf, fainting-fit ; swoon.
Sweer, lazy ; indolent.
Sweetie-wives, **women who attend marriages to sell confections.**
Swick, blame.
Swye, sway ; influence.
Sweype, sweep.
Swyupirt, swift ; sudden ; **abrupt.**
Syne, since.

T

Tack, the lease of a farm ; the farm so leased.
Tacket, a **hobnail** : *tacketie*, **full of** hobnails.
Tae, tea ; **toe** : *tabit*, **toepiece.**
Tak', to take.
Tatie, potato.
Taul, told.
Taupie, simpleton ; a slatternly female.
Ted, toad ; a term of contempt, as applied to a man : the dim. *teddie*, is used as a term of endearment, however, as *O ye bonnie teddie*, addressed to a child.
Tee, too ; likewise.
Teels, tools ; implements.
Teem, empty.
Teen, tune ; humour ; temper.
Terrible, this word is very frequently used in the **sense** of *exceedingly*, as *terrible little*, or *terrible bonnie*.
Tes'ment, testament.
Thack, thatch.
That, used instead of *so : that* **drunk,** *so* drunk, etc. *nae that ill*, **not so bad** (*haud ita male*).
Theets, the traces by which cattle **draw** in a plough, etc. : *oot o' theet*, or *owre the theets*, is acting disorderly or out of rule.
Thegither, together.
Thereoot, outside ; in the open air.
Thig, to beg ; generally applied to the olden practice of begging seed oats **to** sow first **crop on** entering a farm.
Thirl, to astrict **or** bind.
Thole, to suffer ; **to endure** ; **to permit.**
Thoom, thumb : **to keep one's** *thoom* upon, to conceal.
Threep, to insist pertinaciously.
Throu-the-muir, quarrel ; contention.

Ticht, tight.
Tig, to touch lightly ; **to dally** ; to meddle playfully.
Tine, to lose : past part. *tint*, **lost.**
Tinkler, tinker : *tinkler's curse*, **something of no consideration or value.**
Toitin', moving about ploddingly, **or** without energetic action.
Toon, a town ; a farm steading.
Tout, **to** sound as a horn.
Toosht, **a small** undefined quantity of anything : *to toosh't aboot*, to handle carelessly, or be subject to such handling.
Tow, rope.
Towmon, twelvemonths.
Trachel, to draggle ; to abuse through slovenliness.
Trag, persons of mean character ; trash ; worthless stuff.
Trance, **the entrance** ; the lobby or passage.
Transack, transaction ; affair.
Treeshin, calling cattle.
Tribble, trouble ; distress ; affliction ; to trouble.
Troch, small ware ; goods of little value ; to exchange ; to trade in a small way.
Truncher, trencher.
Trypal, tall ; lank, or slovenly person.
Tryst, to appoint a time or place of meeting ; an engagement.
Tyeuk, took.
Turkis, nippers or pincers.
Turnkwite, turncoat ; backslider.
Turra, Turriff, the name of a town.
Twa, **two.**
Twall, twelve.
Tycein, enticing ; treating in **a kindly wheedling manner.**

U

Um'rage, umbrage.
Unce, ounce.
Unco, strange ; **uncommon :** *an unco man*, a stranger.
Un'ersteed, understood.
Upfeshin, upbringing ; **training.**
Upsettin', pretentious.
Uptak, apprehension.
Up-throu', upper part of the country.

V

Veelent, violent.

GLOSSARY.

Vera, very.
Veto-law, Scotch ecclesiastical term, signifying a law to empower a congregation to object to the ordination of a minister over them, should they consider him unsuitable.
Viackle, vehicle ; conveyance.
Vizzy, look : *vizzy backart*, retrospect.
Vokie, jocular ; in exultant spirits.
Vrang, wrong.
Vratch, wretch.
Vreet, *vreetin*, writing.
Vrote, wrote ; written.
Vyaug, a woman of coarse or unruly character.

W

Wainish't-like, vanished-like ; thin ; meagre-looking.
Wale, to select.
Walloch, a characteristic Highland dance.
Walls, wells.
Wallydraggle, an insignificant, untidy person ; an ill-grown animal.
Walthy, wealthy.
Wan, way ; direction : *Ba'dy-fash wan* in the direction of Baldyfash.
Wanworth, unworth : an insignificant price.
Warna, were not.
Warsh or *warsh-like*, insipid ; sickly.
Wa's, walls.
Waucht, draught.
Wauger, to wager ; to bet.
Waur, worse.
Wear-awa', to wear away ; to die.
Wecht, weight.
Weel, well.
Weel-a-wuns, exclamation expressive of soothing and endearment.
Weel-faur't, well-favoured ; comely.
Weer, wire ; knitting-needles.
Weet, wet.
Weirdless worthless ; thriftless.
Went, glance ; blink.
Weesht, whist ! silence.
Whigmaleerie, whim ; fancy.
Whitet or *whitie-broons*, unbleached lint thread.

Wi', with.
Wifie, a little woman, whether a wife or not.
Wil', wild or wildly.
Wile, *wyle*, to wale ; to select.
Wilipen', vilipend ; vilify ; to defame.
Winsome, attractive ; comely.
Win'y, windy ; boastful.
Witter, barb of a dart or hook : *witters* (withers), the throat.
Won'er, wonder.
Woo, call to a horse to stand still.
Wordle, world.
Wordy, worthy ; deserving.
Wormit, wormwood.
Wraith, apparition of a person supposed to be seen immediately before or after his death.
Wud, would : *wudna*, would not.
Wud, mad.
Wudden, wild ; mad.
Wuddie, withe, *i.e.* the withe by which the criminal is hanged ; hence the word is popularly used for the gibbet itself.
Wunt, to want ; to seek.
Wup, to bind round, as with thread, etc.
Wusna, was not.
Wuss, to wish.
Wye, way ; manner.
Wyme, stomach ; belly.
Wyte, to wait ; blame.

Y

Yabble, to speak loudly and rapidly with indistinct utterance.
Yalla, yellow.
Yap, hungry.
Yaucht, to own.
Yauns, arms, *e.g.* of a windmill.
Yawfu', awful.
Yearock, a hen not exceeding a year old ; a pullet.
Yer, your.
Yerl, earl.
Yett, a gate.
Yirnin, rennet ; the stomach of a calf.
Yokit, yoked.
Yule and *Yeel*, Christmas.

THE END.

Printed by R. & R. CLARK, *Edinburgh.*

www.ingramcontent.com/pod-product-compliance
Lightning Source LLC
Chambersburg PA
CBHW030356230426
43664CB00007BB/623